English Grammar in Use

A self-study reference and practice book for intermediate students

D1425847

WITH ANSWERS

Raymond Murphy

SECOND EDITION

CAMBRIDGE
UNIVERSITY PRESS

Published by the Press Syndicate of the University of Cambridge
The Pitt Building, Trumpington Street, Cambridge CB2 1RP
40 West 20th Street, New York, NY 10011-4211, USA
10 Stamford Road, Oakleigh, Melbourne 3166, Australia

© Cambridge University Press 1985, 1994

First published 1985
Fourth printing (with amendments) 1986
Twenty-first printing 1993
Second edition 1994
Reprinted 1994

Printed in Great Britain
by Scotprint Ltd, Musselburgh, Scotland

A catalogue record for this book is available from the British Library

ISBN 0 521 43680 X (with answers)
ISBN 0 521 43681 8 (without answers)

Copyright
The law allows a reader to make a single copy of part of a book
for purposes of private study. It does not allow the copying of
entire books or the making of multiple copies of extracts. Written
permission for any such copying must always be obtained from the
publisher in advance.

CONTENTS

IF YOU ARE NOT SURE WHICH UNITS YOU NEED TO STUDY,
USE THE **STUDY GUIDE** ON PAGE 301.

IF YOU ARE NOT SURE WHICH UNITS YOU NEED TO STUDY,
USE THE **STUDY GUIDE** ON PAGE 301.

IF YOU ARE NOT SURE WHICH UNITS YOU NEED TO STUDY,
USE THE **STUDY GUIDE** ON PAGE 301.

IF YOU ARE NOT SURE WHICH UNITS YOU NEED TO STUDY,
USE THE **STUDY GUIDE** ON PAGE 301.

THANKS

I would like to thank all the students and teachers who used the material that made up the original edition of this book. In particular, I am grateful to my former colleagues at the Swan School of English, Oxford, for all their interest and encouragement. I would also like to thank Adrian du Plessis, Alison Baxter, Barbara Thomas and Michael Swan for their help with the original edition.

Regarding this new edition, I would like to express my thanks to:
  Jeanne McCarten for her help and advice throughout the preparation of the project
  Alison Silver, Geraldine Mark, Peter Donovan, Ruth Carim and Nick Newton of Cambridge University Press
  Gerry Abbot, Richard Fay, Clare West and Pam Murphy for their comments on the manuscript
  Sue André and Paul Heacock for their help with the appendix on American English
  Amanda MacPhail for the illustrations

TO THE STUDENT

This book is for students who want help with English grammar. It is written for you to use without a teacher.

The book will be useful for you if you are not sure of the answers to questions like these:
- What is the difference between *I did* and *I have done*?
- When do we use *will* for the future?
- What is the structure after *I wish*?
- When do we say *used to do* and when do we say *used to doing*?
- When do we use *the*?
- What is the difference between *like* and *as*?

These and many other points of English grammar are explained in the book and there are exercises on each point.

Level
The book is intended mainly for *intermediate* students (students who have already studied the basic grammar of English). It concentrates on those structures which intermediate students want to use but which often cause difficulty. Some advanced students who have problems with grammar will also find the book useful.

The book is *not* suitable for elementary learners.

How the book is organised
There are 136 units in the book. Each unit concentrates on a particular point of grammar. Some problems (for example, the present perfect or the use of *the*) are covered in more than one unit. For a list of units, see the *Contents* at the beginning of the book.

Each unit consists of two facing pages. On the left there are explanations and examples; on the right there are exercises. At the back of the book there is a *Key* for you to check your answers to the exercises (page 310).

There are also seven *Appendices* at the back of the book (pages 274–283). These include irregular verbs, summaries of verb forms, spelling and American English.

Finally, there is a detailed *Index* at the back of the book (page 344).

How to use the book
The units are *not* in order of difficulty, so it is *not* intended that you work through the book from beginning to end. Every learner has different problems and you should use this book to help you with the grammar that *you* find difficult. It is suggested that you work in this way:

- Use the *Contents* and/or *Index* to find which unit deals with the point you are interested in.
- If you are not sure which units you need to study, use the *Study guide* on page 301.
- Study the explanations and examples on the left-hand page of the unit you have chosen.
- Do the exercises on the right-hand page.
- Check your answers with the *Key*.
- If your answers are not correct, study the left-hand page again to see what went wrong.

You can of course use the book simply as a reference book without doing the exercises.

Additional exercises
At the back of the book there are *Additional exercises* (pages 284–300). These exercises bring together some of the grammar points from a number of different units. For example, Exercise 14 brings together grammar points from Units 26–40. You can use these exercises for extra practice after you have studied and practised the grammar in the units concerned.

TO THE TEACHER

English Grammar in Use was written as a self-study grammar book but teachers may also find it useful as additional course material in cases where further work on grammar is necessary.

The book will probably be most useful at middle- and upper-intermediate levels (where all or nearly all of the material will be relevant), and can serve both as a basis for revision and as a means for practising new structures. It will also be useful for some more advanced students who have problems with grammar and need a book for reference and practice. The book is not intended to be used by elementary learners.

The units are organised in grammatical categories (*Present and past*, *Articles and nouns*, *Prepositions* etc.). They are not ordered according to level of difficulty, so the book should *not* be worked through from beginning to end. It should be used selectively and flexibly in accordance with the grammar syllabus being used and the difficulties students are having.

The book can be used for immediate consolidation or for later revision or remedial work. It might be used by the whole class or by individual students needing extra help. The left-hand pages (explanations and examples) are written for the student to use individually but they may of course be used by the teacher as a source of ideas and information on which to base a lesson. The student then has the left-hand page as a record of what has been taught and can refer to it in the future. The exercises can be done individually, in class or as homework. Alternatively (and additionally), individual students can be directed to study certain units of the book by themselves if they have particular difficulties not shared by other students in their class.

This new edition of *English Grammar in Use* contains a set of *Additional exercises* (pages 284–300). These exercises provide 'mixed' practice bringing together grammar points from a number of different units.

A 'classroom edition' of *English Grammar in Use* is also available. It contains no key and some teachers might therefore prefer it for use with their students.

English Grammar in Use Second Edition

While this is a completely new edition of *English Grammar in Use,* the general structure and character of the original book remain the same. The main changes from the original are:

- There are new units on compound nouns (Unit 79), *there* and *it* (Unit 83), *each* and *every* (Unit 90) and *by* (Unit 127).

- Some units have been redesigned, for example Unit 73 (*school* or *the school*) and Unit 94 (relative clauses 4).

- Some of the material has been reorganised. For example, Units 3–4 (present continuous and present simple) and Units 68–69 (countable and uncountable nouns) correspond to single units in the original edition. The material in Units 131–135 (verb + preposition) has been completely rearranged.

- Some of the units have been reordered and nearly all units have a different number from the original edition. A few units have been moved to different parts of the book. For example, Unit 35 (*had better* and *it's time...*) is the new rewritten version of the original Unit 65.

- On the left-hand pages, many of the explanations have been rewritten and many of the examples have been changed.

- Many of the original exercises have been either modified or completely replaced with new exercises.

- There is a new section of *Additional exercises* at the back of the book (see *To the student*).

- In the edition with answers there is a new *Study guide* to help students decide which units to study (see *To the student*). The *Study guide* is only in the edition with answers.

- There are two new appendices on future forms and modal verbs. The other appendices have been revised.

English Grammar in Use

WITH ANSWERS

Present continuous (**I am doing**)

A Study this example situation:

Ann is in her car. She is on her way to work.
She **is driving** to work.

This means: she is driving *now*, at the time of
speaking. The action is not finished.

Am/is/are -ing is the *present continuous*:

I	**am**	(= I**'m**)	driv**ing**
he/she/it	**is**	(= he**'s** etc.)	work**ing**
we/you/they	**are**	(= we**'re** etc.)	do**ing** etc.

B I **am doing** something = I'm in the middle of doing something; I've started doing it and I haven't
finished yet.
Often the action is happening at the time of speaking:

- Please don't make so much noise. **I'm working**. (*not* 'I work')
- 'Where's Margaret?' 'She**'s having** a bath.' (*not* 'she has a bath')
- Let's go out now. It **isn't raining** any more. (*not* 'it doesn't rain')
- (*at a party*) Hello, Jane. **Are** you **enjoying** the party? (*not* 'do you enjoy')
- I'm tired. **I'm going** to bed now. Goodnight!

But the action is not necessarily happening at the time of speaking. For example:

Tom and Ann are talking in a café. Tom says:

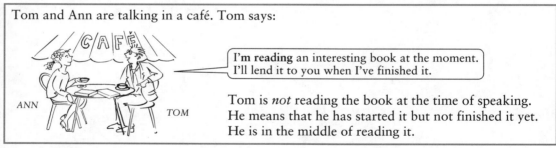

I**'m reading** an interesting book at the moment.
I'll lend it to you when I've finished it.

Tom is *not* reading the book at the time of speaking.
He means that he has started it but not finished it yet.
He is in the middle of reading it.

Some more examples:

- Catherine wants to work in Italy, so she **is learning** Italian. (but perhaps she isn't
learning Italian exactly at the time of speaking)
- Some friends of mine **are building** their own house. They hope it will be finished before
next summer.

C We use the present continuous when we talk about things happening in a period around now
(for example, **today** / **this week** / **this evening** etc.):

- 'You**'re working** hard today.' 'Yes, I have a lot to do.' (*not* 'you work hard today')
- '**Is** Susan **working** this week?' 'No, she's on holiday.'

We use the present continuous when we talk about changes happening around now:

- The population of the world **is rising** very fast. (*not* 'rises')
- **Is** your English **getting** better? (*not* 'does your English get better')

EXERCISES

1.1 *Complete the sentences with one of the following verbs in the correct form:*

come   get   happen   look   make   start   stay   try   ~~work~~

1 'You ...'re working... hard today.' 'Yes, I have a lot to do.'
2 I .... for Christine. Do you know where she is?
3 It .... dark. Shall I turn on the light?
4 They haven't got anywhere to live at the moment. They .... with friends until they find somewhere.
5 'Are you ready, Ann?' 'Yes, I ....'
6 Have you got an umbrella? It .... to rain.
7 You .... a lot of noise. Could you be quieter? I .... to concentrate.
8 Why are all these people here? What ....?

1.2 *Use the words in brackets to complete the questions.*

1 '...Is Colin working... this week?' 'No, he's on holiday.' (Colin/work)
2 Why .... at me like that? What's the matter? (you/look)
3 'Jenny is a student at university.' 'Is she? What ....?' (she/study)
4 .... to the radio or can I turn it off? (anybody/listen)
5 How is your English? .... better? (it/get)

1.3 *Put the verb into the correct form. Sometimes you need the negative (**I'm not doing** etc.).*

1 I'm tired. I ...'m going... (go) to bed now. Goodnight!
2 We can go out now. It ...isn't raining... (rain) any more.
3 'How is your new job?' 'Not so good at the moment. I .... (enjoy) it very much.'
4 Catherine phoned me last night. She's on holiday in France. She .... (have) a great time and doesn't want to come back.
5 I want to lose weight, so this week I .... (eat) lunch.
6 Angela has just started evening classes. She .... (learn) German.
7 I think Paul and Ann have had an argument. They .... (speak) to each other.

1.4 *Read this conversation between Brian and Sarah. Put the verbs into the correct form.*

SARAH: Brian! How nice to see you! What (1) .... (you/do) these days?
BRIAN: I (2) .... (train) to be a supermarket manager.
SARAH: Really? What's it like? (3) .... (you/enjoy) it?
BRIAN: It's all right. What about you?
SARAH: Well, actually I (4) .... (not/work) at the moment.
I (5) .... (try) to find a job but it's not easy.
But I'm very busy. I (6) .... (decorate) my flat.
BRIAN: (7) .... (you/do) it alone?
SARAH: No, some friends of mine (8) .... (help) me.

1.5 *Complete the sentences using one of these verbs:* get   change   rise   fall   increase
You don't have to use all the verbs and you can use a verb more than once.

1 The population of the world ...is rising... very fast.
2 Ken is still ill but he .... better slowly.
3 The world .... Things never stay the same.
4 The cost of living .... Every year things are more expensive.
5 The economic situation is already very bad and it .... worse.

Present simple (**I do**)

A Study this example situation:

Alex is a bus driver, but now he is in bed asleep. So:
He is *not* driving a bus. (He is asleep.)
but He **drives** a bus. (He is a bus driver.)

Drive(s)/work(s)/do(es) etc. is the *present simple*:

I/we/you/they	**drive/work/do** etc.
he/she/it	drives/works/does etc.

B We use the present simple to talk about things in general. We are not thinking only about now. We use it to say that something happens all the time or repeatedly, or that something is true in general. It is not important whether the action is happening at the time of speaking:

- Nurses **look** after patients in hospitals.
- I usually **go** away at weekends.
- The earth **goes** round the sun.

Remember that we say: **he/she/it -s**. Don't forget the **s**:

- I **work**... *but* He works...   They **teach**... *but* My sister teaches...

For spelling (-**s** or -**es**), see Appendix 6.

C We use **do/does** to make questions and negative sentences:

do does	I/we/you/they he/she/it	**work?** **come?** **do?**		I/we/you/they he/she/it	**don't** **doesn't**	**work** **come** **do**

- I come from Canada. Where **do** you **come** from?
- 'Would you like a cigarette?'   'No, thanks. I **don't smoke.**'
- What **does** this word **mean**? (*not* 'What means this word?')
- Rice **doesn't grow** in cold climates.

In the following examples **do** is also the main verb:

- 'What **do** you **do**?' (= What's your job?)   'I work in a shop.'
- He's so lazy. He **doesn't do** anything to help me. (*not* 'He doesn't anything')

D We use the present simple when we say how often we do things:

- I **get** up at 8 o'clock **every morning**. (*not* 'I'm getting')
- **How often do** you **go** to the dentist? (*not* 'How often are you going?')
- Ann **doesn't drink** tea **very often**.
- In summer John **usually plays** tennis **once or twice a week**.

E **I promise / I apologise** etc.

Sometimes we do things by saying something. For example, when you *promise* to do something, you can say '**I promise**...'; when you suggest something, you can say '**I suggest**...'. We use the present simple (**promise/suggest** etc.) in sentences like this:

- I **promise** I won't be late. (*not* 'I'm promising')
- 'What **do** you **suggest** I do?'   'I **suggest** that you...'

In the same way we say: I **apologise**... / I **advise**... / I **insist**... / I **agree**... / I **refuse**... etc.

EXERCISES

2.1 *Complete the sentences using one of the following:*

cause(s)   close(s)   **drink(s)**   live(s)   open(s)   ~~speak(s)~~   take(s) place

1 Ann ....*speaks*.... German very well.
2 I never .... coffee.
3 The swimming pool .... at 9 o'clock and .... at 18.30 every day.
4 Bad driving .... many accidents.
5 My parents .... in a very small flat.
6 The Olympic Games .... every four years.

2.2 *Put the verb into the correct form.*

1 Jane .....*doesn't drink*.... (not/drink) tea very often.
2 What time .... (the banks / close) in Britain?
3 'Where .... (Martin/come) from?'   'He's Scottish.'
4 'What .... (you/do)?'   'I'm an electrical engineer.'
5 It .... (take) me an hour to get to work. How long .... (it/take) you?
6 I .... (play) the piano but I .... (not/play) very well.
7 I don't understand this sentence. What .... (this word/mean)?

2.3 *Use one of the following verbs to complete these sentences. Sometimes you need the negative:*

believe   eat   flow   ~~go~~   ~~grow~~   make   rise   tell   translate

1 The sun ...*goes*... round the earth.
2 Rice ...*doesn't grow*.... in Britain.
3 The sun .... in the east.
4 Bees .... honey.
5 Vegetarians .... meat.
6 An atheist .... in God.
7 An interpreter .... from one language into another.
8 A liar is someone who .... the truth.
9 The River Amazon .... into the Atlantic Ocean.

2.4 *Ask Liz questions about herself and her family.*

1 You know that Liz plays tennis. You want to know how often. Ask her.
   How often ...*do you play tennis?*...
2 Perhaps Liz's sister plays tennis too. You want to know. Ask Liz.
   .... your sister ....
3 You know that Liz reads a newspaper every day. You want to know which one. Ask her.
   ....
4 You know that Liz's brother works. You want to know what he does. Ask Liz.
   ....
5 You know that Liz goes to the cinema a lot. You want to know how often. Ask her.
   ....
6 You don't know where Liz's mother lives. Ask Liz.
   ....

2.5 *Complete using one of the following:*

I apologise   I insist   I promise   I recommend   ~~I suggest~~

1 It's a nice day. ...*I suggest*... we go out for a walk.
2 I won't tell anybody what you said.   ....
3 *(in a restaurant)* You must let me pay for the meal.   ....
4 .... for what I said about you. It wasn't true and I shouldn't have said it.
5 The new restaurant in Hill Street is very good.   .... it.

Present continuous and present simple (1)
(**I am doing** and **I do**)

A Study the explanations and compare the examples:

Present continuous (**I am doing**)	*Present simple* (**I do**)
Use the continuous for something that is happening at or around the time of speaking. The action is not finished.	Use the simple for things in general or things that happen repeatedly.
I am doing *past* *now* *future*	◄------------- I do -------------► *past* *now* *future*
• The water **is boiling**. Can you turn it off? • Listen to those people. What language **are** they **speaking**? • Let's go out. It **isn't raining** now. • 'Don't disturb me. I'm busy.' 'Why? What **are** you **doing**?' • **I'm going** to bed now. Goodnight! • Maria is in Britain at the moment. She's **learning** English.	• Water **boils** at 100 degrees celsius. • Excuse me, **do** you **speak** English? • It **doesn't rain** very much in summer. • What **do** you usually **do** at weekends? • What **do** you **do**? (= What's your job?) • I always **go** to bed before midnight. • Most people **learn** to swim when they are children.
Use the continuous for a *temporary* situation: • **I'm living** with some friends until I find a flat. • 'You're **working** hard today.' 'Yes, I've got a lot to do.'	Use the simple for a *permanent* situation: • My parents **live** in London. They have lived there all their lives. • John isn't lazy. He **works** very hard most of the time.
See Unit 1 for more information.	See Unit 2 for more information.

B **I always do** and **I'm always doing**

Usually we say 'I **always do** something' (= I do it every time):
> • I **always go** to work by car. (*not* 'I'm always going')

You can also say 'I'm **always doing** something', but this has a different meaning. For example:

I've lost my key again. **I'm always losing** things.

'**I'm always losing** things' does *not* mean that I lose things every time. It means that I lose things *too often*, *more often than normal*.

'**You're always -ing**' means that you do something very often, more often than the speaker thinks is normal or reasonable.

> • You're **always watching** television. You should do something more active.
> • John is never satisfied. He's **always complaining**.

EXERCISES

3.1 *Are the underlined verbs right or wrong? Correct the verbs that are wrong.*

1 Water <u>boils</u> at 100 degrees celsius. ...RIGHT...
2 The water <u>boils</u>. Can you turn it off? WRONG: is boiling
3 Look! That man <u>tries</u> to open the door of your car. ....
4 Can you hear those people? What <u>do</u> they <u>talk</u> about? ....
5 The moon <u>goes</u> round the earth. ....
6 I must go now. It <u>gets</u> late. ....
7 I usually <u>go</u> to work by car. ....
8 'Hurry up! It's time to leave.'   'OK, I <u>come</u>.' ....
9 I hear you've got a new job. How <u>do</u> you <u>get</u> on? ....

3.2 *Put the verb in the correct form, present continuous or present simple.*

1 Let's go out. It ...**isn't raining**... (not/rain) now.
2 Julia is very good at languages. She ...**speaks**... (speak) four languages very well.
3 Hurry up! Everybody .... (wait) for you.
4 '.. (you/listen) to the radio?'   'No, you can turn it off.'
5 '.. (you/listen) to the radio every day?'   'No, just occasionally.'
6 The River Nile .... (flow) into the Mediterranean.
7 Look at the river. It .... (flow) very fast today – much faster than usual.
8 We usually .... (grow) vegetables in our garden but this year we .... (not/grow) any.
9 'How is your English?'   'Not bad. It .... (improve) slowly.'
10 Ron is in London at the moment. He .... (stay) at the Park Hotel. He .... (always/stay) there when he's in London.
11 Can we stop walking soon? I .... (start) to feel tired.
12 'Can you drive?'   'I .... (learn). My father .... (teach) me.'
13 Normally I .... (finish) work at 5.00, but this week I .... (work) until 6.00 to earn a bit more money.
14 My parents .... (live) in Bristol. They were born there and have never lived anywhere else. Where .... (your parents/live)?
15 Sonia .... (look) for a place to live. She .... (stay) with her sister until she finds somewhere.
16 'What .... (your father/do)?'   'He's an architect but he .... (not/work) at the moment.'
17 *(at a party)* Usually I .... (enjoy) parties but I .... (not/enjoy) this one very much.
18 The train is never late. It .... (always/leave) on time.
19 Jim is very untidy. He .... (always/leave) his things all over the place.

3.3 *Finish B's sentences. Use **always -ing** (see Section B).*

1 A: I'm afraid I've lost my key again.
   B: Not again! ...**You're always losing your key.**...
2 A: The car has broken down again.
   B: That car is useless! It ....
3 A: Look! You've made the same mistake again.
   B: Oh no, not again! I ....
4 A: Oh, I've left the lights on again.
   B: Typical! You ....

Present continuous and present simple (2)
(**I am doing** and **I do**)

A

We use continuous tenses only for actions and happenings (they **are eating** / it **is raining** etc.).
Some verbs (for example, **know** and **like**) are *not* action verbs. You cannot say 'I am knowing' or
'they are liking'; you can only say 'I **know**', 'they **like**'.

The following verbs are not normally used in continuous tenses:

like	love	hate	want	need	prefer
know	realise	suppose	mean	understand	believe remember
belong	contain	consist	depend	seem	

- I'm hungry. I **want** something to eat. (*not* 'I'm wanting')
- Do you **understand** what I **mean**?
- Ann **doesn't seem** very happy at the moment.

When **think** means 'believe', do *not* use the continuous:
- What **do** you **think** (= believe) will happen? (*not* 'what are you thinking')
but - You look serious. What **are** you **thinking** about? (= What is going on in your mind?)
- I'm **thinking** of giving up my job. (= I am considering)

When **have** means 'possess' etc., do *not* use the continuous (see Unit 17):
- We're enjoying our holiday. We **have** a nice room in the hotel. (*not* 'we're having')
but - We're enjoying our holiday. We**'re having** a great time.

B

See   hear   smell   taste
We normally use the present simple (*not* continuous) with these verbs:
- Do you **see** that man over there? (*not* 'are you seeing')
- This room **smells**. Let's open a window.
We often use **can + see/hear/smell/taste**:
- Listen! **Can** you **hear** something?
But you can use the continuous with **see** (**I'm seeing**) when the meaning is 'having a meeting
with' (especially in the future – see Unit 19A):
- I'm **seeing** the manager tomorrow morning.

C

He is selfish and **He is being selfish**
The present continuous of **be** is **I am being** / **he is being** / **you are being** etc.
I'm being = 'I'm behaving / I'm acting'. Compare:
- I can't understand why he**'s being** so selfish. He isn't usually like that.
  (**being** selfish = behaving selfishly at the moment)
but - He never thinks about other people. He **is** very selfish. (*not* 'he is being')
  (= he is selfish generally, not only at the moment)
We use **am/is/are being** to say how somebody is behaving. It is not usually possible in other
sentences:
- It**'s** hot today. (*not* 'it is being hot')   - Sarah **is** very tired. (*not* 'is being tired')

D

Look and **feel**
You can use the present simple or continuous when you say how somebody looks or feels now:
- You **look** well today. *or* You**'re looking** well today.
- How **do** you **feel** now? *or* How **are** you **feeling** now?
but - I usually **feel** tired in the morning. (*not* 'I'm usually feeling')

Present continuous and simple (1) → **UNIT 3**   **Have** → **UNIT 17**   Present tenses for the future → **UNIT 19**

EXERCISES

4.1 *Are the underlined verbs right or wrong? Correct the ones that are wrong.*

1 I'<u>m seeing</u> the manager tomorrow morning.   ...RIGHT...
2 I'<u>m feeling</u> hungry. Is there anything to eat?   ....
3 <u>Are</u> you <u>believing</u> in God?   ....
4 This sauce is great. It'<u>s tasting</u> really good.   ....
5 I'<u>m thinking</u> this is your key. Am I right?   ....

4.2 *Look at the pictures. Use the words in brackets to make sentences. (You should also study Unit 3 before you do this exercise.)*

1 (you / not / seem / very happy today) **You don't seem very happy today.**	4 (the dinner / smell / good) ....
2 (what / you / do?) .... Be quiet! (I / think)	5 Excuse me. (anybody / sit / here?) .... No, it's free.
3 (who / this umbrella / belong to?) .... I've no idea.	6 Can you ring me back in half an hour? (I / have / dinner) ....

4.3 *Put the verb into the correct form, present continuous or present simple.*

1 Are you hungry? ...Do you want... something to eat? (you/want)
2 Jill is interested in politics but she .... to a political party. (not/belong)
3 Don't put the dictionary away. I .... it. (use)
4 Don't put the dictionary away. I .... it. (need)
5 Who is that man? What ....? (he/want)
6 Who is that man? Why .... at us? (he/look)
7 George says he's 80 years old but nobody .... him. (believe)
8 She told me her name but I .... it now. (not/remember)
9 I .... of selling my car. (think)   Would you be interested in buying it?
10 I .... you should sell your car. (think)   You .... it very often. (not/use)
11 I used to drink a lot of coffee but these days I .... tea. (prefer)
12 Air .... mainly of nitrogen and oxygen. (consist)

4.4 *Complete the sentences using the most suitable form of* **be**. *Sometimes you must use the simple* (**am/is/are**) *and sometimes the continuous is more suitable* (**am/is/are being**).

1 I can't understand why ...he's being... so selfish. He isn't usually like that.
2 Jack .... very nice to me at the moment. I wonder why.
3 You'll like Jill when you meet her. She .... very nice.
4 Normally you are very sensible, so why .... so silly about this matter?
5 Why isn't Sarah at work today? .... ill?

Past simple (**I did**)

A Study this example:

> Wolfgang Amadeus Mozart was an Austrian musician and composer. He **lived** from 1756 to 1791. He **started** composing at the age of five and **wrote** more than 600 pieces of music. He **was** only 35 years old when he **died**.
>
> **Lived/started/wrote/was/died** are all *past simple*.

B Very often the past simple ends in **-ed** (*regular* verbs):
- I work in a travel agency now. Before that I **worked** in a shop.
- We **invited** them to our party but they **decided** not to come.
- The police **stopped** me on my way home last night.
- She **passed** her examination because she **studied** very hard.

For spelling (stop**ped**, stud**ied** etc.), see Appendix 6.

But many verbs are *irregular*. The past simple does *not* end in **-ed**. For example:

write	→	**wrote**	• Mozart **wrote** more than 600 pieces of music.
see	→	**saw**	• We **saw** Rose in town a few days ago.
go	→	**went**	• I **went** to the cinema three times last week.
shut	→	**shut**	• It was cold, so I **shut** the window.

For a list of irregular verbs, see Appendix 1.

C In questions and negatives we use **did/didn't** + *infinitive* (**enjoy/see/go** etc.):

I	**enjoyed**
she	**saw**
they	**went**

did	you	**enjoy?**
	she	**see?**
	they	**go?**

I		**enjoy**
she	**didn't**	**see**
they		**go**

- A: **Did** you **go** out last night?
  B: Yes, I **went** to the cinema but I **didn't enjoy** the film much.
- 'When **did** Mr Thomas **die**?' 'About ten years ago.'
- They **didn't invite** her to the party, so she **didn't go**.
- '**Did** you **have** time to write the letter?' 'No, I **didn't**.'

Be careful when **do** is the main verb in the sentence:
- What **did** you **do** at the weekend? (*not* 'what did you at the weekend')
- I **didn't do** anything. (*not* 'I didn't anything')

D The past of **be** (**am/is/are**) is **was/were**:

I/he/she/it	**was/wasn't**
we/you/they	**were/weren't**

was	I/he/she/it?
were	we/you/they?

Note that we do *not* use **did** in negatives and questions with **was/were**:
- I **was** angry because they **were** late.
- **Was** the weather good when you **were** on holiday?
- They **weren't** able to come because they **were** so busy.
- **Did** you **go** out last night or **were** you too tired?

EXERCISES

5.1 *Read what Sharon says about a typical working day:*

SHARON

> I usually get up at 7 o'clock and have a big breakfast. I walk to work, which takes me about half an hour. I start work at 8.45. I never have lunch. I finish work at 5 o'clock. I'm always tired when I get home. I usually cook a meal in the evening. I don't usually go out. I go to bed at about 11 o'clock. I always sleep well.

Yesterday was a typical working day for Sharon. Write what she did or didn't do yesterday.

1   .**She got up at 7 o'clock.**.
2   She .... a big breakfast.
3   She ....
4   It .... to get to work.
5   .... at 8.45.
6   .... lunch.
7   .... at 5 o'clock.
8   .... tired when .... home.
9   .... a meal yesterday evening.
10 .... out yesterday evening.
11 .... at 11 o'clock.
12 .... well last night.

5.2 *Put one of these verbs in each sentence:*

buy   catch   cost   drink   fall   hurt   sell   spend   teach   throw   win   ~~write~~

1   Mozart ...**wrote**... more than 600 pieces of music.
2   'How did you learn to drive?'   'My father .... me.'
3   We couldn't afford to keep our car, so we .... it.
4   I was very thirsty. I .... the water very quickly.
5   Paul and I played tennis yesterday. He's much better than me, so he .... easily.
6   Don .... down the stairs this morning and .... his leg.
7   Jim .... the ball to Sue, who .... it.
8   Ann .... a lot of money yesterday. She .... a dress which
    .... £100.

5.3 *A friend has just come back from holiday. You ask him about it. Write your questions.*

1   (where/go?) .**Where did you go?**.
2   (go alone?) ....
3   (food/good?) ....
4   (how long / stay there?)
    ....
5   (stay / at a hotel?)
    ....
6   (how/travel?) ....
7   (the weather / fine?)
    ....
8   (what / do in the evenings?)
    ....
9   (meet anybody interesting?)
    ....

5.4 *Complete the sentences. Put the verb into the correct form, positive or negative.*

1   It was warm, so I ...**took**... off my coat. (take)
2   The film wasn't very good. I ...**didn't enjoy**... it very much. (enjoy)
3   I knew Sarah was very busy, so I .... her. (disturb)
4   I was very tired, so I .... to bed early. (go)
5   The bed was very uncomfortable. I .... very well. (sleep)
6   Sue wasn't hungry, so she .... anything. (eat)
7   We went to Kate's house but she .... at home. (be)
8   It was a funny situation but nobody .... (laugh)
9   The window was open and a bird .... into the room. (fly)
10 The hotel wasn't very expensive. It .... very much. (cost)
11 I was in a hurry, so I .... time to phone you. (have)
12 It was hard work carrying the bags. They .... very heavy. (be)

Past continuous (**I was doing**)

A Study this example situation:

Yesterday Karen and Jim played tennis. They began at 10 o'clock and finished at 11.30.
So, at 10.30 they **were playing** tennis.

They **were playing** = 'they were in the middle of playing'. They had not finished playing.

Was/were -ing is the *past continuous*:

I/he/she/it	**was**	play**ing**
we/you/they	**were**	do**ing**
		work**ing** etc.

B We use the past continuous to say that somebody was in the middle of doing something at a certain time. The action or situation had already started before this time but had not finished:

I started doing → *past*   **I was doing**   I finished doing → *past*   *now*

- This time last year I **was living** in Brazil.
- What **were** you **doing** at 10 o'clock last night?
- I waved to her but she **wasn't looking**.

C Compare the past continuous (I **was doing**) and past simple (I **did**):

Past continuous (in the middle of an action)	*Past simple* (complete action)
• I **was walking** home when I met Dave. (= in the middle of walking home)	• I **walked** home after the party last night. (= all the way, completely)
• Ann **was watching** television when the phone rang.	• Ann **watched** television a lot when she was ill last year.

D We often use the past simple and the past continuous together to say that something **happened** in the middle of something else:

- Tom **burnt** his hand when he **was cooking** the dinner.
- I **saw** you in the park yesterday. You **were sitting** on the grass and reading a book.
- While I **was working** in the garden, I **hurt** my back.

But we use the past *simple* to say that one thing happened *after* another:

- I **was walking** along the road when I **saw** Dave. So I **stopped** and we **had** a chat.

Compare:

• When Karen arrived, we **were having** dinner. (= We had already started dinner before Karen arrived.)	• When Karen arrived, we **had** dinner. (= First Karen arrived and then we had dinner.)

E There are some verbs (for example, **know/want/believe**) that are not normally used in the continuous (see Unit 4A):

- We were good friends. We **knew** each other well. (*not* 'we were knowing')
- I was enjoying the party but Chris **wanted** to go home. (*not* 'was wanting')

EXERCISES

6.1 *What were you doing at the following times? Write one sentence as in the examples.*
The past continuous is not always necessary (see the second example).

1 (at 8 o'clock yesterday evening) ....I was having dinner with some friends....
2 (at 5 o'clock last Saturday) ....I was on a train on my way to London....
3 (at 10.15 yesterday morning) ....
4 (at 4.30 this morning) ....
5 (at 7.45 yesterday evening) ....
6 (half an hour ago) ....

6.2 *Use your own ideas to complete these sentences. Use the past continuous.*

1 Tom burnt his hand while he ....was cooking the dinner....
2 The doorbell rang while I ....
3 We saw an accident while we ....
4 Mary fell asleep while she ....
5 The television was on but nobody ....

6.3 *Put the verbs into the correct form, past continuous or past simple.*

1   2   3

I ...saw... (see) Sue in town yesterday but she .... (not/see) me. She .... (look) the other way.

I .... (meet) Tom and Ann at the airport a few weeks ago. They .... (go) to Berlin and I .... (go) to Madrid. We .... (have) a chat while we .... (wait) for our flights.

I .... (cycle) home yesterday when suddenly a man .... (step) out into the road in front of me. I .... (go) quite fast but luckily I .... (manage) to stop in time and .... (not/hit) him.

6.4 *Put the verbs into the correct form, past continuous or past simple.*

1 Jane ...was waiting... (wait) for me when I ...arrived... (arrive).
2 'What .... (you/do) this time yesterday?'   'I was asleep.'
3 '.. (you/go) out last night?'   'No, I was too tired.'
4 'Was Carol at the party last night?'   'Yes, she .... (wear) a really nice dress.'
5 How fast .... (you/drive) when the accident .... (happen)?
6 John .... (take) a photograph of me while I .... (not/look).
7 We were in a very difficult position. We .... (not/know) what to do.
8 I haven't seen Alan for ages. When I last .... (see) him, he .... (try) to find a job in London.
9 I .... (walk) along the street when suddenly I .... (hear) footsteps behind me. Somebody .... (follow) me. I was frightened and I .... (start) to run.
10 When I was young, I .... (want) to be a bus driver.

Present perfect (1) (**I have done**)

A Study this example situation:

Tom is looking for his key. He can't find it.
He **has lost** his key.

'He **has lost** his key' = He lost it and he still hasn't got it.

Have/has lost is the *present perfect simple*:

I/we/they/you	**have**	(= I've etc.)	finished
			lost
he/she/it	**has**	(= he's etc.)	done
			been etc.

The present perfect simple is **have/has** + *past participle*. The past participle often ends in **-ed** (finished/decided etc.), but many important verbs are *irregular* (**lost/done/been/written** etc.). For a list of irregular verbs, see Appendix 1.

B When we use the present perfect there is always a connection with *now*. The action in the past has a result *now*:

● 'Where's your key?'   'I don't know. **I've lost** it.' (I haven't got it *now*)
● He told me his name but **I've forgotten** it. (I can't remember it *now*)
● 'Is Sally here?'   'No, she**'s gone** out.' (she is out *now*)
● I can't find my bag. **Have** you **seen** it? (do you know where it is *now*?)

We often use the present perfect to give new information or to announce a recent happening:

● Ow! **I've cut** my finger.
● The road is closed. There**'s been** (= there **has** been) an accident.
● *(from the news)* The police **have arrested** two men in connection with the robbery.

C You can use the present perfect with **just**, **already** and **yet**:

Just = 'a short time ago':
● 'Would you like something to eat?'   'No, thanks. **I've just had** lunch.'
● Hello. **Have** you **just arrived**?

We use **already** to say that something happened sooner than expected (see also Unit 110D):
● 'Don't forget to post the letter, will you?'   '**I've already posted** it.'
● 'What time is Mark leaving?'   'He**'s already gone**.'

Yet = 'until now' and shows that the speaker is expecting something to happen. Use **yet** only in questions and negative sentences (see also Unit 110C):
● **Has** it **stopped** raining yet?
● I've written the letter but I **haven't posted** it yet.

D Note the difference between **gone (to)** and **been (to)**:

● Jim is away on holiday. He **has gone to** Spain. (= he is there *now* or on his way there)
● Jane is back home from holiday now. She **has been to** Italy. (= she has now come back from Italy)

For **been (to)** see also Units 8 and 125B.

Present perfect → **UNITS 8,11**   Present perfect continuous → **UNITS 9–10**   Present perfect and past → **UNITS 12–14**
American English → **APPENDIX 7**

EXERCISES

7.1 *You are writing a letter to a friend. In the letter you give news about yourself and other people. Use the words given to make sentences. Use the present perfect.*

Dear Chris,

Lots of things have happened since I last wrote to you.

1 I / buy / a new car ...I've bought a new car....
2 my father / start / a new job ....
3 I / give up / smoking ....
4 Charles and Sarah / go / to Brazil ....
5 Suzanne / have / a baby ....

7.2 *Read the situations and write sentences. Choose one of the following:*

arrive   break   go up   grow   improve   ~~lose~~

1 Mike is looking for his key. He can't find it. ...He has lost his key....
2 Margaret can't walk and her leg is in plaster. She ....
3 Maria's English wasn't very good. Now it is much better. ....
4 Tim didn't have a beard last month. Now he has a beard. ....
5 This morning I was expecting a letter. Now I have it. ....
6 Last week the bus fare was 80 pence. Now it is 90. ....

7.3 *Complete B's sentences. Use the verb in brackets + **just/already/yet** (as shown).*   B

	A	
1	Would you like something to eat?	No, thanks. I 've just had... lunch. (just/have)
2	Do you know where Julia is?	Yes, I .... her. (just/see)
3	What time is David leaving?	He .... (already/leave)
4	What's in the newspaper today?	I don't know. I .... (not/read/yet)
5	Is Ann coming to the cinema with us?	No, she .... the film. (already/see)
6	Are your friends here yet?	Yes, they .... (just/arrive)
7	What does Tim think about your plan?	I .... (not/tell/yet)

7.4 *Read the situations and write sentences with **just, already** or **yet**.*

1 After lunch you go to see a friend at her house. She says 'Would you like something to eat?' You say: No, thank you. ...I've just had lunch.... (have lunch)
2 Joe goes out. Five minutes later, the phone rings and the caller says 'Can I speak to Joe?' You say: I'm afraid .... (go out)
3 You are eating in a restaurant. The waiter thinks you have finished and starts to take your plate away. You say: Wait a minute! .... (not/finish)
4 You are going to a restaurant this evening. You phone to reserve a table. Later your friend says 'Shall I phone to reserve a table?' You say: No, ... it. (do)
5 You know that a friend of yours is looking for a job. Perhaps she has been successful. Ask her. You say: ....? (find)
6 Ann went to the bank, but a few minutes ago she returned. Somebody asks 'Is Ann still at the bank?' You say: No, ... (come back)

7.5 *Put in **been** or **gone**.*

1 Jim is on holiday. He's ...gone... to Italy.
2 Hello! I've just .... to the shops. I've bought lots of things.
3 Alice isn't here at the moment. She's .... to the shop to get a newspaper.
4 Tom has .... out. He'll be back in about an hour.
5 'Are you going to the bank?'   'No, I've already .... to the bank.'

Present perfect (2) (**I have done**)

A Study this example conversation:

> DAVE: **Have** you **travelled** a lot, Jane?
> JANE: Yes, I've **been** to lots of places.
> DAVE: Really? **Have** you ever **been** to China?
> JANE: Yes, I've **been** to China twice.
> DAVE: What about India?
> JANE: No, I **haven't been** to India.

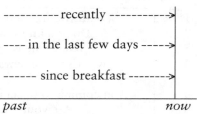

Jane's life
(a period until now)

past   *now*

> When we talk about a period of time that continues from the past until now, we use the
> *present perfect* (**have been / have travelled** etc.). Here, Dave and Jane are talking about the
> places Jane has visited in her life (which is a period that continues until now).

- **Have** you ever **eaten** caviar? (in your life)
- We've never **had** a car.
- '**Have** you **read** *Hamlet*?'   'No, I **haven't read** any of Shakespeare's plays.'
- Susan really loves that film. She'**s seen** it eight times!
- What a boring film! It's the most boring film I'**ve ever seen**.

In the following examples too the speakers are talking about a period that continues until now
(**recently / in the last few days / so far / since breakfast** etc.):

- **Have** you **heard** from George **recently**?
- I'**ve met** a lot of people **in the last few days**.
- Everything is going well. We **haven't had** any
  problems **so far**.
- I'm hungry. I **haven't eaten** anything **since
  breakfast**. (= from breakfast until now)
- It's nice to see you again. We **haven't seen** each
  other **for a long time**.

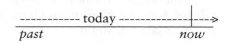

---------- recently ---------->

---- in the last few days ----->

------ since breakfast ------->

past   *now*

B We use the present perfect with **today / this morning / this evening** etc. when these periods are
not finished at the time of speaking (see also Unit 14B):

- I'**ve drunk** four cups of coffee **today**. (perhaps I'll drink more before today is finished)
- **Have** you **had** a holiday **this year** (yet)?
- I **haven't seen** Tom **this morning. Have** you?
- Ron **hasn't worked** very hard **this term**.

----------- today -------------->

past   *now*

C Note that we say 'It's the first time something **has happened**' (*present perfect*). For example:

> Don is having a driving lesson. He is very nervous and unsure
> because it is his first lesson.

- It's **the first time** he **has driven** a car. (*not* 'drives')
- *or*   He **has never driven** a car **before**.

*This is the first time
I've driven a car.*

- Linda has lost her passport again. It's the second time
  this **has happened.** (*not* 'happens')
- This is a lovely meal. It's the first good meal I'**ve had**
  for ages. (*not* 'I have')
- Bill is phoning his girlfriend again. That's the third time
  he'**s phoned** her **this evening**.

Present perfect → UNIT 7   Present perfect + **for/since** → UNITS 11–12   Present perfect and past → UNITS 12–14

American English → APPENDIX 7

EXERCISES

8.1 *You are asking somebody questions about things he or she has done. Make questions from the words in brackets.*

1 (ever / ride / horse?) ....Have you ever ridden a horse?....
2 (ever / be / California?) ....
3 (ever / run / marathon?) ....
4 (ever / speak / famous person?) ....
5 (always / live / in this town?) ....
6 (most beautiful place / ever / visit?)   What ....

8.2 *Complete B's answers. Some sentences are positive and some negative. Use a verb from this list:*
be   be   eat   happen   have   ~~meet~~   play   read   see   see   try

A		B
1	What's George's sister like?	I've no idea. ..I've never met.. her.
2	How is Amy these days?	I don't know. I .... her recently.
3	Are you hungry?	Yes. I .... much today.
4	Can you play chess?	Yes, but .... for ages.
5	Did you enjoy your holiday?	Yes, it's the best holiday .... for a long time.
6	What's that book like?	I don't know. .... it.
7	Is Brussels an interesting place?	I've no idea. .... there.
8	Mike was late for work again today.	Again? He .... every day this week.
9	Do you like caviar?	I don't know. .... it.
10	The car broke down again yesterday.	Not again! That's the second time .... this week.
11	Who's that woman by the door?	I don't know. .... before.

8.3 *Complete these sentences using* **today / this year / this term** *etc.*

1 I saw Tom yesterday but ....I haven't seen him today.....
2 I read a newspaper yesterday but I .... today.
3 Last year the company made a profit but this year ....
4 Tracy worked hard at school last term but ....
5 It snowed a lot last winter but ....
6 Our football team won a lot of games last season but we ....

8.4 *Read the situations and write sentences as shown in the examples.*

1 Jack is driving a car but he's very nervous and not sure what to do.
   You ask: ...Have you driven a car before?...
   He says: ...No, this is the first time I've driven a car....
2 Len is playing tennis. He's not very good and he doesn't know the rules.
   You ask: Have ....
   He says: No, this is the first ....
3 Sue is riding a horse. She doesn't look very confident or comfortable.
   You ask: ....
   She says: ....
4 Maria is in London. She has just arrived and it's very new for her.
   You ask: ....
   She says: ....

Present perfect continuous (**I have been doing**)

A

It has been raining. Study this example situation:

Is it raining?
No, but the ground is wet.

It has been raining.

Have/has been -ing is the *present perfect continuous*:

I/we/they/you	**have**	(= I've etc.)	**been**	**doing**
he/she/it	**has**	(= he's etc.)		**waiting**
				playing etc.

We use the present perfect continuous for an activity that has recently stopped or just stopped.
There is a connection with *now*:

● You're out of breath. **Have** you **been running?** (you're out of breath *now*)
● Paul is very tired. He's **been working** very hard. (he's tired *now*)
● Why are your clothes so dirty? What **have** you **been doing?**
● I've **been talking** to Carol about the problem and she thinks that…

B

It has been raining for two hours. Study this example situation:

It is raining now. It began raining two hours ago and it is
still raining.

How long **has** it **been raining?**
It **has been raining** for two hours.

We often use the present perfect continuous in this way,
especially with **how long, for…** and **since…** . The activity is
still happening (as in this example) or has just stopped.

● **How long have** you **been learning** English? (you're still learning English)
● Tim is still watching television. He's **been watching** television **all day.**
● Where have you been? **I've been looking** for you **for the last half hour.**
● George **hasn't been feeling** well **recently.**

You can use the present perfect continuous for actions repeated over a period of time:
● Debbie is a very good tennis player. She's **been playing since she was eight.**
● Every morning they meet in the same café. They've **been going** there **for years.**

C

Compare **I am doing** (see Unit 1) and **I have been doing**:

I am doing *present continuous* ↓ *now*	I have been doing *present perfect continuous* *now*
● Don't disturb me now. **I'm working.**	● **I've been working** hard, so now I'm going to have a rest.
● We need an umbrella. **It's raining.**	● The ground is wet. **It's been raining.**
● Hurry up! **We're waiting.**	● **We've been waiting** for an hour.

EXERCISES

9.1 *What have these people been doing or what has been happening?*

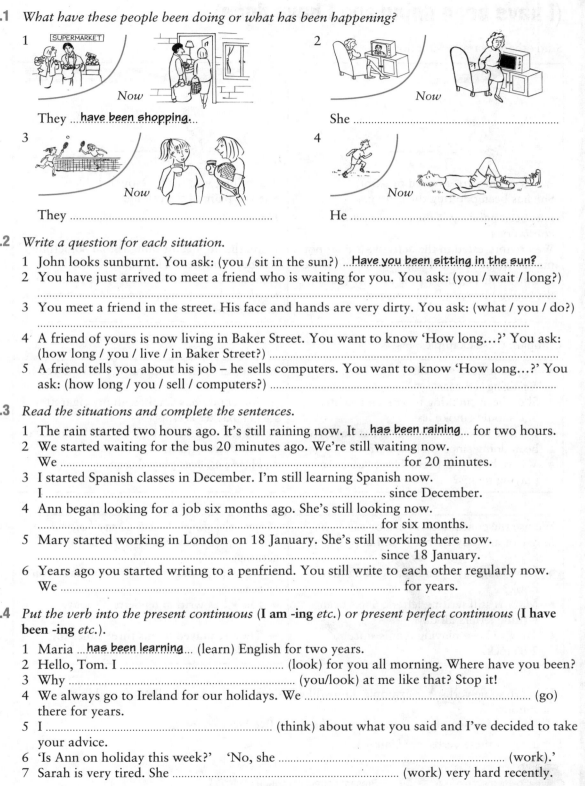

They ...have been shopping...

She ....

They ....

He ....

9.2 *Write a question for each situation.*

1 John looks sunburnt. You ask: (you / sit in the sun?) ...Have you been sitting in the sun?

2 You have just arrived to meet a friend who is waiting for you. You ask: (you / wait / long?)
....

3 You meet a friend in the street. His face and hands are very dirty. You ask: (what / you / do?)
....

4 A friend of yours is now living in Baker Street. You want to know 'How long...?' You ask:
(how long / you / live / in Baker Street?) ....

5 A friend tells you about his job – he sells computers. You want to know 'How long...?' You
ask: (how long / you / sell / computers?) ....

9.3 *Read the situations and complete the sentences.*

1 The rain started two hours ago. It's still raining now. It ...has been raining... for two hours.

2 We started waiting for the bus 20 minutes ago. We're still waiting now.
We .... for 20 minutes.

3 I started Spanish classes in December. I'm still learning Spanish now.
I .... since December.

4 Ann began looking for a job six months ago. She's still looking now.
.... for six months.

5 Mary started working in London on 18 January. She's still working there now.
.... since 18 January.

6 Years ago you started writing to a penfriend. You still write to each other regularly now.
We .... for years.

9.4 *Put the verb into the present continuous (**I am -ing** etc.) or present perfect continuous (**I have been -ing** etc.).*

1 Maria ...has been learning... (learn) English for two years.

2 Hello, Tom. I .... (look) for you all morning. Where have you been?

3 Why .... (you/look) at me like that? Stop it!

4 We always go to Ireland for our holidays. We .... (go)
there for years.

5 I .... (think) about what you said and I've decided to take
your advice.

6 'Is Ann on holiday this week?'   'No, she .... (work).'

7 Sarah is very tired. She .... (work) very hard recently.

Present perfect continuous and simple
(**I have been doing** and **I have done**)

A Study these example situations:

Ann's clothes are covered in paint.
She **has been painting** the ceiling.

Has been painting is the *present perfect continuous*.

We are interested in the activity. It does not matter whether something has been finished or not. In this example, the activity (painting the ceiling) has not been finished.

The ceiling was white. Now it is blue.
She **has painted** the ceiling.

Has painted is the *present perfect simple*.

Here, the important thing is that something has been finished. 'Has painted' is a *completed* action. We are interested in the *result* of the activity (the painted ceiling), not in the activity itself.

Compare these examples:

- My hands are very dirty. I've **been repairing** the car.
- She's **been smoking** too much recently. She should smoke less.
- It's nice to see you again. What **have** you **been doing** since we last met?
- Where have you been? **Have** you **been playing** tennis?

- The car is OK again now. I've **repaired** it.
- Somebody **has smoked** all my cigarettes. The packet is empty.
- Where's the book I gave you? What **have** you **done** with it?
- **Have** you ever **played** tennis?

B We use the continuous to ask or say *how long* (for an activity that is still happening):

- How long **have** you **been reading** that book?
- Mary is still writing letters. She's **been writing** letters **all day**.
- They've **been playing** tennis **since 2 o'clock**.

We use the simple to ask or say *how much*, *how many* or *how many times* (completed actions):

- How many pages of that book **have** you **read**?
- Mary **has written** ten letters today.

- They've **played** tennis three times this week.

C There are some verbs (for example, **know/like/believe**) that are normally not used in the continuous:

- I've **known** about it for a long time. (*not* 'I've been knowing')

For a list of these verbs, see Unit 4A.

Present perfect simple → UNITS 7–8   Present perfect continuous → UNIT 9
Present perfect + **how long/for/since** → UNITS 11–12

EXERCISES

10.1 *Read the situations and write two sentences using the words in brackets.*

1 Tom started reading a book two hours ago. He is still reading it and now he is on page 53.
(read / for two hours) ....He has been reading for two hours.....
(read / 53 pages so far) ...He has read 53 pages so far...

2 Linda is from Australia. She is travelling round Europe at the moment. She began her tour three months ago.
(travel / for three months) She ....
(visit / six countries so far) ....

3 Jimmy is a tennis player. He began playing tennis when he was ten years old. This year he is national champion again – for the fourth time.
(win / the national championship four times) ....
(play / tennis since he was ten) ....

4 When they left college, Mary and Sue started making films together. They still make films.
(make / ten films since they left college) They ....
(make / films since they left college) ....

10.2 *For each situation, ask a question using the words in brackets.*

1 You have a friend who is learning Arabic. You ask:
(how long / learn / Arabic?) ...How long have you been learning Arabic?...

2 You have just arrived to meet a friend. She is waiting for you. You ask:
(how long / wait?) ....

3 You see somebody fishing by the river. You ask:
(how many fish / catch?) ....

4 Some friends of yours are having a party next week. You ask:
(how many people / invite?) ....

5 A friend of yours is a teacher. You ask:
(how long / teach?) ....

6 You meet somebody who is a writer. You ask:
(how many books / write?) ....
(how long / write / books?) ....

7 A friend of yours is saving money to go on holiday. You ask:
(how long / save?) ....
(how much money / save?) ....

10.3 *Put the verb into the more suitable form, present perfect simple (**I have done** etc.) or continuous (**I have been doing** etc.).*

1 Where have you been? ...Have you been playing... (you/play) tennis?
2 Look! Somebody .... (break) that window.
3 You look tired. .... (you/work) hard?
4 '.. (you/ever/work) in a factory?' 'No, never.'
5 'Jane is away on holiday.' 'Oh, is she? Where .... (she/go)?
6 My brother is an actor. He .... (appear) in several films.
7 'Sorry I'm late.' 'That's all right. I .... (not/wait) long.'
8 'Is it still raining?' 'No, it .... (stop).'
9 I .... (lose) my address book. .... (you/see) it anywhere?
10 I .... (read) the book you lent me but I .... (not/finish) it yet.
11 I .... (read) the book you lent me, so you can have it back now.

How long have you (been)...?

A Study this example situation:

Bob and Alice are married. They got married exactly 20 years ago, so today is their 20th wedding anniversary.

They **have been** married **for 20 years.**

We say:

They **are** married. (*present*)

but **How long have** they **been** married? (*present perfect*)
(*not* 'How long are they married?')
They **have been** married **for 20 years.**
(*not* 'They are married for 20 years')

We use the *present perfect* to talk about something that began in the past and still continues now. Compare the *present* and the *present perfect*:

- Amy **is** in hospital.
but She **has been** in hospital **since Monday.** (*not* 'Amy is in hospital since Monday')
- We **know** each other very well.
but We **have known** each other **for a long time.** (*not* 'we know')
- Are you **waiting** for somebody?
but How long have you **been waiting**?

B I **have been doing** something (*present perfect continuous*) = 'I started doing something in the past and I am still doing it (or have just stopped)':

- I've **been learning** English **for a long time.** (*not* 'I am learning')
- Sorry I'm late. **Have** you **been waiting** long?
- It's **been raining** since I got up this morning.

The action can be a repeated action:

- '**How long have** you **been driving?**' 'Since I was 17.'

C I **have done** (*simple*) or I **have been doing** (*continuous*)

The continuous is more usual with **how long, since** and **for** (see also Unit 10B):

- I've **been learning** English for a long time. (*not usually* 'I've learnt')

You can normally use either the continuous or simple with **live** and **work**:

- John **has been living / has lived** in London for a long time.
- How long **have** you **been working / have** you **worked** here?

But we use the *simple* with **always**:

- John **has always lived** in London. (*not* 'has always been living')

You can use the continuous or the simple for actions repeated over a long period:

- I've **been collecting / I've collected** stamps since I was a child.

Some verbs (for example, **know/like/believe**) are not normally used in the continuous:

- How long **have** you **known** Jane? (*not* 'have you been knowing')
- I've **had** a pain in my stomach since I got up this morning.

For a list of these verbs, see Unit 4A. For **have** see Unit 17.

D We use the present perfect *simple* in negative sentences like these:

- I **haven't seen** Tom since Monday. (= Monday was the last time I saw him)
- Jane **hasn't phoned** me for two weeks. (= the last time she phoned was two weeks ago)

EXERCISES

11.1 *Are the <u>underlined</u> verbs right or wrong? Correct them if they are wrong.*

1 Bob is a friend of mine. <u>I know him</u> very well. ...RIGHT...
2 Bob is a friend of mine. <u>I know him</u> for a long time. ...WRONG: I've known him...
3 Sue and Alan <u>are married</u> since July. ....
4 The weather is awful. <u>It's raining</u> again. ....
5 The weather is awful. <u>It's raining</u> all day. ....
6 I like your house. How long <u>are you living</u> there? ....
7 Graham <u>is working</u> in a shop for the last few months. ....
8 I'm going to Paris tomorrow. <u>I'm staying</u> there until next Friday. ....
9 'Do you still smoke?'   'No, I gave it up. <u>I don't smoke</u> for years.' ....
10 That's a very old bicycle. How long <u>do you have</u> it? ....

11.2 *Read the situations and write questions from the words in brackets.*

1 John tells you that his mother is in hospital. You ask him:
   (how long / be / in hospital?) ...How long has your mother been in hospital?...
2 You meet a woman who tells you that she teaches English. You ask her:
   (how long / teach English?) ....
3 You know that Jane is a good friend of Carol's. You ask Jane:
   (how long / know / Carol?) ....
4 Your friend's brother went to Australia some time ago and he's still there. You ask your
   friend: (how long / be / in Australia?) ....
5 Tim always wears the same jacket. It's a very old jacket. You ask him:
   (how long / have / that jacket?) ....
6 You are talking to a friend about Alan. Alan now works at the airport. You ask your friend:
   (how long / work / at the airport?) ....
7 A friend of yours is having driving lessons. You ask him:
   (how long / have / driving lessons?) ....
8 You meet somebody on a train. She tells you that she lives in Glasgow. You ask her:
   (always / live / in Glasgow?) ....

11.3 *Complete B's answers to A's questions.*

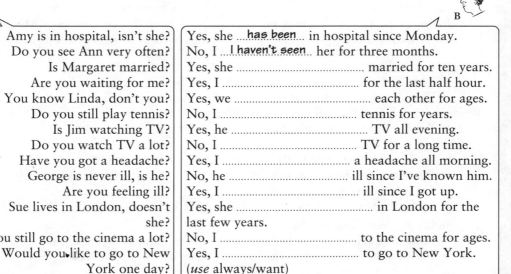

	A	B
1	Amy is in hospital, isn't she?	Yes, she ...has been... in hospital since Monday.
2	Do you see Ann very often?	No, I ...I haven't seen... her for three months.
3	Is Margaret married?	Yes, she .... married for ten years.
4	Are you waiting for me?	Yes, I .... for the last half hour.
5	You know Linda, don't you?	Yes, we .... each other for ages.
6	Do you still play tennis?	No, I .... tennis for years.
7	Is Jim watching TV?	Yes, he .... TV all evening.
8	Do you watch TV a lot?	No, I .... TV for a long time.
9	Have you got a headache?	Yes, I .... a headache all morning.
10	George is never ill, is he?	No, he .... ill since I've known him.
11	Are you feeling ill?	Yes, I .... ill since I got up.
12	Sue lives in London, doesn't she?	Yes, she .... in London for the last few years.
13	Do you still go to the cinema a lot?	No, I .... to the cinema for ages.
14	Would you like to go to New York one day?	Yes, I .... to go to New York. (*use* always/want)

When...? and How long...? For and since

A   Compare **When...?** (+ *past simple*) and **How long...?** (+ *present perfect*):

A: When **did** it **start** raining?
B: It **started** raining   **an hour ago / at 1 o'clock.**
A: **How long has** it **been** raining?
B: It's **been raining**   **for an hour / since 1 o'clock.**

JOE   *CAROL*

A: When **did** Joe and Carol first **meet**?
B: They first **met**   **a long time ago / when they were at school.**
A: **How long have** Joe and Carol **known** each other?
B: They've **known** each other { **for a long time.** / **since they were at school.** }

B   We use both **for** and **since** to say how long something has been happening.

We use **for** when we say a period of time (**two hours, six weeks** etc.): ● I've been waiting **for two hours.**	We use **since** when we say the *start* of a period (**8 o'clock, Monday, 1985** etc.): ● I've been waiting **since 8 o'clock.**
for two hours *two hours ago* ------------------> *now*	**since 8 o'clock** *8 o'clock* ------------------------> *now*

for		**since**	
two hours	a week	8 o'clock	1977
20 minutes	50 years	Monday	Christmas
five days	a long time	12 May	lunchtime
six months	ages	April	they were at school

● Sally's been working here **for six months.** (*not* 'since six months') ● I haven't seen Tom **for three days.** (*not* 'since three days')	● Sally's been working here **since April.** (= from April until now) ● I haven't seen Tom **since Monday.** (= from Monday until now)

It is possible to leave out **for** (but not usually in negative sentences):
- They've been married (for) **ten years.** (with or without **for**)
- They **haven't had** a holiday **for ten years.** (you must use **for**)

We do *not* use **for** + all... (**all day / all my life** etc.):
- I've lived here **all my life.** (*not* 'for all my life')

C   We say '**It's** (a long time / two years etc.) **since** something happened':
- **It's two years since** I last saw Joe. (= **I haven't** seen Joe **for two years** / the last time I saw Joe was two years ago)
- **It's ages since** we went to the cinema. (= We **haven't been** to the cinema for ages)

The question is **How long is it since...?**
- **How long is it since** you last saw Joe? (= When did you last see Joe?)
- **How long is it since** Mrs Hill died? (= When did Mrs Hill die?)

EXERCISES

12.1 *Write questions with* **how long** *and* **when**.

1 It's raining.
(how long ?) ...How long has it been raining?...
(when?) ...When did it start raining?...

2 Kate is learning Italian.
(how long / learn?) ....
(when / start / learn?) ....

3 I know Martin.
(how long / know?) ....
(when / first / meet?) ....

4 Bob and Alice are married.
(how long?) ....
(when?) ....

12.2 *Read the situations and complete the sentences beginning in the way shown.*

1 (It's raining now. It's been raining since lunchtime.)   It started ...raining at lunchtime....

2 (Ann and I are friends. We first met years ago.)   We've ...known each other for years....

3 (Mark is ill. He became ill on Sunday.)   He has ....

4 (Mark is ill. He became ill a few days ago.)   He has ....

5 (Sarah is married. She's been married for two years.)   She got ....

6 (You've got a camera. You bought it ten years ago.)   I've ....

7 (Sue has been in France for the last three weeks.)   She went ....

8 (You're working in a hotel. You started in June.)   I've ....

12.3 *Put in* **for** *or* **since**.

1 It's been raining ...since... lunchtime.

2 Tom's father has been doing the same job .... 20 years.

3 Have you been learning English .... a long time?

4 Sarah has lived in London .... 1985.

5 .... Christmas, the weather has been quite good.

6 Please hurry up! We've been waiting .... an hour.

7 Kevin has been looking for a job .... he left school.

8 The house is very dirty. We haven't cleaned it .... ages.

9 I haven't had a good meal .... last Tuesday.

12.4 *Write B's sentences using the words in brackets.*

1 A: Do you often go on holiday?
B: (no / five years) ...No, I haven't had a holiday for five years....

2 A: Do you often eat in restaurants?
B: (no / ages) No, I ....

3 A: Do you often see Sarah?
B: (no / about a month) No, ...

4 A: Do you often go to the cinema?
B: (no / a long time) ....

Now write B's answers again. This time use **It's...since...** .

5 (1) ...No, it's five years since I had a holiday....

6 (2) No, it's ....

7 (3) No, ...

8 (4) ....

Present perfect and past (1) (**I have done** and **I did**)

A Study this example situation:

Tom is looking for his key. He can't find it.

He **has lost** his key. (*present perfect*)
This means that he doesn't have his key *now*.

Ten minutes later:

Now Tom **has found** his key. He has it now.

Has he **lost** his key? (*present perfect*)
No, he **hasn't**. He **has found** it.

Did he **lose** his key? (*past simple*)
Yes, he **did**.

He **lost** his key (*past simple*)
but now he **has found** it. (*present perfect*)

The *present perfect* is a *present* tense. It always tells us something about *now*. 'Tom **has lost** his key' = he doesn't have his key *now* (see Unit 7).

The *past simple* tells us only about the *past*. If somebody says 'Tom **lost** his key', we don't know whether he has it now or not. We only know that he lost it at some time in the past.

Two more examples:
- Jack **grew** a beard but now he **has shaved** it off. (so he doesn't have a beard *now*)
- They **went** out after lunch and they've just **come** back. (so they are back *now*)

B Do *not* use the present perfect if there is no connection with the present (for example, things that happened a long time ago):
- The Chinese **invented** printing. (*not* 'have invented')
- How many plays **did** Shakespeare **write**? (*not* 'has Shakespeare written')
- Beethoven **was** a great composer. (*not* 'has been')

Compare:
- Shakespeare **wrote** many plays.
- My sister is a writer. She **has written** many books. (she *still* writes books)

C We use the present perfect to give new information (see Unit 7). But if we continue to talk about it, we normally use the past simple:
- A: Ow! I've **burnt** myself.
  B: How **did** you **do** that? (*not* 'have you done')
  A: I **picked** up a hot dish. (*not* 'have picked')
- A: Look! Somebody **has spilt** milk on the carpet.
  B: Well, it **wasn't** me. I **didn't do** it. (*not* 'hasn't been…haven't done')
  A: I wonder who it **was** then. (*not* 'who it has been')

EXERCISES

13.1 *What has happened in these situations?*

1 Jack had a beard. Now he hasn't got a beard. ...He has shaved off his beard...

2 Linda was here five minutes ago. Now she's in bed. She ....

3 The temperature was 25 degrees. Now it is only 17. The temperature ....

4 The light was off. Now it is on. Somebody ....

5 The tree was only three metres high. Now it is four. The tree ....

6 The plane was on the runway a few minutes ago. Now it is in the air.
    The plane ....

13.2 *Put the verbs in brackets in the correct form, present perfect or past simple.*

1 'Where's your key?' 'I don't know. I ...'ve lost... it.' (lose)

2 I ...was... very tired, so I lay down on the bed and went to sleep. (be)

3 Mary .... to Australia for a while but she's back again now. (go)

4 'Where's Ken?' 'He .... out. He'll be back in about an hour.' (go)

5 I did German at school but I .... most of it. (forget)

6 I meant to phone Diane last night but I .... (forget)

7 I .... a headache earlier but I feel fine now. (have)

8 Look! There's an ambulance over there. There .... an accident. (be)

9 They're still building the new road. They .... it. (not/finish)

10 'Is Helen still here?' 'No, she .... out.' (just/go)

11 The police .... three people but later they let them go. (arrest)

12 Ann .... me her address but I'm afraid I.. it. (give, lose)

13 Where's my bike? It .... outside the house. It ....!
    (be, disappear)

14 What do you think of my English? Do you think I ....? (improve)

13.3 *Are the underlined parts of these sentences right or wrong? Correct the ones that are wrong.*

1 Do you know about Sue? She's given up her job. ...RIGHT...

2 The Chinese have invented printing. WRONG: The Chinese invented...

3 How many plays has Shakespeare written? ....

4 Have you read any of Shakespeare's plays? ....

5 Aristotle has been a Greek philosopher. ....

6 Ow! I've cut my finger. It's bleeding. ....

7 My grandparents have got married in London. ....

8 Where have you been born? ....

9 Mary isn't at home. She's gone shopping. ....

10 Albert Einstein has been the scientist who has developed
    the theory of relativity. ....

13.4 *(Section C) Put the verb into the most suitable form, present perfect or past simple.*

1 A: Look! Somebody ...has spilt... (spill) coffee on the carpet.
   B: Well, it ...wasn't... (not/be) me. I ...didn't do... (not/do) it.

2 A: Ben .... (break) his leg.
   B: Really? How .... (that/happen)?
   A: He .... (fall) off a ladder.

3 A: Your hair looks nice. .... (you/have) a haircut?
   B: Yes.
   A: Who .... (cut) it? .... (you/go) to the hairdresser?
   B: No, a friend of mine .... (do) it for me.

Present perfect and past (2) (**I have done** and **I did**)

A   Do *not* use the present perfect (**I have done**) when you talk about a *finished* time (for example, **yesterday / ten minutes ago / in 1985 / when I was a child**). Use a *past* tense:
  - The weather **was** nice **yesterday**. (*not* 'has been nice')
  - They **arrived ten minutes ago**. (*not* 'have arrived')
  - I **ate** a lot of sweets **when I was a child**. (*not* 'have eaten')
  - A: **Did** you **see** the news on television **last night**? (*not* 'Have you seen')
    B: No, I **went** to bed early. (*not* 'have gone')

Use a past tense to ask **When...?** or **What time...?**:
  - **When did** they **arrive**? (*not* 'have they arrived')
  - **What time did** you **finish** work?

Compare:

Present perfect	Past simple
• Tom **has lost** his key. He can't get into the house.	• Tom **lost** his key **yesterday**. He couldn't get into the house.
Here, we are not thinking of the past action. We are thinking of the present result of the action: Tom doesn't have his key *now*.	Here, we are thinking of the action in the past. We don't know from this sentence whether Tom has his key now.

B   Compare present perfect and past:

Present perfect (**have done**)	Past simple (**did**)
• I've **done** a lot of work **today**.	• I **did** a lot of work **yesterday**.
We use the present perfect for a period of time that continues *from the past until now*. For example, **today, this week, since 1985**.	We use the past simple for a *finished* time in the past. For example, **yesterday, last week, from 1985 to 1991**.

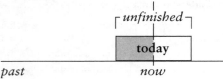 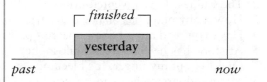

• It **hasn't rained this week**.	• It **didn't rain last week**.
• **Have** you **seen** Ann **this morning**? (it is still morning)	• **Did** you **see** Ann **this morning**? (it is now afternoon or evening)
• **Have** you **seen** Ann **recently**?	• **Did** you **see** Ann **on Sunday**?
• I don't know where Ann is. I **haven't seen** her. (= I haven't seen her recently)	• A: **Was** Ann at the party **on Sunday**? B: I don't think so. I **didn't see** her.
• We've **been waiting** for an hour. (we are still waiting now)	• We **waited** (*or* **were waiting**) for an hour. (we are no longer waiting)
• Ian lives in London. He **has lived** there for seven years.	• Ian **lived** in Scotland for ten years. Now he lives in London.
• I **have never played** golf. (in my life)	• I **didn't play** golf when I was on holiday **last summer**.
The present perfect always has a connection with *now*. See Units 7–12.	The past simple tells us only about the past. See Units 5–6.

EXERCISES

14.1 *Are the <u>underlined</u> parts of these sentences right or wrong? Correct the ones that are wrong.*

1 <u>I've lost</u> my key. I can't find it anywhere. ....**RIGHT**....
2 <u>Have you seen</u> the news on television last night? ...**WRONG: Did you see**...
3 <u>I've bought</u> a new car. Do you want to see it? ....
4 <u>I've bought</u> a new car last week. ....
5 Where <u>have you been</u> yesterday evening? ....
6 Jenny <u>has left</u> school in 1991. ....
7 I'm looking for Mike. <u>Have you seen</u> him? ....
8 I'm very hungry. <u>I haven't eaten</u> anything today. ....
9 Diane <u>hasn't been</u> at work yesterday. ....
10 When <u>has this book been</u> published? ....

14.2 *Make sentences from the words in brackets. Use the present perfect or past simple.*

1 (it / not / rain / this week)   ...**It hasn't rained this week.**...
2 (the weather / be / cold / recently)   The weather ....
3 (it / cold / last week)   It ....
4 (I / not / read / a newspaper yesterday)   I ....
5 (I / not / read / a newspaper today)   ....
6 (Ann / earn / a lot of money / this year)   ....
7 (she / not / earn / so much / last year)   ....
8 (you / have / a holiday recently?)   ....

14.3 *Put the verb into the correct form, present perfect or past simple.*

1 I don't know where Amy is. ....**Have you seen**.... (you/see) her?
2 When I .... (get) home last night, I .... (be)
   very tired and I .... (go) straight to bed.
3 Your car looks very clean. .... (you/wash) it?
4 George .... (not/be) very well last week.
5 Mr Clark .... (work) in a bank for 15 years. Then he gave it up.
6 Molly lives in Dublin. She .... (live) there all her life.
7 '........................ (you/go) to the cinema last night?'   'Yes, but it
   .... (be) a mistake. The film .... (be) awful.'
8 My grandfather .... (die) 30 years ago. I ....
   (never/meet) him.
9 I don't know Carol's husband. I .... (never/meet/him).
10 A: Is your father at home?   B: No, I'm afraid he .... (go) out.
    A: When exactly .... (he/go) out?   B: About ten minutes ago.
11 A: Where do you live?   B: In Boston.
    A: How long .... (you/live) there?   B: Five years.
    A: Where .... (you/live) before that?   B: In Chicago.
    A: And how long .... (you/live) in Chicago?   B: Two years.

14.4 *Write sentences about yourself using the ideas in brackets.*

1 (something you haven't done today)   ...**I haven't eaten any fruit today.**...
2 (something you haven't done today)   ....
3 (something you didn't do yesterday)   ....
4 (something you did yesterday evening)   ....
5 (something you haven't done recently)   ....
6 (something you've done a lot recently)   ....

Past perfect (**I had done**)

A Study this example situation:

At 10.30 | Half an hour later

Bye! | *Hello!*

PAUL | SARAH

Sarah went to a party last week. Paul went to the party too but they didn't see each other. Paul went home at 10.30 and Sarah arrived at 11 o'clock. So:

When Sarah arrived at the party, Paul wasn't there. He **had gone** home.

Had gone is the *past perfect (simple)*:

I/we/they/you he/she/it	had	(= I'd etc.) (= he'd etc.)	**gone** **seen** **finished** etc.

The past perfect simple is **had** + *past participle* (**gone/seen/finished** etc.). For a list of irregular verbs, see Appendix 1.

Sometimes we talk about something that happened in the past:
- Sarah **arrived** at the party.

This is the *starting point* of the story. Then, if we want to talk about things that happened *before* this time, we use the past perfect (**had...**):
- When Sarah arrived at the party, Paul **had** already **gone** home.

Some more examples:
- When we got home last night, we found that somebody **had broken** into the flat.
- Karen didn't want to come to the cinema with us because she **had** already **seen** the film.
- At first I thought **I'd done** the right thing, but I soon realised that **I'd made** a serious mistake.
- The man sitting next to me on the plane was very nervous. He **hadn't flown** before. / He **had** never **flown** before.

B **Had done** (past perfect) is the past of **have done** (present perfect). Compare:

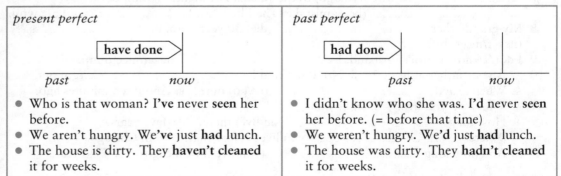

present perfect	*past perfect*
have done →	**had done** →
past *now*	*past* *now*

- Who is that woman? **I've** never **seen** her before.
- We aren't hungry. **We've** just **had** lunch.
- The house is dirty. They **haven't cleaned** it for weeks.

- I didn't know who she was. **I'd** never **seen** her before. (= before that time)
- We weren't hungry. **We'd** just **had** lunch.
- The house was dirty. They **hadn't cleaned** it for weeks.

C Compare the past perfect (**I had done**) and past simple (**I did**):
- 'Was Tom at the party when you arrived?' 'No, he **had** already **gone** home.'
but 'Was Tom there when you arrived?' 'Yes, but he **went** home soon afterwards.'
- Ann wasn't at home when I phoned. She **was** in London.
but Ann **had** just **got** home when I phoned. She **had been** in London.

EXERCISES

15.1 *Read the situations and write sentences from the words in brackets.*

1 You went to Jill's house but she wasn't there. (she / go / out) ...She had gone out....
2 You went back to your home town after many years. It wasn't the same as before.
 (it / change / a lot) ....
3 I invited Rachel to the party but she couldn't come.
 (she / arrange / to do something else) ....
4 You went to the cinema last night. You arrived at the cinema late.
 (the film / already / begin) ....
5 I was very pleased to see Tim again after such a long time.
 (I / not / see / him for five years) ....
6 I offered Sue something to eat but she wasn't hungry.
 (she / just / have / breakfast) ....

15.2 *Read the situations and write sentences ending with* **before**. *Use the verb given in brackets.*

1 The man sitting next to me on the plane was very nervous. It was his first flight.
 (fly) ...He had never flown before. OR He hadn't flown before....
2 A woman walked into the room. She was a complete stranger to me.
 (see) I .... before.
3 Simon played tennis yesterday. He wasn't very good at it because it was his first game.
 (play) He ....
4 Last year we went to Denmark. It was our first time there.
 (be) We ....

15.3 *Use the sentences on the left to complete the paragraphs on the right. These sentences are in the order in which they happened – so (1) happened before (2), (2) before (3) etc. But your paragraph begins with the underlined sentence, so sometimes you need the past perfect.*

1 (1) Somebody broke into the office | We arrived at work in the morning and
     during the night. | found that somebody ...had broken.... into
 (2) <u>We arrived at work in the morning.</u> | the office during the night. So we ....
 (3) We called the police. | ....

2 (1) Ann went out. | I tried to phone Ann this morning but ....
 (2) <u>I tried to phone her</u> this morning. | .... no answer. She ....
 (3) There was no answer. | .... out.

3 (1) Jim came back from holiday a few | I met Jim a few days ago. He .... just
     days ago. | ....
 (2) <u>I met him the same day.</u> | .He ....
 (3) He looked very well. |

4 (1) Kevin wrote to Sally many times. | Yesterday Kevin ....
 (2) She never replied to his letters. | He .... very surprised. He
 (3) <u>Yesterday he had a phone call from her.</u> | .... many times but she
 (4) He was very surprised. | ....

15.4 *Put the verb into the correct form, past perfect (***I had done*** etc.) or past simple (***I did*** etc.).*

1 'Was Tom at the party when you arrived?' 'No, he ...had gone.... (go) home.'
2 I felt very tired when I got home, so I .... (go) straight to bed.
3 The house was very quiet when I got home. Everybody .... (go) to bed.
4 Sorry I'm late. The car .... (break) down on my way here.
5 We were driving along the road when we .... (see) a car which
 .... (break) down, so we .... (stop) to see if we could help.

Past perfect continuous (**I had been doing**)

A Study this example situation:

Yesterday morning

Yesterday morning I got up and looked out of the window. The sun was shining but the ground was very wet.

It **had been raining**.

It was *not* raining when I looked out of the window; the sun was shining. But it **had been** raining before. That's why the ground was wet.

Had been -ing is the *past perfect continuous*:

I/we/you/they he/she/it	had	(= I'd etc.) (= he'd etc.)	been	doing working playing etc.

Some more examples:
- When the boys came into the house, their clothes were dirty, their hair was untidy and one of them had a black eye. They**'d been fighting**.
- I was very tired when I arrived home. I**'d been working** hard all day.

B You can say that something **had been happening** for a period of time *before something else happened*:
- Our game of tennis was interrupted. We**'d been playing** for about half an hour when it started to rain very heavily.
- Ken gave up smoking two years ago. He**'d been smoking** for 30 years.

C **Had been -ing** (*past perfect continuous*) is the past of **have been -ing** (*present perfect continuous*). Compare:

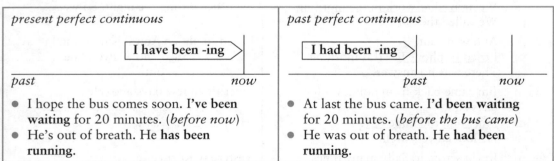

present perfect continuous	*past perfect continuous*

- I hope the bus comes soon. I**'ve been waiting** for 20 minutes. (*before now*)
- He's out of breath. He **has been running**.

- At last the bus came. I**'d been waiting** for 20 minutes. (*before the bus came*)
- He was out of breath. He **had been running**.

D Compare **had been doing** and **was doing** (*past continuous*):
- It **wasn't raining** when we went out. The sun **was shining**. But it **had been raining**, so the ground was wet.
- Ann **was sitting** in an armchair watching television. She was tired because she**'d been working** very hard.

E Some verbs (for example, **know** and **want**) are not normally used in the continuous:
- We were good friends. We **had known** each other for years. (*not* 'had been knowing')

For a list of these verbs, see Unit 4A.

EXERCISES

16.1 *Read the situations and make sentences from the words in brackets.*

1 I was very tired when I arrived home.
(I / work / hard all day) ...I had been working hard all day....

2 The two boys came into the house. They had a football and they were both very tired.
(they / play / football) ....

3 There was nobody in the room but there was a smell of cigarettes.
(somebody / smoke / in the room) ....

4 Ann woke up in the middle of the night. She was frightened and didn't know where she was.
(she / dream) ....

5 When I got home, Mike was sitting in front of the TV. He had just turned it off.
(he / watch / TV) ....

16.2 *Read the situations and complete the sentences.*

1 We played tennis yesterday. Half an hour after we began playing, it started to rain.
We ...had been playing for half an hour... when ...it started to rain....

2 I had arranged to meet Tom in a restaurant. I arrived and waited for him. After 20 minutes I suddenly realised that I was in the wrong restaurant.
I .... for 20 minutes when I ....
....

3 Sarah got a job in a factory. Five years later the factory closed down.
At the time the factory ...., Sarah ....
.... there for five years.

4 I went to a concert last week. The orchestra began playing. After about ten minutes a man in the audience suddenly began shouting.
The orchestra .... when ....
....

5 *This time make your own sentence:*
I began walking along the road. I ....
when ....

16.3 *Put the verb into the most suitable form, past continuous (**I was doing**), past perfect (**I had done**) or past perfect continuous (**I had been doing**).*

1 It was very noisy next door. Our neighbours ...were having... (have) a party.

2 We were good friends. We ...had known... (know) each other for a long time.

3 John and I went for a walk. I had difficulty keeping up with him because he .... (walk) so fast.

4 Mary was sitting on the ground. She was out of breath. She .... (run).

5 When I arrived, everybody was sitting round the table with their mouths full. They .... (eat).

6 When I arrived, everybody was sitting round the table and talking. Their mouths were empty but their stomachs were full. They .... (eat).

7 Jim was on his hands and knees on the floor. He .... (look) for his contact lens.

8 When I arrived, Kate .... (wait) for me. She was rather annoyed with me because I was late and she .... (wait) for a very long time.

9 I was sad when I sold my car. I .... (have) it for a very long time.

10 We were extremely tired at the end of the journey. We .... (travel) for more than 24 hours.

Have and **have got**

A   Have and **have got** (= possess, own etc.)

We often use **have got** rather than **have** alone. So you can say:

- We've **got** a new car.   *or*   We **have** a new car.
- Ann **has got** two sisters.   *or*   Ann **has** two sisters.

We use **have got** or **have** for illnesses, pains etc.:

- I've **got** a headache.   *or*   I **have** a headache.

In questions and negative sentences there are three possible forms:

Have you got any money? **Do you have** any money? **Have you** any money? *(less usual)*	I **haven't got** any money. I **don't have** any money. I **haven't** any money. *(less usual)*
Has she got a car? **Does she have** a car? **Has she** a car? *(less usual)*	She **hasn't got** a car. She **doesn't have** a car. She **hasn't** a car. *(less usual)*

When **have** means 'possess' etc., you cannot use continuous forms (**is having** / **are having** etc.):

- I **have** / I've **got** a headache. (*not* 'I'm having')

For the past we use **had** (usually without 'got'):

- Ann **had** long fair hair when she was a child. (*not* 'Ann had got')

In past questions and negative sentences we normally use **did/didn't**:

- **Did** they **have** a car when they were living in London?
- I **didn't have** a watch, so I didn't know the time.
- Ann **had** long fair hair, **didn't** she?

B   **Have breakfast / have a bath / have a good time** etc.

Have (but not 'have got') is also used for many actions and experiences. For example:

have	breakfast / dinner / a cup of coffee / a cigarette etc. a bath / a shower / a swim / a rest / a party / a holiday / a nice time etc. an accident / an experience / a dream etc. a look (at something) / a chat (with somebody) a baby (= give birth to a baby) difficulty / trouble / fun

- Goodbye! I hope you **have a nice time**.
- Mary **had a baby** recently.

'Have got' is *not* possible in these expressions. Compare:

- I usually **have** a sandwich for my lunch. (**have** = 'eat' – *not* 'have got')

but • I've **got** some sandwiches. Would you like one?

In these expressions, **have** is like other verbs. You can use continuous forms (**is having** / **are having** etc.) where suitable:

- I had a postcard from Fred this morning. He's on holiday. He says he**'s having** a wonderful time. (*not* 'he has a wonderful time')
- The phone rang while we **were having** dinner. (*not* 'while we had')

In questions and negative sentences we normally use **do/does/did**:

- I **don't** usually **have** a big breakfast. (*not* 'I usually haven't')
- What time **does** Ann **have** lunch? (*not* 'has Ann lunch')
- **Did** you **have** any difficulty finding somewhere to live?

EXERCISES

17.1 *Write negative sentences with* **have**. *Some are present* (**can't**) *and some are past* (**couldn't**).

1 I can't make a phone call. (any change)   I haven't got any change.
2 I couldn't read the notice. (my glasses)   I didn't have my glasses.
3 I can't climb up onto the roof. (a ladder)   I ....
4 We couldn't visit the museum. (enough time)   We ....
5 He couldn't find his way to our house. (a map) ....
6 She can't pay her bills. (any money) ....
7 They can't get into the house. (a key) ....
8 I couldn't take any photographs. (a camera) ....

17.2 *Complete these questions with* **have**. *Some are present and some are past.*

1 Excuse me, have you got ..... a pen I could borrow?
2 Why are you holding your face like that? .... a toothache?
3 .... a bicycle when you were a child?
4 '... the time, please?'   'Yes, it's ten past seven.'
5 When you did the exam, ... time to answer all the questions?
6 I need a stamp for this letter. .... one?
7 'It started to rain while I was walking home.'   'Did it? .... an umbrella?'

17.3 *In this exercise you have to write sentences about yourself. Choose four of the following things (or you can choose something else):*

a car   **a bicycle**   **a moped**   **a guitar**   **a computer**   **a camera**   **a driving licence**   **a job**
a dog / a cat (or another animal)
Have you got these things now? Did you have them ten years ago? Write two sentences each time using **I've got / I haven't got** *and* **I had / I didn't have.**

now	ten years ago (or five if you're too young)
1 I've got a car.	I didn't have a car.
2	....
3	....
4	....

17.4 *Complete these sentences. Use an expression from the list and put the verb into the correct form where necessary.*

~~have lunch~~	have a swim	have a nice time	have a chat
have a cigarette	have a rest	have a good flight	have a baby
have a shower	have a party	have a look	

1 I don't eat much during the day. I never ..... have lunch.
2 David likes to keep fit, so he .... every day.
3 We .... last Saturday. It was great – we invited lots of people.
4 Excuse me, can I .... at your newspaper, please?
5 'Where's Jim?'   'He .... in his room. He's very tired.'
6 I met Ann in the supermarket yesterday. We stopped and ....
7 I haven't seen you since you came back from holiday. ....?
8 Suzanne .... a few weeks ago. It's her second child.
9 I don't usually smoke but I was feeling very nervous, so I ....
10 The phone rang but I couldn't answer it because I ....
11 *You meet Tom at the airport. He has just arrived. You say:*
   Hello, Tom. ....?

Used to (do)

A Study this example situation:

A few years ago

Today

Dennis stopped smoking two years ago. He doesn't smoke any more.

But he **used to smoke**.
He **used to smoke** 40 cigarettes a day.

'He **used to smoke**' = he smoked regularly for some time in the past, but he doesn't smoke now. He was a smoker, but now he isn't.

← he **used to smoke** →		he doesn't smoke
past	*2 years ago*	*now*

B 'Something **used to** happen' = something happened regularly in the past but no longer happens:
- I **used to play** tennis a lot but I don't play very often now.
- Diane **used to** travel a lot. These days she doesn't go away so often.
- 'Do you go to the cinema very often?'   'Not now, but I **used to**.' (= I used to go…)

We also use **used to**… for something that was true but is not true any more:
- This building is now a furniture shop. It **used to be** a cinema.
- I **used to think** he was unfriendly but now I realise he's a very nice person.
- I've started drinking coffee recently. I never **used to like** it before.
- Janet **used to have** very long hair when she was a child.

C 'I **used to** do something' is *past*. There is *no* present form. You can*not* say 'I use to do'. To talk about the present, use the present simple (I **do**).

Compare:

past	he **used to smoke**	we **used to live**	there **used to be**
present	he **smokes**	we **live**	there **is**

- We **used to live** in a small village but now we **live** in London.
- There **used to be** four cinemas in the town. Now there **is** only one.

D The normal question form is **did** (you) **use to**…?:
- **Did** you **use to eat** a lot of sweets when you were a child?

The negative form is **didn't use to**… . (**used not to**… is also possible)
- I **didn't use to** like him. (*or* I **used not to** like him.)

E Compare **I used to do** and **I was doing** (see Unit 6):
- I **used to watch** TV a lot. (= I watched TV regularly in the past, but I no longer do this)
- I **was watching** TV when the phone rang. (= I was in the middle of watching TV)

F Do not confuse **I used to do** and **I am used to doing** (see Unit 60). The structures and meanings are different:
- I **used to live** alone. (= I lived alone in the past but I no longer live alone)
- I **am used to living** alone. (= I live alone and I don't find it strange or new because I've been living alone for some time)

EXERCISES

18.1 *Complete these sentences with* **use(d) to...** + *a suitable verb.*

1 Dennis gave up smoking two years ago. He ...*used to smoke*... 40 cigarettes a day.
2 Liz .... a motorbike, but last year she sold it and bought a car.
3 We came to live in Manchester a few years ago. We .... in Nottingham.
4 I rarely eat ice cream now but I .... it when I was a child.
5 Jim .... my best friend but we aren't friends any longer.
6 It only takes me about 40 minutes to get to work since the new road was opened. It .... more than an hour.
7 There .... a hotel opposite the station but it closed a long time ago.
8 When you lived in London, ... to the theatre very often?

18.2 *Brian changed his lifestyle. He stopped doing some things and started doing other things:*

He stopped { studying hard / going to bed early / running three miles every morning }   He started { smoking / going out in the evening / spending a lot of money }

Write sentences about Brian with **used to** *and* **didn't use to.**

1 *He used to study hard.*   4 ....
2 *He didn't use to smoke.*   5 ....
3 ....   6 ....

18.3 *Compare what Carol said five years ago and what she says today:*

FIVE YEARS AGO	*TODAY*
I travel a lot. / I play the piano. / I'm very lazy. / I don't like cheese. / I've got a dog. / I'm a hotel receptionist. / I've got lots of friends. / I never read newspapers. / I don't drink tea. / I go to a lot of parties.	My dog died two years ago. / I eat lots of cheese now. / I work very hard these days. / I don't know many people these days. / I work in a bookshop now. / I don't go away much these days. / I read a newspaper every day now. / I haven't been to a party for ages. / I haven't played the piano for years. / Tea's great! I like it now.

Now write sentences about how Carol has changed. Use **used to / didn't use to / never used to** *in the first part of your sentence.*

1 *She used to travel a lot.* but *she doesn't go away much these days.*
2 She used .... but ....
3 .... but ....
4 .... but ....
5 .... but ....
6 .... but ....
7 .... but ....
8 .... but ....
9 .... but ....
10 .... but ....

Present tenses (**I am doing / I do**) for the future

A *Present continuous* (**I am doing**) with a future meaning

Study this example situation:

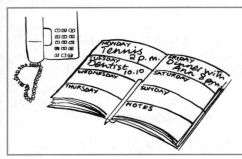

This is Tom's diary for next week.

He **is playing** tennis on Monday afternoon.
He **is going** to the dentist on Tuesday morning.
He **is having** dinner with Ann on Friday.

In all these examples, Tom has already decided and arranged to do these things.

Use the *present continuous* to say what you have already arranged to do. Do not use the present simple (**I do**):

- A: What **are** you **doing** on Saturday evening? (*not* 'what do you do')
  B: **I'm going** to the theatre. (*not* 'I go')
- A: What time **is** Cathy **arriving** tomorrow?
  B: At 10.30. **I'm meeting** her at the station.
- **I'm not working** tomorrow, so we can go out somewhere.
- Ian **isn't playing** football on Saturday. He's hurt his leg.

'(I'm) **going to** (do)' is also possible in these sentences:

- What **are** you **going to do** on Saturday evening?

But the present continuous is more natural for arrangements. See also Unit 20B.

Do not use **will** to talk about what you have arranged to do:

- What **are** you **doing** this evening? (*not* 'what will you do')
- Alex **is getting** married next month. (*not* 'will get')

B *Present simple* (**I do**) with a future meaning

We use the present simple when we talk about timetables, programmes etc. (for example, for public transport, cinemas etc.):

- The train **leaves** Plymouth at 11.30 and **arrives** in London at 14.45.
- What time **does** the film **begin**?
- It's Wednesday tomorrow.

You can use the present simple for people if their plans are fixed like a timetable:

- I **start** my new job on Monday.
- What time **do you finish** work tomorrow?

But the continuous is more usual for personal arrangements:

- What time **are** you **meeting** Ann tomorrow? (*not* 'do you meet')

Compare:

- What time **are you leaving** tomorrow?
but - What time **does the train leave** tomorrow?
- **I'm going** to the cinema this evening.
but - **The film starts** at 8.15 (this evening).

EXERCISES

19.1 *A friend of yours is planning to go on holiday soon. You ask her about her plans. Use the words in brackets to make your questions.*

1	(where/go?) **Where are you going?**	Scotland.
2	(how long/stay?)	Ten days.
3	(when/go?)	Next Friday.
4	(go/alone?)	No, with a friend of mine.
5	(travel/by car?)	No, by train.
6	(where/stay?)	In a hotel.

19.2 *Tom wants you to visit him but you are very busy. Look at your diary for the next few days and explain to him why you can't come.*

MONDAY Volleyball 7.30 pm
TUESDAY Work late (till 9pm)
WEDNESDAY theatre (with mother)
THURSDAY meet Julia 8 pm
FRIDAY
SATURDAY
SUNDAY
NOTES

TOM: Can you come on Monday evening?
YOU: Sorry but ...**I'm playing volleyball.**........................ (1)
TOM: What about Tuesday evening then?
YOU: No, not Tuesday I .... (2)
TOM: And Wednesday evening?
YOU: .... (3)
TOM: Well, are you free on Thursday?
YOU: I'm afraid not. .... (4)

19.3 *Have you arranged to do anything at these times? Write (true) sentences about yourself.*

1 (this evening) ...**I'm going out this evening.**...
  or ..**I'm not doing anything this evening.**.. *or* ..**I don't know what I'm doing this evening.**..
2 (tomorrow morning) I ....
3 (tomorrow evening) ....
4 (next Sunday) ....
5 (*choose another day or time*) ....

19.4 *Put the verb into the more suitable form, present continuous or present simple.*

1 I .**'m going**... (go) to the theatre this evening.
2 ...**Does the film begin**... (the film / begin) at 3.30 or 4.30?
3 We .... (have) a party next Saturday. Would you like to come?
4 The art exhibition .... (open) on 3 May and .... (finish) on 15 July.
5 I .... (not/go) out this evening. I .... (stay) at home.
6 '................................ (you/do) anything tomorrow morning?' 'No, I'm free. Why?'
7 We .... (go) to a concert tonight. It .... (begin) at 7.30.
8 *You are on the train to London and you ask another passenger:*
  Excuse me. What time .... (this train / get) to London?
9 *You are talking to Ann:*
  Ann, I .... (go) to town. .... (you/come) with me?
10 Sue .... (come) to see us tomorrow. She .... (travel) by train and her train .... (arrive) at 10.15. I .... (meet) her at the station.
11 I .... (not/use) the car this evening, so you can have it.
12 *You and a friend are watching television. You say:*
  I'm bored with this programme. When .... (it/finish)?

(I'm) going to (do)

A

'I **am going to do** something' = I have already decided to do it, I intend to do it:

- A: There's a film on television tonight. **Are** you **going to watch** it?
  B: No, I'm tired. **I'm going to have** an early night.
- A: I hear Ruth has won some money. What **is** she **going to do** with it?
  B: She**'s going to buy** a new car.
- A: Have you made the coffee yet?
  B: I'm just **going to make** it. (**just** = right at this moment)
- This food looks horrible. **I'm not going to eat** it.

B

I am doing and **I am going to do**

We normally use **I am doing** (*present continuous*) when we say what we have *arranged* to do –
for example, arranged to meet somebody, arranged to go somewhere (see Unit 19A):

- What time **are you meeting** Ann this evening?
- **I'm leaving** tomorrow. I've got my plane ticket.

'I **am going to** do something' = I've decided to do it (but perhaps not *arranged* to do it):

- 'The windows are dirty.'   'Yes, I know. **I'm going to clean** them later.' (= I've decided to clean them but I haven't *arranged* to clean them)
- I've decided not to stay here any longer. Tomorrow **I'm going to look** for somewhere else to stay.

Often the difference is very small and either form is possible.

C

You can also say that 'something **is going to** happen' in the future. For example:

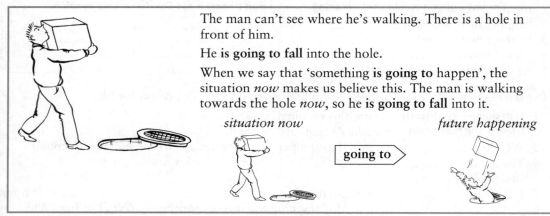

The man can't see where he's walking. There is a hole in front of him.

He **is going to fall** into the hole.

When we say that 'something **is going to** happen', the situation *now* makes us believe this. The man is walking towards the hole *now*, so he **is going to fall** into it.

situation now　　　　　　　　　　　　*future happening*

going to

- Look at those black clouds! It**'s going to rain**. (the clouds are there *now*)
- I feel terrible. I think **I'm going to be** sick. (I feel terrible *now*)

D

'I **was going to** (do something)' = I intended to do it but didn't do it:

- We **were going to travel** by train but then we decided to go by car instead.
- A: Did Peter do the examination?
  B: No, he **was going to do** it but he changed his mind.
- I **was** just **going to cross** the road when somebody shouted 'Stop!'

You can say that something **was going to** happen (but didn't happen):

- I thought it **was going to rain** but then the sun came out.

20.1 *Answer the questions. You are going to do all these things but you haven't done them yet.*
Use **going to** *and the word(s) in brackets.*

1	Have you cleaned the car?	(tomorrow) Not yet. I 'm going to clean it tomorrow.
2	Have you phoned Sally?	(later) Not yet. ....
3	Have you done the shopping?	(this afternoon) Not yet. ....
4	Have you read the paper?	(after dinner) Not ....
5	Have you had dinner?	(just) ....

20.2 *Write a question with* **going to** *for each situation.*

1 Your friend has won some money. You ask:
(what / do with it?) ...**What are you going to do with it?**...

2 Your friend is going to a party tonight. You ask:
(what / wear?) ....

3 Your friend has just bought a new table. You ask:
(where / put it?) ....

4 Your friend has decided to have a party. You ask:
(who / invite?) ....

20.3 *Read the situations and complete the dialogues. Use* **going to**.

1 You have decided to write some letters this evening.
FRIEND: Are you going out this evening? YOU: No, ...**I'm going to write some letters.**...

2 You are a smoker but you have decided to give it up soon.
FRIEND: Smoking is very bad for you.
YOU: I know. ....

3 You have been offered a job but you have decided not to take it.
FRIEND: I hear you've been offered a job.
YOU: That's right, but ....

4 You are in a restaurant. The food is awful and you've decided to complain.
FRIEND: This food is awful, isn't it?
YOU: Yes, it's disgusting. ....

20.4 *What is going to happen in these situations? Use the words in brackets.*

1 There are a lot of black clouds in the sky. (rain) ...**It's going to rain.**...

2 It is 8.30. Jack is leaving his house. He has to be at work at 8.45 but the journey takes 30 minutes. (late) He ....

3 There is a hole in the bottom of the boat. A lot of water is coming in through the hole. (sink) The boat ....

4 Emma is driving. There is very little petrol left in the tank. The nearest petrol station is a long way away. (run out) She ....

20.5 *Complete the sentences with* **was/were going to** + *one of these verbs:*

give up   have   phone   play   ~~travel~~

1 We ...**were going to travel**... by train but then we decided to go by car instead.
2 We .... tennis yesterday but it rained all day.
3 I .... Jim, but I decided to write him a letter instead.
4 When I last saw Tim, he .... his job but in the end he decided not to.
5 We .... a party last week but some of our friends couldn't come, so we cancelled it.

Will/shall (1)

A We use **I'll** (= I **will**) when we decide to do something at the time of speaking:
- Oh, I've left the door open. **I'll go** and shut it.
- 'What would you like to drink?'   '**I'll have** an orange juice, please.'
- 'Did you phone Ruth?'   'Oh no, I forgot. **I'll phone** her now.'

You cannot use the *present simple* (**I do / I go** etc.) in these sentences:
- **I'll go** and shut the door. (*not* 'I go and shut')

We often use **I think I'll...** and **I don't think I'll...**:
- I feel a bit hungry. **I think I'll have** something to eat.
- **I don't think I'll go** out tonight. I'm too tired.

In spoken English the negative of **will** is usually **won't** (= **will not**):
- I can see you're busy, so I **won't stay** long.

B Do *not* use **will** to talk about what you have already decided or arranged to do (see Units 19–20):
- **I'm going** on holiday next Saturday. (*not* 'I'll go')
- **Are** you **working** tomorrow? (*not* 'will you work')

C We often use **will** in these situations:

Offering to do something
- That bag looks heavy. **I'll help** you with it. (*not* 'I help')

Agreeing to do something
- A: You know that book I lent you. Can I have it back if you've finished with it?
- B: Of course. **I'll give** it to you this afternoon. (*not* 'I give')

Promising to do something
- Thanks for lending me the money. **I'll pay** you back on Friday. (*not* 'I pay')
- I **won't tell** anyone what happened. I promise.

Asking somebody to do something (**Will you...?**)
- **Will you** please be quiet? I'm trying to concentrate.
- **Will you** shut the door, please?

You can use **won't** to say that somebody refuses to do something:
- I've tried to advise her but she **won't listen**. (= she refuses to listen)
- The car **won't start**. I wonder what's wrong with it. (= the car 'refuses' to start)

D **Shall I...? Shall we...?**

Shall is used mostly in the questions **shall I...? / shall we...?**

We use **shall I...? / shall we...?** to ask somebody's opinion (especially in offers or suggestions):
- **Shall I** open the window? (= do you want me to open the window?)
- I've got no money. What **shall I** do? (= what do you suggest?)
- '**Shall we** go?'   'Just a minute. I'm not ready yet.'
- Where **shall we** go this evening?

Compare **shall I...?** and **will you...?**:
- **Shall I** shut the door? (= do you want me to shut it?)
- **Will you** shut the door? (= I want you to shut it)

EXERCISES

21.1 *Complete the sentences with* **I'll** + *a suitable verb.*

1 I'm too tired to walk home. I think ...**I'll get**... a taxi.
2 'It's a bit cold in this room.' 'Is it? .... on the heating then.'
3 'We haven't got any milk.' 'Oh, haven't we? .... and get some.'
4 'Do you want me to do the washing-up?' 'No, it's all right. .... it.'
5 'I don't know how to use this computer.' 'OK, ... you.'
6 'Would you like tea or coffee?' '.. coffee, please.'
7 'Goodbye! Have a nice holiday.' 'Thanks. .... you a postcard.'
8 Thank you for lending me your camera. .... it back to you on
   Monday, OK?
9 'Are you coming with us?' 'No, I think .... here.'

21.2 *Read the situations and write sentences with* **I think I'll...** *or* **I don't think I'll...** .

1 It's a bit cold. You decide to close the window. You say: ...**I think I'll close the window.**...
2 You are feeling tired and it's quite late. You decide to go to bed. You say:
   I think ....
3 A friend of yours offers you a lift in his car but you decide to walk. You say:
   Thank you but ....
4 You arranged to play tennis today. Now you decide that you don't want to play. You say:
   I don't think ....
5 You were going to go swimming. Now you decide that you don't want to go.
   ....

21.3 *Which is correct? (If necessary, study Units 19–20 first.)*

1 'Did you phone Ruth?' 'Oh no, I forgot. ~~I phone~~ / I'll phone her now.' (I'll phone *is correct*)
2 I can't meet you tomorrow afternoon. I'm playing / ~~I'll play~~ tennis. (I'm playing *is correct*)
3 'I meet / I'll meet you outside the hotel in half an hour, OK?' 'Yes, that's fine.'
4 'I need some money.' 'OK, I'm lending / I'll lend you some. How much do you need?'
5 I'm having / I'll have a party next Saturday. I hope you can come.
6 'Remember to buy a newspaper when you go out.' 'OK. I don't forget / I won't forget.'
7 What time does your train leave / will your train leave tomorrow?
8 I asked Sue what happened but she doesn't tell / won't tell me.
9 'Are you doing / Will you do anything tomorrow evening?' 'No, I'm free. Why?'
10 I don't want to go out alone. Do you come / Will you come with me?
11 It's a secret between us. I promise I don't tell / I won't tell anybody.

21.4 *What do you say in these situations? Write sentences with* **shall I...?** *or* **shall we...?**

1 You and a friend want to do something this evening but you don't know what. You ask your
   friend. ...**What shall we do this evening?**...
2 You try on a jacket in a shop. You are not sure whether to buy it or not. You ask a friend for
   advice. .... it?
3 It's Ann's birthday next week. You want to give her a present but you don't know what. You
   ask a friend for advice. What ....
4 You and a friend are going on holiday together but you haven't decided where. You ask
   him/her. ....
5 You and a friend are going out. You haven't decided whether to go by car or to walk. You
   ask him/her. .... or ....
6 Your friend wants you to phone later. You don't know what time to phone. You ask
   him/her. ....

Will/shall (2)

A We do *not* use **will** to say what somebody has *already arranged* or *decided to do* in the future:
- Ann **is working** next week. (*not* 'Ann will work')
- **Are** you **going to watch** television this evening? (*not* 'will you watch')

For 'I'm working...' and 'Are you going to...?', see Units 19–20.

But often, when we talk about the future, we are *not* talking about what somebody has decided to do. For example:

CHRIS: Do you think Ann will pass the exam?
JOE: Yes, she**'ll pass** easily.

'She**'ll pass**' does *not* mean 'she has decided to pass'. Joe is saying what he knows or thinks will happen. He is *predicting* the future.
When we predict a future happening or situation, we use **will/won't**.

- Jill has been away a long time. When she returns, she**'ll find** a lot of changes.
- 'Where **will** you **be** this time next year?' 'I**'ll be** in Japan.'
- That plate is very hot. If you touch it, you**'ll burn** yourself.
- Tom **won't pass** the examination. He hasn't worked hard enough for it.
- When **will** you **know** your exam results?

B We often use **will** ('ll) with:

probably	• I**'ll probably** be home late this evening.
I expect	• I haven't seen Carol today. **I expect** she'll phone this evening.
(I'm) sure	• Don't worry about the exam. **I'm sure** you'll pass.
(I) think	• Do you **think** Sarah **will** like the present we bought her?
(I) don't think	• **I don't think** the exam **will** be very difficult.
I wonder	• **I wonder** what **will** happen.

After (**I**) **hope**, we generally use the present:
- **I hope** Carol **phones** this evening.
- **I hope** it **doesn't rain** tomorrow.

C Generally we use **will** to talk about the future, but sometimes we use **will** to talk about *now*. For example:
- Don't phone Ann now. She**'ll be** busy. (= I know she'll be busy *now*)

D **I shall... / we shall...**

Normally we use **shall** only with **I** and **we**.
You can say **I shall** or **I will** (**I'll**), **we shall** or **we will** (**we'll**):
- **I shall** be tired this evening. (*or* I **will** be...)
- **We shall** probably go to Scotland for our holiday. (*or* We **will** probably go...)

In spoken English we normally use **I'll** and **we'll**:
- **We'll** probably go to Scotland.

The negative of **shall** is **shall not** or **shan't**:
- **I shan't** be here tomorrow. (*or* I **won't** be...)

Do not use **shall** with **he/she/it/you/they**:
- She **will** be very angry. (*not* 'she shall be')

Will/shall (1) → UNIT 21   **I will** and **I'm going to** → UNIT 23   **Will be doing / will have done** → UNIT 24
American English → APPENDIX 7

EXERCISES

22.1 *Which form of the verb is correct (or more natural) in these sentences? The verbs are underlined.*

1 Ann isn't free on Saturday. ~~She'll work~~ / She's working. (She's working *is correct*)
2 I'll go / I'm going to a party tomorrow night. Would you like to come too?
3 I think Jane will get / is getting the job. She has a lot of experience.
4 I can't meet you this evening. A friend of mine will come / is coming to see me.
5 A: Have you decided where to go for your holidays?
  B: Yes, we will go / we are going to Italy.
6 There's no need to be afraid of the dog. It won't hurt / It isn't hurting you.

22.2 *Complete the sentences with* **will** *('ll) + one of these verbs:*

be   be   come   get   like   look   meet   ~~pass~~

1 Don't worry about your exam. I'm sure you **'ll pass.**
2 Why don't you try on this jacket? It .... nice on you.
3 You must meet George sometime. I think you .... him.
4 It's raining. Don't go out. You .... wet.
5 They've invited me to their house. They .... offended if I don't go.
6 Goodbye. I expect we .... again before long.
7 I've invited Sue to the party but I don't think she ....
8 I wonder where I .... 20 years from now.

22.3 *Put in* **will** *('ll) or* **won't**.

1 Can you wait for me? I **won't** be very long.
2 There's no need to take an umbrella with you. It .... rain.
3 If you don't eat anything now, you .... be hungry later.
4 I'm sorry about what happened yesterday. It .... happen again.
5 I've got some incredible news! You .... never believe what's happened.
6 Don't ask Margaret for advice. She .... know what to do.

22.4 *Where will you be at these times? Write true sentences about yourself. Use one of these:*

I'll be... *or* **I expect I'll be...** *or* **I'll probably be...** *or* **I don't know where I'll be.** *or*
I'm not sure. I might be... *(For* **might** *see Unit 30.)*

1 (next Monday evening at 7.45) **I'll probably be at home.**
                            or **I'm not sure. I might be at the cinema.**
                            or **I don't know where I'll be.** *(etc.)*
2 (at 5 o'clock tomorrow morning) ....
3 (at 10.30 tomorrow morning) ....
4 (next Saturday afternoon at 4.15) ....
5 (this time next year) ....

22.5 *Write questions using* **do you think...will...?** *+ one of these verbs:*

be back   cost   finish   get married   happen   ~~like~~   rain

1 I've bought Mary a present. **Do you think she'll like it?**
2 The weather doesn't look very good. Do you ....
3 The meeting is still going on. When do you ....
4 My car needs to be repaired. How much ....
5 Sally and David are in love. Do ....
6 'I'm going out now.' 'OK. What time ....'
7 The future situation is uncertain. What ....

45

I will and I'm going to

A Future actions

Study the difference between **will** and **going to**:

Sue is talking to Helen:

> Let's have a party.

> That's a great idea. We**'ll invite** lots of people.

SUE   HELEN

will ('ll): We use **will** when we decide to do something at the time of speaking. The speaker has not decided before. The party is a new idea.

decision now

I'll...

past   now   future

Later that day, Helen meets Dave:

> Sue and I have decided to have a party. We**'re going to invite** lots of people.

HELEN   DAVE

going to: We use (**be**) **going to** when we have *already decided* to do something. Helen had already decided to invite lots of people *before* she spoke to Dave.

decision before

→ I'm going to...

past   now   future

Compare:

- 'George phoned while you were out.'   'OK. I**'ll phone** him back.'
- *but* 'George phoned while you were out.'   'Yes, I know. I**'m going to phone** him back.'
- 'Ann is in hospital.'   'Oh really? I didn't know. I**'ll go** and visit her.'
- *but* 'Ann is in hospital.'   'Yes, I know. I**'m going to visit** her tomorrow.'

B Future happenings and situations (predicting the future)

Sometimes there is not much difference between **will** and **going to**. For example, you can say:

- I think the weather **will** be nice later.
- I think the weather **is going to** be nice later.

When we say 'something **is going to** happen', we know (or think) this because of the situation *now*. For example:

- Look at those black clouds. It**'s going to rain**. (*not* 'it will rain' – we can see the clouds *now*)
- I feel terrible. I think I**'m going to be** sick. (*not* 'I think I'll be sick' – I feel terrible *now*)

Do not use **will** in situations like these. (See also Unit 20C.)

In other situations, it is safer to use **will**:

- Tom **will** probably **arrive** at about 8 o'clock.
- I think Ann **will like** the present we bought for her.

EXERCISES

23.1 *Complete the sentences using* **will** (**'ll**) *or* **going to**.

1 A: Why are you turning on the television?
    B: ...**I'm going to watch**... the news. (I/watch)
2 A: Oh, I've just realised. I haven't got any money.
    B: Haven't you? Well, don't worry. .... you some. (I/lend)
3 A: I've got a headache.
    B: Have you? Wait there and .... an aspirin for you. (I/get)
4 A: Why are you filling that bucket with water?
    B: .... the car. (I/wash)
5 A: I've decided to repaint this room.
    B: Oh, have you? What colour .... it? (you/paint)
6 A: Where are you going? Are you going shopping?
    B: Yes, ... something for dinner. (I/buy)
7 A: I don't know how to use this camera.
    B: It's quite easy. .... you. (I/show)
8 A: What would you like to eat?
    B: .... a sandwich, please. (I/have)
9 A: Did you post that letter for me?
    B: Oh, I'm sorry. I completely forgot. .... it now. (I/do)
10 A: The ceiling in this room doesn't look very safe, does it?
    B: No, it looks as if .... down. (it/fall)
11 A: Has George decided what to do when he leaves school?
    B: Oh, yes. Everything is planned. .... a holiday for a few weeks
    and then .... a computer programming course. (he/have, he/do)

23.2 *Read the situations and complete the sentences using* **will** (**'ll**) *or* **going to**.

1 The phone rings and you answer. Somebody wants to speak to Jim.
    CALLER: Hello. Can I speak to Jim, please?
    YOU: Just a moment. .... him. (I/get)
2 It's a nice day. You've decided to sit in the garden. Before going outside, you tell your friend.
    YOU: The weather's too nice to stay indoors. .... in the garden. (I/sit)
    FRIEND: That's a good idea. I think .... you. (I/join)
3 Your friend is worried because she has lost an important letter.
    YOU: Don't worry about the letter. I'm sure .... it. (you/find)
    FRIEND: I hope so.
4 There was a job advertised in the paper recently. At first you were interested but then you
    decided not to apply.
    FRIEND: Have you decided what to do about that job that was advertised?
    YOU: Yes, ... for it. (I/not/apply)
5 You and a friend come home very late. Other people in the house are asleep. Your friend is
    noisy.
    YOU: Shhh! Don't make so much noise. .... everybody up. (you/wake)
6 John has to go to the airport to catch a plane tomorrow morning.
    JOHN: Ann, I need somebody to take me to the airport tomorrow morning.
    ANN: That's no problem. .... you. (I/take)   What time is your flight?
    JOHN: 10.50.
    ANN: OK. .... at about 9 o'clock then. (we/leave)
    Later that day, Joe offers to take John to the airport.
    JOE: John, do you want me to take you to the airport?
    JOHN: No thanks, Joe. .... me. (Ann/take)

Will be doing and will have done

A Study this example situation:

> Kevin loves football and this evening there is a big football match on television. The match begins at 7.30 and ends at 9.15. Paul wants to see Kevin the same evening and wants to know what time to come to his house.
>
> PAUL: Is it all right if I come at about 8.30?
> KEVIN: No, **I'll be watching** the football then.
> PAUL: Well, what about 9.30?
> KEVIN: Fine. The match **will have finished** by then.

B 'I **will be doing** something' (*future continuous*) = I will be in the middle of doing something. The football match begins at 7.30 and ends at 9.15. So during this time, for example at 8.30, Kevin **will be watching** the match. Another example:

- I'm going on holiday on Saturday. This time next week **I'll be lying** on a beach or **swimming** in the sea.

Compare **will be** (do)**ing** and **will** (do):

- Don't phone me between 7 and 8. We**'ll be having** dinner then.
- Let's wait for Mary to arrive and then we**'ll have** dinner.

Compare **will be -ing** with other continuous forms:

- At 10 o'clock yesterday, Sally **was** in her office. She **was working**. (*past*)
  It's 10 o'clock now. She **is** in her office. She **is working**. (*present*)
  At 10 o'clock tomorrow, she **will be** in her office. She **will be working**.

C We also use **will be doing** in a different way: to talk about *complete* actions in the future:

- A: If you see Sally, can you ask her to phone me?
  B: Sure. **I'll be seeing** her this evening, so I'll tell her then.
- What time **will** your friends **be arriving** tomorrow?

In these examples **will be -ing** is similar to the present continuous for the future. (See Unit 19A.)

You can use **Will you be -ing...?** to ask about somebody's plans, especially if you want something or want them to do something. For example:

- A: **Will you be passing** the post office when you're out?
  B: Probably. Why?
  A: I need some stamps. Could you get me some?
- A: **Will you be using** your bicycle this evening?
  B: No. Do you want to borrow it?

D We use **will have** (**done**) (*future perfect*) to say that something will already be complete. Kevin's football match ends at 9.15. So after this time, for example at 9.30, the match **will have finished**. Some more examples:

- Sally always leaves for work at 8.30 in the morning, so she won't be at home at 9 o'clock. She**'ll have gone** to work.
- We're late. The film **will** already **have started** by the time we get to the cinema.

Compare **will have** (**done**) with other perfect forms:

- Ted and Amy **have been** married for 24 years. (*present perfect*)
  Next year they **will have been** married for 25 years.
  When their first child was born, they **had been** married for three years. (*past perfect*)

EXERCISES

24.1 *Read about Colin. Then you have to tick (✓) the sentences which are true. In each group of sentences at least one is true.*

Colin goes to work every day. He leaves home at 8 o'clock and arrives at work at about 8.45. He starts work immediately and continues until 12.30 when he has lunch (which takes about half an hour). He starts work again at 1.15 and goes home at exactly 4.30. Every day he follows the same routine and tomorrow will be no exception.

1 **At 7.45**
    a he'll be leaving the house
    b he'll have left the house
    c he'll be at home ✓
    d he'll be having breakfast ✓

4 **At 12.45**
    a he'll have lunch
    b he'll be having lunch
    c he'll have finished his lunch
    d he'll have started his lunch

2 **At 8.15**
    a he'll be leaving the house
    b he'll have left the house
    c he'll have arrived at work
    d he'll be arriving at work

5 **At 4 o'clock**
    a he'll have finished work
    b he'll finish work
    c he'll be working
    d he won't have finished work

3 **At 9.15**
    a he'll be working
    b he'll start work
    c he'll have started work
    d he'll be arriving at work

6 **At 4.45**
    a he'll leave work
    b he'll be leaving work
    c he'll have left work
    d he'll have arrived home

24.2 *Put the verb into the correct form,* **will be** (do)**ing** *or* **will have** (done).

1 Don't phone me between 7 and 8. ....*We'll be having*.... (we/have) dinner then.
2 Phone me after 8 o'clock. .... (we/finish) dinner by then.
3 Tomorrow afternoon we're going to play tennis from 3 o'clock until 4.30. So at 4 o'clock,
.... (we/play) tennis.
4 A: Can we meet tomorrow afternoon?
   B: Not in the afternoon. .... (I/work).
5 B *has to go to a meeting which begins at 10 o'clock. It will last about an hour.*
   A: Will you be free at 11.30?
   B: Yes, ... (the meeting/finish) by that time.
6 Tom is on holiday and he is spending his money very quickly. If he continues like this,
.... (he/spend) all his money before the end of his holiday.
7 Chuck came to Britain from the USA nearly three years ago. Next Monday it will be exactly
three years. So on Monday, ... (he/be) in Britain for
exactly three years.
8 Do you think .... (you/still/do) the same job in ten
years' time?
9 Jane is from New Zealand. She is travelling around Europe at the moment. So far she has
travelled about 1,000 miles. By the end of the trip, ...
(she/travel) more than 3,000 miles.
10 If you need to contact me, ... (I/stay) at the Lion Hotel
until Friday.
11 A: .... (you/see) Laura tomorrow?
   B: Yes, probably. Why?
   A: I borrowed this book from her. Can you give it back to her?

When I do / When I've done   When and if

A

Study these examples:

> A: What time will you phone me tomorrow?
> B: I'll phone you **when** I **get** home from work.
>
> 'I'll phone you when I get home from work' is a sentence with two parts:
> > *the main part:* 'I'll phone you'
> > and *the when-part:* '**when** I **get** home from work (tomorrow)'
> The time in the sentence is future ('tomorrow') but we use a *present* tense (**get**) in the **when**-part of the sentence.
> We do *not* use **will** in the **when**-part of the sentence:
> * We'll **go** out **when** it **stops** raining. (*not* 'when it will stop')
> * **When** you **are** in London again, you must come and see us. (*not* 'when you will be')
> * (*said to a child*) What do you want to be **when** you **grow** up? (*not* 'will grow')

The same thing happens after: **while   before   after   as soon as   until** *or* **till**
* I'm going to read a lot of books **while I'm** on holiday. (*not* 'while I will be')
* I'm going back home on Sunday. **Before I go,** I'd like to visit the museum.
* Wait here **until** (*or* **till**) I **come** back.

B

You can also use the *present perfect* (**have done**) after **when / after / until / as soon as**:
* Can I borrow that book **when you've finished** it?
* Don't say anything while Ian is here. Wait **until** he **has gone**.

It is often possible to use the present simple or the present perfect:
* I'll come **as soon as I finish.**   *or*   I'll come **as soon as I've finished.**
* You'll feel better **after** you **have**   *or*   You'll feel better **after** you've **had**
  something to eat.   something to eat.

But do not use the present perfect if two things *happen together*. The present perfect shows that one thing will be complete *before* the other (so the two things do *not* happen together).
Compare:
* **When I've phoned** Kate, we can have dinner.
  (= First I'll phone Kate and after that we can have dinner.)

but * **When I phone** Kate this evening, I'll invite her to the party. (*not* 'when I've phoned')
  (In this example, the two things happen together.)

C

After **if**, we normally use the present simple (**if I do / if I see** etc.) for the future:
* It's raining hard. We'll get wet **if we go** out. (*not* 'if we will go')
* Hurry up! **If** we **don't hurry**, we'll be late.

Compare **when** and **if**:
We use **when** for things which are *sure* to happen:
* I'm going shopping this afternoon. (for sure)   **When** I go shopping, I'll buy some food.

We use **if** (*not* 'when') for things that will *possibly* happen:
* I might go shopping this afternoon. (it's possible)   **If** I go shopping, I'll buy some food.
* **If** it is raining this evening, I won't go out. (*not* 'when it is raining')
* Don't worry **if** I'm late tonight. (*not* 'when I'm late')
* **If** they don't come soon, I'm not going to wait. (*not* 'when they don't come')

EXERCISES

25.1 *Complete these sentences using the verbs in brackets. All the sentences are about the future. Use* **will/won't** *or the present simple* (I **see** / he **plays** / it **is** etc.).

1 I 'll phone.. (phone) you when I ...get... (get) home from work.
2 I want to see Margaret before she .... (go) out.
3 We're going on holiday tomorrow. I .... (tell) you all about it when we .... (come) back.
4 Brian looks very different now. When you .... (see) him again, you .... (not/recognise) him.
5 We must do something soon before it .... (be) too late.
6 I don't want to go without you. I .... (wait) until you .... (be) ready.
7 Sue has applied for the job but she isn't very well qualified for it. I .... (be) surprised if she .... (get) it.
8 I'd like to play tennis tomorrow if the weather .... (be) nice.
9 I'm going out now. If anybody .... (phone) while I .... (be) out, can you take a message?

25.2 *Make one sentence from two.*

1 You will be in London again. You must come and see us then.
   You must come and see us.. when ..you are in London again...
2 I'll find somewhere to live. Then I'll give you my address.
   I .... when ....
3 I'll do the shopping. Then I'll come straight back home.
   .... after ....
4 It's going to start raining. Let's go home before that.
   .... before ....
5 She must apologise to me first. I won't speak to her until then.
   .... until ....

25.3 *Read the situations and complete the sentences.*

1 A friend of yours is going to visit London. You want to know where she is going to stay.
   You ask: Where are you going to stay when ...you are in London?..
2 A friend of yours is visiting you. She has to go soon but maybe there's time for a cup of tea.
   You ask: Would you like a cup of tea before ....?
3 Your friend is reading the newspaper. You'd like it after her.
   You ask: Can I have the newspaper when ....?
4 You want to sell your car. Jim is interested in buying it but he hasn't decided yet.
   You ask: Can you let me know as soon as ....?
5 There are serious traffic problems in your town but they are building a new road.
   You say: I think it will be better when ....

25.4 *Put in* **when** *or* **if**.

1 Don't worry ...if... I'm late tonight.
2 Tom might phone while I'm out this evening. .... he does, can you take a message?
3 I'm going to Rome next week. .... I'm there, I hope to visit a friend of mine.
4 I think Jill will get the job. I'll be very surprised .... she doesn't get it.
5 I'm going shopping. .... you want anything, I can get it for you.
6 I'm going away for a few days. I'll phone you .... I get back.
7 I want you to come to the party but .... you don't want to come, that's all right.
8 We can eat at home or, ... you prefer, we can go to a restaurant.

Can, could and (be) able to

A We use **can** to say that something is possible or that somebody has the ability to do something.
We use **can** + *infinitive* (**can do / can see** etc.):

- We **can see** the lake from our bedroom window.
- **Can** you **speak** any foreign languages?
- I **can come** and see you tomorrow if you like.

The negative is **can't** (= **cannot**):

- I'm afraid I **can't come** to the party on Friday.

B **(Be) able to...** is possible instead of **can**, but **can** is more usual:

- **Are** you **able to speak** any foreign languages?

But **can** has only two forms, **can** *(present)* and **could** *(past)*. So sometimes it is necessary to use **(be) able to...** . Compare:

- I **can't** sleep.
but   I **haven't been able to** sleep recently. (**can** has no present perfect)
- Tom **can** come tomorrow.
but   Tom **might be able to** come tomorrow. (**can** has no infinitive)

C **Could** and **was able to...**

Sometimes **could** is the past of **can**. We use **could** especially with:

see	hear	smell	taste	feel	remember	understand

- When we went into the house, we **could smell** burning.
- She spoke in a very low voice, but I **could understand** what she said.

We also use **could** to say that somebody had the general ability or permission to do something:

- My grandfather **could speak** five languages.
- We were completely free. We **could do** what we wanted. (= we were allowed to do...)

We use **could** for *general* ability. But if we are talking about what happened *in a particular situation*, we use **was/were able to...** or **managed to...** (*not* **could**):

- The fire spread through the building quickly but everybody **was able to escape**.
or ...everybody **managed to escape**. (*but not* 'could escape')
- They didn't want to come with us at first but we **managed to persuade** them.
or ...we **were able to persuade** them. (*but not* 'could persuade')

Compare:
- Jack was an excellent tennis player. He **could beat** anybody. (= he had the general ability to beat anybody)

but
- Jack and Alf had a game of tennis yesterday. Alf played very well but in the end Jack **managed to beat** him. *or* ...**was able to beat** him. (= he managed to beat him in this particular game)

The negative **couldn't** (**could not**) is possible in all situations:

- My grandfather **couldn't swim**.
- We tried hard but we **couldn't persuade** them to come with us.
- Alf played well but he **couldn't beat** Jack.

   Could (do) and **could have (done)** → UNIT 27   **Must** and **can't** → UNIT 28   **Can/Could** you...? → UNIT 36

EXERCISES

26.1 *Complete the sentences using* **can** *or* **(be) able to.** *Use* **can** *if possible; otherwise use* **(be) able to.**

1 George has travelled a lot. He ...**can**... speak four languages.
2 I haven't ...**been able to**... sleep very well recently.
3 Sandra .... drive but she hasn't got a car.
4 I can't understand Martin. I've never .... understand him.
5 I used to .... stand on my head but I can't do it now.
6 I can't see you on Friday but I .... meet you on Saturday morning.
7 Ask Catherine about your problem. She might .... help you.

26.2 *Write sentences about yourself using the ideas in brackets.*

1 (something you used to be able to do) ...**I used to be able to sing well.**...
2 (something you used to be able to do) I used ....
3 (something you would like to be able to do)
   I'd ....
4 (something you have never been able to do)
   I've ....

26.3 *Complete the sentences with* **can / can't / could / couldn't** + *one of these verbs:*

~~come~~   eat   hear   run   sleep   wait

1 I'm afraid I ...**can't come**... to your party next week.
2 When Tim was 16, he was a fast runner. He .... 100 metres in 11 seconds.
3 'Are you in a hurry?'   'No, I've got plenty of time. I ....'
4 I was feeling sick yesterday. I .... anything.
5 Can you speak up a bit? I .... you very well.
6 'You look tired.'   'Yes, I .... last night.'

26.4 *Complete the answers to the questions with* **was/were able to.**

1 A: Did everybody escape from the fire?
   B: Yes, although the fire spread quickly, everybody ...**was able to escape.**...
2 A: Did you have difficulty finding Ann's house?
   B: Not really. Ann had given us good directions and we ....
3 A: Did you finish your work this afternoon?
   B: Yes, there was nobody to disturb me, so ....
4 A: Did the thief get away?
   B: Yes. No one realised what was happening and the thief ....

26.5 *Complete the sentences using* **could, couldn't** *or* **was/were able to.**

1 My grandfather was a very clever man. He ...**could**... speak five languages.
2 I looked everywhere for the book but I ...**couldn't**... find it.
3 They didn't want to come with us at first but we ...**were able to**... persuade them.
4 Laura had hurt her leg and .... walk very well.
5 Sue wasn't at home when I phoned but I .... contact her at her office.
6 I looked very carefully and I .... see a figure in the distance.
7 I wanted to buy some tomatoes. The first shop I went to didn't have any but I
   .... get some in the next shop.
8 My grandmother loved music. She .... play the piano very well.
9 A girl fell into the river but fortunately we .... rescue her.
10 I had forgotten to bring my camera so I .... take any photographs.

Could (do) and could have (done)

A We use **could** in a number of ways. Sometimes **could** is the past of **can** (see Unit 26C):
- Listen. I **can hear** something. *(now)*
- I listened. I **could hear** something. *(past)*

But **could** is not only used in this way. We also use **could** to talk about possible actions *now* or *in the future* (especially to make a suggestion). For example:

> *What shall we do this evening?*
>
> *We could go to the cinema.*

- A: What shall we do this evening?
  B: We **could go** to the cinema.
- It's a nice day. We **could go** for a walk.
- When you go to New York next month, you **could stay** with Barbara.
- A: If you need money, why don't you ask Karen?
  B: Yes, I suppose I **could.**

Can is also possible in these sentences ('We **can** go for a walk.' etc.). **Could** is less sure than **can**. You *must* use **could** (*not* 'can') when you don't really mean what you say. For example:
- I'm so angry with him. I **could** kill him! (*not* 'I can kill him')

B We also use **could** to say that something is possible now or in the future:
- The phone is ringing. It **could be** Tim.
- I don't know when they'll be here. They **could arrive** at any time.

Can is *not* possible in these examples (*not* 'It can be Tim').
In these sentences **could** is similar to **might** (see Units 29–30):
- The phone is ringing. It **might** be Tim.

C Compare **could** (**do**) and **could have** (**done**):
- I'm so tired. I **could sleep** for a week. *(now)*
- I was so tired. I **could have slept** for a week. *(past)*

Most often, we use **could have** (**done**) for things which were possible but did *not* happen:
- Why did you stay at a hotel when you went to New York? You **could have stayed** with Barbara. (= you had the opportunity to stay with her but you didn't)
- Jack fell off a ladder yesterday but he's all right. He's lucky – he **could have hurt** himself badly. (but he didn't hurt himself)
- The situation was bad but it **could have been** worse.

D Sometimes **could** means 'would be able to…':
- We **could go** away if we had enough money. (= we would be able to go away)
- I don't know how you work so hard. I **couldn't do** it.

Could have (**done**) = would **have been** able to (do):
- Why didn't Liz apply for the job? She **could have got** it.
- We **could have gone** away if we'd had enough money.
- The trip was cancelled last week. Paul **couldn't have gone** anyway because he was ill. (= he wouldn't have been able to go)
- You did very well to pass the exam. I'm sure I **couldn't have passed** it. (= I wouldn't have been able to pass it if I had taken it)

Couldn't have (done) → UNIT 28B   **Could** and **might** → UNIT 29C   **Could** I/you…? → UNIT 36
Could with **if** → UNITS 37C, 38E and 39D

EXERCISES

27.1 *Answer the questions with a suggestion. Use* **could**.

1	Where shall we go for our holidays?	(to Scotland) .._We could go to Scotland.._
2	What shall we have for dinner tonight?	(fish) We ....
3	What shall I give Ann for her birthday?	(a book) You ....
4	When shall I phone Angela?	(now) ....
5	When shall we go and see Tom?	(on Friday) ....
6	Where shall we hang this picture?	(in the kitchen) ....

27.2 *Put in* **can** *or* **could**. *Sometimes either word is possible.*

1 'The phone is ringing. Who do you think it is?'   'It ...could... be Tim.'
2 I'm really hungry. I .... eat a horse!
3 If you're very hungry, we .... have dinner now.
4 It's so nice here. I .... stay here all day but unfortunately I have to go.
5 'I can't find my bag. Have you seen it?'   'No, but it .... be in the car.'
6 Peter is a keen musician. He plays the flute and he .... also play the piano.
7 'What shall we do?'   'There's a film on television. We .... watch that.'
8 The weather is nice now but it .... change later.

27.3 *Complete the sentences. Use* **could** *or* **could have** + *a suitable verb.*

1 A: What shall we do this evening?   B: I don't mind. We ...could go... to the cinema.
2 A: I had a very boring evening at home yesterday.
   B: Why did you stay at home? You .... to the cinema.
3 A: There's an interesting job advertised in the paper. You .... for it.
   B: What sort of job is it? Show me the advertisement.
4 A: Did you go to the concert last night?
   B: No. We .... but we decided not to.
5 A: Where shall we meet tomorrow?
   B: Well, I .... to your house if you like.

27.4 *Read this information about Ken:*

Ken didn't do anything on Saturday evening.	Ken was short of money last week.
Ken doesn't know anything about machines.	~~Ken's car was stolen on Monday.~~
Ken was free on Monday afternoon.	Ken had to work on Friday evening.

Some people wanted Ken to do different things last week but they couldn't contact him. So he didn't do any of these things. You have to say whether he could have done or couldn't have done them.

1 Ken's aunt wanted him to drive her to the airport on Tuesday.
   ..._He couldn't have driven her to the airport (because his car had been stolen)._...
2 A friend of his wanted him to go out for a meal on Friday evening.
   Ken ....
3 Another friend wanted him to play tennis on Monday afternoon.
   Ken ....
4 Jack wanted Ken to lend him £50 last week.
   ....
5 Jane wanted Ken to come to her party on Saturday evening.
   He ....
6 Ken's mother wanted him to repair her washing machine.
   ....

Must and **can't**

A Study this example:

My house is very near the motorway.

It **must be** very noisy.

We use **must** to say that we feel sure something is true:

- You've been travelling all day. You **must be** tired. (Travelling is tiring and you've been travelling all day, so you **must** be tired.)
- 'Jim is a hard worker.'   'Jim? A hard worker? You **must be joking**. He's very lazy.'
- Carol **must get** very bored in her job. She does the same thing every day.

We use **can't** to say that we feel sure something is not possible:

- You've just had lunch. You **can't be** hungry already. (People are not normally hungry just after eating a meal. You've just eaten, so you **can't** be hungry.)
- Brian said he would definitely be here before 9.30. It's 10 o'clock now and he's never late. He **can't be coming**.
- They haven't lived here for very long. They **can't know** many people.

Study the structure:

I/you/he (etc.)	**must** **can't**	**be** (tired / hungry / at work etc.) **be** (doing / coming / joking etc.) **do / go / know / have** etc.

B For the past we use **must have** (**done**) and **can't have** (**done**). Study this example:

George is outside his friends' house.
He has rung the doorbell three times but nobody has answered.

They **must have gone** out.
(otherwise they would have answered)

- The phone rang but I didn't hear it. I **must have been** asleep.
- I've lost one of my gloves. I **must have dropped** it somewhere.
- Jane walked past me without speaking. She **can't have seen** me.
- Tom walked straight into a wall. He **can't have been looking** where he was going.

Study the structure:

I/you/he (etc.)	**must** **can't**	**have**	**been** (asleep / at work etc.) **been** (doing / working etc.) **done / gone / known / had** etc.

Couldn't have… is possible instead of **can't have…**:

- She **couldn't have seen** me.
- Tom **couldn't have been looking** where he was going.

Can't ('I can't swim' etc.) → **UNIT 26**   Must ('I must go' etc.) → **UNITS 31–32**

EXERCISES

28.1 *Put in* **must** *or* **can't**.

1 You've been travelling all day. You ...**must**... be very tired.
2 That restaurant .... be very good. It's always full of people.
3 That restaurant .... be very good. It's always empty.
4 You're going on holiday next week. You .... be looking forward to it.
5 It rained every day during their holiday, so they .... have had a very nice time.
6 Congratulations on passing your exam. You .... be very pleased.
7 You got here very quickly. You .... have walked very fast.
8 Bill and Sue go away on holiday very often, so they .... be short of money.

28.2 *Complete the sentences with a verb in the correct form.*

1 I've lost one of my gloves. I must ...**have dropped**... it somewhere.
2 They haven't lived here for long. They can't ...**know**... many people.
3 Ted isn't at work today. He must .... ill.
4 Ted wasn't at work last week. He must .... ill.
5 *(The doorbell rings)* I wonder who that is. It can't .... Mary. She's still at work at this time.
6 Carol knows a lot about films. She must .... to the cinema a lot.
7 Look. Jack is putting on his hat and coat. He must .... out.
8 I left my bike outside the house last night and this morning it isn't there any more. Somebody must .... it.
9 Ann was in a very difficult situation. It can't .... easy for her.
10 There is a man walking behind us. He has been walking behind us for the last 20 minutes. He must .... us.

28.3 *Read the situations and use the words in brackets to write sentences with* **must have** *and* **can't have**.

1 The phone rang but I didn't hear it. (I / asleep)
..*I must have been asleep.*..
2 Jane walked past me without speaking. (she / see / me)
..*She can't have seen me.*..
3 The jacket you bought is very good quality. (it / very expensive)
....
4 I haven't seen the people next door for ages. (they / go away)
....
5 I can't find my umbrella. (I / leave / it in the restaurant last night)
....
6 Don passed the exam without studying for it. (the exam / very difficult)
....
7 She knew everything about our plans. (she / listen / to our conversation)
....
8 Fiona did the opposite of what I asked her to do. (she / understand / what I said)
....
9 When I woke up this morning, the light was on. (I / forget / to turn it off)
....
10 The lights were red but the car didn't stop. (the driver / see / the red light)
....
11 I was woken up in the middle of the night by the noise next door. (the neighbours / have / a party) ....

May and **might** (1)

A

Study this example situation:

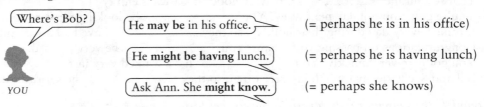

> You are looking for Bob. Nobody is sure where he is but you get some suggestions.
>
> Where's Bob?
> YOU
>
> He **may be** in his office.   (= perhaps he is in his office)
>
> He **might be having** lunch.   (= perhaps he is having lunch)
>
> Ask Ann. She **might know.**   (= perhaps she knows)

We use **may** or **might** to say that something is a possibility. Usually you can use **may** or **might**, so you can say:

- It **may** be true. *or* It **might** be true. (= perhaps it is true)
- She **might** know. *or* She **may** know.

The negative forms are **may not** and **might not** (*or* **mightn't**):

- It **might not** be true. (= perhaps it isn't true)
- I'm not sure whether I can lend you any money. I **may not** have enough. (= perhaps I don't have enough)

Study the structure:

I/you/he (etc.)	may might	(not)	be (true / in his office etc.) be (doing / working / having etc.) do / know / have / want etc.

B

For the past we use **may have** (**done**) or **might have** (**done**):

- A: I wonder why Kay didn't answer the phone.
  B: She **may have been** asleep. (= perhaps she was asleep)
- A: I can't find my bag anywhere.
  B: You **might have left** it in the shop. (= perhaps you left it in the shop)
- A: I was surprised that Sarah wasn't at the meeting.
  B: She **might not have known** about it. (= perhaps she didn't know)
- A: I wonder why Colin was in such a bad mood yesterday.
  B: He **may not have been feeling** well. (= perhaps he wasn't feeling well)

Study the structure:

I/you/he (etc.)	may might	(not) have	been (asleep / at home etc.) been (doing / waiting etc.) done / known / had / seen etc.

C

Sometimes **could** has a similar meaning to **may** and **might**:

- The phone's ringing. It **could be** Tim. (= it may/might be Tim)
- You **could have left** your bag in the shop. (= you may/might have left it...)

But **couldn't** *(negative)* is different from **may not** and **might not**. Compare:

- She was too far away, so she **couldn't have seen** you. (= it is not possible that she saw you)
- A: I wonder why she didn't say hello.
  B: She **might not have seen** you. (= perhaps she didn't see you; perhaps she did)

EXERCISES

29.1 Write these sentences in a different way using **may** or **might**.

1 Perhaps Margaret is in her office. ...She might be in her office...
2 Perhaps Margaret is busy. ....
3 Perhaps she is working. ....
4 Perhaps she wants to be alone. ....
5 Perhaps she was ill yesterday. ....
6 Perhaps she went home early. ....
7 Perhaps she had to go home early. ....
8 Perhaps she was working yesterday. ....

In sentences 9–11 use **may not** or **might not**.

9 Perhaps she doesn't want to see me. ....
10 Perhaps she isn't working today. ....
11 Perhaps she wasn't feeling well yesterday. ....

29.2 Complete the sentences with a verb in the correct form.

1 'Where's Bob?'   'I'm not sure. He might ...be having... lunch.'
2 'Who is that man with Ann?'   'I'm not sure. It might .... her brother.'
3 'Who was the man we saw with Ann yesterday?'   'I'm not sure. It might ....
her brother.'
4 'Why are those people waiting in the street?'   'I don't know. They might ....
for a bus.'
5 'Shall I buy this book for Tim?'   'You'd better not. He might already .... it.'

29.3 Read the situations and make sentences from the words in brackets. Use **may** or **might**.

1 I can't find George anywhere. I wonder where he is.
   a (he / go / shopping) ...He may have gone shopping...
   b (he / play / tennis) ...He might be playing tennis...
2 I'm looking for Helen. Do you know where she is?
   a (she / watch / TV / in her room) ....
   b (she / go / out) ....
3 I can't find my umbrella. Have you seen it?
   a (it / be / in the car) ....
   b (you / leave / in the restaurant last night) ....
4 Why didn't Tom answer the doorbell? I'm sure he was in the house at the time.
   a (he / be / in the bath) ....
   b (he / not / hear / the bell) ....

29.4 Complete the sentences using **might not** or **couldn't**.

1 A: Do you think she saw you?
   B: No, she was too far away. ...She couldn't have seen me...
2 A: I wonder why she didn't say hello. Perhaps she didn't see me.
   B: That's possible. ...She might not have seen you...
3 A: I wonder why Ann didn't come to the party. Perhaps she wasn't invited.
   B Yes, it's possible. She ....
4 A: Tom loves parties. I'm sure he would have come to the party if he'd been invited.
   B: I agree. He ....
5 A: I wonder how the fire started. Do you think it was an accident?
   B: No, the police say it ....
6 A: How did the fire start? I suppose it was an accident.
   B: Well, the police aren't sure. They say it ....

May and **might** (2)

A We use **may** and **might** to talk about possible actions or happenings in the future:
  - I haven't decided yet where to spend my holidays. I **may go** to Ireland. (= perhaps I will go to Ireland)
  - Take an umbrella with you when you go out. It **might rain** later. (= perhaps it will rain)
  - The bus doesn't always come on time. We **might have** to wait a few minutes. (= perhaps we will have to wait)

The negative forms are **may not** and **might not** (**mightn't**):
  - Ann **may not come** to the party tonight. She isn't well. (= perhaps she will not come)
  - There **might not be** a meeting on Friday because the director is ill. (= perhaps there will not be a meeting)

B Usually it doesn't matter whether you use **may** or **might**. So you can say:
  - I **may go** to Ireland. *or* I **might go** to Ireland.
  - Jane **might be** able to help you. *or* Jane **may be** able to help you.

But we use only **might** (*not* **may**) when the situation is *not real*:
  - If I knew them better, I **might** invite them to dinner.
    (The situation here is not real because I *don't* know them very well, so I'm *not* going to invite them. 'May' is not possible in this example.)

C There is also a continuous form: **may/might be -ing**. Compare this with **will be -ing**:
  - Don't phone at 8.30. I'**ll be watching** the football on television.
  - Don't phone at 8.30. I **might be watching** (*or* I **may be watching**) the football on television. (= perhaps I'll be watching it)

For **will be -ing** see Unit 24.

We also use **may/might be -ing** for possible plans. Compare:
  - I'**m going** to Ireland in July. (for sure)
  - I **may be going** (*or* I **might be going**) to Ireland in July. (possible)

But you can also say 'I **may go** (*or* I **might go**) to Ireland…' with little difference of meaning.

D **Might as well / may as well**
Study this example:

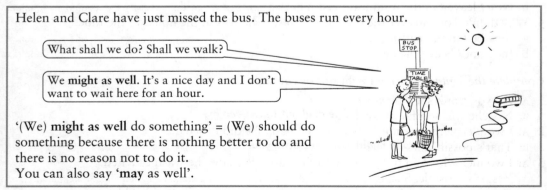

Helen and Clare have just missed the bus. The buses run every hour.

> What shall we do? Shall we walk?

> We **might as well**. It's a nice day and I don't want to wait here for an hour.

'(We) **might as well** do something' = (We) should do something because there is nothing better to do and there is no reason not to do it.
You can also say '**may as well**'.

  - A: What time are you going?
    B: Well, I'm ready, so I **might as well go** now. (*or* …I **may as well go** now)
  - The buses are so expensive these days, you **might as well get** a taxi. (= taxis are just as good, no more expensive)

EXERCISES

30.1 *Write sentences with* **may** *or* **might**.

1 Where are you going for your holidays? (to Ireland???)
   I haven't decided yet. ...**I may go to Ireland.**..

2 What sort of car are you going to buy? (a Mercedes???)
   I'm not sure yet. I ....

3 What are you doing this weekend? (go to London???)
   I haven't decided yet. ....

4 Where are you going to hang that picture? (in the dining room???)
   I haven't made up my mind yet. ....

5 When is Tom coming to see us? (on Saturday???)
   I don't know yet. ....

6 What is Julia going to do when she leaves school? (go to university???)
   She hasn't decided yet. ....

30.2 *Complete the sentences using* **might** + *one of these verbs:*

bite   break   need   ~~rain~~   slip   wake

1 Take an umbrella with you when you go out. It ...**might rain**... later.
2 Don't make too much noise. You .... the baby.
3 Be careful of that dog. It .... you.
4 I don't think we should throw that letter away. We .... it later.
5 Be careful. The footpath is very icy. You ....
6 I don't want the children to play in this room. They .... something.

30.3 *Complete the sentences using* **might be able to** *or* **might have to** + *a suitable verb.*

1 I can't help you but why don't you ask Jill? She ...**might be able to help**... you.
2 I can't meet you this evening but I .... you tomorrow
   evening.
3 I'm not working on Saturday but I .... on Sunday.
4 George isn't well. He .... to hospital for an operation.

30.4 *Write sentences with* **may not** *or* **might not**.

1 (I don't know if Ann will come to the party.) ...**Ann might not come to the party.**..
2 (I don't know if I'll go out this evening.) I ....
3 (I don't know if Tom will like the present I bought for him.)
   Tom ....
4 (I don't know if Sue will be able to meet us this evening.)
   ....

30.5 *Read the situations and make sentences with* **may/might as well**.

1 You and a friend have just missed the bus. The buses run every hour.
   You say: We'll have to wait an hour for the next bus. ...**We might as well walk.**..
2 You have a free ticket for a concert. You're not very keen on the concert but you decide to
   go. You say: I .... to the concert. It's a pity to waste a
   free ticket.
3 You're in a café with a friend. You've finished your drinks. It's a nice café and there is no
   reason to go now, so why not have another drink?
   You say: We .... What would you like?
4 You and a friend are at home. You are bored. There's a film on TV starting in a few minutes.
   You say: .... There's nothing else to do.

Must and have to

A We use **must** and **have to** to say that it is necessary to do something. Sometimes it doesn't matter which you use:

- Oh, it's later than I thought. I **must** go. *or* I **have to** go.

But there is a difference between **must** and **have to** and sometimes this is important:

Must is personal. We use **must** when we give our personal feelings. 'You **must** do something' = 'I (the speaker) say it is necessary': • She's a really nice person. You **must meet** her. (= *I* say this is necessary) • I haven't phoned Ann for ages. I **must phone** her tonight. Compare: • I **must** get up early tomorrow. There are a lot of things I want to do.	**Have to** is impersonal. We use **have to** for *facts*, not for our personal feelings. 'You **have to** do something' because of a rule or the situation: • You can't turn right here. You **have to turn** left. (because of the traffic system) • My eyesight isn't very good. I **have to wear** glasses for reading. • George can't come out with us this evening. He **has to work**. • I **have to** get up early tomorrow. I'm going away and my train leaves at 7.30.

If you are not sure which to use, it is usually safer to use **have to**.

B You can use **must** to talk about the present or future, but not the past:

- We **must go** now.
- We **must go** tomorrow. (*but not* 'We must go yesterday')

You can use **have to** in all forms. For example:

- I **had to go** to hospital. *(past)*
- **Have** you ever **had to go** to hospital? *(present perfect)*
- I **might have to go** to hospital. *(infinitive* after **might**)

In questions and negative sentences with **have to**, we normally use **do/does/did**:

- What **do I have to do** to get a driving licence? (*not* 'What have I to do?')
- Why **did** you **have to go** to hospital?
- Karen **doesn't have to work** on Saturdays.

C **Mustn't** and **don't have to** are completely different:

You **mustn't** do something = it is necessary that you do *not* do it (so, *don't* do it): • You **must** keep it a secret. You **mustn't tell** anyone. (= don't tell anyone) • I promised I would be on time. I **mustn't be** late. (= I must be on time)	You **don't have to** do something = you don't need to do it (but you can if you want): • You can tell me if you want but you **don't have to tell** me. (= you don't need to tell me) • I'm not working tomorrow, so I **don't have to get** up early.

D You can use 'have **got** to' instead of 'have to'. So you can say:

- I've **got to** work tomorrow.   *or*   I **have to** work tomorrow.
- When **has** Ann **got** to go?   *or*   When **does** Ann **have to** go?

Must and can't → UNIT 28   **Must/mustn't/needn't** → UNIT 32

EXERCISES

31.1 *Complete these sentences with* **must** *or* **have to** *(in the correct form). Sometimes it is possible to use either; sometimes only* **have to** *is possible.*

1 It's later than I thought. I ...**must OR have to**... go now.
2 Jack left before the end of the meeting. He ...**had to**... go home early.
3 In Britain many children .... wear uniform when they go to school.
4 When you come to London again, you .... come and see us.
5 Last night Don became ill suddenly. We .... call a doctor.
6 You really .... work harder if you want to pass the examination.
7 I'm afraid I can't come tomorrow. I .... work late.
8 I'm sorry I couldn't come yesterday. I .... work late.
9 Paul doesn't like his new job. Sometimes he .... work at weekends.
10 Caroline may .... go away next week.
11 We couldn't repair the car ourselves. We .... take it to a garage.
12 Julia wears glasses. She .... wear glasses since she was very young.

31.2 *Make questions with* **have to.**

1	I had to go to hospital last week.	Why ...**did you have to go to hospital?**
2	I have to get up early tomorrow.	Why .... early?
3	Ann has to go somewhere now.	Where .... she ....
4	George had to pay a parking fine yesterday.	How much ....
5	I had to wait a long time for the bus.	How long ....
6	I have to phone my sister now.	Why ....
7	Paul has to leave soon.	What time ....

31.3 *Complete these sentences using* **don't / doesn't / didn't have to** + *one of these verbs:*

do   ~~get up~~   **go**   **go**   **pay**   **shave**   **wait**   **work**

1 I'm not working tomorrow, so I ...**don't have to get up**... early.
2 The car park is free – you .... to park your car there.
3 I went to the bank this morning. There was no queue, so I ....
4 Sally is extremely rich. She ....
5 We've got plenty of time. We .... yet.
6 Jack has got a beard, so he ....
7 I'm not particularly busy. I've got a few things to do but I .... them now.
8 A man was slightly injured in the accident but he .... to hospital.

31.4 *Complete these sentences with* **mustn't** *or* **don't/doesn't have to.**

1 I don't want anyone to know. You ...**mustn't**... tell anyone.
2 He ...**doesn't have to get to**... wear a suit to work but he usually does.
3 I can stay in bed tomorrow morning because I .... go to work.
4 Whatever you do, you .... touch that switch. It's very dangerous.
5 There's a lift in the building, so we .... climb the stairs.
6 You .... forget what I told you. It's very important.
7 Sue .... get up early. She gets up early because she wants to.
8 Don't make so much noise. We .... wake the baby.
9 I .... eat too much. I'm supposed to be on a diet.
10 You .... be a good player to enjoy a game of tennis.

Must   mustn't   needn't

A   Must   mustn't   needn't

> 'You **must** do something' = it is necessary that you do it:
> - Don't tell anybody what I said. You **must** keep it a secret.
> - We haven't got much time. We **must** hurry.
>
> 'You **mustn't** do something' = it is necessary that you do *not* do it (so don't do it):
> - You **must** keep it a secret. You **mustn't** tell anybody else. (= don't tell anybody else)
> - It's essential that nobody hears us. We **mustn't** make any noise.
>
> 'You **needn't** do something' = it is *not necessary* that you do it, you don't need to do it:
> - You can come with me if you like but you **needn't come** if you don't want to. (= it is not necessary for you to come)
> - We've got plenty of time. We **needn't hurry**. (= it is not necessary to hurry)

B   Instead of **needn't**, you can use **don't/doesn't need to**. So you can say:
- We **needn't** hurry.   *or*   We **don't need to** hurry.

Remember that we say 'don't need **to do**', but 'needn't **do**' (without **to**).

Needn't and **don't need to** are similar to **don't have to** (see Unit 31C):
- We've got plenty of time. We **don't have to** hurry.

C   Needn't have (**done**)

Study this example situation:

I think it's going to rain. I'll take the umbrella.

I needn't have **brought** the umbrella.

George had to go out. He thought it was going to rain, so he decided to take the umbrella.

But it didn't rain, so the umbrella was not necessary. So:
He **needn't have taken** the umbrella.

'He **needn't have taken** the umbrella' = He took the umbrella but this was not necessary. Of course, he didn't know this when he went out.

Compare **needn't** (do) and **needn't have** (done):
- That shirt isn't dirty. You **needn't wash** it.
- Why did you wash that shirt? It wasn't dirty. You **needn't have washed** it.

D   Didn't need to (**do**) and **needn't have** (**done**)

I **didn't need to...** = it was not necessary for me to... (and I knew this at the time):
- I **didn't need to** get up early, so I didn't.
- I **didn't need to** get up early, but it was a lovely morning, so I did.

'I **needn't have** (**done**) something' = I did something but *now I know* that it was not necessary:
- I got up very early because I had to get ready to go away. But in fact it didn't take me long to get ready. So, I **needn't have got** up so early. I could have stayed in bed longer.

EXERCISES

32.1 *Complete the sentences using* **needn't** + *one of these verbs:*

ask   come   explain   ~~leave~~   tell   walk

1 We've got plenty of time. We ...**needn't leave**... yet.
2 I can manage the shopping alone. You .... with me.
3 We .... all the way home. We can get a taxi.
4 Just help yourself if you'd like something to eat. You .... first.
5 We can keep this a secret between ourselves. We .... anybody else.
6 I understand the situation perfectly. You .... further.

32.2 *Complete the sentences with* **must, mustn't** *or* **needn't.**

1 We haven't got much time. We ...**must**... hurry.
2 We've got plenty of time. We ...**needn't**... hurry.
3 We have enough food at home so we .... go shopping today.
4 Jim gave me a letter to post. I .... remember to post it.
5 Jim gave me a letter to post. I .... forget to post it.
6 There's plenty of time for you to make up your mind. You .... decide now.
7 You .... wash those tomatoes. They've already been washed.
8 This is a valuable book. You .... look after it carefully and you ....
   lose it.
9 'What sort of house do you want to buy? Something big?'   'Well, it .... be big
   – that's not important. But it .... have a nice garden – that's essential.'

32.3 *Read the situations and make sentences with* **needn't have.**

1 George went out. He took an umbrella because he thought it was going to rain. But it didn't
   rain. ...**He needn't have taken an umbrella.**...
2 Ann bought some eggs when she went shopping. When she got home, she found that she
   already had plenty of eggs. She ....
3 A friend got angry with you and shouted at you. You think this was unnecessary. Later you
   say to him/her: You ....
4 Brian had no money, so he sold his car. A few days later he won some money in a lottery.
   He ....
5 When we went on holiday, we took the camera with us but we didn't use it in the end.
   ....
6 I thought I was going to miss my train so I rushed to the station. But the train was late and in
   the end I had to wait 20 minutes. ....

32.4 *Write two sentences for each situation. Use* **needn't have** *in the first sentence and* **could have** *in
the second (as in the example). For* **could have** *see Unit 27.*

1 Why did you rush? Why didn't you take your time?
   ...**You needn't have rushed. You could have taken your time.**...
2 Why did you walk home? Why didn't you take a taxi?
   ....
3 Why did you stay at a hotel? Why didn't you stay with us?
   ....
4 Why did she phone me in the middle of the night? Why didn't she phone me in the morning?
   ....
5 Why did you leave without saying anything? Why didn't you say goodbye to me?
   ....
   ....

Should (1)

A You **should do** something = it is a good thing to do or the right thing to do. You can use **should** to give advice or to give an opinion:

- You look tired. You **should** go to bed.
- The government **should do** more to help homeless people.
- 'Should we invite Susan to the party?' 'Yes, I think we should.'

We often use **should** with **I think / I don't think / Do you think...?**:

- **I think** the government **should do** more to help homeless people.
- **I don't think** you **should work** so hard.
- '**Do you think** I should apply for this job?' 'Yes, **I think you should.**'

'You **shouldn't** do something' = it isn't a good thing to do:

- You **shouldn't believe** everything you read in the newspapers.

Should is not as strong as **must**:

- You **should** apologise. (= it would be a good thing to do)
- You **must** apologise. (= you have no alternative)

B We also use **should** when something is not right or what we expect. For example:

- I wonder where Liz is. She **should be** here by now. (= she isn't here yet, and this is not normal)
- The price on this packet is wrong. It **should be** £1.20, not £1.50.
- Those boys **shouldn't be playing** football at this time. They **should be** at school.

He should be wearing a helmet.

We use **should** to say that we expect something to happen:

- She's been studying hard for the exam, so she **should pass.** (= I expect her to pass)
- There are plenty of hotels in the town. It **shouldn't be** difficult to find somewhere to stay. (= I don't expect that it will be difficult)

C 'You **should have done** something' = you didn't do it but it would have been the right thing to do:

- It was a great party last night. You **should have come.** Why didn't you? (= you didn't come but it would have been good to come)
- I'm feeling sick. I **shouldn't have eaten** so much chocolate. (= I ate too much chocolate)
- I wonder why they're so late. They **should have been** here an hour ago.
- She **shouldn't have been listening** to our conversation. It was private.

Compare **should** (do) and **should have** (done):

- You look tired. You **should go** to bed now.
- You went to bed very late last night. You **should have gone** to bed earlier.

D Ought to...
You can use **ought to** instead of **should** in the sentences on this page. Note that we say 'ought to do...' (with **to**):

- Do you think I **ought to apply** for this job? (= Do you think I **should apply...?**)
- Jack **ought not to go** to bed so late. (= Jack **shouldn't go...**)
- It was a great party last night. You **ought to have come.**
- She's been studying hard for the exam, so she **ought to pass.**

EXERCISES

33.1 *For each situation write a sentence with* **should** *or* **shouldn't** + *one of the following:*

~~go away for a few days~~   go to bed so late   look for another job
put some pictures on the walls   take a photograph   use her car so much

1 (Liz needs a change.) ...*She should go away for a few days.*...
2 (My salary is very low.) You ....
3 (Jack always has difficulty getting up.) He ....
4 (What a beautiful view!) You ....
5 (Sue drives everywhere. She never walks.) She ....
6 (Bill's room isn't very interesting.) ....

33.2 *Read the situations and write sentences with* **I think / I don't think…should… .**

1 Peter and Judy are planning to get married. You think it's a bad idea.
(get married) ...*I don't think they should get married.*...
2 You don't like smoking, especially in restaurants.
(be banned) I think ....
3 I have a very bad cold but I plan to go out this evening. You don't think this is a good idea.
You say to me: (go out) ....
4 You are fed up with the government. You think they have made too many mistakes.
(resign) ....

33.3 *Complete the sentences with* **should** (**have**) + *the verb in brackets.*

1 Margaret ...*should pass*... the exam. She's been studying very hard. (pass)
2 You missed a great party last night. You ...*should have come*... (come)
3 We don't see you enough. You .... and see us more often. (come)
4 I'm in a difficult position. What do you think I ....? (do)
5 I'm sorry that I didn't take your advice. I .... what you said. (do)
6 I'm playing tennis with Jill tomorrow. She .... – she's much better than me. (win)
7 We lost the match but we .... We were the better team. (win)
8 'Is John here yet?'   'Not yet, but he .... here soon.' (be)
9 I posted the letter three days ago, so it .... by now. (arrive)

33.4 *Read the situations and write sentences with* **should/shouldn't.** *Some of the sentences are past and some are present.*

1 I'm feeling sick. I ate too much. ...*I shouldn't have eaten so much.*...
2 That man on the motorbike isn't wearing a helmet. That's dangerous.
He ...*should be wearing a helmet.*...
3 When we got to the restaurant, there were no free tables. We hadn't reserved one.
We ....
4 The notice says that the shop is open every day from 8.30. It is 9 o'clock now but the shop isn't open yet. ....
5 The speed limit is 30 miles an hour, but Catherine is doing 50.
She ....
6 I went to Paris. A friend of mine lives in Paris but I didn't go to see him while I was there.
When I saw him later, he said: You ....
7 I was driving behind another car. Suddenly, the driver in front stopped without warning and I drove into the back of his car. It wasn't my fault. ....
8 I walked into a wall. I wasn't looking where I was going.
....

Should (2)

A You can use **should** after a number of verbs, especially:
suggest   propose   recommend   insist   demand

- They **insisted** that we **should have** dinner with them.
- I **demanded** that he **should apologise**.
- What do you **suggest** I **should do**?

In the same way, you can use **should** after **suggestion/proposal/recommendation** etc.:
- What do you think of Jane's **suggestion** that I **should buy** a car?

and also after 'it's **important/vital/necessary/essential** that...' :
- It's **essential** that **you should be** here on time.

B You can also leave out **should** in all the sentences in Section **A**:

- It's **essential** that **you be** here on time. (= that **you should be** here)
- I **demanded** that **he apologise**.
- What do you **suggest** I **do**?

This form (**you be / he apologise** etc.) is sometimes called the *subjunctive*.

You can also use normal present and past tenses:
- It's **essential** that you **are** here on time.
- I **demanded** that he **apologised**.

Be careful with **suggest**. You cannot use **to...** ('to do / to buy' etc.) after **suggest**:
- What do you **suggest we should do**?
or What do you **suggest we do**? (*but not* 'What do you suggest us to do?')
- Jane **suggested** that I (**should**) **buy** a car.
or Jane **suggested** that I **bought** a car. (*but not* 'Jane suggested me to buy')
For **suggest -ing**, see Unit 52.

C You can use **should** after a number of adjectives, especially:
strange   odd   funny   typical   natural   interesting   surprised   surprising

- It's **strange** that he **should be** late. He's usually on time.
- I was **surprised** that she **should say** such a thing.

D If...should...

You can say 'If something **should** happen...'. For example:
- If Tom **should phone** while I'm out, tell him I'll phone him back later.

'If Tom **should phone**' is similar to 'If Tom **phones**'. With **should**, the speaker feels that the possibility is smaller. Another example:
- I've left the washing outside. If it **should rain**, can you bring it in?

You can also put **should** at the beginning of these sentences (**Should** something happen...):
- **Should** Tom **phone**, can you tell him I'll phone him back later?

E You can use **I should... / I shouldn't...** to give somebody advice. For example:
- 'Shall I leave now?'   'No, **I should** wait a bit longer.'

Here, '**I should wait**' = 'I would wait if I were you, I advise you to wait'. Two more examples:
- It's very cold this morning. **I should wear** a coat when you go out.
- **I shouldn't stay** up too late. You'll be tired tomorrow.

EXERCISES

34.1 *Write a sentence (beginning in the way shown) that means the same as the first sentence.*

1 'I think it would be a good idea to see a specialist,' the doctor said to me.
The doctor recommended that ...I should see a specialist....
2 'You really must stay a little longer,' she said to me.
She insisted that ....
3 'Why don't you visit the museum after lunch?' I said to them.
I suggested that ....
4 'You must pay the rent by Friday,' the landlord said to us.
The landlord demanded that ....
5 'Why don't you go away for a few days?' Jack said to me.
Jack suggested that ....

34.2 *Are these sentences right or wrong?*

1 a Tom suggested that I should look for another job. ...RIGHT...
  b Tom suggested that I look for another job. ....
  c Tom suggested that I looked for another job. ....
  d Tom suggested me to look for another job. ....
2 a Where do you suggest I go for my holiday? ....
  b Where do you suggest me to go for my holiday? ....
  c Where do you suggest I should go for my holiday? ....

34.3 *Complete the sentences using* **should** + *one of these verbs:*

ask   ~~be~~   leave   listen   say   worry

1 It's strange that she ...should be... late. She's usually on time.
2 It's funny that you .... that. I was going to say the same thing.
3 It's only natural that parents .... about their children.
4 Isn't it typical of Ron that he .... without saying goodbye to anybody?
5 I was surprised that he .... me for advice. What advice could I give him?
6 It's very important that everybody .... very carefully.

34.4 *Complete these sentences using* **if...should... .**

1 (It's possible that you'll see Tom this evening.)
...If you should see Tom this evening... , can you ask him to phone me?
2 (It's possible that Ann will arrive before I get home.)
If .... , can you look after her until I come?
3 (Perhaps there will be some letters for me while I'm away.)
.... , can you send them on to this address?
4 (I don't suppose you'll need help but you might.)
.... , let me know.

Write sentences 3 and 4 again, this time beginning with **should.**

5 (3) .... , can you send them on to this address?
6 (4) ....

34.5 *(Section E) Complete the sentences using* **I should** + *one of these verbs:*

buy   keep   phone   ~~wait~~

1 'Shall I leave now?'   'No, ...I should wait... a bit longer.'
2 'Shall I throw these things away?'   'No, ... them. You may need them.'
3 'Shall I go and see Paul?' 'Yes, but .... him first.'
4 'Do you think it's worth repairing this TV set?'   'No, ... a new one.'

Had better   It's time...

A

Had better (**I'd better** / **you'd better** etc.)

I'd better do something = it is advisable to do it. If I don't, there will be a problem or a danger:
- I have to meet Ann in ten minutes. **I'd better go** now or I'll be late.
- 'Shall I take an umbrella?'   'Yes, **you'd better**. It might rain.'
- **We'd better stop** for petrol soon. The tank is almost empty.

The negative is **I'd better not** (= I **had** better not):
- A: Are you going out tonight?
  B: **I'd better not**. I've got a lot of work to do.
- You don't look very well. **You'd better not go** to work today.

You can use **had better** when you warn somebody that they must do something:
- You**'d better** be on time. / You**'d better not** be late. (or I'll be very angry)

Note that:

> The form is '**had** better' (usually '**I'd** better / **you'd** better' etc. in spoken English):
> - **I'd better** phone Carol, **hadn't** I?
>
> **Had** is a past form, but in this expression the meaning is present or future, *not* past:
> - **I'd better go** to the bank **now/tomorrow**.
>
> We say 'I'd better **do**...' (*not* 'to do'):
> - It might rain. We'd better **take** an umbrella. (*not* 'we'd better to take')

B

Had better and **should**

Had better is similar to **should** (see Unit 33A) but not exactly the same.
We use **had better** only for a particular situation (not for things in general).
You can use **should** in all types of situation to give an opinion or to give advice:
- It's cold today. You**'d better** wear a coat when you go out. (a particular situation)
- I think all drivers **should** wear seat belts. (in general – *not* 'had better wear')

Also, with **had better**, there is always a danger or a problem if you don't follow the advice.
Should only means 'it is a good thing to do'. Compare:
- It's a great film. You **should** go and see it. (but no danger, no problem if you don't)
- The film starts at 8.30. You**'d better** go now or you'll be late.

C

It's time...

You can say '**It's time** (for somebody) **to do** something':
- It's time **to go** home. / It's time for us **to go** home.

You can also say:
- It's late. It's time **we went** home.

Here we use the past (**went**) but the meaning is present or future, *not* past:
- It's 10 o'clock and he's still in bed. **It's time** he **got** up. (*not* 'It's time he gets up')

It's time you did something = 'you should have done it already or started it'. We often use this structure to criticise or to complain:
- **It's time** the children **were** in bed. It's long after their bedtime.
- The windows are very dirty. I think **it's time** we **cleaned** them.

You can also say: **It's about time...** / **It's high time...** . This makes the criticism stronger:
- Jack is a great talker. But **it's about time** he **did** something instead of just talking.
- You're very selfish. **It's high time** you **realised** that you're not the most important person in the world.

EXERCISES

35.1 *Complete the sentences. Sometimes you need only one word, sometimes two.*

1 a I need some money. I'd better ...go... to the bank.
  b John is expecting you to phone him. You .... better do it now.
  c 'Shall I leave the window open?'   'No, you'd better .... it.'
  d We'd better leave as soon as possible, ... we?
2 a It's time the government .... something about the problem.
  b It's time something .... about the problem.
  c I think it's about time you .... about me instead of only thinking about
     yourself.

35.2 *Read the situations and write sentences with* **had better**. *Use the words in brackets.*

1 You're going out for a walk with Tom. It might rain. You say to Tom:
   (an umbrella) ...We'd better take an umbrella...
2 Jack has just cut himself. It's quite a bad cut. You say to him:
   (a plaster) ....
3 You and Ann plan to go to a restaurant this evening. It's a very popular restaurant. You say
   to Ann: (reserve) We ....
4 Jill doesn't look very well – not well enough to go to work. You say to her:
   (work) ....
5 You received your phone bill four weeks ago but you haven't paid it yet. If you don't pay
   very soon, you could be in trouble. You say to yourself: (pay)
   ....
6 You want to go out but you're expecting an important phone call. You say to your friend:
   (go out) I ....
7 You and Fiona are going to the theatre. You've missed the bus and you don't want to be late.
   You say to Fiona: (a taxi) ....

35.3 *Put in* **had better** *or* **should**. *Sometimes either is possible.*

1 I have an appointment in ten minutes. I 'd better.. go now or I'll be late.
2 It's a great film. You ...should... go and see it. You'll really like it.
3 I .... get up early tomorrow. I've got a lot to do.
4 When people are driving, they .... keep their eyes on the road.
5 Thank you for coming to see us. You .... come more often.
6 She'll be upset if we don't invite her to the wedding, so we .... invite her.
7 These biscuits are delicious. You .... try one.
8 I think everybody .... learn a foreign language.

35.4 *Read the situations and write sentences with* **It's time** *(somebody* **did** *something).*

1 You think the children should be in bed. It's already 11 o'clock.
   ...It's time the children were in bed...
2 You haven't had a holiday for a very long time. You need one now.
   It's time I ....
3 You're waiting for Mary. She is late. Why isn't she here yet?
   It's time she ....
4 You're sitting on a train waiting for it to leave the station. It's already five minutes late.
   ....
5 You enjoy having parties. You haven't had one for a long time.
   ....
6 The company you work for is badly run. You think there should be some changes.
   ....

Can / Could / Would you...? etc.
(Requests, offers, permission and invitations)

A *Asking people to do things (requests)*
We often use **can** or **could** to ask people to do things:

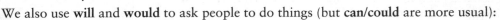

- **Can you** wait a moment, please? *or*
  Could you wait a moment, please?
- Liz, **can you** do me a favour?
- Excuse me, **could you** tell me how to get
  to the station?
- I wonder if **you could** help me.

Note that we say '**Do you think** (you) **could**...? (not
usually 'can'):
- **Do you think you could** lend me some
  money until next week?

> Could you open the door, please?

We also use **will** and **would** to ask people to do things (but **can/could** are more usual):
- Liz, **will you** do me a favour?
- **Would you** please be quiet? I'm trying to concentrate.

B *Asking for things*
To ask for something we use **Can I have...?** or **Could I have...?**:
- *(in a shop)* **Can I have** these postcards, please?
- *(during a meal)* **Could I have** the salt, please?

May I have...? is also possible (but less usual):
- **May I have** these postcards, please?

C *Asking for and giving permission*
To ask for permission to do something, we use **can**, **could** or **may**:
- *(on the phone)* Hello, **can I** speak to Tom, please?
- '**Could I** use your phone?' 'Yes, of course.'
- **Do you think I could** borrow your bike?
- '**May I** come in?' 'Yes, please do.'

To give permission, we use **can** or **may**:
- **You can** use the phone. *or* **You may** use the phone.

May is formal and less usual than **can** or **could**.

D *Offering to do things*
To offer to do something, we sometimes use **Can I...?**:
- '**Can I** get you a cup of coffee?' 'Yes, that would be very nice.'
- '**Can I** help you?' 'No, it's all right. I can manage.'

You can also use **I'll...** to offer to do things (see Unit 21C):
- You look tired. **I'll get** you a cup of coffee.

E *Offering and inviting*
To offer or to invite we use **Would you like...?** (*not* 'do you like')
- '**Would you like** a cup of coffee?' 'Yes, please.'
- '**Would you like** to come to dinner tomorrow evening?' 'Yes, I'd love to.'

I'd like... is a polite way of saying what you want:
- *(at a tourist information office)* **I'd like** some information about hotels, please.
- *(in a shop)* **I'd like** to try on this jacket, please.

EXERCISES

36.1 *Read the situations and write questions beginning* **Can...** *or* **Could...** .

1 You're carrying a lot of things. You can't open the door yourself. There's a man standing near the door. You say to him: ...*Could you open the door, please?*...

2 You phone Ann but somebody else answers. Ann isn't there. You want to leave a message for her. You say: ....

3 You are a tourist. You want to go to the station but you don't know where it is. You ask at your hotel. You say: ....

4 You are in a clothes shop. You see some trousers you like and you want to try them on. You say to the shop assistant: ....

5 You have a car. You have to go to the same place as John, who hasn't got a car. You want to give him a lift. You say to John: ....

36.2 *Read the situations and write questions beginning* **Do you think...** .

1 You want to borrow your friend's camera. What do you say to him?
Do you think ...*I could borrow your camera?*...

2 You are at a friend's house and you want to use her phone. What do you say?

....

3 You've written a letter in English. Before you send it, you want an English friend to check it. What do you ask him? ....

4 You want to leave work early because you have some things to do. What do you ask your boss? ....

5 The woman in the next room is playing music. It's very loud. You want her to turn it down. What do you say to her? ....

6 You are phoning the owner of a flat which was advertised in a newspaper. You are interested in the flat and you want to come and see it today. What do you say to the owner?

....

36.3 *What would you say in these situations?*

1 John has come to see you in your flat. You offer him something to eat.
YOU: ....
JOHN: No, thank you. I'm not hungry.

2 You need help to change the film in your camera. You ask Ann.
YOU: Ann, I don't know how to change the film. ....
ANN: Sure. It's easy. All you have to do is this.

3 You're on a train. The woman next to you has finished reading her newspaper. Now you want to have a look at it. You ask her.
YOU: Excuse me, ...
WOMAN: Yes, of course. I've finished with it.

4 You're on a bus. You have a seat but an elderly man is standing. You offer him your seat.
YOU: ....
MAN: Oh, that's very kind of you. Thank you very much.

5 You're the passenger in a car. Your friend is driving very fast. You ask her to slow down.
YOU: You're making me very nervous. ....
DRIVER: Oh, I'm sorry. I didn't realise I was going so fast.

6 You've finished your meal in a restaurant and now you want the bill. You ask the waiter:
YOU: ....
WAITER: Right. I'll get it for you now.

7 A friend of yours is interested in one of your books. You invite him to borrow it.
FRIEND: This book looks very interesting.
YOU: Yes, it's very good. ....

If I do... and If I did...

A Compare these examples:

> (1) Sue has lost her watch. She thinks it may be at Ann's house.
> SUE: I think I left my watch at your house. Have you seen it?
> ANN: No, but I'll have a look when I get home. **If I find** it, I'll tell you.
>
> In this example, Ann feels there is a real possibility that she will find the watch. So she says:
> If I **find**..., I'll... .

> (2) Ann says: **If I found** a wallet in the street, I'd take it to the police.
>
> This is a different type of situation. Here, Ann is not thinking about a real possibility; she is
> *imagining* the situation and doesn't expect to find a wallet in the street. So she says:
> If I **found**..., I'd (= I **would**)... (*not* 'If I find..., I'll...').

When you imagine something like this, you use **if** + *past*
(**if** I **found** / **if** you **were** / **if** we **didn't** etc.). But the
meaning is *not* past:

If I won a million pounds...

- What would you do **if** you **won** a million pounds?
  (we don't really expect this to happen)
- I don't really want to go to their party, but I probably
  will go. They'd be offended **if** I **didn't** go.
- Sarah has decided not to apply for the job. She isn't
  really qualified for it, so she probably wouldn't get
  it **if** she **applied**.

B We do not normally use **would** in the if-part of the sentence:

- I'd be very frightened **if** somebody **pointed** a gun at me. (*not* 'if somebody would point')
- **If** I **didn't** go to their party, they'd be offended. (*not* 'If I wouldn't go')

But it is possible to say '**if**... **would**' when you ask somebody to do something:

- *(from a formal letter)* I would be grateful **if** you **would send** me your brochure as soon as
  possible.
- 'Shall I close the door?' 'Yes, please, **if** you **would**.'

C In the other part of the sentence (not the **if**-part) we use **would** ('**d**) / **wouldn't**:

- If you took more exercise, you'**d** (= you **would**) probably feel healthier.
- **Would** you **mind** if I used your phone?
- I'm not tired enough to go to bed yet. I **wouldn't** sleep (if I went to bed now).

Could and **might** are also possible:

- If you took more exercise, you **might feel** healthier. (= it is possible that you would feel
  healthier)
- If it stopped raining, we **could go** out. (= we would be able to go out)

D Do not use **when** in sentences like those on this page:

- They would be offended **if** we didn't accept their invitation. (*not* 'when we didn't')
- What would you do **if** you were bitten by a snake? (*not* 'when you were bitten')

For **if** and **when** see also Unit 25C.

EXERCISES

37.1 *Put the verb into the correct form.*

1 They would be rather offended if I ...**didn't go**... to see them. (not/go)
2 If you took more exercise, you ...**would feel**... better. (feel)
3 If I was offered the job, I think I .... it. (take)
4 I'm sure Amy will lend you the money. I'd be very surprised if she ....
  (refuse)
5 If I sold my car, I .... much money for it. (not/get)
6 A lot of people would be out of work if the factory .... (close down)
7 What would happen if I .... that red button? (press)
8 Liz gave me this ring. She .... very upset if I lost it. (be)
9 Mark and Carol are expecting us. They would be disappointed if we
  .... (not/ come)
10 Would Tim mind if I .... his bicycle without asking him? (borrow)
11 If somebody .... in here with a gun, I'd be very frightened. (walk)
12 I'm sure Sue .... if you explained the situation to her. (understand)

37.2 *You ask a friend questions. Use* **What would you do if...?**

1 (Maybe one day your friend will win a lot of money.)
  ...**What would you do if you won a lot of money?**...
2 (Your friend's car has never been stolen but perhaps one day it will be.)
  What ....
3 (Perhaps one day your friend will lose his/her passport.)
  ....
4 (There has never been a fire in the building.)
  ....

37.3 *Answer the questions in the way shown.*

1 A: Shall we catch the 10.30 train?
  B: No. (arrive / too early)   **If we caught the 10.30 train, we'd arrive too early.**
2 A: Is Ken going to take the examination?
  B: No. (fail)   If he ....
3 A: Why don't we stay at a hotel?
  B: No. (cost too much money)   If ....
4 A: Is Sally going to apply for the job?
  B: No. (not / get it)   If ....
5 A: Let's tell them the truth.
  B: No. (not / believe us)   If ....
6 A: Why don't we invite Bill to the party?
  B: No. (have to invite his friends too)
  ....

37.4 *Use your own ideas to complete these sentences.*

1 If you took more exercise, ...**you'd feel better.**...
2 I'd feel very angry if ....
3 If I didn't go to work tomorrow, ...
4 Would you go to the party if ....
5 If you bought some new clothes, ...
6 Would you mind if ....

If I knew...   I wish I knew...

A Study this example situation:

> Sue wants to phone Paul but she can't do this because she doesn't know his number. She says:
>
> **If I knew** his number, I **would phone** him.
>
> Sue says: **If I knew** his number... . This tells us that she *doesn't* know his number. She is imagining the situation. The *real* situation is that she doesn't know his number.

If I knew his number...

When you imagine a situation like this, you use **if** + *past* (**if** I **knew** / **if** you **were** / **if** we **didn't** etc.). But the meaning is present, not past:

- Tom would read more **if** he **had** more time. (but he doesn't have much time)
- **If** I **didn't** want to go to the party, I wouldn't go. (but I want to go)
- We wouldn't have any money **if** we **didn't** work. (but we work)
- **If** you **were** in my position, what would you do?
- It's a pity you can't drive. It would be useful **if** you **could**.

B We use the past in the same way after **wish** (I **wish** I **knew** / I **wish** you **were** etc.). We use **wish** to say that we regret something, that something is not as we would like it to be:

I wish I had an umbrella.

- I **wish** I **knew** Paul's phone number.
  (= I don't know it and I regret this)
- Do you ever **wish** you **could** fly?
  (you can't fly)
- It rains a lot here. I **wish** it **didn't** rain so often.
- It's very crowded here. I **wish** there **weren't** so many people. (but there are a lot of people)
- I **wish** I **didn't** have to work. (but I have to work)

C After **if** and **wish**, you can use **were** instead of **was** (**if** I **were** / I **wish** it **were** etc.). So you can say:

- If I **were** you, I wouldn't buy that coat.   *or*   If I **was** you...
- I'd go out **if** it **weren't** raining.   *or*   ...**if** it **wasn't** raining.
- I **wish** it **were** possible.   *or*   I **wish** it **was** possible.

D We do not normally use **would** in the **if**-part of the sentence or after **wish**:

- **If** I **were** rich, I **would** have a yacht. (*not* 'If I would be rich')
- I **wish** I **had** something to read. (*not* 'I wish I would have')

Sometimes **wish...would** is possible ('I **wish you would listen**'). See Unit 40C.

E Note that **could** sometimes means 'would be able to' and sometimes 'was/were able to':

- You **could** get a job more easily   (you **could** get = you would be able to get)
  if you **could** speak a foreign language.   (you **could** speak = you were able to speak)

EXERCISES

38.1 *Put the verb into the correct form.*

1 If I ...**knew**... his number, I would phone him. (know)
2 I ...**wouldn't buy**.... that coat if I were you. (not/buy)
3 I .... you if I could, but I'm afraid I can't. (help)
4 We would need a car if we .... in the country. (live)
5 If we had the choice, we .... in the country. (live)
6 This soup isn't very good. It .... better if it wasn't so salty. (taste)
7 I wouldn't mind living in England if the weather .... better. (be)
8 If I were you, I .... (not/wait). I .... now. (go)
9 You're always tired. If you .... to bed so late every night, you
   wouldn't be tired all the time. (not/go)
10 I think there are too many cars. If there .... so many cars (not/be),
   there .... so much pollution. (not/be)

38.2 *Write a sentence with* **If...** *for each situation.*

1 We don't visit you very often because you live so far away.
   ..**If you didn't live so far away, we'd visit you more often.**..
2 He doesn't speak very clearly – that's why people don't understand him.
   If he .... more ...., people ....
3 That book is too expensive, so I'm not going to buy it.
   If the book ...., I ....
4 We don't go out very often because we can't afford it.
   ....
5 It's raining, so we can't have lunch in the garden.
   ....
6 I have to work tomorrow evening, so I can't meet you.
   ....

38.3 *Write sentences beginning* **I wish...** .

1 I don't know many people (and I'm lonely). ...**I wish I knew more people.**..
2 I don't have a key (and I need one). I wish ....
3 Ann isn't here (and I need to see her). ....
4 It's cold (and I hate cold weather). ....
5 I live in a big city (and I don't like it). ....
6 I can't go to the party (and I'd like to). ....
7 I have to work tomorrow (but I'd like to stay in bed). ....
8 I don't know anything about cars (and my car has just broken down).
   ....
9 I'm not lying on a beautiful sunny beach (and that's a pity).
   ....

38.4 *Write your own sentences beginning* **I wish...** .

1 (somewhere you'd like to be now – on the beach, in New York, in bed etc.)
   I wish I ....
2 (something you'd like to have – a computer, a job, lots of money etc.)
   ....
3 (something you'd like to be able to do – sing, speak a language, fly etc.)
   ....
4 (something you'd like to be – beautiful, strong, rich etc.)
   ....

If I had known... I wish I had known...

A Study this example situation:

> Last month Gary was in hospital for an operation. Liz didn't know this, so she didn't go to visit him. They met a few days ago. Liz said:
>
> If I **had known** you were in hospital, I **would have gone** to visit you.
>
> Liz said: **If I had known** you were in hospital... . The *real* situation was that she *didn't* know he was in hospital.

When you are talking about the past, you use **if + had** ('d)... (**if I had known/been/done** etc.):
- I didn't see you when you passed me in the street. **If I'd seen** you, of course I would have said hello. (but I didn't see you)
- I decided to stay at home last night. I would have gone out **if I hadn't been** so tired. (but I was tired)
- **If he had been looking** where he was going, he wouldn't have walked into the wall. (but he wasn't looking)
- The view was wonderful. **If I'd had** a camera, I would have taken some photographs. (but I didn't have a camera)

Compare:
- I'm not hungry. **If I was** hungry, I would eat something. *(now)*
- I wasn't hungry. **If I had been** hungry, I would have eaten something. *(past)*

B Do not use **would** in the **if**-part of the sentence. We use **would** in the other part of the sentence:
- **If I had seen** you, I **would have said** hello. (*not* 'If I would have seen you')

Note that **'d** can be **would** or **had**:
- If I**'d seen** you, (I'd seen = I **had** seen)
  I**'d have said** hello. (I'd have said = I **would** have said)

C We use **had** (**done**) in the same way after **wish**. **I wish** something **had happened** = I am sorry that it didn't happen:
- **I wish I'd known** that Gary was ill. I would have gone to see him. (but I didn't know)
- I feel sick. **I wish I hadn't eaten** so much cake. (I ate too much cake)
- Do you **wish** you **had studied** science instead of languages? (you didn't study science)
- The weather was cold while we were away. **I wish it had been** warmer.

Do not use **would have**... after **wish** in these sentences:
- I wish it **had been** warmer. (*not* 'I wish it would have been')

D Compare **would** (**do**) and **would have** (**done**):
- If I had gone to the party last night, I **would be** tired now. (I am not tired now – *present*)
- If I had gone to the party last night, I **would have met** lots of people. (I didn't meet lots of people – *past*)

Compare **would have**, **could have** and **might have**:
- If the weather hadn't been so bad, { we **would have gone** out.
  we **could have gone** out.
  (= we would have been able to go out)
  we **might have gone** out.
  (= perhaps we would have gone out) }

EXERCISES

39.1 *Put the verb into the correct form.*

1 I didn't know you were in hospital. If ...**I'd known**... (I/know), ...**I would have gone**.... (I/go) to visit you.

2 Ken got to the station in time to catch his train. If .... (he/miss) it, ... (he/be) late for his interview.

3 It's good that you reminded me about Ann's birthday. .... (I/forget) if .... (you/not/remind) me.

4 Unfortunately, I didn't have my address book with me when I was in New York. If .... (I/have) your address, ... (I/send) you a postcard.

5 A: How was your holiday? Did you have a nice time?
   B: It was OK, but .... (we/enjoy) it more if .... (the weather/be) better.

6 I took a taxi to the hotel but the traffic was very bad. .... (it/be) quicker if .... (I/walk).

7 I'm not tired. If .... (I/be) tired, I'd go home now.

8 I wasn't tired last night. If .... (I/be) tired, I would have gone home earlier.

39.2 *Write a sentence with* **if** *for each situation.*

1 I wasn't hungry, so I didn't eat anything.
   ...**If I'd been hungry, I would have eaten something.**...

2 The accident happened because the driver in front stopped so suddenly.
   If the driver in front ....

3 I didn't know that George had to get up early, so I didn't wake him up.
   If I ....

4 I was able to buy the car only because Jim lent me the money.
   ....

5 Margaret wasn't injured in the crash because she was wearing a seat belt.
   ....

6 You didn't have any breakfast – that's why you're hungry now.
   ....

7 I didn't get a taxi because I didn't have any money on me.
   ....

39.3 *Imagine that you are in these situations. For each situation, write a sentence with* **I wish**... .

1 You've eaten too much and now you feel sick.
   You say: ...**I wish I hadn't eaten so much.**...

2 There was a job advertised in the newspaper. You decided not to apply for it. Now you think that your decision was wrong.
   You say: I wish I ....

3 When you were younger, you didn't learn to play a musical instrument. Now you regret this.
   You say: ....

4 You've painted the gate red. Now you think that it doesn't look very nice.
   You say: ....

5 You are walking in the country. You would like to take some photographs but you didn't bring your camera. You say: ....

6 You have some unexpected guests. They didn't tell you they were coming. You are very busy and you are not prepared for them.
   You say (to yourself): ....

Would   I wish...would

A
We use **would** (**'d**) when we imagine a situation or action:
- It **would be** nice to have a holiday but we can't afford it.
- I'm not going to bed yet. I'm not tired and I **wouldn't sleep**.

We use **would have** (**done**) when we imagine situations or actions in the past:
- They helped me a lot. I don't know what I **would have done** without their help.
- I didn't go to bed. I wasn't tired, so I **wouldn't have slept**.

For **would** in sentences with **if** see Units 37–39.

B
Compare **will** (**'ll**) and **would** (**'d**):
- **I'll stay** a bit longer. I've got plenty of time.
- **I'd stay** a bit longer but I really have to go now. (so I can't stay longer)

Sometimes **would/wouldn't** is the past of **will/won't**. Compare:

present
- TOM: **I'll phone** you on Sunday.
- ANN: I promise I **won't be** late.
- LIZ: Damn! The car **won't start**.

past
- → Tom said he**'d phone** me on Sunday.
- → Ann promised that she **wouldn't be** late.
- → Liz was angry because the car **wouldn't start**.

C
I wish...would...

Study this example situation:

I wish it would stop raining.

It is raining. Jill wants to go out, but not in the rain. She says:

I wish it **would stop** raining.

This means that Jill is complaining about the rain and wants it to stop.

We use **I wish...would...** when we want something to happen or when we want somebody to do something. The speaker is not happy with the present situation.

- The phone has been ringing for five minutes. **I wish** somebody **would answer** it.
- **I wish** you **would do** something instead of just sitting and doing nothing.

You can use **I wish...wouldn't...** to complain about things people do repeatedly:
- **I wish** you **wouldn't keep** interrupting me.

We use **I wish...would...** for actions and changes, *not* situations. Compare:
- I wish Sarah **would** come. (= I want her to come)
but
- I wish Sarah **were** (*or* **was**) here now. (*not* 'I wish Sarah would be...')
- I wish somebody **would buy** me a car.
but
- I wish I **had** a car. (*not* 'I wish I would have...')

For 'I **wish...were/had** (etc.)' see Units 38B and 39C.

D
You can also use **would** when you talk about things that happened regularly in the past:
- When we were children, we lived by the sea. In summer, if the weather was fine, we **would** all get up early and go for a swim. (= we did this regularly)
- Whenever Arthur was angry, he **would** walk out of the room.

With this meaning, **would** is similar to **used to** (see Unit 18):
- Whenever Arthur was angry, he **used to walk** out of the room.

EXERCISES

40.1 *Complete the sentences using* **would** + *one of the following verbs in the correct form:*

be ~~do~~ enjoy enjoy phone stop

1 They helped me a lot. I don't know what I ...would have done... without their help.
2 You should go and see the film. You .... it.
3 It's a pity you couldn't come to the party last night. You .... it.
4 I .... you last night but I didn't have your number.
5 Why don't you go and see Clare? She .... very pleased to see you.
6 I was in a hurry when I saw you. Otherwise I .... to talk.

40.2 *Write sentences using* **promised**.

1 I wonder why she's late. ...She promised she wouldn't be late.
2 I wonder why Tom hasn't written to me. He promised ....
3 I'm surprised they didn't wait for us. They ....
4 Why did you tell Jill what I said? You ....

40.3 *What do you say in these situations? Write sentences with* **I wish…would…** .

1 It's raining. You want to go out, but not in the rain. You say: ...I wish it would stop raining.
2 You're waiting for John. He's late and you're getting impatient.
   You say (to yourself): I wish ....
3 You can hear a baby crying and you're trying to study.
   You say: ....
4 You're looking for a job – so far without success. Nobody will give you a job.
   You say: I wish somebody ....
5 Brian has been wearing the same clothes for years. You think he needs some new clothes.
   You say (to Brian): ....

   For the following situations, write sentences with **I wish…wouldn't…** .
6 Your friend drives very fast. You don't like this.
   You say (to your friend): I wish you ....
7 Jack always leaves the door open. This annoys you.
   You say (to Jack): ....
8 A lot of people drop litter in the street. You don't like this.
   You say: I wish people ....

40.4 *Are these sentences right or wrong? Correct the ones that are wrong.*

1 I wish Sarah would be here now.   ...WRONG: I wish Sarah were here now.
2 I wish you would listen to me.   ....
3 I wish I would have more money.   ....
4 I wish it wouldn't be so cold today.   ....
5 I wish the weather would change.   ....
6 I wish you wouldn't complain all the time. ....
7 I wish everything wouldn't be so expensive. ....

40.5 *These sentences are about things that often happened in the past. Complete the sentences using* **would** + *one of these verbs:* **forget shake share ~~walk~~**

1 Whenever Arthur was angry, he ...would walk... out of the room.
2 I used to live next to a railway line. Whenever a train went past, the house ....
3 You could never rely on George. It didn't matter how many times you reminded him to do
   something, he .... always ....
4 Brenda was always very generous. She didn't have much but she ....
   what she had with everyone else.

Passive (1) (**is done / was done**)

A Study this example:

This house **was built** in 1930.

'**Was built**' is *passive*. Compare active and passive:

Somebody **built** this house in 1930. *(active)*
    subject   object

This house **was built** in 1930. *(passive)*
    subject

We use an *active* verb to say *what the subject does*:
- My grandfather was a builder. **He built** this house in 1930.
- It's a big company. **It employs** two hundred people.

We use a *passive* verb to say *what happens to the subject*:
- This house is quite old. **It was built** in 1930.
- **Two hundred people are employed** by the company.

B When we use the passive, who or what causes the action is often unknown or unimportant:
- A lot of money **was stolen** in the robbery. (somebody stole it but we don't know *who*)
- **Is** this room **cleaned** every day? (does somebody clean it? – it's not important *who*)

If we want to say who does or what causes the action, we use **by…**:
- This house was built **by my grandfather**.
- Two hundred people are employed **by the company**.

C The passive is **be** (**is/was/have been** etc.) + the *past participle* (**done/cleaned/seen** etc.):
(**be**) **done**   (**be**) **cleaned**   (**be**) **seen**   (**be**) **damaged**   (**be**) **built** etc.
For irregular past participles (**done/known/seen** etc.), see Appendix 1.

Study the active and passive forms of the *present simple* and *past simple*:

Present simple *active:* **clean(s)/see(s)** etc.	Somebody **cleans** this room every day.
passive: **am/is/are cleaned/seen** etc.	This room **is cleaned** every day.

- Many accidents **are caused** by careless driving.
- I'**m not** often **invited** to parties.
- How **is** this word **pronounced**?

Past simple *active:* **cleaned/saw** etc.	Somebody **cleaned** this room yesterday.
passive: **was/were cleaned/seen** etc.	This room **was cleaned** yesterday.

- We **were woken** up by a loud noise during the night.
- 'Did you go to the party?' 'No, I **wasn't invited**.'
- How much money **was stolen**?

EXERCISES

41.1 *Complete the sentences using one of these verbs in the correct form:*
~~cause~~   damage   hold   include   invite   make   overtake   show
translate   write

1   Many accidents ...**are caused**... by dangerous driving.
2   Cheese .... from milk.
3   The roof of the building .... in a storm a few days ago.
4   There's no need to leave a tip. Service .... in the bill.
5   You .... to the wedding. Why didn't you go?
6   A cinema is a place where films ....
7   In the United States, elections for President .... every four years.
8   Originally the book .... in Spanish and a few years ago it
    .... into English.
9   We were driving along quite fast but we .... by lots of other cars.

41.2 *Write questions using the passive. Some are present and some are past.*

1   Ask about the telephone. (when/invent?)   ...**When was the telephone invented?**...
2   Ask about glass. (how/make?)   How ....
3   Ask about Australia. (when/discover?)   ....
4   Ask about silver. (what/use for?)   ....
5   Ask about television. (when/invent?)   ....

41.3 *Put the verb into the correct form, present simple or past simple, active or passive.*

1   It's a big factory. Five hundred people ...**are employed**... (employ) there.
2   Water .... (cover) most of the Earth's surface.
3   Most of the Earth's surface .... (cover) by water.
4   The park gates .... (lock) at 6.30 p.m. every evening.
5   The letter .... (post) a week ago and it .... (arrive) yesterday.
6   The boat .... (sink) quickly but fortunately everybody
    .... (rescue).
7   Ron's parents .... (die) when he was very young. He and his sister
    .... (bring) up by their grandparents.
8   I was born in London but I .... (grow) up in the north of England.
9   While I was on holiday, my camera .... (steal) from my hotel room.
10 While I was on holiday, my camera .... (disappear) from my hotel room.
11 Why .... (Sue/resign) from her job? Didn't she enjoy it?
12 Why .... (Bill/sack) from his job? What did he do wrong?
13 The company is not independent. It .... (own) by a much larger company.
14 I saw an accident last night. Somebody .... (call) an ambulance but
    nobody .... (injure) so the ambulance .... (not/need).
15 Where .... (these photographs/take)? In London?
    .... (you/take) them?

41.4 *Rewrite these sentences. Instead of using* 'somebody/they/people' *etc. write a passive sentence.*

1   Somebody cleans the room every day.   ...**The room is cleaned every day.**...
2   They cancelled all flights because of fog.   All ....
3   People don't use this road very often.   ....
4   Somebody accused me of stealing money.   I ....
5   How do people learn languages?   How ....
6   People advised us not to go out alone.   ....

Passive (2) (**be/been/being done**)

Study the following active and passive forms:

A

> *Infinitive*
> *active:*   (to) **do/clean/see** etc.   Somebody will clean the room later.
> *passive:*   (to) **be done/cleaned/seen** etc.   The room **will be cleaned** later.
>
> - The situation is serious. Something must **be done** before it's too late.
> - A mystery is something that can't **be explained**.
> - The music was very loud and could **be heard** from a long way away.
> - A new supermarket is going **to be built** next year.
> - Please go away. I want **to be left** alone.

B

> *Perfect infinitive*
> *active:*   **have** done/cleaned/seen etc.   Somebody **should have cleaned** the room.
> *passive:*   **have been** done/cleaned/seen etc.   The room **should have been cleaned**.
>
> - I haven't received the letter yet. It might **have been** sent to the wrong address.
> - If you hadn't left the car unlocked, it wouldn't **have been stolen**.
> - There were some problems at first but they seem **to have been solved**.

C

> *Present perfect*
> *active:*   **have/has (done)**   The room looks nice. Somebody **has cleaned** it.
> *passive:*   **have/has been (done)**   The room looks nice. It **has been cleaned**.
>
> - Have you heard the news? The President **has been shot**!
> - **Have** you ever **been bitten** by a dog?
> - 'Are you going to the party?'   'No, I **haven't been invited**.'

> *Past perfect*
> *active:*   **had (done)**   The room looked nice. Somebody **had cleaned** it.
> *passive:*   **had been (done)**   The room looked nice. It **had been cleaned**.
>
> - The vegetables didn't taste very good. They **had been cooked** for too long.
> - The car was three years old but **hadn't been used** very much.

D

> *Present continuous*
> *active:*   **am/is/are (do)ing**   Somebody **is cleaning** the room at the moment.
> *passive:*   **am/is/are being (done)**   The room **is being cleaned** at the moment.
>
> - There's somebody walking behind us. I think we **are being followed**.
> - (*in a shop*) 'Can I help you, madam?'   'No, thank you. I'm **being served**.'

> *Past continuous*
> *active:*   **was/were (do)ing**   Somebody **was cleaning** the room when I arrived.
> *passive:*   **was/were being (done)**   The room **was being cleaned** when I arrived.
>
> - There was somebody walking behind us. We **were being followed**.

EXERCISES

42.1 *What do these words mean? Use* **it can...** *or* **it can't...** . *Use a dictionary if necessary.*

If something is
1 **washable,** ...it can be washed...   4 **unusable,** ....
2 **unbreakable,** it ....   5 **invisible,** ....
3 **edible,** it ....   6 **portable,** ....

42.2 *Complete these sentences with one of the following verbs (in the correct form):*

carry   cause   ~~do~~   make   repair   ~~send~~   spend   wake up

Sometimes you need **have** *('might* **have***', 'could* **have***' etc.).*

1 The situation is serious. Something must ...be done... before it's too late.
2 I haven't received the letter. It might ...have been sent... to the wrong address.
3 A decision will not .... until the next meeting.
4 I told the hotel receptionist that I wanted to .... at 6.30 the next morning.
5 Do you think that less money should .... on armaments?
6 This road is in very bad condition. It should .... a long time ago.
7 The injured man couldn't walk and had to ....
8 It's not certain how the fire started but it might .... by an electrical fault.

42.3 *Rewrite these sentences. Instead of using 'somebody' or 'they',* *write a passive sentence.*

1 Somebody has cleaned the room.   ..The room has been cleaned...
2 They have postponed the concert. The ....
3 Somebody is using the computer at the moment. The computer ....
4 I didn't realise that somebody was recording our conversation.
   I didn't realise that ....
5 When we got to the stadium we found that they had cancelled the game.
   When we got to the stadium, we found that ....
6 They are building a new ring road round the city.
   ....
7 They have built a new hospital near the airport.
   ....

42.4 *Make sentences from the words in brackets. Sometimes the verb is active, sometimes passive.* *(This exercise also includes the past simple – see Unit 41C.)*

1 There's somebody behind us.   (I think / we / follow) ...I think we're being followed...
2 This room looks different.   (you / paint?) ...Have you painted it?
3 My car has disappeared.   (it / steal!) It ....
4 My umbrella has disappeared.   (somebody / take) Somebody ....
5 Tom gets a higher salary now.   (he / promote) ....
6 Ann can't use her office at the moment.   (it / redecorate) ....
7 The photocopier broke down yesterday, but now it's OK.   (it / work / again;   it / repair)
   ....
8 The police have found the people they were looking for.   (two people / arrest / last night)
   ....
9 A tree was lying across the road.   (it / blow down / in the storm)
   ....
10 The man next door disappeared six months ago.   (nobody / see / since then)
   ....
11 I was mugged on my way home a few nights ago.   (you / ever / mug?)
   ....

Passive (3)

A   **I was born...**

We say: **I was** born... (*not* 'I am born'):
- **I was born** in Chicago.
- Where **were** you **born**? (*not* 'where are you born') } *past simple*

but
- How many babies **are born** every day?   *present simple*

B   Some verbs can have two objects. For example, **give**:
- We gave   **the police**   **the information**. (= We gave the information to the police.)
      object 1   object 2

So it is possible to make two passive sentences:
- **The police** were given the information.   *or*   **The information** was given to the police.

Other verbs which can have two objects are: **ask   offer   pay   show   teach   tell**

When we use these verbs in the passive, most often we begin with the *person*:
- **I was offered** the job but I refused it. (= they offered me the job)
- **You will be given** plenty of time to decide. (= we will give you plenty of time)
- **Have you been shown** the new machine? (= has anybody shown you...?)
- **The men were paid** £200 to do the work. (= somebody paid the men £200)

C   **I don't like being...**

The passive of **doing/seeing** etc. is **being done / being seen** etc. Compare:

active: I don't like **people telling me** what to do.

passive: I don't like **being told** what to do.

- I remember **being given** a toy drum on my fifth birthday. (= I remember somebody giving me a toy drum...)
- Mr Miller hates **being kept** waiting. (= he hates people keeping him waiting)
- We managed to climb over the wall without **being seen**. (= ...without anybody seeing us)

D   **Get**

Sometimes you can use **get** instead of **be** in the passive:
- There was a fight at the party but nobody **got hurt**. (= nobody **was** hurt)
- I don't often **get invited** to parties. (= **I'm** not often invited)
- I'm surprised Ann **didn't get offered** the job. (...Ann **wasn't offered** the job)

You can use **get** to say that something happens to somebody or something, especially if this is unplanned or unexpected:
- Our dog **got run** over by a car.

You can use **get** only when things happen or change. For example, you cannot use **get** in these sentences:
- Jill **is liked** by everybody. (*not* 'gets liked' – this is not a 'happening')
- He was a mystery man. Nothing **was known** about him. (*not* 'got known')

We use **get** mainly in informal spoken English. You can use **be** in all situations.

We also use **get** in the following expressions (which are not passive in meaning):
   get married   get divorced
   get dressed (= put on your clothes)   **get changed** (= change your clothes)

EXERCISES

43.1 *When were they born? Choose five of these people and write a sentence for each. (Two of them were born in the same year.)*

Beethoven	Galileo	Elvis Presley	1452	1869	1929
Agatha Christie	Mahatma Gandhi	Leonardo da Vinci	1564	1891	1935
~~Walt Disney~~	Martin Luther King	William Shakespeare	1770	~~1901~~	

1   ..Walt Disney was born in 1901...
2   ....
3   ....
4   ....
5   ....
6   ....
7   And you? I

43.2 *Write these sentences in another way, beginning in the way shown.*

1   They didn't give me the money.   I ..wasn't given the money...
2   They asked me some difficult questions at the interview.
    I ....
3   Janet's colleagues gave her a present when she retired.
    Janet ....
4   Nobody told me that George was ill.
    I wasn't ....
5   How much will they pay you?
    How much will you ....
6   I think they should have offered Tom the job.
    I think Tom ....
7   Has anybody shown you what to do?
    Have you ....

43.3 *Complete the sentences using* **being** + *one of these verbs:*

ask   attack   give   invite   ~~keep~~   pay

1   Mr Miller doesn't like ...**being kept**... waiting.
2   They went to the party without ....
3   Most people like .... presents.
4   It's a dangerous city. People won't go out after dark because they are afraid of
    ....
5   I don't like .... stupid questions.
6   Few people are prepared to work without ....

43.4 *Complete the sentences using* **get/got** + *one of these verbs (in the correct form):*

ask   break   damage   ~~hurt~~   pay   steal   sting   stop   use

1   There was a fight at the party but nobody ...**got hurt**....
2   Ted .... by a bee while he was sitting in the garden.
3   How did that window ....?
4   These tennis courts don't .... very often. Not many people want to play.
5   I used to have a bicycle but it ....
6   Last night I .... by the police as I was driving home.
7   How much did you .... last month?
8   Please pack these things very carefully. I don't want them to ....
9   People often want to know what my job is. I often .... that question.

It is said that...   He is said to...   (be) supposed to...

A   Study this example situation:

Henry is very old. Nobody knows exactly how old he is, but:

It is said that he is 108 years old.

or   He **is said to be** 108 years old.

Both these sentences mean: 'People say that he is 108 years old.'

You can use these structures with a number of other verbs, especially:

thought   believed   considered   reported   known   expected   alleged   understood

Compare the two structures:

- Cathy works very hard.
  It is said that she works 16 hours a day.   *or*   **She is said to work** 16 hours a day.
- The police are looking for a missing boy.
  It is believed that the boy is wearing a   *or*   **The boy is believed to be wearing** a white pullover and blue jeans.   white pullover and blue jeans.
- The strike started three weeks ago.
  It is expected that it will end soon.   *or*   **The strike is expected to end** soon.
- A friend of mine has been arrested.
  It is alleged that he kicked a policeman.   *or*   **He is alleged to have kicked** a policeman.
- Those two houses belong to the same family.
  It is said that there is a secret tunnel   *or*   **There is said to be** a secret tunnel between them.   between them.

These structures are often used in news reports. For example, in a report about an accident:

- **It is reported that** two people were   *or*   Two people **are reported to have been** injured in the explosion.   **injured** in the explosion.

B   **(Be) supposed to**

Sometimes **it is supposed to...** = it is said to...:

- Let's go and see that film. It's **supposed to be** very good. (= it is said to be very good)
- 'Why was he arrested?'   'He's **supposed to have kicked** a policeman.' (= he is said to have kicked a policeman)

But sometimes **supposed to** has a different meaning. 'Something **is supposed to** happen' = it is planned, arranged or expected. Often this is different from what *really* happens:

- I'd better hurry. It's nearly 8 o'clock and I'm **supposed to be meeting** Ann at 8.15.
  (= I have arranged to meet Ann, I said I would meet her)
- The train **was supposed to arrive** at 11.30 but it was an hour late. (= the train was expected to arrive at 11.30 according to the timetable)
- You **were supposed to clean** the windows. Why didn't you do it?

'You're **not supposed to** do something' = it is not allowed or advisable for you to do it:

- You're **not supposed to park** your car here. It's private parking only.
- Mr Bond is much better after his illness but he's still **not supposed to do** any heavy work. (= his doctors have advised him not to...)

EXERCISES

44.1 *Write these sentences in another way, beginning as shown. Use the <u>underlined</u> word in your sentence.*

1 It is <u>expected</u> that the strike will end soon. The strike ...<u>is expected to end soon.</u>...

2 It is <u>expected</u> that the weather will be good tomorrow.
The weather is ....

3 It is <u>believed</u> that the thieves got in through the kitchen window.
The thieves ....

4 It is <u>reported</u> that many people are homeless after the floods.
Many people ....

5 It is <u>thought</u> that the prisoner escaped by climbing over a wall.
The prisoner ....

6 It is <u>alleged</u> that the man drove through the town at 90 miles an hour.
The man is ....

7 It is <u>reported</u> that the building has been badly damaged by fire.
The building ....

8 a It is <u>said</u> that the company is losing a lot of money.
  The company ....

  b It is <u>believed</u> that the company lost a lot of money last year.
  The company ....

  c It is <u>expected</u> that the company will lose money this year.
  The company ....

44.2 *People say a lot of things about Arthur. For example:*

1 Arthur eats spiders.
2 He is very rich.
3 He writes poetry.
4 He has 12 children.
5 He robbed a bank a long time ago.

ARTHUR

Nobody knows for sure whether these things are true or not. Write sentences about Arthur using (be) **supposed to.**

1 ...<u>Arthur is supposed to eat spiders.</u>...
2 He ....
3 ....
4 ....
5 ....

44.3 *Now you have to use* (be) **supposed to** *with its other meaning. In each example what happens is different from what is supposed to happen. Use* (be) **supposed to** *+ one of these verbs:*
~~arrive~~   be   block   come   ~~park~~   phone   start
Some of the sentences are negative (like the first example).

1 You ...<u>'re not supposed to park</u>... here. It's private parking only.
2 The train ...<u>was supposed to arrive</u>... at 11.30, but it was an hour late.
3 What are the children doing at home? They .... at school at this time.
4 We .... work at 8.15, but we rarely do anything before 8.30.
5 This door is a fire exit. You .... it.
6 Oh dear! I .... Ann but I completely forgot.
7 They arrived very early – at 2 o'clock. They .... until 3.30.

Have something done

A Study this example situation:

The roof of Jill's house was damaged in a storm, so she arranged for somebody to repair it. Yesterday a workman came and did the job.

Jill **had the roof repaired** yesterday.

This means: Jill arranged for somebody else to repair the roof. She didn't repair it herself.

We use **have something done** to say that we arrange for somebody else to do something for us. Compare:
- Jill **repaired** the roof. (= she repaired it herself)
- Jill **had the roof repaired**. (= she arranged for somebody else to repair it)

Study these sentences:
- Did Ann make the dress herself or **did she have it made?**
- 'Are you going to repair the car yourself?'   'No, I'm going to **have it repaired**.'

Be careful with word order. The *past participle* (**repaired/cut** etc.) is after the *object* (**the roof / your hair** etc.):

	have	+	object	+	past participle	
Jill	had		the roof		repaired	yesterday.
Where	did you **have**		your hair		cut?	
Your hair looks nice.	Have you **had**		it		cut?	
Julia	has just **had**		central heating		installed	in her house.
We	are **having**		the house		painted	at the moment.
How often	do you **have**		your car		serviced?	
I think you should	have		that coat		cleaned	soon.
I don't like	having		my photograph		taken.	

B You can also say '**get** something done' instead of '**have** something done' (mainly in informal spoken English):
- When are you going to **get the roof repaired?** (= have the roof repaired)
- I think you should **get your hair cut**.

C Sometimes **have something done** has a different meaning. For example:
- Jill and Eric **had all their money stolen** while they were on holiday.

Of course this does *not* mean that they *arranged* for somebody to steal their money. 'They **had all their money stolen**' means only: 'All their money was stolen from them.'

With this meaning, we use **have something done** to say that something happens to somebody or their belongings. Usually what happens is not nice:
- George **had his nose broken** in a fight.
- Have you ever **had your passport stolen?**

EXERCISES

45.1 Tick (✓) the correct sentence, (a) or (b), for each picture.

1 	2	3	4

1 SARAH
a Sarah is cutting her hair.
b Sarah is having her hair cut.

2 BILL
a Bill is cutting his hair.
b Bill is having his hair cut.

3 JOHN
a John is cleaning his shoes.
b John is having his shoes cleaned.

4 SUE
a Sue is taking a photograph.
b Sue is having her photograph taken.

45.2 Why did you do these things? Answer using 'have something done'. Use one of these verbs:

clean   cut   repair   ~~service~~

1 Why did you take your car to the garage?   To have it serviced.
2 Why did you take your jacket to the cleaner's?   To ....
3 Why did you take your watch to the jeweller's?   ....
4 Why did you go to the hairdresser?   ....

45.3 Write sentences in the way shown.

1 Jill didn't repair the roof herself.   She had it repaired.
2 I didn't cut my hair myself.   I ....
3 They didn't paint the house themselves.   They ....
4 Sue didn't make the curtains herself.   ....

45.4 Use the words in brackets to complete the sentences. Use the structure 'have something done'.

1 We are having the house painted (the house / paint) at the moment.
2 I lost my key. I'll have to .... (another key / make).
3 When was the last time you .... (your hair / cut)?
4 You look different.   .... (you / your hair / cut)?
5 .... (you / a newspaper / deliver) to your house or do you go to the shop to buy one?
6 A: What are those workmen doing in your garden?
   B: Oh, we .... (a swimming pool / build).
7 A: Can I see the photographs you took when you were on holiday?
   B: I'm afraid I .... (not / the film / develop) yet.
8 This coat is dirty. I must .... (it / clean).
9 If you want to wear earrings, why don't you .... (your ears / pierce)?

45.5 Now you have to use 'have something done' with its second meaning (see Section C).

1 George's nose was broken in a fight.
   What happened to George? He had his nose broken in a fight.
2 Sarah's bag was stolen on a train.
   What happened to Sarah? She ....
3 Fred's hat was blown off in the wind.
   What happened to Fred? ....
4 Diane's passport was taken away from her by the police.
   What happened to Diane? ....

Reported speech (1) (**He said that...**)

A Study this example situation:

I'm feeling ill.

You want to tell somebody else what Tom said.
There are two ways of doing this:
You can repeat Tom's words (*direct* speech):
Tom said 'I'm feeling ill.'
Or you can use *reported* speech:
Tom said that he was feeling ill.

Compare:

direct: Tom said ' I   am feeling ill.'   *In writing we use these to show direct speech.*

reported: Tom said that he was feeling ill.

B When we use reported speech, the main verb of the sentence is usually past (Tom **said** that... / I **told** her that... etc.). The rest of the sentence is usually past too:
- Tom **said** that he **was feeling** ill.
- I **told** her that I **didn't have** any money.

You can leave out **that**:
- Tom said (that) he was feeling ill.
- I told her (that) I didn't have any money.

In general, the *present* form in direct speech changes to the *past* form in reported speech:

am/is → **was**   do/does → **did**   will → **would**
are → **were**   have/has → **had**   can → **could**
want/like/know/go etc. → **wanted/liked/knew/went** etc.

Compare direct speech and reported speech:

You met Judy. Here are some of the things she said to you in *direct speech*:	Later you tell somebody what Judy said. You use *reported* speech:
'My parents **are** very well.'	• Judy said that her parents **were** very well.
'I'm going to learn to drive.'	• She said that she **was** going to learn to drive.
'John **has** given up his job.'	• She said that John **had** given up his job.
'I **can't** come to the party on Friday.'	• She said that she **couldn't** come to the party on Friday.
'I **want** to go away for a holiday but I **don't** know where to go.'	• She said that she **wanted** to go away for a holiday but (she) **didn't** know where to go.
'I'm going away for a few days. I'll phone you when I **get** back.'	• She said that she **was** going away for a few days and **would** phone me when she **got** back.

JUDY

C The *past simple* (**did/saw/knew** etc.) can usually stay the same in reported speech, or you can change it to the *past perfect* (**had done / had seen / had known** etc.):
direct   Tom said: 'I **woke** up feeling ill, so I **didn't go** to work.'
reported Tom said (that) he **woke** up feeling ill, so he **didn't go** to work.   *or*
            Tom said (that) he **had woken** up feeling ill, so he **hadn't gone** to work.

EXERCISES

46.1 *Yesterday you met a friend of yours, Charlie. Here are some of the things Charlie said to you:*

1 I'm living in London now.
2 My father isn't very well.
3 Sharon and Paul are getting married next month.
4 Margaret has had a baby.
5 I don't know what Fred is doing.
6 I saw Helen at a party in June and she seemed fine.

CHARLIE

7 I haven't seen Diane recently.
8 I'm not enjoying my job very much.
9 You can come and stay at my flat if you are ever in London.
10 My car was stolen a few weeks ago.
11 I want to go on holiday but I can't afford it.
12 I'll tell Ann I saw you.

<u>*Later that day*</u> *you tell another friend what Charlie said. Use reported speech.*

1 ..Charlie said that he was living in London now...
2 He said that ....
3 He ....
4 ....
5 ....
6 ....
7 ....
8 ....
9 ....
10 ....
11 ....
12 ....

46.2 *Somebody says something to you which is the opposite of what they said before. Write a suitable answer beginning* **I thought you said… .**

1 A: That restaurant is expensive.
   B: Is it? ..I thought you said it was cheap...
2 A: Ann is coming to the party tonight.
   B: Is she? I thought you said she ....
3 A: Ann likes Paul.
   B: Does she? I thought ....
4 A: I know lots of people.
   B: Do you? I thought you said you ....
5 A: I'll be here next week.
   B: Will you? ....
6 A: I'm going out this evening.
   B: Are you? ....
7 A: I can speak a little French.
   B: Can you? ....
8 A: I haven't been to the cinema for ages.
   B: Haven't you? ....

Reported speech (2)

A It is not always necessary to change the verb when you use reported speech. If you report something and it is still true, you do not need to change the verb:

- *direct*   Tom said 'New York **is** more lively than London.'
  reported Tom said that New York **is** more lively than London.
  (New York is *still* more lively. The situation hasn't changed.)
- *direct*   Ann said 'I want to go to New York next year.'
  reported Ann said that she **wants** to go to New York next year.
  (Ann still wants to go to New York next year.)

Note that it is also correct to change the verb into the past:

- Tom said that New York **was** more lively than London.
- Ann said that she **wanted** to go to New York next year.

But you *must* use a past form when there is a difference between what was said and what is really true. Study this example situation:

> You met Sonia a few days ago.
> She said: '**Jim is ill.**' *(direct speech)*
>
> YOU   SONIA   Jim is ill.
>
> Later that day you see Jim. He is looking well and carrying a tennis racket.
> You say:
> 'I didn't expect to see you, Jim. Sonia
> said you **were** ill.'
> (*not* ' Sonia said you are ill', because
> clearly he is not ill.)   YOU   Sonia said you were ill.

B **Say** and **tell**

If you say *who* you are talking to, use **tell**:

- Sonia **told me** that you were ill. (*not* 'Sonia said me')   **TELL** <u>SOMEBODY</u>
- What did you **tell the police**? (*not* 'say the police')

Otherwise use **say**:

- Sonia **said** that you were ill. (*not* 'Sonia told that…')   **SAY** ~~SOMEBODY~~
- What did you **say**?

But you can '**say** something **to** somebody':

- Ann **said** goodbye **to** me and left. (*not* 'Ann said me goodbye')
- What did you **say to** the police?

C **Tell/ask** somebody **to** do something

We also use the infinitive (**to do / to stay** etc.) in reported speech, especially with **tell** and **ask** (for orders and requests):

- *direct*   '**Stay** in bed for a few days,' the doctor said to me.
  reported The doctor **told me to** stay in bed for a few days.
- *direct*   '**Don't shout**,' I said to Jim.
  reported I **told Jim not to** shout.
- *direct*   'Please **don't tell** anybody what happened,' Ann said to me.
  reported Ann **asked me not to** tell anybody what (had) happened.

'…**said to** do something' is also possible:

- The doctor **said to stay** in bed for a few days. (*but not* 'The doctor said me…')

EXERCISES

47.1 *Here are some things that Ann said to you:*

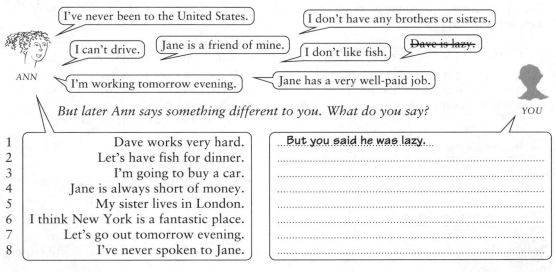

I've never been to the United States.

I don't have any brothers or sisters.

I can't drive.

Jane is a friend of mine.

I don't like fish.

~~Dave is lazy.~~

ANN

I'm working tomorrow evening.

Jane has a very well-paid job.

YOU

But later Ann says something different to you. What do you say?

1	Dave works very hard.	But you said he was lazy.
2	Let's have fish for dinner.	....
3	I'm going to buy a car.	....
4	Jane is always short of money.	....
5	My sister lives in London.	....
6	I think New York is a fantastic place.	....
7	Let's go out tomorrow evening.	....
8	I've never spoken to Jane.	....

47.2 *Complete the sentences with* **say** *or* **tell** *(in the correct form). Use only one word each time.*

1 Ann ...**said**... goodbye to me and left.
2 .... us about your holiday. Did you have a nice time?
3 Don't just stand there! .... something!
4 I wonder where Sue is. She .... she would be here at 8 o'clock.
5 Jack .... me that he was fed up with his job.
6 The doctor .... that I should rest for at least a week.
7 Don't .... anybody what I .... It's a secret just between us.
8 'Did she .... you what happened?' 'No, she didn't .... anything to me.'
9 George couldn't help me. He .... me to ask Kate.
10 George couldn't help me. He .... to ask Kate.

47.3 *(Section C) The following sentences are direct speech:*

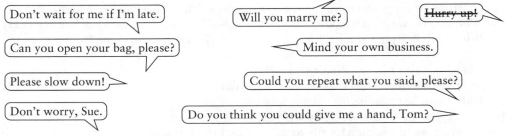

Don't wait for me if I'm late.

Will you marry me?

~~Hurry up!~~

Can you open your bag, please?

Mind your own business.

Please slow down!

Could you repeat what you said, please?

Don't worry, Sue.

Do you think you could give me a hand, Tom?

Now choose one of these to complete each sentence below. Use <u>reported</u> *speech.*

1 Bill was taking a long time to get ready, so I ...**told him to hurry up.**...
2 Sarah was driving too fast, so I asked ....
3 Sue was very pessimistic about the situation. I told ....
4 I couldn't move the piano alone, so I ....
5 The customs officer looked at me suspiciously and ....
6 I had difficulty understanding him, so I ....
7 I didn't want to delay Ann, so I ....
8 John was very much in love with Mary, so he ....
9 He started asking me personal questions, so ....

Questions (1)

A We usually make questions by changing the word order: we put the first *auxiliary verb (AV)* before the *subject (S)*:

	S + AV		AV + S	
Tom	will	→	will	Tom?
you	have	→	have	you?
I	can	→	can	I?
the house	was	→	was	the house?

- **Will Tom** be here tomorrow?
- **Have you** been working hard?
- What **can I** do? (*not* 'What I can do?')
- When **was the house** built?
  (*not* 'When was built the house?')

B In *present simple* questions, we use **do/does**:

you	live	→	**do**	you live?
the film	begins	→	**does**	the film begin?

- **Do** you **live** near here?
- What time **does** the film **begin**? (*not* 'What time begins…?')

In *past simple* questions, we use **did**:

you	sold	→	**did**	you sell?
the accident	happened	→	**did**	the accident **happen**?

- **Did** you **sell** your car?
- How **did** the accident happen?

But do not use **do/does/did** in questions if **who/what/which** is the *subject* of the sentence. Compare:

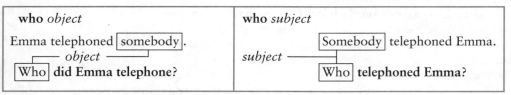

In these examples, **who/what/which** is the *subject*:
- **Who wants** something to eat? (*not* 'Who does want')
- **What happened** to you last night? (*not* 'What did happen')
- **Which bus** goes to the city centre? (*not* 'Which bus does go')

C Note the position of prepositions in questions beginning **Who/What/Which/Where…?**:
- **Who** do you want to speak **to**?
- **Which** job has Jane applied **for**?
- **What** was the weather **like** yesterday?
- **Where** do you come **from**?

D *Negative questions* (**isn't it**…? / **didn't you**…?)
We use negative questions especially to show surprise:
- **Didn't you** hear the bell? I rang it four times.

or when we expect the listener to agree with us:
- '**Haven't we** met somewhere before?' 'Yes, I think we have.'
- **Isn't it** a beautiful day! (= It's a beautiful day, isn't it?)

Note the meaning of **yes** and **no** in answers to negative questions:
- **Don't you** want to go to the party? { **Yes.** (= Yes, I want to go)
  No. (= No, I don't want to go) }

Note the word order in negative questions beginning **Why…?**:
- **Why don't we** go out for a meal tonight? (*not* 'Why we don't…')
- **Why wasn't Mary** at work yesterday? (*not* 'Why Mary wasn't…')

EXERCISES

48.1 *Ask Liz questions. (Look at her answers before you write the questions.)*

1	(where / from?) .Where are you from?	From London originally.
2	(where / live / now?) Where	In Manchester.
3	(married?)	Yes.
4	(how long / married?)	12 years.
5	(children?)	Yes, three boys.
6	(how old / they?)	4, 7 and 9.
7	(what / husband / do?)	He's a policeman.
8	(he / enjoy his job?)	Yes, very much.
9	(arrest anyone yesterday?)	
	....	I don't know.
10	(how often / go / on holiday?)	Usually once a year.
11	(where / next year?)	We don't know yet.

LIZ

48.2 *Make questions with* **who** *or* **what**.

1	Somebody hit me.	.Who hit you?
2	I hit somebody.	.Who did you hit?
3	Somebody gave me the key.	Who ....
4	Something happened.	What ....
5	Diane told me something.	....
6	This book belongs to somebody.	....
7	Somebody lives in that house.	....
8	I fell over something.	....
9	Something fell on the floor.	....
10	This word means something.	....
11	I borrowed the money from somebody.	....
12	I'm worried about something.	....

48.3 *Put the words in brackets in the correct order. All the sentences are questions.*

1 (when / was / built / this house) ...When was this house built?
2 (how / cheese / is / made) ....
3 (when / invented / the computer / was) ....
4 (why / Sue / working / isn't / today) ....
5 (what time / coming / your friends / are) ....
6 (why / was / cancelled / the concert) ....
7 (where / your mother / was / born) ....
8 (why / you / to the party / didn't / come) ....
9 (how / the accident / did / happen) ....
10 (why / this machine / doesn't / work) ....

48.4 *Write negative questions from the words in brackets. In each situation you are surprised.*

1 A: We won't see Ann this evening.
  B: Why not? (she / not / come / to the party?) ...Isn't she coming to the party?
2 A: I hope we don't meet Brian tonight.
  B: Why? (you / not / like / him?) ....
3 A: Don't go and see that film.
  B: Why not? (it / not / good) ....
4 A: I'll have to borrow some money.
  B: Why? (you / not / have / any?) ....

Questions (2) (**Do you know where...**? / **She asked me where...**)

A

When we ask for information, we often say **Do you know...?** / **Could you tell me...?** etc. If you begin a question like this, the word order is different from a simple question. Compare:

Where **has Tom** gone?   (*simple question*)

but   **Do you know** where **Tom has** gone?   (*not* 'Do you know where has Tom gone?')

When the question (**Where has Tom gone?**) is part of a longer sentence (**Do you know...?** / **I don't know... / Can you tell me...?** etc.), it loses the normal question word order. Compare:

- What time **is it**?   *but*   Do you know what time **it is**?
- Who **is that woman**?   I don't know who **that woman is**.
- Where **can I** find Linda?   Can you tell me where **I can** find Linda?
- How much **will it** cost?   Have you any idea how much **it will** cost?

Be careful with **do/does/did** questions:

- What time **does the film begin**?   *but*   Do you know what time **the film begins**?
                                                                    (*not* 'Do you know what time does...')
- What **do you mean**?   Please explain what **you mean**.
- Why **did Ann leave** early?   I wonder why **Ann left** early.

Use **if** or **whether** where there is no other question word (**what, why** etc.):
- Did anybody see you?   *but*   Do you know **if** (*or* **whether**) anybody saw you?

B

The same changes in word order happen in *reported* questions:

direct   The police officer said to us, 'Where are you going ?'

reported   The police officer asked us where we were going .

direct   Clare said, 'What time do the banks close ?'

reported   Clare wanted to know what time the banks closed .

In reported questions, the verb usually changes to the past (**were, closed**). See Unit 46.

Study these examples. You had an interview for a job and these were some of the questions the interviewer asked you:

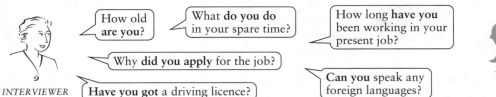

How old **are you**?

What **do you do** in your spare time?

How long **have you** been working in your present job?

Why **did you apply** for the job?

INTERVIEWER   **Have you got** a driving licence?

Can you speak any foreign languages?

YOU

Later you tell a friend what the interviewer asked you. You use *reported* speech:
- She asked (me) how old **I was**.
- She wanted to know what **I did** in my spare time.
- She asked (me) how long **I had** been working in my present job.
- She asked (me) why **I had** applied for the job. (*or* ...why **I applied**)
- She wanted to know whether (*or* if) **I could** speak any foreign languages.
- She asked whether (*or* if) **I had** a driving licence. (*or* ...**I had got**...)

EXERCISES

49.1 *Make a new sentence from the question in brackets.*

1 (Where has Tom gone?)   Do you know ...*where Tom has gone?*...
2 (Where is the post office?)   Could you tell me where ....
3 (What's the time?)   I wonder ....
4 (What does this word mean?)   I want to know ....
5 (What time did they leave?)   Do you know ....
6 (Is Sue going out tonight?)   I don't know ....
7 (Where does Carol live?)   Have you any idea ....
8 (Where did I park the car?)   I can't remember ....
9 (Is there a bank near here?)   Can you tell me ....
10 (What do you want?)   Tell me ....
11 (Why didn't Kay come to the party?)   I don't know ....
12 (Do you have to pay to park here?)   Do you know ....
13 (Who is that woman?)   I've no idea ....
14 (Did Ann receive my letter?)   Do you know ....
15 (How far is it to the airport?)   Can you tell me ....

49.2 *You are making a phone call. You want to speak to Sue but she isn't there. Somebody else answers the phone. You want to know three things:*
(1) **Where has she gone?** *(2)* **When will she be back?** *and (3)* **Did she go out alone?**
Complete the conversation:

A: Do you know where ....(1)?
B: Sorry, I've got no idea.
A: Never mind. I don't suppose you know ....(2).
B: No, I'm afraid not.
A: One more thing. Do you happen to know ....(3)?
B: I'm afraid I didn't see her go out.
A: OK. Well, thank you anyway. Goodbye.

49.3 *You have been away for a while and have just come back to your home town. You meet Gerry, a friend of yours. He asks you a lot of questions:*

1 How are you?   5 Where are you living?   6 Why did you come back?
2 Where have you been?   7 Are you glad to be back?
3 How long have you been back?   8 Do you have any plans to go away again?
4 What are you doing now?   *GERRY*   9 Can you lend me some money?

Now you tell another friend what Gerry asked you. Use reported speech.

1 ...*He asked me how I was.*...
2 He asked me ....
3 He ....
4 ....
5 ....
6 ....
7 ....
8 ....
9 ....

Auxiliary verbs (**have/do/can** etc.)
I think so / **I hope so** etc.

A There are two verbs in each of these sentences:

I	**have**	**lost**	my keys.
She	**can't**	**come**	to the party.
The hotel	**was**	**built**	ten years ago.
Where	**do** you	**live?**	

In these examples **have/can't/was/do** are *auxiliary* (= helping) *verbs*.

You can use an auxiliary verb (without the rest of the sentence) when you don't want to repeat something:

- 'Have you locked the door?' 'Yes, I **have**.' (= I have *locked the door*)
- George wasn't working but Janet **was**. (= Janet was *working*)
- She could lend me the money but she **won't**. (= she won't *lend me the money*)
- 'Are you angry with me?' 'Of course I**'m not**.' (= I'm not *angry*)

Use **do/does/did** for the present and past simple:

- 'Do you like onions?' 'Yes, I **do**.' (= I *like onions*)
- 'Does Mark smoke?' 'He **did** but he **doesn't** any more.'

B We use **have you?** / **isn't she?** / **do they?** etc. to show polite interest in what somebody has said:

- 'I've just met Simon.' 'Oh, **have you?** How is he?'
- 'Liz isn't very well today.' 'Oh, **isn't she?** What's wrong with her?'
- 'It rained every day during our holiday.' '**Did it?** What a pity!'

Sometimes we use these 'short questions' to show surprise:

- 'Jim and Nora are getting married.' '**Are they?** Really?'

C We use auxiliary verbs with **so** and **neither**:

- 'I'm feeling tired.' '**So am I**.' (= I'm feeling tired too)
- 'I never read newspapers.' '**Neither do I**.' (= I never read newspapers either)
- Sue hasn't got a car and **neither has Martin**.

Note the word order after **so** and **neither** (*verb* before *subject*):

- I passed the exam and **so did Tom**. (*not* 'so Tom did')

You can use **nor** instead of **neither**:

- 'I can't remember his name.' '**Nor** can I.' *or* '**Neither** can I.'

You can also use '...**not**...**either**':

- 'I haven't got any money.' '**Neither** have I.' *or* '**Nor** have I.' *or* 'I haven**'t either**.'

D **I think so** / **I hope so** etc.

After some verbs you can use **so** when you don't want to repeat something:

- 'Are those people English?' '**I think so**.' (= I think *they are English*)
- 'Will you be at home tomorrow morning?' '**I expect so**.' (= I expect *I'll be at home...*)
- 'Do you think Kate has been invited to the party?' '**I suppose so**.'

You can also say **I hope so**, **I guess so** and **I'm afraid so**.

The usual negative forms are:

I think so / I expect so	→	I **don't** think so / I **don't** expect so
I hope so / I'm afraid so / I guess so	→	I hope **not** / I'm afraid **not** / I guess **not**
I suppose so	→	I **don't** suppose so *or* I suppose **not**

- 'Is that woman American?' '**I think so**. / **I don't think so**.'
- 'Do you think it's going to rain?' '**I hope so**. / **I hope not**.' (*not* 'I don't hope so')

EXERCISES

50.1 Complete the sentences with an auxiliary verb (**do/was/could/should** etc.). Sometimes the verb must be negative (**don't/wasn't** etc.).

1 I wasn't tired but my friends ...were....
2 I like hot weather but Ann ....
3 'Is Colin here?' 'He .... five minutes ago but I think he's gone home now.'
4 She might phone later this evening but I don't think she ....
5 'Are you and Chris coming to the party?' 'I .... but Chris ....'
6 I don't know whether to apply for the job or not. Do you think I ....?
7 'Please don't tell anybody what I said.' 'Don't worry.   I ....'
8 'You never listen to me.' 'Yes, I ....!'
9 'Can you play a musical instrument?' 'No, but I wish I ....'
10 'Please help me.' 'I'm sorry. I .... if I .... but I ....'

50.2 You never agree with Sue. Answer in the way shown.

1   I'm hungry.   Are you? I'm not.
2   I'm not tired.   Aren't you? I am.
3   I like football.   ....
4 SUE   I didn't enjoy the film.   ....
5   I've never been to South America.   ....
6   I thought the exam was quite easy.   .... YOU

50.3 You are talking to Tina. Write <u>true</u> sentences about <u>yourself</u>. Reply with **So…** or **Neither…** if suitable. Study the two examples carefully.

1   I feel really tired.   So do I.
2   I'm working hard.   Are you? I'm not.
3   I watched television last week.   ....
4 TINA   I won't be in London next week.   ....
5   I live in a small town.   ....
6   I'd like to go to the moon.   .... YOU
7   I can't play the trumpet.   ....

50.4 In these conversations, you are B. Read the information in brackets and then answer with **I think so, I hope not** etc.

1 (You don't like rain.)   A: Is it going to rain?   B: (hope) ...I hope not....
2 (You need more money quickly.)
   A: Do you think you'll get a pay rise soon?   B: (hope) ....
3 (You think Diane will probably get the job that she applied for.)
   A: I wonder if Diane will get the job.   B: (expect) ....
4 (You're not sure whether Jill is married – probably not.)
   A: Is Jill married?   B: (think) ....
5 (You are the receptionist at a hotel. The hotel is full.)
   A: Have you got a room for tonight?   B: (afraid) ....
6 (You're at a party. You have to leave early.)
   A: Do you have to leave already?   B: (afraid) ....
7 (Ann normally works every day, Monday to Friday. Tomorrow is Wednesday.)
   A: Is Ann working tomorrow?   B: (suppose) ....
8 (You are going to a party. You can't stand John.)
   A: Do you think John will be at the party?   B: (hope) ....
9 (You're not sure what time the concert is – probably 7.30.)
   A: Is the concert at 7.30?   B: (think) ....

Question tags (**do you? isn't it?** etc.)

A Study these examples:

You haven't seen Mary today, **have you?**

No, I'm afraid not.

Yes, I really enjoyed it.

It was a good film, **wasn't it?**

Have you? and **wasn't it?** are *question tags* (= mini-questions that we often put on the end of a sentence in spoken English). In question tags, we use an auxiliary verb (**have/was/will** etc.). We use **do/does/did** for the present and past simple (see also Unit 50):

- 'Karen plays the piano, **doesn't she?**'   'Well, yes, but not very well.'
- 'You didn't lock the door, **did you?**'   'No, I forgot.'

B Normally we use a *negative* question tag after a *positive* sentence:

positive sentence +	*negative tag*
Mary **will** be here soon,	**won't she?**
There **was** a lot of traffic,	**wasn't there?**
Jim **should** pass the exam,	**shouldn't he?**

...and a *positive* question tag after a *negative* sentence:

negative sentence +	*positive tag*
Mary **won't** be late,	**will she?**
They **don't** like us,	**do they?**
You **haven't** got a car,	**have you?**

Notice the meaning of **yes** and **no** in answer to a negative sentence:

- You're **not** going out today, **are you?** { **Yes.** (= Yes, I am going out)
  No. (= No, I am not going out) }

C The meaning of a question tag depends on how you say it. If your voice goes *down*, you aren't really asking a question; you are only inviting the listener to agree with you:

- 'It's a nice day, **isn't it?**'   'Yes, lovely.'
- 'Tim doesn't look well today, **does he?**'   'No, he looks very tired.'
- She's very pretty. She's got beautiful eyes, **hasn't she?**

But if the voice goes *up*, it is a real question:

- 'You haven't seen Mary today, **have you?**'   'No, I'm afraid not.'
  (= Have you seen Mary today by any chance?)

We often use a *negative sentence + positive tag* to ask for things or information, or to ask somebody to do something. The voice goes *up* at the end of the tag in sentences like these:

- 'You haven't got a pen, **have you?**'   'Yes, here you are.'
- 'You couldn't do me a favour, **could you?**'   'It depends what it is.'
- 'You don't know where Karen is, **do you?**'   'Sorry, I've no idea.'

D After **Let's**... the question tag is ...**shall we?**:

- **Let's** go for a walk, **shall we?**

After the imperative (**Do**... / **Don't do**... etc.), the tag is usually ...**will you?**:

- **Open** the door, **will you?**   - **Don't** be late, **will you?**

Note that we say ...**aren't I?** (= am I not?):

- I'm late, **aren't I?**

51.1 *Put a question tag on the end of these sentences.*

1 Tom won't be late, ...will he?...	No, he's never late.
2 You're tired, ...aren't you?...	Yes, a little.
3 You've got a camera, ...?	Yes, why? Do you want to borrow it?
4 You weren't listening, ...?	Yes, I was!
5 Sue doesn't know Ann, ...?	No, they've never met.
6 Jack's on holiday, ...?	Yes, he's in Portugal.
7 Ann's applied for the job, ...?	Yes, but she won't get it.
8 You can speak German, ...?	Yes, but not very fluently.
9 He won't mind if I use his phone, ...?	No, of course he won't.
10 There are a lot of people here, ...?	Yes, more than I expected.
11 Let's go out tonight, ...?	Yes, let's.
12 This isn't very interesting, ...?	No, not very.
13 I'm too impatient, ...?	Yes, you are sometimes.
14 You wouldn't tell anyone, ...?	No, of course not.
15 Listen, ...?	OK, I'm listening.
16 I shouldn't have lost my temper, ...?	No, but never mind.
17 Don't drop that vase, ...?	No, don't worry.
18 He'd never met her before, ...?	No, that was the first time.

51.2 *Read the situation and write a sentence with a question tag. In each situation you are asking your friend to agree with you.*

1 You look out of the window. The sky is blue and the sun is shining. What do you say to your friend? (beautiful day) ...It's a beautiful day, isn't it?...

2 You're with a friend outside a restaurant. You're looking at the prices, which are very high. What do you say? (expensive) It ....

3 You've just come out of the cinema with a friend. You really enjoyed the film. What do you say to your friend? (great) The film ....

4 You and a friend are listening to a woman singing. You like her voice very much. What do you say to your friend? (a lovely voice) She ....

5 You are trying on a jacket. You look in the mirror and you don't like what you see. What do you say to your friend? (not / look / very good) It ....

6 Your friend's hair is much shorter than when you last met. What do you say to her/him? (have / your hair / cut) You ....

7 You and a friend are walking over a wooden bridge. It is very old and some parts are broken. What do you say? (not / very safe) This bridge ....

51.3 *In these situations you are asking for information and asking people to do things. Make sentences like those in Section C.*

1 You need a pen. Perhaps Jane has got one. Ask her. ...Jane, you haven't got a pen, have you?...

2 Jack is just going out. You want him to get you some stamps. Ask him.
Jack, you ....

3 You're looking for Ann. Perhaps Kate knows where she is. Ask her.
Kate, you ....

4 You need a bicycle pump. Perhaps Helen has got one. Ask her.
Helen, ...

5 You're looking for your keys. Perhaps Robin has seen them. Ask him.
....

Verb + -ing (enjoy doing / stop doing etc.)

A Look at these examples:
- I **enjoy** danc**ing**. (*not* 'I enjoy to dance')
- Would you **mind** clos**ing** the door? (*not* 'mind to close')
- Ian **suggested** go**ing** to the cinema. (*not* 'suggested to go')

After **enjoy**, **mind** and **suggest**, we use **-ing** (*not* **to...**).

Here are some more verbs that are followed by **-ing**:

stop	delay	fancy	consider	admit	miss	involve
finish	postpone	imagine	avoid	deny	risk	practise

- Suddenly everybody **stopped** talk**ing**. There was silence.
- I'll do the shopping when I've **finished** clean**ing** the flat.
- He tried to **avoid** answer**ing** my question.
- I don't **fancy** go**ing** out this evening.
- Have you ever **considered** go**ing** to live in another country?

Note the negative form **not -ing**:
- When I'm on holiday, I **enjoy not** hav**ing** to get up early.

B We also use **-ing** after:

> **give up** (= stop)
> **put off** (= postpone)
> **carry on / go on** (= continue)
> **keep** *or* **keep on** (= do something continuously or repeatedly)

- Paula has **given up** smok**ing**.
- We must do something. We can't **go on** liv**ing** like this! (*or* ...**carry on** living...)
- Don't **keep** interrupt**ing** me while I'm speaking. (*or* Don't **keep on** interrupting...)

C With some verbs you can use the structure *verb* + somebody + **-ing**:
- I can't **imagine George** rid**ing** a motorbike.
- You can't **stop me** do**ing** what I want.
- 'Sorry to **keep you** wait**ing** so long.'   'That's all right.'

Note the passive form (**being done/seen/kept** etc.):
- I don't **mind being kept** waiting. (= I don't mind **people** keep**ing** me...)

D When you are talking about finished actions, you can say **having done/stolen/said** etc.:
- She admitted **having stolen** the money.

But it is not necessary to use **having** (done). You can also use the simple **-ing** form for finished actions:
- She admitted **stealing** the money.
- I now **regret saying** (*or* **having said**) what I said.

For **regret**, see Unit 55B.

E After some of the verbs on this page (especially **admit/deny/suggest**) you can use **that...**:
- She **denied that** she had stolen the money. (*or* She **denied** stealing...)
- Ian **suggested that** we went to the cinema. (*or* Ian **suggested going**...)

For **suggest**, see also Unit 34.

EXERCISES

52.1 *Complete each sentence with one of these verbs:*

~~answer~~   apply   be   be   listen   make   see   try   use   wash   work   write

1 He tried to avoid ...**answering**... my question.
2 Could you please stop .... so much noise?
3 I enjoy .... to music.
4 I considered .... for the job but in the end I decided against it.
5 Have you finished .... your hair yet?
6 If you walk into the road without looking, you risk .... knocked down.
7 Jim is 65 but he isn't going to retire yet. He wants to carry on ....
8 I don't mind you .... the phone as long as you pay for all your calls.
9 Hello! Fancy .... you here! What a surprise!
10 I've put off .... the letter so many times. I really must do it today.
11 What a stupid thing to do! Can you imagine anybody .... so stupid?
12 Sarah gave up .... to find a job in this country and decided to go abroad.

52.2 *Complete the sentences for each situation using -ing.*

1   What shall we do? / We could go to the cinema.   She suggested ...**going**...
...**to the cinema.**...

2   Do you want to play tennis? / No, not really.   He didn't fancy ....
....

3   You were driving too fast. / Yes, it's true. Sorry!   She admitted ....
....

4   Why don't we go for a swim? / Good idea!   She suggested ....
....

5   You broke into the shop. / No, I didn't!   He denied ....
....

6   Can you wait a few minutes? / Sure, no problem.   They didn't mind ....
....

52.3 *Complete the sentences so that they mean the same as the first sentence. Use -ing.*

1 I can do what I want and you can't stop me. You ...**can't stop me doing what I want.**...
2 It's not a good idea to travel during the rush hour.
  It's better to avoid ....
3 Shall we go away tomorrow instead of today?
  Shall we postpone .... until ....?
4 The driver of the car said it was true that he didn't have a licence.
  The driver of the car admitted ....
5 Could you turn the radio down, please?
  Would you mind ....?
6 Please don't interrupt me all the time.
  Would you mind ....?

52.4 *Use your own ideas to complete these sentences. Use -ing.*

1 She's a very interesting person. I always enjoy ...**talking to her.**...
2 I'm not feeling very well. I don't fancy ....
3 I'm afraid there aren't any chairs. I hope you don't mind ....
4 It was a lovely day, so I suggested ....
5 It was very funny. I couldn't stop ....
6 My car isn't very reliable. It keeps ....

Verb + **to...** (**decide to do / forget to do** etc.)

A

offer	decide	hope	deserve	attempt	promise
agree	plan	aim	afford	manage	threaten
refuse	arrange	learn	forget	fail	

If these verbs are followed by another verb, the structure is usually *verb + to... (infinitive)*:
- It was late, so we **decided to take** a taxi home.
- Simon was in a difficult situation, so I **agreed to lend** him some money.
- How old were you when you **learnt to drive**? (*or* 'learnt **how** to drive')
- I waved to Karen but **failed to attract** her attention.

Note these examples with the *negative* **not to...**:
- We **decided not to go** out because of the weather.
- I **promised not to be** late.

With many verbs you cannot normally use **to...** . For example, **enjoy/think/suggest**:
- I **enjoy** dancing. (*not* 'enjoy to dance')
- Ian **suggested going** to the cinema. (*not* 'suggested to go')
- Are you **thinking of buying** a car? (*not* 'thinking to buy')

For verb + **-ing**, see Unit 52. For verb + preposition + **-ing**, see Unit 61.

B

We also use **to...** after: **seem appear tend pretend claim**. For example:
- They **seem to have** plenty of money.
- I like George but I think he **tends to talk** too much.
- Ann **pretended not to see** me as she passed me in the street.

There is also a *continuous* infinitive (**to be doing**) and a *perfect* infinitive (**to have done**):
- I **pretended to be** reading the newspaper. (= I pretended that I **was reading**)
- You **seem to have lost** weight. (= it seems that you **have lost** weight)

C

We say '**decide to do** something', '**promise to do** something' etc. In the same way, we say 'a **decision to do** something', 'a **promise to do** something' etc. (*noun + to...*):
- I think his **decision to give** up his job was stupid.
- George has a **tendency to talk** too much.

D

After **dare** you can use the infinitive with or without **to**:
- I wouldn't **dare to tell** him.   *or*   I wouldn't **dare tell** him.

But after **daren't** (*or* **dare not**), you must use the infinitive without **to**:
- I **daren't tell** him what happened. (*not* 'I daren't to tell him')

E

After the following verbs you can use a question word (**what/whether/how** etc.) + **to...**:
ask decide know remember forget explain learn understand wonder

We **asked**	how	to get	to the station.
Have you **decided**	where	to go	for your holidays?
I don't **know**	whether	to apply	for the job or not.
Do you **understand**	what	to do?	

Also: **show / tell / ask / advise / teach** somebody **what / how / where** to do something:
- Can somebody **show me how to change** the film in this camera?
- Ask Jack. He'll **tell you what to do**.

EXERCISES

53.1 *Complete the sentences for each situation.*

1 Shall we get married? — Yes, let's. They decided ...*to get*...
   ...*married.*...

2 Please help me. — OK. She agreed ....
   ....

3 Can I carry your bag for you? — No, thanks. I can manage. He offered ....
   ....

4 Let's meet at 8 o'clock. — OK, fine. They arranged ....
   ....

5 What's your name? — I'm not going to tell you. She refused ....
   ....

53.2 *Complete each sentence with a suitable verb.*

1 Don't forget ...*to post*... the letter I gave you.
2 There was a lot of traffic but we managed .... to the airport in time.
3 Jill has decided not .... a car.
4 We've got a new computer in our office. I haven't learnt .... it yet.
5 I wonder where Sue is. She promised not .... late.
6 We were all too afraid to speak. Nobody dared .... anything.

53.3 *Put the verb into the correct form, to... or -ing. (See Unit 52 for verb + -ing.)*

1 When I'm tired, I enjoy ...*watching*... television. It's relaxing. (watch)
2 It was a nice day, so we decided .... for a walk. (go)
3 It's a nice day. Does anyone fancy .... for a walk? (go)
4 I'm not in a hurry. I don't mind .... (wait)
5 They don't have much money. They can't afford .... out very often. (go)
6 I wish that dog would stop .... It's driving me mad. (bark)
7 Our neighbour threatened .... the police if we didn't stop the noise. (call)
8 We were hungry, so I suggested .... dinner early. (have)
9 Hurry up! I don't want to risk .... the train. (miss)
10 I'm still looking for a job but I hope .... something soon. (find)

53.4 *Make a new sentence using the verb in brackets.*

1 He has lost weight.   (seem)   ...*He seems to have lost weight.*...
2 Tom is worried about something. (appear) Tom appears ....
3 You know a lot of people.   (seem)   You ....
4 My English is getting better.   (seem)   ....
5 That car has broken down.   (appear) ....
6 David forgets things.   (tend)   ....
7 They have solved the problem.   (claim)   ....

53.5 *Complete each sentence using* **what/how/whether** + *one of these verbs:*
do ~~get~~ **go** **ride** **say** **use**

1 Do you know ...*how to get*... to John's house?
2 Can you show me .... this washing machine?
3 Would you know .... if there was a fire in the building?
4 You'll never forget .... a bicycle once you have learned.
5 I was really astonished. I didn't know ....
6 I've been invited to the party but I don't know .... or not.

Verb + (object) + **to...** (I **want (you) to do** etc.)

want	ask	help	would like	would love
expect	beg	**mean** (= intend)	would prefer	would hate

These verbs are followed by **to...** (*infinitive*). The structure can be:

verb + **to...**   or   *verb* + *object* + **to...**

- We **expected to be** late.
- **Would** you **like to go** now?
- He doesn't **want to know**.

- We expected **Tom to be** late.
- Would you like **me to go** now?
- He doesn't want **anybody to know**.

Be careful with **want**. Do not say 'want that...':

- Do you **want me to come** with you? (*not* 'Do you want that I come')

After **help** you can use the infinitive with or without **to**. So you can say:

- Can you help me **to move** this table? *or* Can you help me **move** this table?

tell	remind	force	enable	teach
order	warn	invite	persuade	get (= persuade, arrange for)

These verbs have the structure *verb* + *object* + **to...**:

- Can you **remind me to phone** Ann tomorrow?
- Who **taught you to drive**?
- I didn't move the piano by myself. I **got somebody to help** me.
- Jim said the switch was dangerous and **warned me not to touch** it.

In the next example, the verb is *passive* (**was warned**):

- I **was warned not to touch** the switch.

Note that you cannot use **suggest** with the structure *verb* + *object* + **to...**:

- Jane **suggested that I should buy** a car. (*not* 'Jane suggested me to buy')

For **suggest**, see Units 34 and 52.

advise	recommend	encourage	allow	permit	forbid

There are two possible structures after these verbs. Compare:

verb + **-ing** (without an object)

- I wouldn't **recommend** staying in that hotel.
- She doesn't **allow** smoking in the house.

verb + *object* + **to...**

- I wouldn't **recommend anybody to stay** in that hotel.
- She doesn't **allow us to smoke** in the house.

Compare these examples with **(be) allowed** *(passive)*:

- Smoking **isn't allowed** in the house.
- We **aren't allowed to smoke** in the house.

Make and **let**

These verbs have the structure *verb* + *object* + *infinitive* (without **to**):

- The customs officer **made Sally open** her case. (*not* 'to open')
- Hot weather **makes me feel** tired. (= causes me to feel tired)
- Her parents wouldn't **let her go** out alone. (= wouldn't allow her to go out)
- **Let me carry** your bag for you.

We say '**make** somebody **do**...' (*not* 'to do'), but the *passive* is '(be) **made to do**...' (infinitive *with* **to**):

- Sally **was made to open** her case (by the customs officer).

EXERCISES

54.1 *Complete the questions. Use* **do you want me to...?** *or* **would you like me to...?** *with one of these verbs (+ any other necessary words):* ~~come~~ lend repeat show shut wait

1 Do you want to go alone or ...*do you want me to come with you?*...
2 Have you got enough money or do you want ....?
3 Shall I leave the window open or would you ....?
4 Do you know how to use the machine or would ....?
5 Did you hear what I said or do ....?
6 Can I go now or do ....?

54.2 *Complete the sentences for each situation.*

1 Lock the door. ▷ ◁ OK.   She told ...*him to lock*
....*the door.*

2 Why don't you come and stay with us for a few days? ▷ ◁ Yes, I'd love to.   They invited him ....
....

3 Can I use your phone? ▷ ◁ No!   She wouldn't let ....
....

4 Be careful. ▷ ◁ Don't worry. I will.   She warned ....
....

5 Can you give me a hand? ▷ ◁ Yes, of course.   He asked ....
....

54.3 *Complete these sentences so that the meaning is similar to the first sentence.*

1 My father said I could use his car.   My father allowed ...*me to use his car.*...
2 I was surprised that it rained.   I didn't expect ....
3 Don't stop him doing what he wants.   Let ....
4 He looks older when he wears glasses.   Glasses make ....
5 I think you should know the truth.   I want ....
6 Don't let me forget to phone my sister.   Remind ....
7 At first I didn't want to apply for the job but Sarah persuaded me.
   Sarah persuaded ....
8 My lawyer said I shouldn't say anything to the police.
   My lawyer advised ....
9 I was told that I shouldn't believe everything he says.
   I was warned ....
10 If you've got a car, you are able to travel round more easily.
   Having a car enables ....

54.4 *Put the verb in the right form: -ing or infinitive (with or without to).*

1 She doesn't allow ...*smoking*... in the house. (smoke)
2 I've never been to Iceland but I'd like .... there. (go)
3 I'm in a difficult position. What do you advise me ....? (do)
4 She said the letter was personal and wouldn't let me .... it. (read)
5 We were kept at the police station for two hours and then we were allowed
   .... (go)
6 Where would you recommend me .... for my holidays? (go)
7 I wouldn't recommend .... in that restaurant. The food is awful. (eat)
8 The film was very sad. It made me .... (cry)
9 Carol's parents always encouraged her .... hard at school. (study)

Verb + **-ing** or to **to...** (1) (**remember/regret** etc.)

A When one verb follows another verb, the structure is usually *verb* + **-ing** or *verb* + **to...** . Compare:

verb + **-ing**	*verb* + **to...**
● They **denied stealing** the money.	● They **decided to steal** the money.
● I **enjoy going** out.	● I **want to go** out.
Often we use **-ing** for an action that happens *before* the first verb or at the same time:	Often we use **to...** for an action that *follows* the first verb:
stealing ← denied { enjoy going ↗ }	decided → to steal want → to go

This difference is often helpful (see Section B) but does not explain all uses of **-ing** and **to...** .

B Some verbs can be followed by **-ing** or **to...** with a difference of meaning:

remember

I remember doing something = I did it and now I remember this. You **remember doing** something *after* you have done it: ● I'm absolutely sure I locked the door. I clearly **remember locking** it. (= I locked it, and now I remember this) ● He could **remember driving** along the road just before the accident happened, but he couldn't remember the accident itself.	**I remembered to do** something = I remembered that I had to do it, and so I did it. You **remember to do** something *before* you do it: ● I **remembered to lock** the door when I left but I forgot to shut the windows. (= I remembered that I had to lock the door and so I locked it) ● Please **remember to post** the letter. (= don't forget to post it)

regret

I regret doing something = I did it and now I'm sorry about it: ● I now **regret saying** what I said. I shouldn't have said it.	**I regret to say / to tell** you / **to inform** you = I'm sorry that I have to say (etc.): ● *(from a formal letter)* We **regret to inform** you that we are unable to offer you the job.

go on

Go on doing something = continue doing the same thing: ● The minister **went on talking** for two hours. ● We must change our ways. We can't **go on living** like this.	**Go on to do** something = do or say something new: ● After discussing the economy, the minister then **went on to talk** about foreign policy.

C begin   start   intend   continue   bother
These verbs can be followed by **-ing** or **to...** with little or no difference in meaning. So you can say:
   ● It has **started raining**.   *or*   It has **started to rain**.
   ● John **intends buying** a house.   *or*   John **intends to buy**...
   ● Don't **bother locking** the door.   *or*   Don't **bother to lock**...
But normally we do not use **-ing** after **-ing**:
   ● It's starting **to rain**. (*not* 'it's starting raining')

55.1 *Put the verb into the correct form, -ing or to... . Sometimes either form is possible.*

1 They denied ...**stealing**... the money. (steal)
2 I don't enjoy .... very much. (drive)
3 I don't want .... out tonight. I'm too tired. (go)
4 I can't afford .... out tonight. I haven't got enough money. (go)
5 Has it stopped .... yet? (rain)
6 Can you remind me .... some coffee when we go out? (buy)
7 Why do you keep .... me questions? Can't you leave me alone? (ask)
8 Please stop .... me questions! (ask)
9 I refuse .... any more questions. (answer)
10 One of the boys admitted .... the window. (break)
11 The boy's father promised .... for the window to be repaired. (pay)
12 Ann was having dinner when the phone rang. She didn't answer the phone; she just carried
    on .... (eat)
13 'How did the thief get into the house?'   'I forgot .... the window.' (shut)
14 I've enjoyed .... you. (meet) I hope .... you again soon. (see)
15 The baby began .... in the middle of the night. (cry)
16 Julia has been ill but now she's beginning .... better. (get)

55.2 *Here is some information about Tom when he was a child.*

1 He was in hospital when he was four.   4 He cried on his first day at school.
2 He went to Paris when he was eight.   5 He said he wanted to be a doctor.
3 Once he fell into a river.   6 Once he was bitten by a dog.

He can still remember 1, 2 and 4. But he can't remember 3, 5 and 6. Write sentences beginning
He can remember... *or* **He can't remember... .**

1 ...He can remember being in hospital when he was four...
2 ....
3 ....
4 ....
5 ....
6 ....

55.3 *Complete these sentences with a suitable verb in the correct form, -ing or to... .*

1 a Please remember ...**to lock**... the door when you go out.
   b A: You lent me some money a few months ago.
      B: Did I? Are you sure? I don't remember .... you any money.
   c A: Did you remember .... your sister?
      B: Oh no, I completely forgot. I'll phone her tomorrow.
   d When you see Mandy, remember .... her my regards, won't you?
   e Someone must have taken my bag. I clearly remember .... it by the
      window and now it has gone.
2 a I believe that what I said was fair. I don't regret .... it.
   b *(after a driving test)* I regret .... that you have failed the test.
3 a Keith joined the company 15 years ago. He was quickly promoted and became assistant
      manager after two years. A few years later he went on .... manager of the
      company.
   b I can't go on .... here any more. I want a different job.
   c When I came into the room, Liz was reading a newspaper. She looked up and said hello to
      me, and then went on .... her newspaper.

Verb + **-ing** or to **to…** (2) (**try/need/help**)

A Try to… and try -ing

> **Try to do** = attempt to do, make an effort to do:
> - I was very tired. I **tried to keep** my eyes open but I couldn't.
> - Please **try to be** quiet when you come home. Everyone will be asleep.
>
> **Try** also means 'do something as an experiment or test'. For example:
> - These cakes are delicious. You must **try** one. (= you must have one to see if you like it)
> - We couldn't find anywhere to stay. We **tried** every hotel in the town but they were all full. (= we went to every hotel to see if they had a room)
>
> If **try** (with this meaning) is followed by a verb, we say **try -ing**:
> - A: The photocopier doesn't seem to be working.
>   B: **Try pressing** the green button. (= press the green button – perhaps this will help to solve the problem)
>
> Compare:
> - I **tried to move** the table but it was too heavy. (so I couldn't move it)
> - I didn't like the way the furniture was arranged, so I **tried moving** the table to the other side of the room. But it still didn't look right, so I moved it back again.

B Need to… and need -ing

> I **need to do** something = it is necessary for me to do it:
> - I **need to take** more exercise.
> - He **needs to work** harder if he wants to make progress.
> - I don't **need to come** to the meeting, do I?
>
> Something **needs doing** = something needs to be done:
> - The batteries in the radio **need changing**.
>   (= they need to be changed)
> - Do you think my jacket **needs cleaning**?
>   (= …needs to be cleaned)
> - It's a difficult problem. It **needs thinking** about very carefully. (= it needs to be thought about)

This room needs tidying.

C Help and can't help

> You can say 'help to do' or 'help do' (infinitive with or without **to**):
> - Everybody **helped to clean** up after the party. *or* Everybody **helped clean** up…
> - Can you **help** me **to move** this table? *or* Can you **help** me **move**…
>
> There is also an expression '**can't/couldn't help** doing something'. '**I can't help doing** something' = I can't stop myself from doing it:
> - I don't like him but he has a lot of problems. I **can't help feeling** sorry for him.
> - She tried to be serious but she **couldn't help laughing**. (= she couldn't stop herself from laughing)
> - I'm sorry I'm so nervous. I **can't help it**. (= I can't help **being** nervous)

56.1 *Make helpful suggestions. Each time write a sentence using* **try** + *one of the following*
suggestions: phone him at work   move the aerial   ~~change the batteries~~
                        turn it the other way   take an aspirin

1   The radio isn't working. I wonder what's wrong with it.   ...Have you tried changing the batteries?...

2   I can't open the door. The key won't turn.   Try ....

3   The TV picture isn't very good. What can I do about it?   Have you ....

4   I can't contact Fred. He's not at home. What shall I do?   Why don't you ....

5   I've got a terrible headache. I wish it would go.   Have you ....

56.2 *For each picture write a sentence with* **need(s)** + *one of the following verbs:*
    ~~clean~~   cut   empty   redecorate   tighten

1	2	3	4	5

1   Her jacket is dirty. ...It needs cleaning...
2   The grass is very long. It ....
3   The room isn't very nice. ....
4   The screws are loose. ....
5   The bin is full. ....

56.3 *Put the verb into the correct form,* **-ing** *or* **to…** .

1   a   I was very tired. I tried ...to keep... (keep) my eyes open but I couldn't.
    b   I rang the doorbell but there was no answer. Then I tried ....
      (knock) on the door, but there was still no answer.
    c   We tried .... (put) the fire out but we were unsuccessful. We
      had to call the fire brigade.
    d   Sue needed to borrow some money. She tried .... (ask) Gerry
      but he was short of money too.
    e   I tried .... (reach) the shelf but I wasn't tall enough.
    f   Please leave me alone. I'm trying .... (concentrate).

2   a   I need a change. I need .... (go) away for a while.
    b   She isn't able to look after herself. She needs .... (look) after.
    c   The windows are dirty. They need .... (clean).
    d   Why are you leaving now. You don't need .... (go) yet, do you?
    e   You don't need .... (iron) that shirt. It doesn't need
      .... (iron).

3   a   They were talking very loudly. I couldn't help .... (overhear) them.
    b   Can you help me .... (get) the dinner ready?
    c   He looks so funny. Whenever I see him, I can't help .... (smile).
    d   The fine weather helped .... (make) it a very enjoyable holiday.

Verb + -ing or to to... (3) (like / would like etc.)

A

| like | love | hate | can't bear | enjoy | dislike | mind | can't stand |

These verbs and expressions all mean 'like' or 'not like'. They are often followed by -ing:
- Ann **hates** fly**ing**.
- Why do you **dislike** liv**ing** here?
- I don't **like** people shout**ing** at me. (= I don't like **being shouted** at.)

After **love, hate** and **can't bear**, you can also use **to...** . So you can say:
- I **love** meet**ing** people.   *or*   I **love to meet** people.
- She **can't bear** be**ing** alone.   *or*   She **can't bear to be** alone.

But after **enjoy / dislike / mind / can't stand**, we use only -ing (*not* '**to...**'):
- I **enjoy** be**ing** alone. (*not* 'I enjoy to be')
- Tom doesn't **mind** work**ing** at night. (*not* 'mind to work')

B   **Like**

You can say 'I **like** do**ing** something' or 'I **like to do** something'. Often it doesn't matter which you use, so you can say:
- I **like** gett**ing** up early.   *or*   I **like to get** up early.

In British English, there is sometimes a difference between 'I **like doing**' and 'I **like to do**'.
'I **like doing** something' means 'I enjoy it':
- Do you **like** cook**ing**? (= do you enjoy it?)
- I **like** liv**ing** here. (= I enjoy it)
'I **like to do** something' means 'I think it is good or right to do it':
- I **like to clean** the kitchen as often as possible. (This doesn't mean that I *enjoy* it; it means that I think it is a good thing to do.)
- Mary **likes** people **to be** on time.

C   **Would like / would love / would hate / would prefer** are usually followed by **to...** (*infinitive*):
- I **would like to be** rich.
- **Would** you **like to come** to dinner on Friday?
- I'd **love** (= would love) **to be** able to travel round the world.
- **Would** you **prefer to have** dinner now or later?

Compare **I like** and **I would like**:
- I **like playing / to play** tennis. (= I enjoy it in general)
- I **would like to play** tennis today. (= I want to play today)

Note that **would mind** is followed by -ing (*not* **to...**):
- **Would** you **mind** clos**ing** the door, please?

D   You can also say 'I would like **to have done** something' (= I regret now that I didn't or couldn't do something):
- It's a pity we didn't see Val when we were in London. I **would like to have seen** her again.
- We'**d like to have gone** on holiday but we didn't have enough money.
You can use the same structure after **would love / would hate / would prefer**:
- Poor old Tom! I **would hate to have been** in his position.
- I'd **love to have gone** to the party but it was impossible.

EXERCISES

57.1 *Complete the sentences with* **likes...** *or* **doesn't like...** + *one of the following (in the correct form):*

be kept waiting   do nothing   drive   ~~fly~~   ~~solve mysteries~~
take photographs   take risks   work in the open air

1 George is a detective. He enjoys his work. He ...*likes solving mysteries.*...
2 Ann very rarely travels by plane. She ...*doesn't like flying.*...
3 Rose always carries her camera with her. She ....
4 Christine doesn't use her car very often. She ....
5 Dave is a gardener. He likes his job. He ....
6 Jennifer is a very cautious person. She ....
7 Ted is extremely lazy. He ....
8 Helen is very impatient. She ....

57.2 *Write sentences about yourself. Say whether you like or don't like these activities. Choose one of these verbs for each sentence:* (**don't**) **like** **love** **hate** **enjoy** **don't mind**

1 (flying)   I *don't like flying.*...
2 (playing cards)   ....
3 (doing the ironing)   ....
4 (going to museums)   ....
5 (lying on the beach all day)   ....

57.3 *How would you feel about doing these jobs? In your sentences use one of these:*
I'd like / I wouldn't like   **I'd love**   **I'd hate**   **I wouldn't mind**

1 (a teacher)   ...*I wouldn't like to be a teacher.*...
2 (a dentist)   ....
3 (a hairdresser)   ....
4 (an airline pilot)   ....
5 (a tourist guide)   ....

57.4 *Put in a suitable verb in the correct form,* **-ing** *or* **to...** . *Sometimes either form is possible.*

1 It's nice to be with other people but sometimes I enjoy ...*being*... alone.
2 I'm not quite ready yet. Do you mind .... a little longer?
3 When I was a child, I hated .... to bed early.
4 I don't enjoy .... letters. I can never think what to write.
5 I need a new job. I can't stand .... here any more.
6 I would love .... to your wedding but I'm afraid it isn't possible.
7 Caroline never wears a hat. She doesn't like .... hats.
8 'Would you like .... down?' 'No, thanks. I'll stand.'
9 When I have to catch a train, I'm always worried that I'll miss it. So I like
.... to the station in plenty of time.
10 Have you got a moment? I'd like .... to you about something.

57.5 *Write sentences like those in Section* **D**. *Use the verb in brackets.*

1 It's a pity I couldn't go to the wedding. (like)   *I would like to have gone to the wedding.*
2 It's a pity I didn't see the programme. (like)   ....
3 I'm glad I didn't lose my watch. (hate)   ....
4 It's a pity I didn't meet Ann. (love)   ....
5 I'm glad I wasn't alone. (not/like)   ....
6 It's a pity I couldn't travel by train. (prefer)   ....

Prefer and would rather

A **Prefer to do** and **prefer doing**
You can use '**prefer to** (do)' or '**prefer -ing**' to say what you prefer in general:
- I don't like cities. I **prefer to live** in the country.   *or*   I **prefer living** in the country.

Study the differences in structure after **prefer**. We say:

	I prefer	something	**to**	something else.
	I prefer	**doing** something	**to**	**doing** something else.
but	I prefer	**to do** something	**rather than**	(**do**) something else.

- I **prefer** this coat **to** the coat you were wearing yesterday.
- I **prefer** driving **to** travelling by train.
- *but* I **prefer to drive rather than travel** by train.
- Ann **prefers to live** in the country **rather than** (**live**) in a city.

B **Would prefer** (**I'd prefer…**)
We use '**would** prefer' to say what somebody wants in a particular situation (not in general):
- '**Would** you **prefer** tea or coffee?'   'Coffee, please.'

We say 'would prefer **to do**' (*not* 'doing'):
- 'Shall we go by train?'   'Well, **I'd prefer to go** by car.' (*not* 'I'd prefer going')
- **I'd prefer to stay** at home tonight **rather than go** to the cinema.

C **Would rather** (**I'd rather…**)
Would rather (do) = **would prefer** (to do). After **would rather** we use the infinitive *without* **to**.
Compare:
- 'Shall we go by train?'   { 'I'd **prefer to go** by car.'
                              'I'd **rather go** by car.' (*not* 'to go')
- '**Would** you **rather have** tea or coffee?'   'Coffee, please.'

The negative is 'I'**d rather not** (do something)':
- I'm tired. I'**d rather not go** out this evening, if you don't mind.
- 'Do you want to go out this evening?'   'I'**d rather not**.'

Study the structure after **would rather**:

	I'd rather	**do** something	**than**	(**do**) something else.

- I'**d rather stay** at home tonight **than go** to the cinema.

D **I'd rather you did** something
When you want somebody to do something, you can say '**I'd rather you did** something':
- 'Shall I stay here?'   'I'**d rather** you **came** with us.'
- 'Shall I tell them the news?'   'No. I'**d rather** they **didn't** know.'
- Shall I tell them or **would** you **rather** they **didn't** know?

In this structure we use the *past* (**came, did** etc.), but the meaning is present or future, *not* past.
Compare:
- I'd rather **cook** the dinner now.
- *but* I'd rather **you cooked** the dinner now. (*not* 'I'd rather you cook')

The negative is 'I'd rather you **didn't**…':
- I'**d rather you didn't tell** anyone what I said.
- 'Do you mind if I smoke?'   'I'**d rather you didn't**.'

58.1 *Which do you prefer? Write sentences using* '**I prefer** (something) **to** (something else)'. *Put the verb into the correct form where necessary.*

1 (drive / travel by train)   ...I prefer driving to travelling by train...
2 (tennis / football)   I prefer ....
3 (phone people / write letters)   I .... to ....
4 (go to the cinema / watch films on TV)

   ....

   Now rewrite sentences 3 and 4 using the structure '**I prefer** (to do something)...'.

5 (1) ...I prefer to drive rather than travel by train...
6 (3) I prefer to ....
7 (4) ....

58.2 *Write sentences using* **I'd prefer...** *or* **I'd rather...** + *one of the following:*

eat at home   ~~get a taxi~~   go alone   go for a swim   listen to some music
stand   think about it for a while   wait a few minutes   ~~wait till later~~

1	Shall we walk home?	(prefer)	I'd prefer to get a taxi.
2	Do you want to eat now?	(rather)	I'd rather wait till later.
3	Shall we watch TV?	(prefer)	....
4	What about a game of tennis?	(rather)	....
5	Shall we leave now?	(rather)	....
6	Do you want to go to a restaurant?	(prefer)	....
7	I think we should decide now?	(rather)	....
8	Would you like to sit down?	(rather)	....
9	Do you want me to come with you?	(prefer)	....

   Now write sentences using **than** *and* **rather than**.

10 (get a taxi / walk home)   I'd prefer ...to get a taxi rather than walk home...
11 (go for a swim / play tennis)   I'd rather ....
12 (wait a few minutes / leave now)
   I'd rather ....
13 (eat at home / go to a restaurant)
   I'd prefer ....
14 (think about it for a while / decide now)
   I'd rather ....

58.3 *Complete the sentences using* **would you rather I...** .

1 Are *you* going to cook the dinner or ...would you rather I cooked it?...
2 Are *you* going to tell Ann what happened or would you rather ....?
3 Are *you* going to do the shopping or ....?
4 Are *you* going to answer the phone or ....?

58.4 *Use your own ideas to complete these sentences.*

1 'Shall I tell Ann the news?'   'No, I'd rather she ...didn't... know.'
2 Do you want me to go now or would you rather I .... here?
3 Do you want to go out this evening or would you rather .... at home?
4 This is a private letter addressed to me. I'd rather you .... read it.
5 It's quite a nice house but I'd rather it .... a bit bigger.
6 'Do you mind if I turn on the radio?'   'I'd rather you ....   I'm trying to study.'

Preposition (**in/for/about** etc.) + **-ing**

A   If a preposition (**in/for/about** etc.) is followed by a verb, the verb ends in -ing. For example:

	preposition	*verb* (**-ing**)	
Are you interested	**in**	working	for us?
I'm not very good	**at**	learning	languages.
She must be fed up	**with**	studying.	
What are the advantages	**of**	having	a car?
This knife is only	**for**	cutting	bread.
How	**about**	playing	tennis tomorrow?
I bought a new bicycle	**instead of**	going	away on holiday.
Carol went to work	**in spite of**	feeling	ill.

You can also say 'interested in **somebody** (do)ing…', 'fed up with **you** (do)ing…' etc.:
- I'm fed up **with you** telling me what to do.

B   Note the use of the following prepositions + -ing:

> **before -ing** and **after -ing**:
> - **Before** going out, I phoned Sarah. (*not* 'Before to go out')
> - What did you do **after** leaving school?
> You can also say '**Before I went** out…' and '…**after you left** school'.
>
> **by -ing** (to say *how* something happens):
> - The burglars got into the house **by** breaking a window and climbing in.
> - You can improve your English **by** reading more.
> - She made herself ill **by** not **eating** properly.
>
> **without -ing**:
> - I ran ten kilometres **without** stopping.
> - They climbed through the window **without** anybody seeing them. (*or* …**without** being seen.)
> - She needs to work **without** people disturbing her. (*or* …**without** being disturbed.)
> - It's nice to go on holiday **without** having to worry about money.

C   **To -ing**

To is often part of the *infinitive* (**to** do / **to** see etc.):
- We decided **to go** out.
- Would you like **to play** tennis?

But **to** is also a *preposition* (like **in/for/about/from** etc.). For example:
- We drove from London **to Edinburgh**.
- I prefer tea **to coffee**.
- Are you looking forward **to the weekend**?

If a preposition is followed by a verb, the verb ends in -ing (**in** doing / **about** going etc.– see Section **A**). So, when **to** is a preposition and it is followed by a verb, you must say **to -ing**:
- I prefer driving **to** travelling by train. (*not* 'to travel')
- Are you looking forward **to** seeing Ann again? (*not* 'looking forward to see')

For **be/get used to -ing**, see Unit 60.

EXERCISES

59.1 *Complete the sentences so that they mean the same as the sentence(s) in brackets.*

1 (Why is it useful to have a car?) What are the advantages of ...having a car?..
2 (I don't intend to lend you any money.) I have no intention of ....
3 (Helen has a good memory for names.) Helen is good at ....
4 (Mark won't pass the exam. He has no chance.)
   Mark has no chance of ....
5 (Did you get into trouble because you were late?)
   Did you get into trouble for ....
6 (We didn't eat at home. We went to a restaurant instead.)
   Instead of ....
7 (Tom thinks that working is better than doing nothing.)
   Tom prefers working to ....
8 (They got married. They didn't tell any of their friends.)
   They got married without ....
9 (Our team played well but we lost the game.)
   Our team lost the game in spite of ....

59.2 *Complete the sentences using* **by -ing**. *Use one of the following (with the verb in the correct form):*   borrow too much money   ~~break a window~~   drive too fast
        put some posters up on the walls   stand on a chair   turn a key

1 The burglars got into the house ...by breaking a window...
2 I was able to reach the top shelf ....
3 You start the engine of a car ....
4 Kevin got himself into financial difficulty ....
5 You can put people's lives in danger ....
6 We made the room look nicer ....

59.3 *Complete the sentences with a suitable word. Use only one word each time.*

1 I ran ten kilometres without ...stopping...
2 He left the hotel without .... his bill.
3 It's a nice morning. How about .... for a walk?
4 I was surprised that she left without .... goodbye to anyone.
5 Before .... to bed, I like to have a hot drink.
6 We were able to translate the letter into English without .... a dictionary.
7 It was a very long journey. I was very tired after .... on a train for 36 hours.
8 I was annoyed because the decision was made without anybody .... me.
9 After .... the same job for ten years, I felt I needed a change.

59.4 *For each situation write a sentence with* **I'm (not) looking forward to**.

1 You are going on holiday next week. How do you feel about this?
   ...I'm looking forward to going on holiday...
2 Diane is a good friend of yours and she is coming to visit you soon. So you will see her again soon. How do you feel about this?   I'm ....
3 You are going to the dentist tomorrow. You don't like visits to the dentist. How do you feel about this?   I'm not ....
4 Carol is a student at school. She hates it but she is leaving school next summer. How does she feel about this? ....
5 You've arranged to play tennis tomorrow. You like tennis. How do you feel about this?
   ....

Be/get used to something (I'm used to...)

A Study this example situation:

WELCOME
KEEP LEFT
TENIR A GAUCHE
LINKS FAHREN

Jane is American but she has lived in Britain for three years. When she first drove a car in Britain, she found it very difficult because she had to drive on the left instead of on the right. Driving on the left was strange and difficult for her because:

She **wasn't used to it**.
She **wasn't used to driving** on the left.

But after a lot of practice, driving on the left became less strange. So:
She **got used to driving** on the left.

Now after three years, it's no problem for Jane:
She **is used to driving** on the left.

I'm used to something = it is not new or strange for me:
- Frank lives alone. He doesn't mind this because he has lived alone for 15 years. It is not strange for him. He **is used to it**. He **is used to living** alone.
- I bought some new shoes. They felt a bit strange at first because I **wasn't used to them**.
- Our new flat is on a very busy street. I expect we'll **get used to the noise**, but at the moment it's very disturbing.
- Diane has a new job. She has to get up much earlier now than before – at 6.30. She finds this difficult because she **isn't used to getting** up so early.
- Brenda's husband is often away from home. She doesn't mind this. She **is used to him** be**ing** away.

B After **be/get used** you cannot use the infinitive (**to do / to drive** etc.). We say:
- She is used **to driving** on the left. (*not* 'she is used to drive')

When we say 'I **am used to**...', '**to**' is a *preposition*, not a part of the infinitive (see Unit 59C). So we say:
- Frank is used **to living** alone. (*not* 'Frank is used to live')
- Jane had to get used **to driving** on the left. (*not* 'get used to drive')

C Do not confuse **I am used to doing** (be/get used to) and **I used to do**. They are different in structure and meaning.

> **I am used to (doing) something** = something isn't strange or new for me:
> - I **am** used **to the weather** in this country.
> - I **am** used **to driving** on the left because I've lived in Britain for a long time.
>
> **I used to do something** = I did something regularly in the past but no longer do it (see Unit 18). You can use this structure only for the past, *not* for the present. The structure is 'I **used to do**' (*not* 'I **am** used to do'):
> - I **used to drive** to work every day, but these days I usually go by bike.
> - We **used to live** in a small village, but now we live in London.

EXERCISES

60.1 *Read the situations and complete the sentences. Use* (**be/get**) **used to** *as in the example.*

1 Jane is American. She came to Britain and at first she found driving on the left difficult.
   When she arrived in Britain, she ...**wasn't used to driving**... on the left, but she soon
   ...**got used to**... it. Now she has no problems. She ...**is used to driving**.... on the left.

2 Juan is Spanish and came to live in England. In Spain he always had dinner late in the
   evening, but in England dinner was at 6 o'clock. This was very early for him.
   When Juan first came to England, he .... dinner so early,
   but after some time he .... it. Now he finds it quite normal.
   He .... at six o'clock.

3 Julia is a nurse. A year ago she started working nights. At first she found it hard.
   At first Julia didn't like it. She .... nights and it took her a
   few months to .... it. Now, after a year, she's quite happy.
   She .... nights.

60.2 *What do you say in these situations? Use* **I'm** (not) **used to...** .

1 You live alone. You don't mind this. You have always lived alone.
   FRIEND: Do you get a bit lonely sometimes?   YOU: No, ...**I'm used to living alone.**...

2 You sleep on the floor. You don't mind this. You have always slept on the floor.
   FRIEND: Wouldn't you prefer to sleep in a bed?
   YOU: No, I ....

3 You have to work hard. This is not a problem for you. You have always worked hard.
   FRIEND: You have to work very hard in your job, don't you?
   YOU: Yes, but I don't mind that. I ....

4 You normally go to bed early. Last night you went to bed very late (for you) and as a result
   you are very tired this morning.
   FRIEND: You look tired this morning.
   YOU: Yes, ...

60.3 *Read the situation and complete the sentences using* **used to**.

1 Some friends of yours have just moved into a flat on a busy street. It is very noisy.
   They'll have to ...**get used to the noise.**...

2 Jack once went to the Middle East. It was very difficult for him at first because of the heat.
   He wasn't ....

3 Sue moved from a big house to a much smaller one. She found it strange at first.
   She had to .... in a much smaller house.

4 The children at school had a new teacher. She was different from the teacher before her but this
   wasn't a problem for the children. The children soon ....

5 Somebody from Britain is thinking of going to live in your country. Warn him/her!
   You would have to ....

60.4 *(Section C) Complete the sentences using* <u>only one word</u> *each time.*

1 Jane had to get used to ...**driving**.... on the left.
2 We used to .... in a small village but now we live in London.
3 Tom used to .... a lot of coffee. Now he prefers tea.
4 I feel very full after that meal. I'm not used to .... so much.
5 I wouldn't like to share an office. I'm used to .... my own office.
6 I used to .... a car but I sold it a few months ago.
7 When we were children, we used to .... swimming every day.
8 There used to .... a cinema here but it was knocked down a few years ago.
9 I'm the boss here! I'm not used to .... told what to do.

Verb + preposition + -ing (succeed in -ing/ accuse somebody of -ing etc.)

A Many verbs have the structure *verb + preposition* (**in/for/about** etc.) *+ object*. For example:

verb +	*preposition*	*+ object*
We **talked**	about	the problem.
You must **apologise**	for	what you said.

If the *object* is another verb, it ends in **-ing**:

verb +	*preposition*	*+ -ing (object)*
We **talked**	about	going to America.
She **apologised***	for	**not telling** the truth.

Here are some more verbs with this structure:

succeed (in)	Have you **succeeded**	in	finding a job yet?
insist (on)	They **insisted**	on	paying for the meal.
think (of)	I'm **thinking**	of	buying a house.
dream (of)	I wouldn't **dream**	of	asking them for money.
approve (of)	She doesn't **approve**	of	gambling.
decide (against)	We have **decided**	against	moving to London.
feel (like)	Do you **feel**	like	going out tonight?
look forward (to)	I'm **looking forward**	to	meeting her.

* We say 'apologise **to** somebody for…':
- She **apologised to me** for not telling the truth. (*not* 'she apologised me')

B With some of the verbs in **A**, you can use the structure *verb + preposition* + somebody + **-ing**:

verb +	*preposition*	**somebody**	*+ -ing*
She doesn't **approve**	of	me	gambling.
We are all **looking forward**	to	Liz	coming home.

C The following verbs can have the structure *verb + object + preposition + -ing*:

	verb +	*object +*	*preposition*	*+ -ing*
congratulate (on)	I **congratulated**	Ann	on	passing the exam.
accuse (of)	They **accused**	me	of	telling lies.
suspect (of)	Nobody **suspected**	the man	of	being a spy.
prevent (from)	What **prevented**	him	from	coming to see us?
stop (from*)	The police **stopped**	everyone	from	leaving the building.
thank (for)	I forgot to **thank**	them	for	helping me.
forgive (for)	Please **forgive**	me	for	not writing to you.
warn (against)	They **warned**	us	against	buying the car.

* You can also say '**stop** somebody **doing**' (*without* from). So you can say:
- You can't **stop me doing** what I want.   *or*   …stop me **from** doing what I want.

Some of these verbs are often used in the *passive*. For example:
- **I was accused of** telling lies.
- **The man was suspected of** being a spy.
- **We were warned against** buying the car.

EXERCISES

61.1 *Complete each sentence using only one word.*

1 Our neighbours apologised for ...**making**.... so much noise.
2 I feel lazy. I don't feel like .... any work.
3 I wanted to go out alone but Joe insisted on .... with me.
4 I'm fed up with my job. I'm thinking of .... something else.
5 We have decided against .... a new car because we can't really afford it.
6 I hope you write to me soon. I'm looking forward to .... from you.
7 The weather was extremely bad and this prevented us from .... out.
8 The man who has been arrested is suspected of .... a false passport.
9 I think you should apologise to Sue for .... so rude to her.
10 Some parents don't approve of their children .... a lot of television.
11 I'm sorry I can't come to your party but thank you very much for .... me.

61.2 *Complete the sentences using a preposition + one of the following verbs (in the correct form):*

cause   escape   ~~go~~   help   interrupt   live   play   solve   spend   walk

1 Do you feel ...**like going**.... out this evening?
2 It took us a long time but we finally succeeded .... the problem.
3 I've always dreamed .... in a small house by the sea.
4 The driver of the other car accused me .... the accident.
5 There was a fence around the lawn to stop people .... on the grass.
6 Forgive me .... you but may I ask you something?
7 Where are you thinking .... your holiday this year?
8 The guards weren't able to prevent the prisoner ....
9 I wanted to cook the meal by myself but Dave insisted .... me.
10 I'm sorry we've had to cancel our game of tennis tomorrow. I was really looking forward
....

61.3 *Complete the sentences on the right.*

1 YOU GEORGE
It was nice of you to help me. Thanks very much.
George thanked ...**me for helping him.**...

2 ANN TOM
I'll drive you to the station. I insist.
Tom insisted ....
....

3 YOU JIM
I hear you passed your exam. Congratulations!
Jim congratulated me ....
....

4 SUE MRS BOND
It was nice of you to come to see me. Thank you.
Mrs Bond thanked ....
....

5 JACK YOU
Don't stay at the hotel near the airport.
I warned ....
....

6 YOU MARY
I'm sorry I didn't phone you earlier.
Mary apologised ....
....

7 YOU JANE
You're selfish.
Jane accused ....
....

Expressions + -ing

A When these expressions are followed by a verb, the verb ends in **-ing**:

It's no use… / It's no good…:
- There's nothing you can do about the situation, so **it's no use** worry**ing** about it.
- **It's no good** try**ing** to persuade me. You won't succeed.

There's no point in…:
- **There's no point in** hav**ing** a car if you never use it.
- **There was no point in** wait**ing** any longer, so we went.

It's (not) worth…:
- I live only a short walk from here, so **it's not worth** tak**ing** a taxi.
- It was so late when we got home, **it wasn't worth** go**ing** to bed.

You can say 'a film is **worth** see**ing**', 'a book is **worth** read**ing**', etc.
- What was the film like? Was it **worth** see**ing**?
- I don't think newspapers are **worth** read**ing**.

B **(Have) difficulty -ing**

We say 'have difficulty **doing** something' (*not* 'to do'):
- I had **difficulty** find**ing** a place to live. (*not* 'I had difficulty to find')
- Did you have any **difficulty** gett**ing** a visa?
- People often have great **difficulty** read**ing** my writing.

We usually say 'have **difficulty**' (*not* 'have difficulties'):
- I'm sure you'll have no **difficulty** pass**ing** the exam. (*not* 'have no difficulties')

C We use **-ing** after:

a waste of money… / a waste of time… (**to…** is also possible):
- It was a **waste of time** read**ing** that book. It was rubbish.
- It's a **waste of money** buy**ing** things you don't need.

spend/waste (time)…
- He **spent hours** try**ing** to repair the clock.
- I **waste a lot of time** daydream**ing**.

(be) busy…:
- She said she couldn't see me. She was too **busy** do**ing** other things.

D **Go swimming / go fishing** etc.

We use **go -ing** for a number of activities (especially sports). For example, you can say:
go swimm**ing** / **go** sail**ing** / **go** fish**ing** / **go** climb**ing** / **go** ski**ing** / **go** jogg**ing** etc.
also: **go** shopp**ing** / **go** sightsee**ing**.
- I'd like to **go** ski**ing**.
- When did you last **go** shopp**ing**?
- I've never **been** sail**ing**. (For **been** and **gone**, see Unit 7D.)

You can also say '**come** swimming / **come** skiing' etc.:
- Why don't you **come** swimm**ing** with us?

EXERCISES

62.1 *Complete the sentences on the right.*

1	Shall we get a taxi home?	No, it isn't far. It's not worth ...**getting a taxi.**
2	If you need help, why don't you ask Tom?	It's no use .... He won't be able to help us.
3	I don't really want to go out tonight.	Well, stay at home! There's no point .... if you don't want to.
4	Shall I phone Ann now?	No, it's no good....................................... She won't be at home.
5	Are you going to complain about what happened?	No, it's not worth .... Nobody will do anything about it.
6	Do you ever read newspapers?	No. I think it's a waste ....

62.2 *Make sentences with* **worth -ing** *or* **not worth -ing.** *Choose one of these verbs:*
consider   keep   read   repair   ~~see~~   visit

1 The film isn't very good. ...**It's not worth seeing.**
2 It would cost too much to repair this watch. It's not worth ....
3 If you have time, you should go to the museum. It's worth ....
4 It's quite an interesting suggestion. ....
5 There's an interesting article in the paper today. ....
6 We can throw these old clothes away. They ....

62.3 *Make sentences beginning* **There's no point... .**

1 Why have a car if you never use it? ...**There's no point in having a car if you never use it.**
2 Don't eat if you're not hungry. There's no ....
3 Why work if you don't need money? ....
4 Don't study if you feel tired. ....

62.4 *Write sentences using* **difficulty.**

1 I managed to get a visa but it was difficult. ...**I had difficulty getting a visa.**
2 I can't remember people's names. I have difficulty ....
3 Lucy managed to get a job without difficulty. She had no ....
4 Do you find it difficult to understand him? Do you have ....
5 It won't be difficult to get a ticket for the concert.
  You won't have any ....

62.5 *Complete the sentences. Use only one word each time.*

1 It's a waste of money ...**buying**... things you don't need.
2 Every morning I spend about an hour .... the newspaper.
3 'What's Carol doing?'   'She's busy .... letters.'
4 I think you waste too much time .... television.
5 There's a beautiful view from that hill. It is worth .... to the top.

62.6 *Complete these sentences with one of the following (with the verb in the correct form):*
go skiing   go shopping   go swimming   ~~go sailing~~   go riding

1 Barry lives by the sea and he's got a boat, so he often ...**goes sailing.**
2 There's plenty of snow in the mountains so we'll be able to ....
3 It was a very hot day, so we .... in the river.
4 Margaret has got two horses. She often ....
5 The shops are shut now. It's too late to ....

To..., for... and **so that...** (purpose)

A   We use **to...** to say why somebody does something (= the *purpose* of an action):
- 'Why did you go out?'   '**To post** a letter.'
- A friend of mine phoned **to invite** me to a party.
- We shouted **to warn** everybody of the danger.

We use **to...** to say why something exists or why somebody has/wants/needs something:
- This wall is **to keep** people out of the garden.
- The President has a team of bodyguards **to protect** him.
- I need a bottle opener **to open** this bottle.

B   We use **to...** to say what can be done or must be done with something:
- It's difficult to find **a place to park** in the city centre. (= a place where you can park)
- Would you like **something to eat**?
- Have you got **much work to do**? (= work that you must do)
- I get lonely if there's **nobody to talk to**.

Also: **money/time/chance/opportunity/energy/courage** etc. **to** (do something):
- They gave us **some money to buy** some food.
- Do you have **much opportunity** to practise your English?
- I need **a few days to think** about your proposal.

C   **For...** and **to...**
Compare:
- I'm going to Spain **for a holiday**.

but   I'm going to Spain **to learn** Spanish. (*not* 'for learn Spanish', *not* 'for learning Spanish')

We use **for** + *noun* (**for a holiday**) but **to** + *verb* (**to learn**). Some more examples:
- What would you like **for dinner**?

but   What would you like **to eat**? (*not* 'for eat')
- Let's go to the pool **for a swim**.

but   Let's go to the pool **to have** a swim.

Note that you can say ...**for** (somebody) **to** (do something):
- There weren't any chairs **for us to sit on**, so we had to sit on the floor.

You can use **for -ing** to say what the *general* purpose of a thing is. **To...** is also possible:
- This knife is only **for cutting** bread. (*or* ...**to cut** bread.)

You can use **What...for?** to ask about purpose:
- **What** is this switch **for**?   • **What** did you do that **for**?

D   **So that**
Sometimes you have to use **so that** for purpose. We use **so that** (*not* **to...**):

i)   when the purpose is *negative* (**so that...won't/wouldn't**):
- I hurried **so that** I **wouldn't** be late. (= because I didn't want to be late)
- Leave early **so that** you **won't** (*or* **don't**) miss the bus.

ii) with **can** and **could** (**so that...can/could**)
- She's learning English **so that** she **can** study in Canada.
- We moved to London **so that** we **could** visit our friends more often.

iii) when one person does something **so that** *another* person does something else:
- **I** gave her my address **so that she** could contact me.
- **He** wore glasses and a false beard **so that nobody** would recognise him.

63.1 *Use a sentence from Box A and a sentence from Box B to make a new sentence.*

A
1	~~I shouted~~
2	I had to go to the bank
3	I'm saving money
4	I went into hospital
5	I'm wearing two pullovers
6	I phoned the police station

B
| I want to keep warm |
| I wanted to report that my car had been stolen |
| I want to go to Canada |
| I had to have an operation |
| I needed to get some money |
| ~~I wanted to warn people of the danger~~ |

1 ...I shouted to warn people of the danger....
2 I had to go to the bank ....
3 I ....
4 ....
5 ....
6 ....

63.2 *Complete these sentences using a suitable verb.*

1 The President has a team of bodyguards ...to protect.... him.
2 I didn't have enough time .... the newspaper today.
3 I came home by taxi. I didn't have the energy ....
4 'Would you like something ....?' 'Yes, please. A cup of coffee.'
5 We need a bag .... these things in.
6 There will be a meeting next week .... the problem.
7 I wish we had enough money .... a new car.
8 I saw Helen at the party but we didn't have a chance .... to each other.
9 I need some new clothes. I haven't got anything nice ....
10 They've just passed their exams. They're having a party ....
11 I can't do all this work alone. I need somebody .... me.

63.3 *Put in* **to** *or* **for.**

1 I'm going to Spain ...for... a holiday.
2 You need a lot of experience .... this job.
3 You need a lot of experience .... do this job.
4 We'll need more time .... make a decision.
5 I went to the dentist .... a check-up.

6 I had to put on my glasses .... read the letter.
7 Do you wear glasses .... reading?
8 I wish we had a garden .... the children .... play in.

63.4 *Write sentences with* **so that.**

1 I hurried. I didn't want to be late.   ...I hurried so that I wouldn't be late.
2 We wore warm clothes. We didn't want to get cold.
  We wore ....
3 The man spoke very slowly. He wanted me to understand what he said.
  The man ....
4 I whispered. I didn't want anybody else to hear our conversation.
  .... nobody ....
5 Please arrive early. We want to be able to start the meeting on time.
  Please ....
6 She locked the door. She didn't want to be disturbed.
  ....
7 I slowed down. I wanted the car behind to be able to overtake.
  ....

Adjective + **to...**

A

Difficult to understand etc.

Compare sentences **a** and **b**:

- Jim doesn't speak very clearly. $\begin{cases} \text{It is } \textbf{difficult to understand} \boxed{\text{him}}. \textbf{(a)} \\ \boxed{\text{He}} \text{ is } \textbf{difficult to understand.} \textbf{(b)} \end{cases}$

Sentences **a** and **b** have the same meaning. But note that we say:
- He is difficult **to understand**. (*not* 'He is difficult to understand *him*.')

You can use the structures in the box with:
difficult   easy   hard   impossible   dangerous   safe   expensive   cheap
and a number of other adjectives (for example, **nice/interesting/exciting**):
- Do you think it is **safe to drink this water**?
  Do you think this water is **safe to drink**? (*not* 'to drink it')
- Your writing is awful. It is **impossible to read it**. (= to read your writing)
  Your writing is **impossible to read**. (*not* 'to read it')
- I like being with Jill. It's very **interesting to talk to** her.
  Jill is very **interesting to talk to**. (*not* 'to talk to her')

You can also use this structure with an adjective + *noun*:
- This is a **difficult question** (for me) **to answer**. (*not* 'to answer it')

B

(It's) nice (of you) to...
You can use this structure to say what you think of what somebody does:
- It was **nice of you to take** me to the station. Thank you very much.
You can use many other adjectives in this way. For example:
kind   clever   sensible   mean   silly   stupid   careless   unfair   considerate:
- It's **silly of Mary to give** up her job when she needs the money.
- I think it was very **unfair of him to criticise** me.

C

(I'm) sorry to...
You can use this structure to say how somebody reacts to something:
- I was **sorry to hear** that your father is ill.
You can use many other adjectives in this way. For example:
**happy   glad   pleased   delighted   sad   disappointed   surprised   amazed
astonished   relieved**:
- Was Tom **surprised to see** you when you went to see him?
- We were **delighted to get** your letter last week.

D

The **first** (person) **to know**, the **next** train **to arrive**
We use **to...** after **the first/second/third** etc. and also after **the next, the last, the only**:
- If I have any more news, you will be **the first** (person) **to know**.
- **The next** train **to arrive** at platform 4 will be the 6.50 to Cardiff.
- Everybody was late except me. I was **the only** one **to arrive** on time.

E

You can say that something is **sure / certain / bound / likely to** happen:
- She's very intelligent. She's **sure / certain / bound to pass** the exam.
- I'm **likely to be** late home this evening. (= I will probably be late home)

64.1 *(Section A) Write these sentences in another way, beginning as shown.*

1 It's difficult to understand him.   He is difficult to understand.
2 It's quite easy to use this machine.   This machine is ....
3 It was very difficult to open the window.   The window ....
4 It's impossible to translate some words.   Some words ....
5 It's not safe to stand on that chair.   That chair ....
6 It's expensive to maintain a car.   A ....

64.2 *(Section A) Complete the second sentence using the adjective in brackets. Use* **a/an** *+ adjective + noun +* **to…** *(as in the example).*

1 I couldn't answer the question.   (difficult) It was a difficult question to answer.
2 Everybody makes that mistake.   (easy) It's an ....
3 I like living in this place.   (nice) It's a ....
4 We enjoyed watching the game.   (good) It was ....

64.3 *(Section B) Make a new sentence beginning* **It…** *. Use one of these adjectives each time:*
careless   considerate   ~~kind~~   nice

1 You did my shopping for me.   It was kind of you to do my shopping for me.
2 You make the same mistake again and again.
  It ....
3 Don and Jenny invited me to stay with them.
  ....
4 John made so much noise when I was trying to sleep.
  It wasn't very ....

64.4 *(Section C) Use the following words to complete these sentences:*
sorry/hear   glad/hear   ~~delighted/get~~   surprised/see

1 We were delighted to get your letter last week.
2 Thank you for your letter. I .... that you're keeping well.
3 We .... Pauline at the party. We didn't expect her to come.
4 I .... that your mother isn't well. I hope she gets well soon.

64.5 *(Section D) Complete the second sentence using the words in brackets +* **to…** *.*

1 Nobody left before me.   (the first) I was the first person to leave.
2 Everybody else arrived before Paul.   (the last) Paul was the ....
3 Fiona passed the exam. All the other students failed.   (the only)
  Fiona was ....
4 I complained to the restaurant manager about the service. Another customer had already
  complained before me.   (the second) I was ....
5 Neil Armstrong walked on the moon in 1969. Nobody had done this before him.
  (the first) Neil Armstrong was ....

64.6 *(Section E) Complete these sentences using the word in brackets and a suitable verb.*

1 Diane is very intelligent. She is bound to pass the exam. (bound)
2 I'm not surprised you're tired. After such a long journey you .... tired.
  (bound)
3 Tom's got a very bad memory. He .... what you told him. (sure)
4 I don't think you need to take an umbrella. It .... (not likely)
5 The holidays begin this weekend. There .... a lot of traffic on the
  roads. (likely)

To... (afraid **to do**) and preposition + **-ing** (afraid **of -ing**)

A   **Afraid to** (do) and **afraid of** (do)**ing**

I am **afraid to do** something = I *don't want* to do it because it is dangerous or the result could be bad. We use **afraid to do** for things we do intentionally:

● A lot of people are **afraid to go** out at night. (= they don't want to go out because it is dangerous – so they don't go out)
● He was **afraid to tell** his parents about the broken window. (= he didn't want to tell them because he knew they would be angry)

I am **afraid of** something **happening** = it is possible that something bad will happen (for example, an accident). We do not use **afraid of -ing** for things we do intentionally:

● The path was icy, so we walked very carefully. We were **afraid of falling**. (= it was possible that we would fall – *not* 'we were afraid to fall')
● I don't like dogs. I'm always **afraid of being** bitten. (*not* 'afraid to be bitten')

So, you are **afraid to do** something because you are **afraid of something happening** as a result:

● I was **afraid to go** near the dog because I **was afraid of being** bitten.

B   **Interested in** (do)**ing** and **interested to** (do)

I'm **interested in doing** something = I'm thinking of doing it, I'd like to do it:
● I'm trying to sell my car but nobody is **interested in buying** it. (*not* 'to buy')

We use **interested to** especially with **hear/see/know/read/learn**. I was **interested to hear** it = 'I heard it and it was interesting for me':
● I was **interested to hear** that Diane has got a new job.
● Ask George for his opinion. I would be **interested to know** what he thinks. (= it would be interesting for me to know)

This structure is the same as **surprised to / delighted to...** etc. (see Unit 64C):
● I was **surprised to hear** that Diane has got a new job.

C   **Sorry to** (do) and **sorry for** (do)**ing**

We usually say **sorry to...** to apologise when (or just before) we do something:
● I'm **sorry to bother** you, but I need to talk to you.

We use **sorry to** (**hear/read** etc.) to show sympathy with somebody (see Unit 64C):
● I was **sorry to hear** that Fiona lost her job. (= I was sorry when I heard...)

You can use **sorry for** (doing something) to apologise for something you did before:
● (I'm) **sorry for shouting** at you yesterday. (*not* 'Sorry to shout...')

You can also say:
● (I'm) **sorry I shouted** at you yesterday.

D   Note that we say:

I **want to** (do) / I'd **like to** (do)	*but*	I'm **thinking of** (do)**ing** / I **dream of** (do)**ing**
I **failed to** (do)	*but*	I **succeeded in** (do)**ing**
I **allowed** them **to** (do)	*but*	I **prevented** them **from** (do)**ing**

For examples, see Units 53–54 and 61.

EXERCISES

65.1 *Read the situation and use the words in brackets to write a sentence with* **afraid**.

1 The streets are unsafe at night.
(a lot of people / afraid / go / out) ...A lot of people are afraid to go out...

2 We walked very carefully along the icy path.
(we / afraid / fall) ...We were afraid of falling...

3 I don't usually carry my passport with me.
(I / afraid / lose / it) ....

4 The sea was very rough.
(we / afraid / go / swimming) ....

5 We rushed to the station.
(we / afraid / miss / our train) ....

6 In the middle of the film there was a particularly horrifying scene.
(we / afraid / look) ....

7 The glasses were very full, so Jane carried them very carefully.
(she / afraid / spill / the drinks) ....

8 I didn't like the look of the food on my plate.
a (I / afraid / eat / it) ....
b (I / afraid / make / myself ill) ....

65.2 *Complete the sentences using one of these verbs:*

~~buy~~   get   go   hear   read   start

1 I'm trying to sell my car but nobody is interested ...in buying... it.

2 Julia is interested .... her own business.

3 I was interested .... your letter in the newspaper last week.

4 Bill wants to stay single. He's not interested .... married.

5 You must tell me what you think. I'm always interested .... your opinion.

6 There's a party tonight but I'm not interested ....

65.3 *Complete the sentences using the verb in brackets.*

1 I'm sorry ...for shouting... at you yesterday. (shout)

2 Sorry .... you but have you got a pen I could borrow? (disturb)

3 Sorry .... late last night. I didn't realise the time. (be)

4 I'm sorry .... what I said yesterday. I didn't really mean it. (say)

5 'I've just had my exam results. I failed.'   'Oh? I'm sorry .... that.' (hear)

65.4 *Complete the sentences using the verb in brackets.*

1 a We wanted ...to leave... the building. (leave)
  b We weren't allowed .... the building. (leave)
  c We were prevented .... the building. (leave)

2 a Fred failed .... the problem. (solve)
  b Amy succeeded .... the problem. (solve)

3 a I'm thinking .... away next week. (go)
  b I'm hoping .... away next week. (go)
  c I'm looking forward .... away next week. (go)
  d I'd like .... away next week. (go)

4 a Mary wanted .... me a drink. (buy)
  b Mary promised .... me a drink. (buy)
  c Mary insisted .... me a drink. (buy)
  d Mary wouldn't dream .... me a drink. (buy)

See somebody do and see somebody doing

A   Study this example situation:
Tom got into his car and drove away. You saw this.
You can say:
  ● I saw Tom **get** into his car and **drive** away.

In this structure we use **get/drive/do** etc. (infinitive without '**to**'):

YOU

Somebody **did** something	+	I saw this

  I saw somebody **do** something.

Note that we use the infinitive *without* **to**:
  ● We saw them **go** out. (*not* 'to go')
But after a *passive* ('they **were seen**') etc., we use **to**:
  ● They were seen **to** go out.

B   Study this example situation:
Yesterday you saw Ann. She was waiting for a bus.
You can say:
  ● I saw Ann **waiting** for a bus.

In this structure we use **-ing** (wait**ing**):

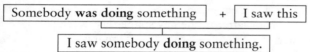

Somebody **was doing** something	+	I saw this

  I saw somebody **doing** something.

C   Study the difference in meaning between the two structures:

'I saw him **do** something' = he **did** something (*past simple*) and I saw this. I saw the complete action from beginning to end:
● He **fell** off the wall. I saw this. → I saw him **fall** off the wall.
● The accident **happened**. Did you see this? → Did you see the accident **happen**?

'I saw him **doing** something' = he **was doing** something (*past continuous*) and I saw this. I saw him when he was in the middle of doing it. This does not mean that I saw the complete action:
● He **was walking** along the street.
   I saw this when I drove past in my car. } → I saw him **walking** along the street.

Sometimes the difference is not important and you can use either form:
● I've never seen her **dance**. *or* I've never seen her **dancing**.

D   We use these structures with **see** and **hear**, and a number of other verbs:
  ● I didn't **hear** you **come** in.
  ● Liz suddenly **felt** something **touch** her on the shoulder.
  ● Did you **notice** anyone **go** out?

  ● I could **hear** it **raining**.
  ● The missing boys were last **seen playing** near the river.
  ● **Listen to** the birds **singing**!
  ● Can you **smell** something **burning**?
  ● I **found** Sue in my room **reading** my letters.

EXERCISES

66.1 *Complete the answers to the questions.*

1	Did anybody go out?
2	Has Jill arrived yet?
3	How do you know I took the money?
4	Did the doorbell ring?
5	Can Tom play the piano?
6	Did I lock the door when I went out?
7	How did the woman fall in the river?

1 I don't think so. I didn't see ...*anybody go out.*...
2 Yes, I think I heard her ....
3 I know because I saw you ....
4 I'm not sure. I didn't hear ....
5 I've never heard ....
6 Yes, you did. I saw ....
7 I don't know. I didn't see ....

66.2 *In each of these situations you and a friend saw, heard or smelt something. Look at the pictures and complete the sentences.*

1   ...*We saw Ann waiting for a bus.*...
2 We saw Dave and Helen ....
3 We saw .... in a restaurant.
4 We heard ....
5 We could ....
6 ....

66.3 *Complete these sentences. Use one of these verbs (in the correct form):*

climb   ~~come~~   crawl   cry   cycle   explode   happen
open   run   say   ~~sing~~   slam   sleep   tell

1 Listen to the birds ...*singing.*...
2 I didn't hear you ...*come*... in.
3 Did anybody see the accident ....?
4 We listened to the old man .... his story from beginning to end.
5 Listen! Can you hear a baby ....?
6 I looked out of the window and saw Tim on his bike .... along the road.
7 'Why did you turn round suddenly?'   'I thought I heard somebody .... my name.'
8 We watched the two men .... across the garden, ... a window and .... through it into the house.
9 Everybody heard the bomb ....   It was a tremendous noise.
10 Oh! I can feel something .... up my leg! It must be an insect.
11 I heard somebody .... the door in the middle of the night. It woke me up.
12 When we got home, we found a cat .... on the kitchen table.

-ing clauses (**Feeling tired**, I went to bed early.)

A A *clause* is a part of a sentence. Some sentences have two or more clauses:

- Jim hurt his arm **playing tennis**.
  └─ *main clause* ─┘ └─ *-ing clause* ─┘

- **Feeling tired**, I went to bed early.
  └ *-ing clause* ─┘ └── *main clause* ──┘

'Play**ing** tennis' and 'feel**ing** tired' are -ing clauses.
If the -ing clause is first (as in the second example), we write a comma (,) between the clauses.

B When two things happen at the same time, you can use -ing for one of the verbs. The main clause usually comes first:
- I've just seen Carol. She's in the bar **having a drink**. (= she is in the bar *and* she is having a drink)
- A man ran out of the house **shouting**. (= he ran out of the house *and* he was shouting)
- Do something! Don't just stand there **doing** nothing!

We also use -ing when one action happens during another action. We use -ing for the longer action. The longer action is the second part of the sentence:
- Jim hurt his arm **playing tennis**. (= while he was playing)
- Did you cut yourself **shaving**? (= while you were shaving)
You can also use -ing after **while** or **when**:
- Jim hurt his arm **while playing** tennis.
- Be careful **when crossing** the road. (= when you are crossing)

C When one action happens before another action, we use **having** (**done**) for the first action:
- **Having found** a hotel, we looked for somewhere to have dinner.
- **Having finished** her work, she went home.
You can also say **after -ing**:
- **After finishing** her work, she went home.

If one short action follows another short action, you can use the simple -ing form (**doing** instead of **having done**) for the first action:
- **Taking** a key out of his pocket, he opened the door.

These structures are used more in written English than in spoken English.

D You can use an -ing clause to explain something or to say why somebody does something. The -ing clause usually comes first:
- **Feeling** tired, I went to bed early. (= because I felt tired)
- **Being** unemployed, he hasn't got much money. (= because he is unemployed)
- **Not having** a car, she finds it difficult to get around. (= because she doesn't have a car)
- **Having** already **seen** the film twice, I didn't want to go to the cinema. (= because I had already seen it twice)

These structures are used more in written English than in spoken English.

67.1 *Join a sentence from Box A with one from Box B to make one sentence. Use an* **-ing** *clause.*

A	1 ~~Carol was in the bar.~~	B	She was feeling very tired.
	2 Emma was sitting in an armchair.		She looked at the sights and took photographs.
	3 Sue got home late.		She said she would be back in an hour.
	4 Sarah went out.		She was reading a book.
	5 Linda was in London for two years.		~~She was having a drink.~~
	6 Mary walked round the town.		She worked as a tourist guide.

1 Carol was in the bar having a drink.
2 Emma was sitting ....
3 Sue ....
4 ....
5 ....
6 ....

67.2 *Make one sentence from two using an* **-ing** *clause.*

1 Jim was playing tennis. He hurt his arm. Jim hurt his arm playing tennis.
2 I was watching television. I fell asleep. I ....
3 The man slipped. He was getting off a bus. The man ....
4 I was walking home in the rain. I got wet. I ....
5 Margaret was driving to work yesterday. She had an accident.

....

6 Two firemen were overcome by smoke. They were trying to put out the fire.

....

67.3 *Make sentences beginning* **Having…** .

1 She finished her work. Then she went home. Having finished her work, she went home.
2 We bought our tickets. Then we went into the theatre.

....

3 They continued their journey after they'd had dinner.

....

4 After Lucy had done all her shopping, she went for a cup of coffee.

....

67.4 *Make sentences beginning* **-ing** *or* **Not -ing** *(like those in Section D). Sometimes you need to begin with* **Having** *(done something).*

1 I felt tired. So I went to bed early. Feeling tired, I went to bed early.
2 I thought they might be hungry. So I offered them something to eat.

....

3 She is a foreigner. So she needs a visa to stay in this country.

....

4 I didn't know his address. So I wasn't able to contact him.

....

5 Sarah has travelled a lot. So she knows a lot about other countries.

....

6 The man wasn't able to understand English. So he didn't know what I wanted.

....

7 We had spent nearly all our money. So we couldn't afford to stay in a hotel.

....

Countable and uncountable nouns (1)

A   A noun can be *countable* or *uncountable*. Compare:

Countable	*Uncountable*
● I eat **a banana** every day.	● I eat **rice** every day.
● I like **bananas**.	● I like **rice**.
Banana is a *countable* noun.	**Rice** is an *uncountable* noun.
A countable noun can be singular (**banana**) or plural (**bananas**).	An uncountable noun has only one form (**rice**).
Countable nouns are things we can count. So we can say 'one banana', 'two bananas' etc.	Uncountable nouns are things we cannot count. We cannot say 'one rice', 'two rices' etc.

Examples of nouns usually countable:	Examples of nouns usually uncountable:
● There's **a beach** near here.	● There's **sand** in my shoes.
● Ann was singing **a song**.	● Ann was listening to (some) **music**.
● Have you got **a ten-pound note**?	● Have you got any **money**?
● It wasn't your fault. It was **an accident**.	● It wasn't your fault. It was bad **luck**.
● There are no **batteries** in the radio.	● There is no **electricity** in this house.
● We haven't got enough **cups**.	● We haven't got enough **water**.

B

You can use **a/an** with singular countable nouns:	You cannot normally use **a/an** with uncountable nouns. We do not say 'a sand' or 'a music'. But you can often use **a...of**:
a beach **a student** **an umbrella**	**a bowl of** rice **a drop** of water **a piece of** music **a game** of tennis etc.
You cannot use singular countable nouns alone (without **a/the/my** etc.):	You can use uncountable nouns alone (without **the/my/some** etc.):
● I want **a banana**. (*not* 'I want banana')	● I eat **rice** every day.
● There's been **an accident**. (*not* 'There's been accident')	● There's **blood** on your shirt.
	● Can you hear **music**?
You can use *plural* countable nouns alone:	See also Unit 74.
● I like **bananas**. (= bananas in general)	
● **Accidents** can be prevented.	
See also Unit 74.	

C

You can use **some** and **any** with *plural* countable nouns:	You can use **some** and **any** with uncountable nouns:
● We sang **some songs**.	● We listened to **some music**.
● Did you buy **any apples**?	● Did you buy **any apple juice**?
We use **many** and **few** with plural countable nouns:	We use **much** and **little** with uncountable nouns:
● We didn't take **many** photographs.	● We didn't do **much shopping**.
● I have **a few** jobs to do.	● I have **a little work** to do.

EXERCISES

68.1 *Some of these sentences need **a/an**. Correct the sentences which are wrong. If the sentence is already correct, put 'RIGHT'.*

1 Jim goes everywhere by bike. He hasn't got car. ...a car...
2 Ann was listening to music when I arrived. ...RIGHT...
3 We went to very nice restaurant last weekend. ....
4 I clean my teeth with toothpaste. ....
5 I use toothbrush to clean my teeth. ....
6 Can you tell me if there's bank near here? ....
7 My brother works for insurance company in London. ....
8 I don't like violence. ....
9 Can you smell paint? ....
10 We need petrol. I hope we come to petrol station soon. ....
11 I wonder if you can help me. I have problem. ....
12 John has got interview for job tomorrow. ....
13 Liz doesn't usually wear jewellery but yesterday she was wearing necklace. ....
14 I think volleyball is very good game. ....

68.2 *Complete the sentences using one of the following words. Use **a/an** where necessary.*

~~accident~~   biscuit   blood   coat   decision   electricity   key   letter   moment
~~music~~   question   sugar

1 It wasn't your fault. It was ...an accident...
2 Listen! Can you hear ...music?...
3 I couldn't get into the house because I didn't have ....
4 It's very warm today. Why are you wearing ....?
5 Do you take .... in your coffee?
6 Are you hungry? Would you like .... with your coffee?
7 Our lives would be very difficult without ....
8 I didn't phone them. I wrote .... instead.
9 The heart pumps .... through the body.
10 Excuse me, but can I ask you ....?
11 I'm not ready yet. Can you wait ...., please?
12 We can't delay much longer. We have to make .... soon.

68.3 *Complete the sentences using one of the following words. Sometimes the word needs to be plural (-s).*

air   country   day   friend   meat   language   letter   patience   people
~~photograph~~   queue   space

1 I had my camera but I didn't take many ...photographs...
2 There are seven .... in a week.
3 A vegetarian is a person who doesn't eat ....
4 Outside the cinema there was .... of people waiting to see the film.
5 I'm not very good at writing ....
6 Last night I went out with some .... of mine.
7 There were very few .... in the shops today. They were almost empty.
8 I'm going out for a walk. I need some fresh ....
9 George always wants things quickly. He's got no ....
10 Do you speak any foreign ....?
11 Jane travels a lot. She has been to many ....
12 Our flat is very small. We haven't got much ....

Countable and uncountable nouns (2)

A   Many nouns can be used as countable or uncountable nouns, usually with a difference in meaning. Compare:

Countable	Uncountable
● Did you hear **a noise** just now? (= a particular noise)	● I can't work here. There's too much **noise**. (*not* 'too many noises')
● I bought **a paper** to read. (= a newspaper)	● I need **some paper** to write on. (= material for writing on)
● There's **a hair** in my soup! (= one single hair)	● You've got very long **hair**. (*not* 'hairs') (= all the hair on your head)
● You can stay with us. There is **a spare room**. (= a room in a house)	● You can't sit here. There isn't **room**. (= space)
● I had some interesting **experiences** while I was away. (= things that happened to me)	● They offered me the job because I had a lot of **experience**. (*not* 'experiences')
● Enjoy your holiday. Have **a good time**!	● I can't wait. I haven't got **time**.

B   **Coffee/tea/beer/juice** etc. (drinks) are normally uncountable:
- ● I don't drink **coffee** very often.

But they can be countable when you are thinking of **a cup** / **a glass** etc. So you can say:
- ● *(in a restaurant)* **Two** coffees and **an orange juice**, please.

C   There are some nouns that are usually uncountable in English but often countable in other languages. For example:

accommodation	behaviour	damage	luck	permission	traffic
advice	bread	furniture	luggage	progress	weather
baggage	chaos	information	news	scenery	work

These nouns are usually *uncountable*, so:
i) you cannot use **a/an** with them (you cannot say 'a bread', 'an advice' etc.) and
ii) they are not normally plural (we do not say 'breads', 'advices' etc.):
- ● I'm going to buy **some bread**.   *or*   ...**a loaf of bread**. (*not* 'a bread')
- ● Enjoy your holiday! I hope you have good **weather**. (*not* 'a good weather')
- ● Where are you going to put all your **furniture**? (*not* 'furnitures')

News is uncountable, not plural:
- ● The **news was** very depressing. (*not* 'the news were')

Travel *(noun)* means 'travelling in general'. You cannot say 'a travel' to mean **a journey** or **a trip**:
- ● We had **a very good journey**. (*not* 'a good travel')

Compare these countable and uncountable nouns:

Countable	Uncountable
● I'm looking for **a job**.	● I'm looking for **work**. (*not* 'a work')
● What **a beautiful view**!	● What beautiful **scenery**!
● It's **a nice day** today.	● It's nice **weather** today.
● We had a lot of **bags** and **cases**.	● We had a lot of **luggage**. (*not* 'luggages')
● **These chairs** are mine.	● **This furniture** is mine.
● It was **a good suggestion**.	● It was good **advice**.

69.1 *Which of the underlined parts of these sentences is correct?*

1 'Did you hear ~~noise~~ / a noise just now?'   'No, I didn't hear anything.' ('a noise' *is correct*)
2 a If you want to know the news, you can read paper / a paper.
  b I want to write some letters but I haven't got a paper / any paper to write on.
3 a I thought there was somebody in the house because there was light / a light on inside.
  b Light / A light comes from the sun.
4 a I was in a hurry this morning. I didn't have time / a time for breakfast.
  b 'Did you enjoy your holiday?'   'Yes, we had wonderful time / a wonderful time.'
5 Sue was very helpful. She gave us some very useful advice / advices.
6 We had very good weather / a very good weather while we were on holiday.
7 We were very unfortunate. We had bad luck / a bad luck.
8 It's very difficult to find a work / job at the moment.
9 Our travel / journey from London to Istanbul by train was very tiring.
10 When the fire alarm rang, there was total chaos / a total chaos.
11 I had to buy a / some bread because I wanted to make some sandwiches.
12 Bad news don't / doesn't make people happy.
13 Your hair is / Your hairs are too long. You should have it / them cut.
14 Nobody was hurt in the accident but the damage / the damages to the car was / were quite bad.

69.2 *Complete the sentences using these words. Sometimes you need the plural (-s).*

chair   experience   experience   furniture   hair   information
job   ~~luggage~~   permission   progress   work

1 I didn't have much ....luggage... – just two small bags.
2 They'll tell you all you want to know. They'll give you plenty of ....
3 There is room for everybody to sit down. There are plenty of ....
4 We have no .... , not even a bed or a table.
5 'What does Alan look like?'   ' He's got a long beard and very short ....'
6 Carla's English is better than it was. She's made ....
7 George is unemployed. He's looking for a ....
8 George is unemployed. He's looking for ....
9 If you want to leave work early, you have to ask for ....
10 I don't think Ann will get the job. She hasn't got enough ....
11 Rita has done many interesting things. She should write a book about her ....

69.3 *What do you say in these situations? Complete the sentences using one of the words from Section C.*

1 Your friends have just arrived at the station. You can't see any suitcases or bags.
  You ask them: Have ...you got any luggage?...
2 You go into the tourist office. You want to know about places to see in the town. You say:
  I'd like ....
3 You are a student at school. You want your teacher to advise you about which examinations to take. You say: Can you give me ....?
4 You want to watch the news on TV but you don't know what time it is on. You ask your friend: What time ....?
5 You are standing at the top of a mountain. You can see a very long way. It's lovely. You say:
  It ...., isn't it?
6 You look out of the window. The weather is horrible: cold, wet and windy. You say to your friend: What ....!

Countable nouns with **a/an** and **some**

A Countable nouns can be *singular* or *plural*:

a **dog**   a **child**   the **evening**   this **party**   an **umbrella**
dogs   some **children**   the **evenings**   these **parties**   two **umbrellas**

B Before singular countable nouns you can use **a/an**:

- Goodbye! Have **a** nice **evening**.
- Do you need **an** umbrella?

You cannot use singular countable nouns alone (without **a/the/my** etc.):

- She never wears **a** hat. (*not* 'She never wears hat')
- Be careful of **the** dog. (*not* 'Be careful of dog')
- What **a** beautiful day!
- I've got **a** headache.

C We use **a/an…** to say what kind of thing or person something/somebody is:

- A dog is **an animal**.
- I'm **an optimist**.
- Tim's father is **a doctor**.
- Are you **a good driver**?
- Jill is **a really nice person**.
- What **a lovely dress**!

We say that somebody has **a** long **nose** / **a** nice **face** / **a** strong **heart** etc.:

- Jack has got **a** long **nose**. (*not* 'the long nose')

In sentences like these, we use plural nouns alone (*not* with 'some'):

- Dogs are **animals**.
- Most of my friends are **students**.
- Jill's parents are **really nice people**.
- What **awful shoes**!
- Jack has got **blue eyes**. (*not* 'the blue eyes')

Remember to use **a/an** when you say what somebody's job is:

- Sandra is **a nurse**. (*not* 'Sandra is nurse')
- Would you like to be **an English teacher**?

D You can use **some** with plural countable nouns. We use **some** in two ways:

i) **Some** = a number of / a few of / a pair of:

- I've seen **some** good **films** recently. (*not* 'I've seen good films')
- **Some friends** of mine are coming to stay at the weekend.
- I need **some** new **sunglasses**. (= a new pair of sunglasses)

Do *not* use **some** when you are talking about things in general (see also Unit 74):

- I love **bananas**. (*not* 'some bananas')
- My aunt is a writer. She writes **books**. (*not* 'some books')

Sometimes you can make sentences with or without **some** (with no difference in meaning):

- There are (**some**) eggs in the fridge if you're hungry.

ii) **Some** = some *but not all*

- **Some children** learn very quickly. (but not all children)
- **Some police officers** in Britain carry guns, but most of them don't.

EXERCISES

70.1 *What are these things? Try and find out if you don't know.*

  1 an ant? ...**It's an insect.**...

  2 ants? bees? ...**They're insects.**...

  3 a cauliflower? ....

  4 chess? ....

  5 a violin? a trumpet? a flute?

    ....

  6 a skyscraper? ....

  7 Earth? Mars? Venus? Jupiter?

    ....

  8 a tulip? ....

  9 the Rhine? the Nile? the Mississippi?

    ....

10 a pigeon? an eagle? a crow?

    ....

Who were these people?

11 Beethoven? ...**He was a composer.**...

12 Shakespeare? ....

13 Albert Einstein? ....

14 Washington? Lincoln? John Kennedy?

    ....

15 Marilyn Monroe? ....

16 Elvis Presley? John Lennon? ....

17 Van Gogh? Renoir? Gauguin? ....

70.2 *Read about what these people do and say what their jobs are. Choose one of these jobs:*

driving instructor   **interpreter**   **journalist**   ~~**nurse**~~   **pilot**   **plumber**
travel agent   **waiter**

1 Stella looks after patients in hospital. ...**She's a nurse.**...

2 George works in a restaurant. He brings the food to the tables. He ....

3 Mary arranges people's holidays for them. She ....

4 Ron works for an airline. He flies aeroplanes. ....

5 Linda teaches people how to drive. ....

6 Dave fits and repairs water pipes. ....

7 Jenny writes articles for a newspaper. ....

8 John translates what people are saying from one language into another, so that they can understand each other. ....

70.3 *Put in* **a/an** *or* **some** *where necessary. If no word is necessary, leave the space empty (–).*

  1 I've seen ...**some**... good films recently.

  2 What's wrong with you? Have you got ...**a**... headache?

  3 I know a lot of people. Most of them are ...**–**... students.

  4 When I was .... child, I used to be very shy.

  5 Would you like to be .... actor?

  6 Do you collect .... stamps?

  7 What .... beautiful garden!

  8 .... birds, for example the penguin, cannot fly.

  9 I've been walking for three hours. I've got .... sore feet.

10 I don't feel very well this morning. I've got .... sore throat.

11 It's a pity we haven't got .... camera. I'd like to take .... photograph of that house.

12 Those are .... nice shoes. Where did you get them?

13 I'm going shopping. I want to buy .... new shoes.

14 You need .... visa to visit .... countries, but not all of them.

15 Jane is .... teacher. Her parents were .... teachers too.

16 Do you enjoy going to .... concerts?

17 When we got to the city centre, ... shops were still open but most of them were closed.

18 I don't believe him. He's .... liar. He's always telling .... lies.

A/an and **the**

A Study this example:

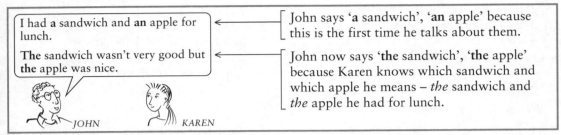

I had **a** sandwich and **an** apple for lunch. ← John says '**a** sandwich', '**an** apple' because this is the first time he talks about them.

The sandwich wasn't very good but **the** apple was nice. ← John now says '**the** sandwich', '**the** apple' because Karen knows which sandwich and which apple he means – *the* sandwich and *the* apple he had for lunch.

JOHN   KAREN

Compare **a** and **the** in these examples:
- **A** man and **a** woman were sitting opposite me. **The** man was American but I think **the** woman was British.
- When we were on holiday, we stayed at **a** hotel. Sometimes we had our evening meal at **the** hotel and sometimes we went to **a** restaurant.

B We use **the** when we are thinking of one particular thing. Compare **a/an** and **the**:
- Tom sat down on a chair. (perhaps one of many chairs in the room)

but   Tom sat down on **the** chair **nearest the door**. (a particular chair)
- Ann is looking for **a** job. (not a particular job)

but   Did Ann get **the** job **she applied for**? (a particular job)
- Have you got **a** car? (not a particular car)

but   I cleaned **the** car yesterday. (= my car)

For **a** see also Units 70 and 72A.

C We use **the** when it is clear in the situation which thing or person we mean. For example, in a room we talk about '**the** light / **the** floor / **the** ceiling / **the** door / **the** carpet' etc.:
- Can you turn off **the** light, please? (= the light in this room)
- I took a taxi to **the** station. (= the station in that town)
- I'd like to speak to **the** manager, please. (= the manager of this shop etc.)

In the same way, we say (go to) **the bank, the post office**:
- I must go to **the bank** to get some money and then I'm going to **the post office** to get some stamps. (The speaker is usually thinking of a particular bank or post office.)

Also: **the doctor, the dentist**:
- Carol isn't very well. She's gone to **the doctor**. (= her usual doctor)
- I hate going to **the dentist**.

Compare **a**:
- Is there **a bank** near here?
- My sister is **a dentist**.

Don't forget **the**:
- Susan works in **the** city centre. (*not* 'in city centre')
- My brother is in **the** army. (*not* 'in army')

D We say 'once **a** week / three times **a** day / £1.20 **a** kilo' etc.:
- 'How often do you go to the cinema?'   'About once **a** month.'
- 'How much are those potatoes?'   '£1.20 **a** kilo.'
- She works eight hours **a** day, six days **a** week.

EXERCISES

71.1 *Put in* **a/an** *or* **the**.

1 This morning I bought ...**a**... newspaper and .... magazine. .... newspaper is in my bag but I don't know where I put .... magazine.
2 I saw .... accident this morning. .... car crashed into .... tree. .... driver of .... car wasn't hurt but .... car was badly damaged.
3 There are two cars parked outside: .... blue one and .... grey one. .... blue one belongs to my neighbours; I don't know who .... owner of .... grey one is.
4 My friends live in .... old house in .... small village. There is .... beautiful garden behind .... house. I would like to have .... garden like that.

71.2 *Put in* **a/an** *or* **the**.

1 a This house is very nice. Has it got .... garden?
   b It's a beautiful day. Let's sit in .... garden.
   c I like living in this house but it's a pity that .... garden is so small.
2 a Can you recommend .... good restaurant?
   b We had dinner in .... very nice restaurant.
   c We had dinner in .... most expensive restaurant in town.
3 a She has .... French name but in fact she's English, not French.
   b What's .... name of that man we met yesterday?
   c We stayed at a very nice hotel – I can't remember .... name now.
4 a There isn't .... airport near where I live. .... nearest airport is 70 miles away.
   b Our plane was delayed. We had to wait at .... airport for three hours.
   c Excuse me, please. Can you tell me how to get to .... airport?
5 a 'Are you going away next week?' 'No, ... week after next.'
   b I'm going away for .... week in September.
   c George has a part-time job. He works three mornings .... week.

71.3 *Put in* **a/an** *or* **the** *in these sentences where necessary.*

1 Would you like apple? ...**an apple**...
2 How often do you go to dentist? ....
3 Could you close door, please? ....
4 I'm sorry. I didn't mean to do that. It was mistake. ....
5 Excuse me, where is bus station, please? ....
6 I've got problem. Can you help me? ....
7 I'm just going to post office. I won't be long. ....
8 There were no chairs, so we had to sit on floor. ....
9 Have you finished with book I lent you? ....
10 My sister has just got job in bank in Manchester. ....
11 We live in small flat near city centre. ....
12 There's small supermarket at end of street I live in. ....

71.4 *Answer these questions about yourself. Where possible, use the structure in Section D* (**once a week / three times a day** *etc.*).

1 How often do you go to the cinema? ..**Three or four times a year.**..
2 How much does it cost to hire a car in your country? ..**About £30 a day.**..
3 How often do you go away on holiday? ....
4 What's the speed limit in towns in your country? ....
5 How much sleep do you need? ....
6 How often do you go out in the evening? ....
7 How much television do you watch (on average)? ....

The (1)

A We use **the...** when there is only one of something:
- What is **the** longest river in **the** world? (there is only one longest river)
- **The** earth goes round **the** sun and **the** moon goes round **the** earth.
- I'm going away at **the** end of this month.

Don't forget **the**:
- Paris is **the** capital of France. (*not* 'Paris is capital of...')

But we use **a/an** to say what kind of thing something is (see Unit 70C). Compare **the** and **a**:
- **The** sun is **a** star. (= one of many stars)
- **The** hotel we stayed at was **a** very nice hotel.

B We say: **the sky the sea the ground the country the environment:**
- We looked up at all the stars in **the sky**. (*not* 'in sky')
- Would you rather live in a town or in **the country**?
- We must do more to protect **the environment**. (= the natural world around us)

Note that we say **space** (without 'the') when we mean 'space in the universe':
- There are millions of stars **in space**. (*not* 'in the space')

but • I tried to park my car but **the space** was too small.

C We use **the** before **same** (**the same**):
- Your pullover is **the same** colour as mine. (*not* 'is same colour')
- These two photographs are **the same**. (*not* 'are same')

D We say: (go to) **the cinema, the theatre:**
- I often go to **the cinema** but I haven't been to **the theatre** for ages.

When we say **the cinema / the theatre**, we do not necessarily mean one particular cinema or theatre.

We usually say **the radio**, but **television** (without 'the'):
- I often listen to **the radio**.
- I often watch **television**.
- We heard the news on **the radio**.
- We watched the news on **television**.

but • Can you turn off **the television**, please? (= the television set)

Compare **a**:
- There isn't **a theatre** in this town.
- I'm going to buy **a** new **radio / television** (set).

E Breakfast lunch dinner

We do *not* normally use **the** with the names of meals (**breakfast, lunch** etc.):
- What did you have for **breakfast**?
- We had **lunch** in a very nice restaurant.
- What time is **dinner**?

But we use **a** if there is an adjective before **breakfast, lunch** etc.:
- We had **a** very **nice lunch**. (*not* 'we had very nice lunch')

F Platform 5 Room 126 etc.

We do *not* use 'the' before *noun + number*. For example, we say:
- Our train leaves from **Platform 5**. (*not* 'the Platform 5')
- (*in a shop*) Have you got these shoes in **size 43**? (*not* 'the size 43')

In the same way, we say: **Room 126** (in a hotel) **page 29** (of a book) **Section A** etc.

A and the → UNIT 71   **The** (2), (3) and (4) → UNITS 73–75   **The** with names → UNITS 76–77

EXERCISES

72.1 *Put in* **the** *or* **a/an** *where necessary. If no word is necessary, leave the space empty (–).*

1 A: Where did you have ...—... lunch?   B: We went to ...a... restaurant.
2 A: Did you have .... nice holiday?   B: Yes, it was .... best holiday I've ever had.
3 A: Where's .... nearest shop?   B: There's one at .... end of this street.
4 A: Do you often listen to .... radio?   B: No. In fact I haven't got .... radio.
5 A: Would you like to travel in .... space?   B: Yes, I'd love to go to .... moon.
6 A: Do you go to .... cinema very often?
   B: No, not very often. But I watch a lot of films on .... television.
7 A: It was .... nice day yesterday, wasn't it?
   B: Yes, it was beautiful. We went for a walk by .... sea.
8 A: What did you have for .... breakfast this morning?
   B: Nothing. I never eat .... breakfast.
9 A: Can you tell me where .... Room 25 is, please?
   B: It's on .... second floor.
10 A: We spent all our money because we stayed at .... most expensive hotel in town.
   B: Why didn't you stay at .... cheaper hotel?

72.2 *Put in* **the** *where necessary. If you don't need* **the**, *leave the space empty (–).*

1 I haven't been to ...the... cinema for ages.
2 I lay down on .... ground and looked up at .... sky.
3 Sheila spends most of her free time watching .... television.
4 .... television was on but nobody was watching it.
5 Have you had .... dinner yet?
6 Mary and I arrived at .... same time.
7 You'll find .... information you need at .... top of .... page 15.
8 Peru is .... country in South America. .... capital is Lima.

72.3 *Put in* **the** *or* **a/an** *where necessary. If the sentence is already correct, put* 'RIGHT'. *(If necessary, see Unit 71 for* **a/an** *and* **the**.)

1 Sun is star. ...The sun is a star...
2 Tim lives in small village in country. ....
3 Moon goes round earth every 27 days. ....
4 What is highest mountain in world? ....
5 I'm fed up with doing same thing every day. ....
6 It was very hot day. It was hottest day of year. ....
7 I don't usually have lunch but I always eat good breakfast. ....
8 If you live in foreign country, you should try and learn language. ....
9 We missed our train because we were waiting on wrong platform. We were on Platform 3 instead of Platform 8. ....

72.4 *Complete the sentences using one of the following. Use* **the** *if necessary.*

~~breakfast~~   cinema   dinner   gate   Gate 21   Question 8   sea

1 I didn't have time for ...breakfast... this morning because I was in a hurry.
2 'I'm going to .... this evening.'   'Are you? What film are you going to see?'
3 There was no wind, so .... was very calm.
4 'Are you going out this evening?'   'Yes, after ....'
5 The examination paper wasn't too difficult but I couldn't answer ....
6 Oh, ... is open. I must have forgotten to shut it.
7 *(airport announcement)* 'Flight BA123 to Vienna is now boarding at ....'

145

The (2) (School / the school)

A   Compare **school** and **the school**:

ALISON

Alison is ten years old. Every day she goes to **school**. She's at **school** now. **School** begins at 9 and finishes at 3.

We say a child goes to **school** or is at **school** (as a pupil). We are not necessarily thinking of a particular school. We are thinking of **school** as a general idea.

Today Alison's mother wants to speak to her daughter's teacher. So she has gone to **the school** to see her. She's at **the school** now.

Alison's mother is not a pupil. She is not 'at school', she doesn't 'go to school'. But if she wants to see Alison's teacher, she goes to **the school** (= Alison's school, a particular school).

B   We use **prison**, **hospital**, **university**, and **church** in a similar way. We do *not* use **the** when we are thinking of the general idea of these places and what they are used for. Compare:

- Ken's brother is in **prison** for robbery. (He is a prisoner. We are not thinking of a particular prison.)
- Jack had an accident last week. He was taken to **hospital**. He's still in **hospital** now. (as a patient)
- When I leave **school**, I want to go to **university**.
- Mrs Kelly goes to **church** every Sunday. (to a religious service)

- Ken went to **the prison** to visit his brother. (He went as a visitor, not as a prisoner.)
- Jill has gone to **the hospital** to visit Jack. She's at **the hospital** now. (as a visitor)
- Excuse me, where is **the university**, please? (= the university buildings)
- The workmen went to **the church** to repair the roof. (not for a religious service)

With most other places, you need **the**. For example, **the cinema**, **the bank**, **the station**. See Units 71C and 72D.

C   Bed   work   home
We say: 'go to **bed** / be in **bed**' etc. (*not* 'the bed'):
- It's time to go to **bed** now.
- This morning I had breakfast **in bed**.

but ● I sat down on **the bed**. (a particular piece of furniture)

'go to **work** / be at **work** / start **work** / finish **work**' etc. (*not* 'the work'):
- Ann didn't go to **work** yesterday.
- What time do you usually finish **work**?

'go **home** / come **home** / arrive **home** / be at **home**' etc.:
- It's late. Let's go **home**.
- Will you be at **home** tomorrow afternoon?

D   We say 'go to **sea** / be at **sea**' (without 'the') when the meaning is 'go/be on a voyage':
- Keith is a seaman. He spends most of his life at **sea**.

but ● I'd like to live near **the sea**.
- It can be dangerous to swim in **the sea**.

EXERCISES

73.1 *Complete the sentences using a preposition (**to/at/in** etc.) + one of the following words:*
bed   home   hospital   prison   school   university   work
You can use the words more than once.

1 Two people were injured in the accident and were taken ...**to hospital.**...
2 In Britain, children from the age of five have to go ....
3 Mark didn't go out last night. He stayed ....
4 I'll have to hurry. I don't want to be late ....
5 There is a lot of traffic in the morning when everybody is going ....
6 Cathy's mother has just had an operation. She is still ....
7 When Julia leaves school, she wants to study economics ....
8 Bill never gets up before 9 o'clock. It's 8.30 now, so he is still ....
9 If you commit a serious crime, you could be sent ....

73.2 *Complete the sentences with the word given (**school** etc.). Use **the** where necessary.*

1 (**school**)
   a Every term parents are invited to ...**the school**... to meet the teachers.
   b Why aren't your children at ...**school**... today? Are they ill?
   c When he was younger, Ted hated ....
   d What time does .... start in the mornings in your country?
   e A: How do your children get home from ....? By bus?
      B: No, they walk. .... isn't very far.
   f What sort of job does Jenny want to do when she leaves ....?
   g There were some people waiting outside .... to meet their children.
2 (**university**)
   a In your country, do many people go to ....?
   b If you want to get a degree, you normally have to study at ....
   c This is only a small town but .... is the biggest in the country.
3 (**hospital**)
   a Nora works as a cleaner at ....
   b When Ann was ill, we all went to .... to visit her.
   c My brother has always been very healthy. He's never been in ....
   d Peter was injured in an accident and was kept in .... for a few days.
4 (**church**)
   a John's mother is a regular churchgoer. She goes to .... every Sunday.
   b John himself doesn't go to ....
   c John went to .... to take some photographs of the building.
5 (**prison**)
   a In many places people are in .... because of their political opinions.
   b The other day the fire brigade were called to .... to put out a fire.
   c The judge decided to fine the man £500 instead of sending him to ....
6 (**home/work/bed**)
   a I like to read in .... before I go to sleep.
   b It's nice to travel around but there's no place like ....!
   c Shall we meet after .... tomorrow evening?
   d If I'm feeling tired, I go to .... early.
   e What time do you usually start .... in the morning?
   f The economic situation is very bad. Many people are out of ....
7 (**sea**)
   a There's a nice view from the window. You can see ....
   b It was a long voyage. We were at .... for four weeks.
   c I love swimming in ....

The (3) (Children / the children)

A When we are talking about things or people in general, we do *not* use 'the':
- I'm afraid of **dogs.** (*not* 'the dogs')
  (**dogs** = dogs in general, not a particular group of dogs)
- **Doctors** are paid more than **teachers.**
- Do you collect **stamps?**
- **Crime** is a problem in most big cities. (*not* 'the crime')
- **Life** has changed a lot in the last 30 years. (*not* 'the life')
- Do you often listen to **classical music?** (*not* 'the classical music')
- Do you like **Chinese food / French cheese / Swiss chocolate?**
- My favourite sport is **football/skiing/athletics.** (*not* 'the football / the skiing' etc.)
- My favourite subject at school was **history/physics/English.**

We say '**most** people / **most** books / **most** cars' etc. (*not* 'the most...' – see also Unit 87A).
- **Most people** like George. (*not* 'the most people')

B We use **the** when we mean particular things or people. Compare:

In general (without 'the')		Particular people or things (with **the**)
• **Children** learn a lot from playing. (= children in general)	*but*	• We took **the children** to the zoo. (= a particular group, perhaps the speaker's own children)
• I often listen to **music.**	*but*	• The film wasn't very good but I liked **the music.** (= the music in the film)
• All **cars** have wheels.	*but*	• All **the cars** in this car park belong to people who work here.
• **Sugar** isn't very good for you.	*but*	• Can you pass **the sugar**, please? (= the sugar on the table)
• Do **English people** work hard? (= English people in general)	*but*	• Do **the English people** you know work hard? (= only the English people you know, not English people in general)

C The difference between 'something in general' and 'something in particular' is not always very clear. Compare these sentences:

In general (without 'the')	Particular people or things (with **the**)
• I like working with **people.** (= people in general)	
• I like working with **people who are lively.** (not all people, but 'people who are lively' is still a general idea)	• I like **the people I work with.** (= a particular group of people)
• Do you like **coffee?** (= coffee in general)	
• Do you like **strong black coffee?** (not all coffee, but 'strong black coffee' is still a general idea)	• Did you like **the coffee we had after our meal last night?** (= particular coffee)

The (1) and (2) → **UNITS 72–73**   The + adjective (**the young / the English** etc.) → **UNIT 75**

74.1 *In this exercise you have to write whether you like or dislike these things:*

| boxing | cats | fast food restaurants | football | hot weather |
| mathematics | opera | small children | rock music | zoos |

Choose FOUR of these things and begin your sentences with one of these:

I like… / I don't like…   I don't mind…
I love… / I hate…   I'm interested in… / I'm not interested in…

1 I don't like hot weather very much.
2 ....
3 ....
4 ....
5 ....

74.2 *Complete the sentences using one of the following. Use* **the** *where necessary.*

(the) basketball   (the) **questions**   (the) **history**   (the) **hotels**   (the) **meat**   (the) **lies**
(the) information   (the) **patience**   (the) **people**   (the) **water**   (the) **grass**   (the) **spiders**

1 My favourite sport is ...basketball..
2 ...The information... we were given wasn't correct.
3 Many people are afraid of ....
4 A vegetarian is somebody who doesn't eat ....
5 The test wasn't very difficult. I answered all .... without difficulty.
6 Do you know .... who live next door?
7 .... is the study of the past.
8 George always tells the truth. He never tells ....
9 We couldn't find anywhere to stay in the town. All .... were full.
10 .... in the pool didn't look very clean, so we didn't go for a swim.
11 Don't sit on .... It's wet after the rain.
12 You need .... to teach young children.

74.3 *Choose the correct form, with or without* **the.**

1 I'm afraid of dogs / the dogs. ('dogs' *is correct*)
2 Can you pass salt / the salt, please? ('the salt' *is correct*)
3 Apples / The apples are good for you.
4 Look at apples / the apples on that tree! They're very big.
5 Women / The women live longer than men / the men.
6 I don't drink tea / the tea. I don't like it.
7 We had a very nice meal. Vegetables / The vegetables were especially good.
8 Life / The life is strange sometimes. Some very strange things happen.
9 I like skiing / the skiing but I'm not very good at it.
10 Who are people / the people in this photograph?
11 What makes people / the people violent? What causes aggression / the aggression?
12 All books / All the books on the top shelf belong to me.
13 Don't stay in that hotel. It's very noisy and beds / the beds are very uncomfortable.
14 A pacifist is somebody who is against war / the war.
15 First World War / The First World War lasted from 1914 until 1918.
16 One of our biggest social problems is unemployment / the unemployment.
17 Ron and Brenda got married but marriage / the marriage didn't last very long.
18 Most people / The most people believe that marriage / the marriage and family life / the family life are the basis of society / the society.

The (4) (The giraffe / the telephone / the piano etc.; the + adjective)

A Study these sentences:
- **The giraffe** is the tallest of all animals.
- **The bicycle** is an excellent means of transport.
- When was **the telephone** invented?
- **The dollar** is the currency (= money) of the United States.

In these examples, **the...** does not mean one particular thing. **The giraffe** = one particular type of animal, *not* one particular giraffe. We use **the** (+ a singular countable noun) in this way to talk about a type of animal, machine etc.

In the same way we use **the** for musical instruments:
- Can you play **the** guitar?
- **The piano** is my favourite instrument.

Compare **a**:
- I'd like to have **a guitar**.
- We saw **a giraffe** at the zoo.

Note that we use **man** (= human beings in general / the human race) without 'the':
- What do you know about the origins of **man**? (*not* 'the man')

B The + *adjective*

We use **the** + adjective (without a noun) to talk about groups of people, especially:

the young	the old	the elderly	
the rich	the poor	the unemployed	the homeless
the sick	the disabled	the injured	the dead

The young = young people, **the rich** = rich people etc.:
- Do you think **the rich** should pay more taxes to help **the poor**?
- **The homeless** need more help from the government.

These expressions are always *plural* in meaning. You cannot say 'a young' or 'an unemployed'. You must say '**a young man**', '**an unemployed woman**' etc.
Note also that we say 'the **poor**' (*not* 'the poors'), 'the **young**' (*not* 'the youngs') etc.

C The + *nationality*

You can use **the** with some nationality adjectives to mean 'the people of that country'. For example:
- **The French** are famous for their food. (= the people of France)
- Why do **the English** think they are so wonderful? (= the people of England)

In the same way you can say:

the Spanish	the Dutch	the British	the Irish	the Welsh

Note that **the French / the English** etc. are plural in meaning. You can*not* say 'a French / an English'. You have to say '**a Frenchman / an Englishwoman**' etc.

You can also use **the** + nationality words ending in -ese (**the Chinese / the Sudanese** etc.):
- **The Chinese** invented printing.

These words can also be singular (**a Japanese, a Sudanese**).
Also: **the Swiss / a Swiss** (plural or singular)

With other nationalities, the plural noun ends in -s. For example:

an Italian	**a** Mexican	**a** Scot	**a** Turk
(the) Italians	(the) Mexicans	(the) Scots	(the) Turks

EXERCISES

75.1 *Answer the questions. Choose the right answer from the box. Don't forget* **the.** *Use a dictionary if necessary.*

1	*animals*		2	*birds*		3	*inventions*		4	*currencies*	
	tiger	elephant		eagle	penguin		telephone	wheel		dollar	lira
	rabbit	cheetah		swan	owl		telescope	laser		escudo	rupee
	giraffe	kangaroo		parrot	robin		helicopter	typewriter		peseta	yen

1 a Which of the animals is tallest? ...the giraffe...
 b Which animal can run fastest? ....
 c Which of these animals is found in Australia? ....
2 a Which of these birds has a long neck? ....
 b Which of these birds cannot fly? ....
 c Which bird flies at night? ....
3 a Which of these inventions is oldest? ....
 b Which one is most recent? ....
 c Which one is especially important for astronomy? ....
4 a What is the currency of India? ....
 b What is the currency of Portugal? ....
 c What is the currency of your country? ....

75.2 *Put in* **the** *or* **a** *where necessary. If the sentence is already complete leave an empty space (–).*

1 When was ...the... telephone invented?
2 Can you play .... musical instrument?
3 Jill plays .... violin in an orchestra.
4 There was .... piano in the corner of the room.
5 Can you play .... piano?
6 Our society is based on .... family.
7 Martin comes from .... large family.
8 When was .... paper first made?
9 .... computer has changed the way we live.

75.3 *Complete these sentences using* **the** *+ one of these adjectives:*
injured   poor   rich   sick   unemployed   ~~young~~

1 ...The young... have the future in their hands.
2 Ambulances arrived at the scene of the accident and took .... to hospital.
3 Life is all right if you have a job, but things are not so easy for ....
4 Julia has been a nurse all her life. She has spent her life caring for ....
5 In England there is an old story about a man called Robin Hood. It is said that he robbed
.... and gave the money to ....

75.4 *What do you call the people of these countries?*

		one person (a/an...)	*the people in general*
1	Canada?	...a Canadian...	...the Canadians...
2	Germany?	....	....
3	France?	....	....
4	Russia?	....	....
5	China?	....	....
6	Brazil?	....	....
7	England?	....	....
8	*and your country?*	....	....

Names with and without **the** (1)

A We do not use 'the' with names of people ('Ann', 'Ann Taylor' etc.). In the same way, we do not normally use 'the' with names of places. For example:

continents	Africa (*not* 'the Africa'), Europe, South America
countries	France (*not* 'the France'), Japan, Switzerland
states, regions etc.	Texas, Cornwall, Tuscany, Central Europe
islands	Corsica, Sicily, Bermuda
cities, towns etc.	Cairo, New York, Madrid
mountains	Everest, Etna, Kilimanjaro

But we use **the** in names with 'Republic', 'Kingdom', 'States' etc.:
    the United **States** of America (**the** USA)   **the** United **Kingdom** (**the** UK)
    the Dominican **Republic**
Compare:
    ● We visited **Canada** and **the United States**.

B When we use **Mr/Mrs/Captain/Doctor** etc. + *a name*, we do *not* use 'the'. So we say:
    Mr Johnson / **Doctor** Johnson / **Captain** Johnson / **President** Johnson etc. (*not* 'the…')
    Uncle Robert / **Aunt** Jane / **Saint** Catherine / **Princess** Anne etc. (*not* 'the…')
Compare:
    ● We called **the doctor**. *but* We called **Doctor** Johnson. (*not* 'the Doctor Johnson')

We use **mount** (= mountain) and **lake** in the same way (without 'the'):
    Mount Everest (*not* 'the…')   **Mount** Etna   **Lake** Superior   **Lake** Constance
    ● They live near **the lake**. *but* They live near **Lake** Constance. (*without* 'the')

C We use **the** with the names of oceans, seas, rivers and canals (see also Unit 77B):

the Atlantic (Ocean)	**the** Mediterranean (Sea)	**the** Red Sea
the Indian Ocean	**the** Channel (between France and Britain)	**the** Suez Canal
the (River) Amazon	**the** (River) Thames **the** Nile	**the** Rhine

D We use **the** with *plural* names of people and places:

people	**the** Taylors (= the Taylor family), **the** Johnsons
countries	**the** Netherlands, **the** Philippines, **the** United States
groups of islands	**the** Canaries / **the** Canary Islands, **the** Bahamas, **the** British Isles
mountain ranges	**the** Rocky Mountains / **the** Rockies, **the** Andes, **the** Alps

    ● The highest mountain in **the Alps** is **Mont Blanc**. (*not* 'the Mont Blanc')

E North/northern etc.
We say: **the north** (of France)   *but*   **northern** France (*without* 'the')
            the south-east (of Spain) *but*   **south-eastern** Spain
Compare:
    ● Sweden is in **northern** Europe; Spain is in **the south**.
Also: **the** Middle East   **the** Far East
You can also use **north/south** etc. + a place name (without 'the'):
    North America   **West Africa**   **South-East Spain**

Note that on maps, **the** is not usually included in the name.

EXERCISES

76.1 *Put in* **the** *where necessary. Leave a space (–) if the sentence is already complete.*

1 Who is ...—... Doctor Johnson? (*The sentence is complete without* **the**.)
2 I was ill, so I went to see .... doctor.
3 .... President is the most powerful person in .... United States.
4 .... President Kennedy was assassinated in 1963.
5 Do you know .... Wilsons? They're a very nice couple.
6 Do you know .... Professor Brown's phone number?

76.2 *Some of these sentences are correct, but some need* **the** *(perhaps more than once). Correct the sentences where necessary. Put* '*RIGHT*' *if the sentence is already correct.*

1 Everest was first climbed in 1953. ...RIGHT...
2 Milan is in north of Italy. ...the north of Italy...
3 Africa is much larger than Europe. ....
4 Last year I visited Mexico and United States. ....
5 South of England is warmer than north. ....
6 Portugal is in western Europe. ....
7 France and Britain are separated by Channel. ....
8 Jim has travelled a lot in Middle East. ....
9 Chicago is on Lake Michigan. ....
10 The highest mountain in Africa is Kilimanjaro (5,895 metres). ....
11 Next year we are going skiing in Swiss Alps. ....
12 United Kingdom consists of Great Britain and Northern Ireland. ....
13 Seychelles are a group of islands in Indian Ocean. ....
14 River Volga flows into Caspian Sea. ....

76.3 *Here are some geography questions. Choose the right answer from one of the boxes and write* **the** *if necessary. You do not need all the names in the boxes. Use an atlas if necessary.*

continents	countries	oceans and seas	mountains	rivers and canals	
Africa	Canada	Atlantic	Alps	Amazon	Rhine
Asia	Denmark	Indian Ocean	Andes	Danube	Thames
Australia	Indonesia	Pacific	Himalayas	Nile	Volga
Europe	Sweden	Black Sea	Rockies	Suez Canal	
North America	Thailand	Mediterranean	Urals	Panama Canal	
South America	United States	Red Sea			

1 What do you have to cross to travel from Europe to America? ...The Atlantic...
2 Where is Argentina? ....
3 Which is the longest river in Africa? ....
4 Of which country is Stockholm the capital? ....
5 Of which country is Washington the capital? ....
6 What is the name of the mountain range in the west of North America? ....
7 What is the name of the sea between Africa and Europe? ....
8 Which is the smallest continent in the world? ....
9 What is the name of the ocean between America and Asia? ....
10 What is the name of the ocean between Africa and Australia? ....
11 Which river flows through London? ....
12 Which river flows through Vienna, Budapest and Belgrade? ....
13 Of which country is Bangkok the capital? ....
14 What joins the Atlantic and Pacific Oceans? ....
15 Which is the longest river in South America? ....

Names with and without **the** (2)

A *Names without 'the'*

We do not use 'the' with names of most streets/roads/squares/parks etc.:

    Union **Street** (*not* 'the...')   Fifth **Avenue**   Piccadilly **Circus**   Hyde **Park**

    Blackrock **Road**   **Broadway**   Times **Square**   Waterloo **Bridge**

Many names (especially names of important buildings and institutions) are two words:

    Kennedy Airport   **Cambridge University**

The first word is usually the name of a person ('Kennedy') or a place ('Cambridge'). We do not usually use 'the' with names like these. Some more examples:

    Victoria Station (*not* 'the...')   **Edinburgh Castle**   **London Zoo**

    Westminster Abbey   **Buckingham Palace**   **Canterbury Cathedral**

But we say '**the** White House', '**the** Royal Palace', because 'white' and 'royal' are not names like 'Kennedy' and 'Cambridge'. This is only a general rule and there are exceptions.

B Most other names (of places, buildings etc.) have names with **the**:

            adjective or
the + *name etc.* + *noun*

the	Hilton	**Hotel**
	National	**Theatre**
	Sahara	**Desert**
	Atlantic	**Ocean**

These places usually have names with **the**:

hotels/restaurants/pubs	**the** Station **Hotel, the** Bombay **Restaurant, the** Red Lion (pub)
theatres/cinemas	**the** Palace **Theatre, the** Odeon **Cinema**
museums/galleries	**the** British **Museum, the** Tate **Gallery**
other buildings	**the** Empire State **Building, the** Festival **Hall, the** White **House**
oceans/seas/canals	**the** Indian **Ocean, the** Mediterranean **Sea, the** Suez **Canal**

also:

newspapers	**the** Washington **Post, the** Financial **Times**
organisations (but see also Section D)	**the** European **Community, the** BBC (= the British Broadcasting **Corporation**)

Sometimes we leave out the noun: **the Hilton** (Hotel), **the Sahara** (Desert)

Sometimes the name is only **the** + *noun*: **the Vatican** *(in Rome),* **the Sun** *(British newspaper)*

Names with **...of...** usually have **the**. For example:

    the Bank **of** England   **the** Tower **of** London   **the** Museum **of** Modern Art

    the Houses **of** Parliament **the** Great Wall **of** China   **the** Tropic **of** Capricorn

    the Gulf **of** Mexico   **the** University **of** London *(but* ~~the~~ London University)

C Many shops, restaurants, hotels, banks etc. are named after the people who started them. These names end in -'s or -s. We do *not* use 'the' with these names:

    Lloyds Bank (*not* the Lloyds Bank)   McDonalds   Jack's Guest House   Harrods (shop)

Churches are often named after saints:

    St John's Church (*not* the St John's Church)   St Paul's Cathedral

D Names of companies, airlines etc. are usually without 'the':

    Fiat (*not* the Fiat)   **Sony**   **Kodak**   **British Airways**   **IBM**

EXERCISES

77.1 Use the map to answer the questions in the way shown. Write the name of the place and the street it is in. On maps we do not normally use **the**. In your sentences, use **the** if necessary.

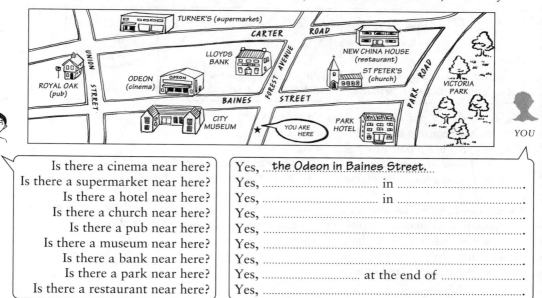

1	Is there a cinema near here?	Yes, __the Odeon in Baines Street.__
2	Is there a supermarket near here?	Yes, ... in ....
3	Is there a hotel near here?	Yes, ... in ....
4	Is there a church near here?	Yes, ...
5	Is there a pub near here?	Yes, ...
6	Is there a museum near here?	Yes, ...
7	Is there a bank near here?	Yes, ...
8	Is there a park near here?	Yes, ... at the end of ....
9	Is there a restaurant near here?	Yes, ...

77.2 Where are these streets and buildings? Choose from the box to complete the sentences. Use **the** where necessary.

Acropolis	Broadway	Buckingham Palace	Eiffel Tower
Vatican	White House	St Mark's Cathedral	~~Trafalgar Square~~

1 ...Trafalgar Square... is in London.
2 .... is in Paris.
3 .... is in Rome.
4 .... is in London.
5 .... is in New York.
6 .... is in Washington.
7 .... is in Athens.
8 .... is in Venice.

77.3 Choose the correct form, with or without **the**.

1 Have you ever been to ~~British Museum~~ / the British Museum. (**the...** is correct)
2 Hyde Park / The Hyde Park is a very large park in central London.
3 Another park in central London is St James's Park / the St James's Park.
4 Grand Hotel / The Grand Hotel is in Baker Street / the Baker Street.
5 We flew to New York from Gatwick Airport / the Gatwick Airport near London.
6 Frank is a student at Liverpool University / the Liverpool University.
7 If you're looking for a good clothes shop, I would recommend Harrison's / the Harrison's.
8 If you're looking for a good pub, I would recommend Ship Inn / the Ship Inn.
9 Statue of Liberty / The Statue of Liberty is at the entrance to New York harbour / the New York harbour.
10 You should go to Science Museum / the Science Museum. It's very interesting.
11 John works for IBM / the IBM now. He used to work for British Telecom / the British Telecom.
12 'Which cinema are you going to this evening?'   'Classic / The Classic.'
13 I'd like to go to China and see Great Wall / the Great Wall.
14 Which newspaper shall I buy – Independent / the Independent or Herald / the Herald?
15 This book is published by Cambridge University Press / the Cambridge University Press.

Singular and plural

A Sometimes we use a *plural* noun for *one* thing that has *two* parts. For example:

trousers *(two legs)* *also* jeans/tights/shorts/pants	pyjamas *(top and bottom)*	glasses *(or* spectacles*)*	binoculars	scissors

These words are plural, so they take a plural verb:
- My trousers **are** too long. (*not* 'is too long')

You can also use **a pair of** + these words:
- **Those are** nice **jeans**.   *or*   **That's a nice pair of** jeans. (*not* 'a nice jeans')
- I need **some** new **glasses**.   *or*   I need **a** new **pair of** glasses.

B Some nouns end in -ics but are *not* usually plural. For example: **athletics   gymnastics   mathematics** (*or* **maths**)   **physics   electronics   economics   politics**
- **Gymnastics is** my favourite sport.

News is not plural (see Unit 69C):
- What time **is** the **news** on television? (*not* 'are the news')

Some words ending in -s can be singular or plural. For example:

means	**a means** of transport	**many means** of transport
series	**a** television **series**	**two** television **series**
species	**a species** of bird	**200 species** of bird

C Some singular nouns are often used with a plural verb. For example:
government   staff   team   family   audience   committee   company   firm

These nouns are all *groups* of people. We often think of them as a number of people (= 'they'), not as one thing (= 'it'). So we often use a plural verb:
- **The government** (= they) **want** to increase taxes.
- **The staff** at the school (= they) **are** not happy with **their** new working conditions.

In the same way, we often use a plural verb after the name of a sports team or a company:
- **Scotland are** playing France next week (in a football match).
- **Shell have** increased the price of petrol.

A singular verb (The government **wants**… / Shell **has**… etc.) is also possible.

We always use a plural verb with **police**:
- The police **have** arrested a friend of mine. (*not* 'The police has')
- Do you think the police **are** well-paid?

Note that a person in the police is 'a policeman / a policewoman / a police officer' (*not* 'a police').

D We do not often use the plural of **person** ('persons'). We normally use **people** (a *plural* word):
- He's **a** nice **person**.   *but*   They are nice **people**.
- **Many people don't** have enough to eat. (*not* 'doesn't have')

E We think of a sum of money, a period of time, a distance etc. as *one* thing. So we use a singular verb:
- **Twenty thousand pounds** (= it) **was** stolen in the robbery. (*not* 'were stolen')
- **Three years** (= it) **is** a long time to be without a job. (*not* 'Three years are…')
- **Six miles is** a long way to walk every day.

EXERCISES

78.1 *Complete the sentences using a word from Sections A or B. Sometimes you need* **a** *or* **some**.

1 My eyes aren't very good. I need ...glasses....
2 This plant is ...a... very rare ...species...
3 Footballers don't wear trousers when they play. They wear ....
4 The bicycle is .... of transport.
5 The bicycle and the car are .... of transport.
6 I want to cut this piece of material. I need ....
7 Ann is going to write .... of articles for her local newspaper.
8 There are a lot of American TV .... shown on British television.
9 While we were out walking, we saw 25 different .... of bird.

78.2 *In each example the words on the left are connected with an activity (for example, a sport or an academic subject). Write the name of the activity. Each time the beginning of the word is given.*

1 calculate   algebra   equation   m...athematics...
2 government   election   minister   p..
3 finance   trade   industry   e..
4 running   jumping   throwing   a..
5 light   heat   gravity   ph..
6 exercises   somersault   parallel bars   gy..
7 computer   silicon chip   video games   el..

78.3 *Choose the correct form of the verb, singular or plural. In one sentence either the singular or plural verb is possible.*

1 Gymnastics is/~~are~~ my favourite sport. ('is' *is correct*)
2 The trousers you bought for me doesn't/don't fit me.
3 The police want/wants to interview two men about the robbery last week.
4 Physics was/were my best subject at school.
5 Can I borrow your scissors? Mine isn't/aren't sharp enough.
6 Fortunately the news wasn't/weren't as bad as we expected.
7 Where does/do your family live?
8 Three days isn't/aren't long enough for a good holiday.
9 I can't find my binoculars. Do you know where it is / they are?
10 Do you think the people is/are happy with the government?
11 Does/Do the police know how the accident happened?
12 I don't like very hot weather. Thirty degrees is/are too warm for me.

78.4 *Most of these sentences are wrong. Correct them where necessary; put* 'RIGHT' *if the sentence is already correct.*

1 The government want to increase taxes. ...RIGHT ('wants' is also correct)...
2 Susan was wearing a black jeans. ....
3 Brazil are playing Italy in a football match next Wednesday. ....
4 I like Martin and Jill. They're very nice persons. ....
5 I need more money than that. Ten pounds are not enough. ....
6 I'm going to buy a new pyjama. ....
7 The committee haven't made a decision yet. ....
8 Many people has given up smoking. ....
9 There was a police standing at the corner of the street. ....
10 Has the police arrived yet? ....
11 This scissors is not very sharp. ....

Noun + noun (a **tennis ball** / a **headache** etc.)

A

We often use two nouns together (*noun + noun*) to mean *one* thing/person/idea etc. For example:
a **tennis ball**   a **bank manager**   a **road accident**   income **tax**   the **city centre**

The first noun is like an adjective – it tells us *what kind* of thing/person/idea etc. For example:
a **tennis ball** = a **ball** used to play **tennis**
a **road accident** = an **accident** that happens on the **road**
income tax = **tax** that you pay on your **income**
a **London doctor** = a **doctor** from **London**

So you can say:
a **television** camera   a **television** programme   a **television** studio   a **television** producer
(all different things or people to do with television)
language **problems**   marriage **problems**   health **problems**   work **problems**
(all different kinds of problems)

Compare:
garden vegetables (= **vegetables** that are grown in a garden)
a **vegetable garden** (= a **garden** where vegetables are grown)

Often the first word ends in **-ing**. Usually these are things used for doing something. For example:
a **washing** machine   a **frying** pan   a **swimming** pool   the **dining** room

Sometimes the first noun tells us *which* thing etc. is meant. For example:
● The **garage roof** needs repairing. (= the **roof** of the **garage**)
● The **sea temperature** today is 18 degrees. (= the **temperature** of the **sea**)

Sometimes there are more than two nouns together:
● I waited at the **hotel reception desk**. (= a desk)
● We watched the **World Swimming Championships** on television.
● If you want to play **table tennis** (= a game), you need a **table tennis table** (= a table).

B

When nouns are together like this, sometimes we write them as one word and sometimes as two separate words. For example:
a **headache**   **toothpaste**   a **weekend**   a **stomach ache**   **table tennis**
There are no clear rules for this. If you are not sure, it is usually better to write *two* words.
You can often put a hyphen (-) between the two words (but this is not usually necessary):
a **dining-room**   the **city-centre**

C

Note the difference between:
a **wine glass** (perhaps empty) and a **glass of wine** (= a glass with wine in it)
a **shopping bag** (perhaps empty) and a **bag of shopping** (= a bag full of shopping)

D

When we use *noun + noun*, the first noun is like an *adjective*. It is normally singular but the meaning is often plural. For example, a **book**shop is a shop where you can buy books, an **apple** tree is a tree that has apples.
In the same way we say:
a three-**hour** journey (*not* 'a three-hours journey')
a ten-**pound** note (*not* 'pounds')   two 14-**year**-old girls (*not* 'years')
a four-**week** English course (*not* 'weeks')   a three-**page** letter (*not* 'pages')

So we say:
● It was **a three-hour** journey.   *but*   The journey took three **hours**.

For the structure 'I've got three **weeks**' holiday', see Unit 80E.

EXERCISES

79.1 *What do we call these things and people? Use the structure noun + noun.*

   1 A ticket for a concert is ....**a concert ticket.**...

   2 A magazine about computers is ....

   3 Photographs taken on your holiday are your ....

   4 Chocolate made with milk is ....

   5 Somebody whose job is to inspect factories is ....

   6 A hotel in central London is ....

   7 The results of your examinations are your ....

   8 The carpet in the dining room is ....

   9 A scandal involving a football club is ....

  10 A question that has two parts is ....

  11 A girl who is seven years old is ....

79.2 *Write the correct word for each picture. Each word has two parts and these are given above the pictures. In **1a** for example, you must decide whether the word is* **boathouse** *or* **houseboat**.

boat/house   horse/race   card/phone

1a   1b   2a   2b   3a   3b

....

79.3 *Answer the questions using two of the following words each time:*

~~accident~~   belt   card   credit   editor   forecast   newspaper

number   ~~road~~   room   seat   shop   weather   window

  1 This can be caused by bad driving.   ...**A road accident**...

  2 If you're staying at a hotel, you need to remember this. Your ....

  3 You should wear this when you're in a car. A ....

  4 You can sometimes use this to pay for things instead of cash. A ....

  5 If you want to know if it's going to rain, you can read or listen to this. The ....

  6 This person is a top journalist. A ....

  7 You might stop to look in this when you're walking along a street. A ....

79.4 *Complete the sentences using one of the following:*

    15 minute(s) 60 minute(s) two hour(s) five day(s) two year(s) 500 year(s)

    six mile(s) 20 pound(s) five course(s) ~~ten page(s)~~ ~~450 page(s)~~

*Sometimes you need the singular (***day/page*** etc.) and sometimes the plural (***days/pages*** etc.).*

   1 It's quite a long book. There are ...**450 pages.**...

   2 A few days ago I received a ...**ten-page**... letter from Julia.

   3 I didn't have any change. I only had a .... note.

   4 At work in the morning I usually have a .... break for coffee.

   5 There are .... in an hour.

   6 It's only a .... flight from London to Madrid.

   7 It was a big meal. There were ....

   8 Mary has just started a new job. She's got a .... contract.

   9 The oldest building in the city is the .... old castle.

  10 I work .... a week. Saturday and Sunday are free.

  11 We went for a .... walk in the country.

-'s (**the girl's** name) and **of...** (the name **of the book**)

A We normally use -'s for people or animals (**the girl's...** / **the horse's...** etc.):

the girl's name   **the horse's** tail   **Mr Evans's** daughter
a woman's hat   **the manager's** office   **Sarah's** eyes

- Where is **the manager's** office? (*not* 'the office of the manager')
- What colour are **Sarah's** eyes? (*not* 'the eyes of Sarah')

Note that you can use -'s without a following noun:

- This isn't my book. It's **my brother's**. (= my brother's book)

We do not always use -'s for people. For example, we would use **of...** in this sentence:

- What is the name **of the man who lent us the money**? ('the man who lent us the money'
 is too long to be followed by -'s)

Note that we say **a woman's hat** (= a hat for a woman), **a boy's name** (= a name for a boy), **a
bird's egg** (= an egg laid by a bird) etc.

B For things, ideas etc. we normally use of (...**of the book** / ...**of the restaurant** etc.):

the roof **of the garage** (*not* 'the garage's roof')
the name **of the book**   the owner **of the restaurant**

Sometimes you can use the structure *noun + noun* (see Unit 79):

the **garage door**   the **restaurant owner**

We normally use of (not *noun + noun*) with **the beginning / end / top / bottom / front / back /
middle / side** etc. So we say:

the back of the car (*not* 'the car back')
the beginning of the month

C You can usually use -'s or **of...** for an organisation (= a group of people). So you can say:

the government's decision   *or*   the decision **of the government**
the company's success   *or*   the success **of the company**

It is also possible to use -'s for places. So you can say:

the city's new theatre   **the world's** population   **Italy's** largest city

D After a *singular* noun we use -'s:

my **sister's** room (= **her** room – *one* sister)   Mr **Carter's** house

After a *plural* noun (sisters, friends etc.) we put ' (an *apostrophe*) after the s (s'):

my **sisters'** room (= **their** room – *two or more* sisters)
the **Carters'** house (Mr and Mrs Carter)

If a plural noun does not end in -s (for example, **men / women / children / people**) we use -'s:

the **men's** changing room   a **children's** book (= a book for children)

Note that you can use -'s after more than one noun:

Jack and Jill's wedding   **Mr and Mrs Carter's** house

E You can also use -'s with time expressions (**yesterday** / **next week** etc.)

- Have you still got **yesterday's** newspaper?
- **Next week's** meeting has been cancelled.

In the same way, you can say **today's...** / **tomorrow's...** / **this evening's...** / **Monday's...** etc.

We also use -'s (or -s' with plural words) with periods of time:

- I've got **a week's** holiday starting on Monday.
- Jill has got **three weeks'** holiday.
- I live near the station – it's only about **ten minutes'** walk.

Compare this structure with '**a three-hour** journey', '**a ten-minute** walk' etc. (see Unit 79D).

EXERCISES

80.1 *Join the two (or three) nouns. Sometimes you have to use -'s or -s'; and sometimes you have to use ...of... .*

1 the owner / that car   ..the owner of that car..
2 the mother / Ann   ...Ann's mother...
3 the jacket / that man ....
4 the top / the page ....
5 the daughter / Charles ....
6 the cause / the problem ....
7 the newspaper / yesterday ....
8 the birthday / my father ....
9 the name / this street ....
10 the toys / the children ....
11 the new manager / the company ....
12 the result / the football match ....
13 the garden / our neighbours ....
14 the ground floor / the building ....
15 the children / Don and Mary ....
16 the economic policy / the government ....
17 the husband / Catherine ....
18 the husband / the woman talking to Mary ....
19 the car / the parents / Mike. ....
20 the wedding / the friend / Helen ....

80.2 *What is another way of saying these things? Use -'s.*

1 a hat for a woman ...a woman's hat..
2 a name for a boy ....
3 clothes for children ....
    ....

4 a school for girls ....
5 a nest for a bird ....
6 a magazine for women ....

80.3 *Read each sentence and write a new sentence beginning with the <u>underlined</u> words.*

1 The meeting <u>tomorrow</u> has been cancelled.
  ..Tomorrow's meeting has been cancelled...
2 The storm <u>last week</u> caused a lot of damage.
  Last ....
3 The only cinema in <u>the town</u> has closed down.
  The ....
4 Exports from <u>Britain</u> to the United States have fallen recently.
  ....
5 Tourism is the main industry in <u>the region</u>.
  ....

80.4 *Use the information given to complete the sentences.*

1 If I leave my house at 9 o'clock and drive to London, I arrive at about 12.
  So it's about ...three hours' drive... to London from my house. (drive)
2 If I leave my house at 8.55 and walk to the station, I get there at 9 o'clock.
  So it's only .... from my house to the station. (walk)
3 I'm going on holiday on the 12th. I have to be back at work on the 26th.
  So I've got .... (holiday)
4 I went to sleep at 3 o'clock this morning and woke up an hour later. After that I couldn't
  sleep. So last night I only had .... (sleep)

A friend **of mine**   **My own** house   **On my own / by myself**

A

A friend of mine / a friend of Tom's etc.

We say 'a friend **of mine/yours/his/hers/ours/theirs**' (*not* 'a friend of me/you/him' etc.)

- I'm going to a wedding on Saturday. **A friend of mine** is getting married. (*not* 'a friend of me')
- We went on holiday with **some friends of ours.** (*not* 'some friends of us')
- Michael had an argument with **a neighbour of his.**
- It was **a good idea of yours** to go swimming this afternoon.

In the same way we say 'a friend **of Tom's**', 'a friend **of my sister's**' etc.:

- It was **a good idea of Tom's** to go swimming.
- That woman over there is **a friend of my sister's.**

B

My own… / your own… etc.

We use **my/your/his/her/its/our/their** before **own:**

   my own house   **your own** car   **her own** room

You cannot say 'an own…' ('an own house', 'an own car' etc.).

My own… / your own… (etc.) = something that is only mine/yours (etc.), not shared or borrowed:

- I don't want to share a room with anybody. I want **my own room.**
- Vera and George would like to have **their own house.** (*not* 'an own house')
- It's a pity that the flat hasn't got **its own entrance.**
- It's **my own fault** that I've got no money. I buy too many things I don't need.
- Why do you want to borrow my car? Why can't you use **your own?**(= your own car)

You can also use …**own**… to say that you do something yourself instead of somebody else doing it for you. For example:

- Brian usually cuts **his own hair.**
  (= he cuts it himself; he doesn't go to
  the hairdresser)
- I'd like to have a garden so that I could
  grow **my own vegetables.**
  (= grow them myself instead of
  buying them from shops)

C

On my own / by myself

On my own and **by myself** both mean 'alone'. We say:

on	my / your his / her / its our / their	own	=	by	myself / yourself (*singular*) himself / herself / itself ourselves / yourselves (*plural*) / themselves

- I like living **on my own / by myself.**
- Did you go on holiday **on your own / by yourself?**
- Jack was sitting **on his own / by himself** in a corner of the café.
- Learner drivers are not allowed to drive **on their own / by themselves.**

EXERCISES

81.1 *Write new sentences using the structure in Section A (a friend of mine etc.).*

1 I am writing to <u>one of my friends</u>.   I'm writing to a friend of mine.
2 We met <u>one of your relations</u>.   We met a ....
3 Henry borrowed <u>one of my books</u>.   Henry ....
4 Ann invited <u>some of her friends</u> to her flat.   Ann ....
5 We had dinner with <u>one of our neighbours</u>.   ....
6 I went on holiday with <u>two of my friends</u>.   ....
7 Is that man <u>one of your friends</u>?   ....
8 I met <u>one of Jane's friends</u> at the party.   ....

81.2 *Complete the sentences using* **my own / your own** *etc. + one of the following:*
business   ideas   money   private jet   parliament   ~~room~~   television

1 I don't want to share a room. I want ...my own room.
2 I don't watch television with the rest of the family. I've got ....
   in my room.
3 Sue doesn't need to borrow from me. She's got ....
4 Julia is fed up with working for other people. She wants to start ....
5 Henry is extremely rich. He's got ....
6 You can give him advice but he won't listen. He's got ....
7 The Isle of Man is an island off the coast of Britain. It is not completely independent but it
   has ....

81.3 *Complete the sentences using* **my own / your own** *etc.*

1 Why do you want to borrow my car?   Why can't you ...use your own car?
2 How can you blame me? It's not my fault.   It's ....
3 He's always using my ideas.   Why can't he use .... ?
4 Please don't worry about my problems.   You've got ....
5 I can't make her decisions for her.   She must make ....

81.4 *Complete the sentences using* **my own / your own** *etc. Choose one of these verbs:*
bake   ~~cut~~   make   write

1 Brian never goes to the hairdresser.   He usually ...cuts his own hair.
2 Mary doesn't often buy clothes.   She usually ....
3 Paul is a singer.   He sings songs written by other people but he also ....
   ....
4 We don't often buy bread from a bakery.   We ....

81.5 *Complete the sentences using* **on my own / by myself** *etc.*

1 Did you go on holiday on ...your own?
2 I'm glad I live with other people. I wouldn't like to live on ....
3 The box was too heavy for me to lift by ....
4 'Who was Tom with when you saw him?'   'Nobody. He was by ....'
5 Very young children should not go swimming by ....
6 I don't think she knows many people. When I see her, she is always by ....
7 I don't like strawberries with cream. I like them on ....
8 Do you like working with other people or do you prefer working by .... ?
9 We had no help decorating the flat. We did it completely on ....
10 I went out with Sally because she didn't want to go out on ....

Myself/yourself/themselves etc.

A Study this example:

George cut **himself** when he was shaving this morning.

We use **myself/yourself/himself** etc. *(reflexive pronouns)* when the *subject* and *object* are the same:

subject → ⟨George⟩ cut ⟨himself⟩. ← *object*

The reflexive pronouns are:
singular: my**self**   your**self** *(one person)*   him**self**/her**self**/it**self**
plural: our**selves**   your**selves** *(more than one person)*   them**selves**

- I don't want you to pay for me. I'll pay for **myself**. (*not* 'I'll pay for me')
- Julia had a great holiday. **She** enjoyed **herself** very much.
- Do **you** sometimes talk to **yourself**? (*said to one person*)
- If **you** want more to eat, help **yourselves**. (*said to more than one person*)

Compare:
- It's not our fault. **You** can't blame **us**.
- It's our own fault. **We** blame **ourselves**.

Note that we do *not* use **myself/yourself** etc. after '**bring/take** something **with...**':
- It might rain. I'll **take** an umbrella **with me**. (*not* 'with myself')

B We do *not* use **myself** etc. after **concentrate/feel/relax/meet**:
- You must try and **concentrate**. (*not* 'concentrate yourself')
- 'Do you **feel** nervous?'   'Yes, I can't **relax**.'
- What time shall we **meet**? (*not* 'meet ourselves', *not* 'meet us')

We normally use **wash/shave/dress** *without* **myself** etc.:
- He got up, **washed**, **shaved** and **dressed**. (*not* 'washed himself' etc.)

But we say 'I **dried myself**'.

C Study the difference between **-selves** and **each other**:
- Tom and Ann stood in front of the mirror and looked at **themselves**. (= *Tom and Ann* looked at *Tom and Ann*)
but - Tom looked at Ann; Ann looked at Tom. They looked at **each other**.

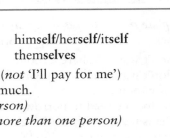

themselves

each other

You can use **one another** instead of **each other**:
- How long have you and Bill known **one another**? (*or* ...known **each other**)
- Sue and Ann don't like **each other**. (*or* ...don't like **one another**)

D We also use **myself/yourself** etc. in another way. For example:
- 'Who repaired your bicycle for you?'   'Nobody. I repaired it **myself**.'

'I repaired it **myself**' = I repaired it, not anybody else. Here, **myself** is used to *emphasise* **I** (= it makes it stronger). Some more examples:
- I'm not going to do it for you. **You** can do it **yourself**. (= you, not me)
- **Let's** paint the house **ourselves**. It will be much cheaper.
- **The film itself** wasn't very good but I liked the music.
- I don't think Sue will get the job. **Sue herself** doesn't think she'll get it. (*or* **Sue** doesn't think she'll get it **herself**.)

EXERCISES

82.1 *Complete each sentence using* **myself/yourself** *etc. with one of these verbs (in the correct form):*
blame   burn   ~~cut~~   enjoy   express   hurt   put

1 George ...*cut himself*... while he was shaving this morning.
2 Bill fell down some steps but fortunately he didn't .... badly.
3 It isn't her fault. She really shouldn't ....
4 Please try and understand how I feel.   .... in my position.
5 They had a great time. They really ....
6 Be careful! That pan is very hot. Don't ....
7 Sometimes I can't say exactly what I mean. I wish I could .... better.

82.2 *Put in* **myself/yourself/ourselves** *etc. or* **me/you/us** *etc.*

1 Julia had a great holiday. She enjoyed ...*herself*... .
2 It's not my fault. You can't blame ....
3 What I did was very wrong. I'm ashamed of ....
4 We've got a problem. I hope you can help ....
5 'Can I take another biscuit?'   'Of course. Help ....!'
6 Take some money with .... in case you need it.
7 Don't worry about Tom and me. We can look after ....
8 I gave them a key to our house so that they could let .... in.
9 When they come to visit us, they always bring their dog with ....

82.3 *Complete these sentences. Use* **myself/yourself** *etc. only where necessary. Use one of these verbs (in the correct form):* **concentrate   defend   dry   feel   meet   relax   ~~shave~~   wash**

1 Martin decided to grow a beard because he was fed up with ...*shaving*... .
2 I wasn't very well yesterday but I .... much better today.
3 She climbed out of the swimming pool and .... with a towel.
4 I tried to study but I just couldn't ....
5 If somebody attacks you, you need to be able to ....
6 I'm going out with Chris this evening. We're .... at the station at 7.30.
7 You're always rushing around. Why don't you sit down and .... ?
8 There was no water, so we couldn't ....

82.4 *Complete the sentences with* **-selves** *or* **each other**.

1 How long have you and Bill known ...*each other?*...
2 If people work too hard, they can make .... ill.
3 I need you and you need me. We need ....
4 In Britain friends often give .... presents at Christmas.
5 Some people are very selfish. They only think of ....
6 Nora and I don't see .... very often these days.
7 We couldn't get back into the house. We had locked .... out.
8 They've had an argument. They're not speaking to .... at the moment.
9 We'd never met before, so we introduced .... to ....

82.5 *Complete the answers to the questions using* **myself/yourself/itself** *etc.*

1	Who repaired the bicycle for you?	Nobody. I ...*repaired it myself*... .
2	Did Brian have his hair cut by a hairdresser?	No. He cut ....
3	Do you want me to post that letter for you?	No, I'll ....
4	Who told you that Linda was getting married?	Linda ....
5	Can you phone John for me?	Why can't you .... ?

There... and it...

A There and it

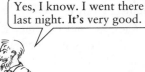

> There's a new restaurant in King Street.

> Yes, I know. I went there last night. It's very good.

We use **there...** when we talk about something for the first time, to say that it exists:

- **There's** a new restaurant in King Street. (*not* 'A new restaurant is in King Street')
- The journey took a long time. **There was** a lot of traffic. (*not* 'It was a lot of traffic')
- Things are much more expensive now. **There has been** a big rise in the cost of living.

It = a particular thing, place, fact, situation etc. (but see also Section **C**):

- We went to the new restaurant. **It's** very good. (**it** = the restaurant)
- 'Was the traffic bad?' 'Yes, **it was** terrible.' (**it** = the traffic)
- I wasn't expecting them to come. **It** (= that they came) was a complete surprise.

Compare:

- I don't like this town. **There's** nothing to do here. **It's** a boring place.

Note that **there** also means 'to/at/in that place':

- The new restaurant is very good. I went **there** (= to the restaurant) last night.
- When we arrived at the party, there were already a lot of people **there** (= at the party).

B You can say **there will be, there must be, there used to be** etc.

- **Will there be** many people at the party?
- '**Is there** a flight to Paris this evening?' '**There might be.** I'll phone the airport.'
- If people drove more carefully, **there wouldn't be** so many accidents.

Also: **there must have been, there should have been** etc.:

- **There was** a light on. **There must have been** somebody at home.

Compare **there** and **it**:

- They live on a busy road. **There must be** a lot of noise from the traffic.
  They live on a busy main road. **It must be** very noisy.
- **There used to be** a cinema in King Street but it closed a few years ago.
  That building is now a supermarket. **It used to be** a cinema.

You can also say **there is sure/certain/likely to be** something (see also Unit 64E):

- **There is sure to be** a flight to Paris this evening.

C We use **it** in sentences like this:

- **It's** dangerous **to walk in the road.** (**It** = to walk in the road)

It is unusual to say 'To walk in the road is dangerous.' Normally we begin with **It...**:

- **It** didn't take us long **to get here.** (**It** = to get here)
- **It's** a pity (**that**) Sandra can't come to the party. (**It** = that Sandra can't come)
- Let's go. **It's** not worth **waiting any longer.** (**It** = waiting any longer)

We use **it** to talk about distance, time and weather:

- **It's** a long way from here to the airport.
- What day is **it** today?
- **It's** going to be a nice day.
- How far is **it** to the airport?
- **It's** a long time since I last saw you.
- **It** was windy. (*but* '**There** was **a cold wind.**')

EXERCISES

83.1 *Put in* there is/was *or* it is/was. *Some sentences are questions* (is there...? / is it...? *etc.*) *and some are negative* (isn't/wasn't).

1 The journey took a long time. ...There was... a lot of traffic.
2 What's the new restaurant like? ...Is it... good?
3 '.......................... a bookshop near here?' 'Yes, ... one in Hill Street.'
4 When we got to the cinema, ... a queue outside. .... a very long queue, so we decided not to wait.
5 I couldn't see anything. .... completely dark.
6 .... trouble at the club last night. They had to call the police.
7 How far .... from Milan to Rome?
8 .... Keith's birthday yesterday. We had a party.
9 .... three years since I last went to the theatre.
10 I wanted to visit the museum but .... enough time.
11 '........................ time to go?' 'Yes, ... nearly midnight.'
12 A few days ago .... a storm. .... a lot of damage.
13 .... a beautiful day yesterday. We had a picnic.
14 .... anything on television, so I turned it off.
15 .... an accident in King Street but .... very serious.

83.2 *Read the first sentence and then write a sentence beginning* There... .

1 The roads were busy today. ...There was a lot of traffic.
2 This soup is very salty. There .... in the soup.
3 The box was empty. .... in the box.
4 The film was very violent. ....
5 The shops were very crowded. ....
6 I like this town – it's lively. ....

83.3 *Complete the sentences. Use* **there will be, there would be** *etc. Choose from:*

will   might   ~~would~~   wouldn't   should   used to   (be) going to

1 If people drove more carefully, ...there would be... fewer accidents.
2 'Have we got any eggs?' 'I'm not sure. .... some in the fridge.'
3 I think everything will be OK. I don't think .... any problems.
4 Look at the sky. .... a storm.
5 'Is there a school in the village?' 'Not now. .... one but it closed.'
6 People drive too fast on this road. I think .... a speed limit.
7 If people weren't aggressive, ... any wars.

83.4 *Are these sentences right or wrong? Change* it *to* there *where necessary.*

1 They live on a busy road. It must be a lot of noise. ...WRONG: There must be...
2 Last winter it was very cold and it was a lot of snow. ....
3 I wish it was warmer. I hate cold weather. ....
4 It used to be a church here, but it was knocked down. ....
5 It's a long way from my house to the nearest shop. ....
6 Why was she so unfriendly? It must have been a reason. ....
7 I don't know who will win but it's sure to be a good match. ....
8 'Where can we park the car?' 'Don't worry. It's sure to be a car park somewhere.' ....
9 After the lecture it will be an opportunity to ask questions. ....
10 I like the place where I live but it would be nicer to live by the sea. ....
11 I was told that it would be somebody to meet me at the station but it wasn't anybody.
....

Some and any

A

In general we use **some** (*also* **somebody/someone/something**) in positive sentences and **any** (*also* **anybody** etc.) in negative sentences (but see also Sections **C** and **D**):

some	any
• We bought **some** flowers.	• We didn't buy **any** flowers.
• He's busy. He's got **some** work to do.	• He's lazy. He **never** does **any** work.
• There's **somebody** at the door.	• There isn't **anybody** at the door.
• I'm hungry. I want **something** to eat.	• I'm not hungry. I **don't** want **anything** to eat.

We use **any** in the following sentences because the meaning is negative:
- She went out **without any** money. (She did**n't** take **any** money with her.)
- He **refused** to eat **anything**. (He did**n't** eat **anything**.)
- **Hardly anybody** passed the examination. (= almost nobody passed)

B

In most questions we use **any**:
- 'Have you got **any** luggage?'   'No, I haven't.'
- 'Has **anybody** seen my bag?'   'Yes, it's under the table.'

But we use **some** in questions when we expect the answer 'yes':
- What's wrong? Have you got **something** in your eye? (It seems that you have got something in your eye and I expect you to answer 'yes'.)

We use **some** in questions when we offer or ask for things:
- Would you like **something** to eat?   • Can I have **some** sugar, please?

C

We often use **any** after **if**:
- **If** there are **any** letters for me, can you send them on to this address?
- **If anyone** has any questions, I'll be pleased to answer them.
- Let me know **if** you need **anything**.

The following sentences have the idea of **if**:
- I'm sorry for **any** trouble I've caused. (= if I have caused any trouble)
- **Anyone** who wants to do the exam must give me their names today. (= if there is anyone)

D

We also use **any** with the meaning 'it doesn't matter which':
- You can catch **any** bus. They all go to the centre. (= it doesn't matter which bus you catch)
- 'Sing a song.'   'Which song shall I sing?'   '**Any** song. I don't mind.' (= it doesn't matter which song)
- Come and see me **any** time you want.
- 'Let's go out somewhere.'   'Where shall we go?'   '**Anywhere**. I don't mind.'
- We left the door unlocked. **Anybody** could have come in.

Compare **something** and **anything**:
- A: I'm hungry. I want **something** to eat.
  B: What would you like?
  A: I don't mind. **Anything**. (= something, but it doesn't matter what)

E

Somebody/someone/anybody/anyone are singular words:
- **Someone is** here to see you.

But we often use **they/them/their** after these words:
- **Someone** has forgotten **their** umbrella. (= his or her umbrella)
- If **anybody** wants to leave early, **they** can. (= he or she can)

Not...any → UNIT 85   Some of... / any of... → UNIT 87   Hardly any → UNIT 100C

84.1 *Complete the sentences with* **some** *or* **any**.

1 We didn't buy ...**any**... flowers.
2 This evening I'm going out with .... friends of mine.
3 'Have you seen .... good films recently?' 'No, I haven't been to the cinema for ages.'
4 I didn't have .... money, so I had to borrow ....
5 Can I have .... milk in my coffee, please?
6 I was too tired to do .... work.
7 You can cash these traveller's cheques at .... bank.
8 Can you give me .... information about places of interest in the town?
9 With the special tourist train ticket, you can travel on .... train you like.
10 If there are .... words you don't understand, use a dictionary.

84.2 *Complete the sentences with* **some-** *or* **any-** + **-body/-thing/-where**.

1 I was too surprised to say ...**anything**... .
2 There's .... at the door. Can you go and see who it is?
3 Does .... mind if I open the window?
4 I wasn't feeling hungry, so I didn't eat ....
5 You must be hungry. Would you like .... to eat?
6 Quick, let's go! There's .... coming and I don't want .... to see us.
7 Sally was upset about .... and refused to talk to ....
8 This machine is very easy to use. .... can learn to use it in a very short time.
9 There was hardly .... on the beach. It was almost deserted.
10 'Do you live .... near Jim?' 'No, he lives in another part of town.'
11 We slept in a park because we didn't have .... to stay.
12 'Where shall we go on holiday?' 'Let's go .... warm and sunny.'
13 They stay at home all the time. They never seem to go ....
14 I'm going out now. If .... phones while I'm out, can you tell them I'll be back at 11.30?
15 Why are you looking under the bed? Have you lost .... ?
16 .... who saw the accident should contact the police.
17 Sue is very secretive. She never tells .... *(2 words)*

84.3 *Complete the sentences. Use* **any** *(+ noun) or* **anybody/anything/anywhere**.

1	Which bus do I have to catch?	...**Any bus**... They all go to the centre.
2	Which day shall I come?	I don't mind. ....
3	What do you want to eat?	.... I don't mind. Whatever you have.
4	Where shall I sit?	It's up to you. You can sit .... you like.
5	What sort of job are you looking for?	.... It doesn't matter.
6	What time shall I phone tomorrow?	.... I'll be in all day.
7	Who shall I invite to the party?	I don't mind. .... you like.
8	Which newspaper shall I buy?	.... Whatever they have in the shop.

No/none/any

A

No   none   nothing   nobody/no one   nowhere

You can use these negative words at the beginning of a sentence or alone:

- **No** cars are allowed in the city centre.
- **None** of this money is mine.
- 'What did you say?'   '**Nothing.**'
- **Nobody** (*or* **No one**) came to visit me while I was in hospital.
- 'Where are you going?'   '**Nowhere.** I'm staying here.'

You can also use these words after a verb, especially after **be** and **have**:

- The house is empty. There**'s nobody** living there.
- She **had no** difficulty finding a job.

No/nothing/nobody etc. = **not + any/anything/anybody** etc.:

- We haven**'t** got **any** money. (= We've got **no** money.)
- I didn**'t** say **anything.** (= I said **nothing.**)
- She didn**'t** tell **anybody** about her plans. (= She told **nobody**…)
- The station isn**'t anywhere** near here. (= …is **nowhere** near here)

When you use **no/nothing/nobody** etc., do *not* use a negative verb (isn**'t**, didn**'t**, can**'t** etc.):

- I said **nothing.** (*not* 'I didn't say nothing')
- **Nobody** tells me anything. (*not* 'Nobody doesn't tell…')

B

We also use **any/anything/anybody** etc. (without 'not') to mean 'it doesn't matter which/ what/who' (see Unit 84D). Compare **no-** and **any-**:

- 'What do you want to eat?'   '**Nothing.** I'm not hungry.'
  I'm so hungry. I could eat **anything.** (= it doesn't matter what)
- The exam was extremely difficult. **Nobody** passed. (= everybody failed)
  The exam was very easy. **Anybody** could have passed. (= it doesn't matter who)

C

No and none

We use **no** + a noun. **No** = **not a** or **not any**:

- We had to walk home because there was **no bus.** (= there wasn**'t a** bus)
- I can**'t** talk to you now. I've got **no time.** (= I haven**'t** got **any** time)
- There were **no shops** open. (= there weren**'t any** shops open)

We use **none** alone (without a noun):

- 'How much money have you got?'   '**None.**' (= no money)
- All the tickets have been sold. There are **none** left. (= no tickets left)

Or we use **none of**…:

none of these shops   none of my money   none of it/them/us/you

After **none of** + a *plural* word ('none of **the shops**', 'none of **them**' etc.) you can use a singular or a plural verb. A plural verb is more usual:

- **None of the shops were** (*or* **was**) open.

D

After **nobody/no one** you can use **they/them/their**:

- **Nobody** phoned, did **they**? (= did he or she)
- The party was a disaster. **Nobody** enjoyed **themselves**. (= himself or herself)
- **No one** in the class did **their** homework. (= his or her homework)

85.1 *Answer these questions using* **none/nobody/nothing/nowhere.**

1 What did you do?   ...Nothing...
2 Who were you talking to?   ....
3 Where are you going?   ....
4 How much luggage have you got?   ....
5 How many children have they got?   ....
6 Who did you meet?   ....
7 What did you buy?   ....

Now write full sentences using **any/anybody/anything/anywhere.**

8 (1) ...I didn't do anything...
9 (2) I ....
10 (3) ....
11 (4) ....
12 (5) ....
13 (6) ....
14 (7) ....

85.2 *Complete these sentences with* **no, none** *or* **any.**

1 It was a public holiday, so there were ...no... shops open.
2 I haven't got ...any... money. Can you lend me some?
3 I couldn't make an omelette because there were .... eggs.
4 I couldn't make an omelette because there weren't .... eggs.
5 'How many eggs have we got?' '............................. I'll go and buy some from the shop if you like.'
6 We took a few photographs but .... of them were very good.
7 What a stupid thing to do! .... intelligent person would do such a thing.
8 I'll try and answer .... questions you ask me.
9 I couldn't answer .... of the questions they asked me.
10 We cancelled the party because .... of the people we invited were able to come.

85.3 *Complete these sentences with* **no-** *or* **any-** *+* **-body/-thing/-where.**

1 I don't want ...anything... to drink. I'm not thirsty.
2 The bus was completely empty. There was .... on it.
3 'Where did you go for your holidays?' '............................. I stayed at home.'
4 I went to the shops but I didn't buy.............................
5 'What did you buy?' '............................. I couldn't find .... I wanted.'
6 The town was still the same when I returned years later. .... had changed.
7 Have you seen my watch? I've looked all over the house but I can't find it ....
8 There was complete silence in the room. .... said.............................

85.4 *Choose the right word.*

1 She didn't tell ~~nobody~~ / anybody about her plans. (anybody *is correct*)
2 The accident looked serious but fortunately nobody / anybody was injured.
3 I looked out of the window but I couldn't see nobody / anybody.
4 My job is very easy. Nobody / Anybody could do it.
5 'What's in that box?' 'Nothing / Anything. It's empty.'
6 The situation is uncertain. Nothing / Anything could happen.
7 I don't know nothing / anything about economics.

Much, many, little, few, a lot, plenty

A   We use **much** and **little** with uncountable nouns:

much time   **much** luck   **little** energy   **little** money

We use **many** and **few** with plural nouns:

many friends   **many** people   **few** cars   **few** countries

B   We use **a lot of** / **lots of** / **plenty of** with uncountable and plural nouns:

a lot of luck   **lots of** time   **plenty of** money
a lot of friends   **lots of** people   **plenty of** ideas

Plenty = more than enough:

- There's no need to hurry. We've got **plenty of time**.
- I've had **plenty** to eat. I don't want any more.

C   We use **much/many** especially in negative sentences and questions. **A lot (of)** is also possible:

- We did**n't** spend **much** money. (*or* We didn't spend **a lot of** money.)
- Do you know **many** people? (*or* Do you know **a lot of** people?)
- I don't go out **much**. (*or* I don't go out **a lot**.)

In positive sentences **a lot (of)** is more usual. **Much** is unusual in positive sentences in spoken English:

- We spent **a lot of** money. (*not* 'We spent much money')
- He goes out **a lot**. (*not* 'He goes out much')

You can use **many** in positive sentences, but **a lot (of)** is more usual in spoken English:

- **A lot of** people (*or* **Many** people) drive too fast.

But note that we use **too much** and **so much** in positive sentences:

- We spent **too much** money.

D   **Little** and **few** (without 'a') are negative ideas (= not much / not many):

- We must be quick. There is **little** time. (= not much, not enough time)
- He isn't popular. He has **few** friends. (= not many, not enough friends)

You can say **very little** and **very few**:

- There is **very little** time.
- He has **very few** friends.

A little and **a few** are more positive. **A little** = some, a small amount:

- Let's go and have a drink. We've got **a little** time before the train leaves.
  (a little time = some time, enough time to have a drink)
- 'Do you speak English?'   '**A little**.' (so we can talk a bit)

A few = some, a small number:

- I enjoy my life here. I have **a few** friends and we meet quite often.
  (a few friends = not many but enough to have a good time)
- 'When did you last see Clare?'   '**A few** days ago.' (= some days ago)

Compare:

- He spoke **little** English, so it was difficult to communicate with him.
  He spoke **a little** English, so we were able to communicate with him.
- She's lucky. She has **few** problems. (= not many problems)
  Things are not going so well for her. She has **a few** problems. (= some problems)

Note that '**only a little**' and '**only a few**' have a negative meaning:

- We must be quick. We've **only** got **a little** time.
- The village was very small. There were **only a few** houses.

EXERCISES

86.1 *In some of these sentences* **much** *is incorrect or unnatural. Change* **much** *to* **many** *or* **a lot (of)** *where necessary. Put* 'RIGHT' *if the sentence is correct.*

1 We didn't spend much money. ...RIGHT...
2 Sue drinks much tea. ...a lot of tea...
3 Jim always puts much salt on his food. ....
4 We'll have to hurry. We haven't got much time. ....
5 Did it cost much to repair the car? ....
6 It cost much to repair the car. ....
7 I don't know much people in this town. ....
8 I use the phone much at work. ....
9 They've got so much money they don't know what to do with it. ....

86.2 *Complete the sentences using* **plenty (of)** + *one of the following:*

hotels   money   room   ~~time~~   to learn   things to see

1 There's no need to hurry.   ...We've got plenty of time...
2 He's got no financial problems.   He's got ....
3 Come and sit with us.   There's ....
4 She knows a lot but she still has ....
5 It's an interesting town to visit.   There ....
6 I'm sure we'll find somewhere to stay. ....

86.3 *Put in* **much**, **many**, **few** *or* **little**.

1 He isn't very popular. He has ...few... friends.
2 Ann is very busy these days. She has .... free time.
3 Did you take .... photographs when you were on holiday?
4 I'm not very busy today. I haven't got .... to do.
5 The museum was very crowded. There were too .... people.
6 Most of the town is modern. There are .... old buildings.
7 The weather has been very dry recently. We've had .... rain.

86.4 *Some of these sentences need* **a**. *Put in* **a** *where necessary. Put* 'RIGHT' *if the sentence is already complete.*

1 She's lucky. She has <u>few problems</u>.   ...RIGHT...
2 Things are not going so well for her. She has <u>few problems</u>.   ...a few problems...
3 Can you lend me <u>few dollars</u>? ....
4 I can't give you a decision yet. I need <u>little time</u> to think. ....
5 There was <u>little traffic</u>, so the journey didn't take very long. ....
6 It was a surprise that he won the match. <u>Few people</u> expected him to win. ....
7 I don't know much Spanish – <u>only few words</u>. ....

86.5 *Put in* **little** / **a little** / **few** / **a few**.

1 We must be quick. We have ...little... time.
2 Listen carefully. I'm going to give you .... advice.
3 Do you mind if I ask you .... questions?
4 This town is not a very interesting place to visit, so .... tourists come here.
5 I don't think Jill would be a good teacher. She's got .... patience.
6 'Would you like milk in your coffee?'   'Yes, please. ....'
7 This is a very boring place to live. There's .... to do.
8 'Have you ever been to Paris?'   'Yes, I've been there .... times.'

All / all of   most / most of   no / none of etc.

| all | some | any | most | much/many | little/few |

A   You can use the words in the box (and also **no**) with *a noun* (**some food** / **few books** etc.):
- **All cars** have wheels.
- **Some cars** can go faster than others.
- (*on a notice*) **No cars.** (= no cars allowed)
- **Many people** drive too fast.
- I don't go out very often. I'm at home **most days.**

You cannot say 'all *of* cars', 'most *of* people' etc. (see also Section B):
- **Some people** are very unfriendly. (*not* 'some of people')

Note that we say **most** (*not* 'the most'):
- **Most tourists** don't visit this part of the town. (*not* 'the most tourists')

B   **Some of... / most of... / none of...** etc.
You can use the words in the box (also **none** and **half**) with **of**. You can say **some of** (the people),
most of (my friends), **none of** (this money) etc.

We use **some of, most of** (etc.) + **the / this / that / these / those / my / his / Ann's...** etc.
So we say:

>   **some of the** people, **some of those** people (*but not* 'some of people')
>   **most of my** friends, **most of Ann's** friends (*but not* 'most of friends')
>   **none of this** money, **none of their** money (*but not* 'none of money')

For example:
- **Some of the** people I work with are very friendly.
- **None of this** money is mine.
- Have you read **any of these** books?
- I wasn't well yesterday. I spent **most of the day** in bed.

You don't need **of** after **all** or **half**. So you can say:
- **All my friends** live in London.   *or*   All **of** my friends...
- **Half this money** is mine.   *or*   Half **of** this money...

See also Section C.

Compare **all...** and **all (of) the...**:
- **All flowers** are beautiful. (= all flowers in general)
- **All (of) the flowers** in this garden are beautiful. (= a particular group of flowers)

C   You can use **all of / some of / none of** etc. + **it/us/you/them**:
- 'How many of these people do you know?'   '**None of them.**' / '**A few of them.**'
- Do **any of you** want to come to a party tonight?
- 'Do you like this music?'   '**Some of it. Not all of it.**'

Before **it/us/you/them** you need **of** after **all** and **half** (all **of**, half **of**):
>   all **of** us (*not* 'all us')   half **of** them (*not* 'half them')

D   You can use the words in the box (and also **none**) alone, *without* a noun:
- Some cars have four doors and **some** have two.
- A few of the shops were open but **most** (of them) were closed.
- Half (of) this money is mine, and **half** (of it) is yours. (*not* 'the half')

Some/any → UNIT 84   **No/none →** UNIT 85   **Much/many/little/few →** UNIT 86   **All →** UNITS 89, 109C
All of whom / most of which etc. → UNIT 95B

174

EXERCISES

87.1 *Put in* of *where necessary. Leave an empty space (–) if the sentence is already complete.*

1 All ......—.... cars have wheels.
2 None ...**of**... this money is mine.
3 Some .... people get angry very easily.
4 Some .... the people I met at the party were very interesting.
5 I have lived in London most .... my life.
6 Many .... people watch too much TV.
7 Are any .... those letters for me?
8 Most .... days I get up before 7 o'clock.
9 Jim thinks that all .... museums are boring.

87.2 *Choose from the list and complete the sentences. Use* of *(some of / most of etc.) where necessary.*

| accidents | ~~cars~~ | her friends | the people I invited | birds | my dinner | the houses |
| the population | ~~these books~~ | European countries | her opinions | my spare time |

1 I haven't read many ...**of these books.**...
2 All ...**cars**.... have wheels.
3 I spend most .... gardening.
4 It's a historic town. Many .... are over 400 years old.
5 Many .... are caused by bad driving.
6 When she got married, she kept it a secret. She didn't tell any ....
7 Not many people live in the north of the country. Most .... live in the south.
8 Not all .... can fly. For example, the penguin can't fly.
9 None .... to the party could come, so I cancelled it.
10 Julia and I have very different ideas. I don't agree with many ....
11 Sarah travels a lot. She has been to most ....
12 I had no appetite. I could only eat half ....

87.3 *Complete the sentences using the words in brackets. Sometimes no other words are necessary. Sometimes you need* the *or* of the.

1 I wasn't well yesterday. I spent ...**most of the day**.... in bed. (most/day)
2 ...**Some cars**... can go faster than others. (some/cars)
3 .... drive too fast. (many/people)
4 .... you took on holiday were very good. (some/photographs)
5 .... learn more quickly than others. (some/people)
6 We've eaten .... we bought. There's very little left. (most/food)
7 Have you spent .... you borrowed? (all/money)
8 Peter can't stop talking. He talks .... (all/time)
9 We had a lazy holiday. We spent .... on the beach. (most/time)
10 George is easy to get on with. .... like him. (most/people)
11 The exam was difficult. I could only answer .... (half/questions)

87.4 *Complete the sentences. Use* all/some/none + it/them/us *(all of it / some of them etc.).*

1 These books are all Jane's. ...**None of them**... belong to me.
2 'How many of these books have you read?' '.. Every one.'
3 We all got wet in the rain because .... had an umbrella.
4 Some of this money is yours and .... is mine.
5 I asked some people for directions but .... were able to help me.
6 She made up the whole story from beginning to end. .... was true.
7 Not all the tourists in the group were Spanish. .... were French.
8 I watched most of the film but not ....

Both / both of   neither / neither of   either / either of

A

We use **both/neither/either** for *two* things. You can use these words with a *noun* (**both books, neither book** etc.).

For example, you are talking about going out to eat this evening. There are two restaurants where you can go. You say:

- **Both restaurants** are very good. (*not* 'the both restaurants')
- **Neither restaurant** is expensive.
- We can go to **either restaurant**. I don't mind. (**either** = one or the other, it doesn't matter which one)

B

Both of... / neither of... / either of...

When you use **both/neither/either + of**, you always need **the... / these/those... / my/your/his/Tom's...** (etc.). You cannot say 'both of restaurants'. You have to say 'both of **the** restaurants', 'both of **those** restaurants' etc.:

- **Both of these** restaurants are very good.
- **Neither of the** restaurants we went to was (*or* were) expensive.
- I haven't been to **either of those** restaurants. (= I haven't been to one or the other)

You don't need **of** after **both**. So you can say:

- **Both my parents** are from London.   *or*   Both **of** my parents...

You can use **both of / neither of / either of + us/you/them**:

- *(talking to two people)* Can **either of you** speak Spanish?
- I asked two people the way to the station but **neither of them** knew.

You must say 'both of' before **us/you/them** (**of** is necessary):

- **Both of us** were very tired. (*not* 'Both us were...')

After **neither of...** a singular or a plural verb is possible:

- Neither of the children **wants** (*or* **want**) to go to bed.

C

You can also use **both/neither/either** alone:

- I couldn't decide which of the two shirts to buy. I liked **both**. (*or* I liked **both** of them.)
- 'Is your friend British or American?'   '**Neither**. She's Australian.'
- 'Do you want tea or coffee?'   '**Either**. I don't mind.'

D

You can say:

both...and...:	• **Both** Ann **and** Tom were late.
	• I was **both** tired **and** hungry when I arrived home.
neither...nor...:	• **Neither** Liz **nor** Robin came to the party.
	• She said she would contact me but she **neither** wrote **nor** phoned.
either...or...:	• I'm not sure where he's from. He's **either** Spanish **or** Italian.
	• **Either** you apologise **or** I'll never speak to you again.

E

Compare **either/neither/both** (*two things*) and **any/none/all** (*more than two*):

• There are **two** good hotels in the town. You can stay at **either** of them.	• There are **many** good hotels in the town. You can stay at **any** of them.
• We tried **two** hotels. **Neither** of them had any rooms. / **Both** of them were full.	• We tried **a lot of** hotels. **None** of them had any rooms. / **All** of them were full.

88.1 *Complete the sentences with* **both/neither/either**.

1 'Do you want tea or coffee?' '...**Either.**... I really don't mind.'
2 'What day is it today – the 18th or the 19th?' '............................. It's the 20th.'
3 'There are two sandwiches here. Do you mind which I take?' 'No, take ....'
4 A: Where did you go for your holidays – Scotland or Ireland?
   B: We went to .... A week in Scotland and a week in Ireland.
5 'When shall I phone you, morning or afternoon?' '............................. I'll be in all day.'
6 'Where's Kate? Is she at work or at home?' '............................. She's away on holiday.'

88.2 *Complete the sentences with* **both/neither/either**. *Use* of *where necessary*.

1 ...**Both (of)**... my parents are from London.
2 To get to the town centre, you can go along the footpath by the river or you can go along the
   road. You can go .... way.
3 I tried twice to phone George but .... times he was out.
4 .... Tom's parents is English. His father is Polish and his mother is Italian.
5 I saw an accident this morning. One car drove into the back of another. Fortunately
   .... driver was injured but .... cars were quite badly damaged.
6 I've got two sisters and a brother. My brother is working but .... my
   sisters are still at school.

88.3 *Complete the sentences with* **both/neither/either of us/them**.

1 I asked two people the way to the station but ....**neither of them**... could help me.
2 I was invited to two parties last week but I didn't go to ....
3 There were two windows in the room. It was very warm, so I opened ....
4 Sarah and I play tennis together regularly but .... can play very well.
5 I tried two bookshops for the book I wanted but .... had it.

88.4 *Write sentences with* **both...and...** / **neither...nor...** / **either...or...** .

1 Tom was late. So was Ann.   ...**Both Tom and Ann were late.**...
2 She didn't write and she didn't phone.   ...**She neither wrote nor phoned.**...
3 Jim is on holiday and so is Carol.   Both ....
4 George doesn't smoke and he doesn't drink.   ....
5 Jim hasn't got a car. Carol hasn't got a car either.   ....
6 It was a very boring film. It was very long too.   The film ....
7 Is that man's name Richard? Or is it Robert? It's one of the two.
   That man's name ....
8 I haven't got time to go on holiday. And I haven't got the money.
   I've got ....
9 We can leave today or we can leave tomorrow – whichever you prefer.
   We ....

88.5 *Complete the sentences with* **neither/either/none/any**.

1 We tried a lot of hotels but ....**none**... of them had any rooms.
2 I took two books with me on holiday but I didn't read .... of them.
3 I took five books with me on holiday but I didn't read .... of them.
4 There are a few shops at the end of the street but .... of them sell newspapers.
5 You can phone me at .... time during the evening. I'm always at home.
6 I can meet you on the 6th or 7th. Would .... of those days be convenient for you?
7 John and I couldn't get into the house because .... of us had a key.
8 There were a few letters this morning but .... of them were for me.

UNIT
89

All, every and whole

A   All and everybody/everyone
We do not normally use **all** to mean **everybody/everyone**:
- **Everybody** enjoyed the party. (*not* 'All enjoyed...')

But note that we say **all of us/you/them**, not 'everybody of...':
- **All of us** enjoyed the party. (*not* 'everybody of us')

B   All and everything
Sometimes you can use **all** or **everything**:
- I'll do **all I can** to help.   *or*   I'll do **everything I can** to help.

You can say 'all **I can**' / 'all **you need**' etc. but we do not normally use **all** *alone*:
- He thinks he knows **everything**. (*not* 'he knows all')
- Our holiday was a disaster. **Everything** went wrong. (*not* 'All went wrong')

We use **all** in the expression **all about**:
- They told us **all about** their holiday.

We also use **all** (*not* 'everything') to mean **the only thing**(s):
- **All** I've eaten today is a sandwich. (= the only thing I've eaten today)

C   **Every/everybody/everyone/everything** are *singular* words, so we use a *singular* verb:
- **Every seat** in the theatre **was** taken.
- **Everybody has** arrived. (*not* 'have arrived')

But we often use **they/them/their** after **everybody/everyone**:
- **Everybody** said **they** enjoyed **themselves**. (= he or she enjoyed himself or herself)

D   All and whole
Whole = complete, entire. Most often we use **whole** with *singular* nouns:
- Did you read **the whole book**? (= all the book, not just a part of it)
- She has lived **her whole life** in Scotland.

We normally use **the/my/her** etc. before **whole**. Compare **whole** and **all**:
   the whole book / **all the** book   **her whole** life / **all her** life
You can also use: **a whole...**:
- Jack was so hungry, he ate **a whole packet** of biscuits. (= a complete packet)

We do not normally use **whole** with *uncountable* nouns. We say:
- I've spent **all the money** you gave me. (*not* 'the whole money')

E   Every/all/whole with time words
We use **every** to say how often something happens. So we say **every day / every Monday / every ten minutes / every three weeks** etc.:
- When we were on holiday, we went to the beach **every day**. (*not* 'all days')
- The bus service is very good. There's a bus **every ten minutes**.
- Ann gets paid **every four weeks**.

All day / the whole day = the complete day from beginning to end:
- We spent **all day / the whole day** on the beach.
- He was very quiet. He didn't say a word **all evening / the whole evening**.

Note that we say **all day** (*not* 'all the day'), **all week** (*not* 'all the week') etc.

Compare **all the time** and **every time**:
- They never go out. They are at home **all the time**. (= always – *not* 'every time')
- **Every time** I see you, you look different. (= each time, on every occasion)

178   **All/all of** → UNIT 87   **Each and every** → UNIT 90   **Every one** → UNIT 90   **All** (word order) → UNIT 109C

EXERCISES

89.1 *Complete these sentences with* **all**, **everything** *or* **everybody/everyone**.

1 It was a good party. ...Everybody.... enjoyed it.
2 ...All... I've eaten today is a sandwich.
3 .... has got their faults. Nobody is perfect.
4 Nothing has changed. .... is the same as it was.
5 Margaret told me .... about her new job. It sounds quite interesting.
6 Can .... write their names on a piece of paper, please?
7 Why are you always thinking about money? Money isn't ....
8 I didn't have much money with me. .... I had was ten pounds.
9 When the fire alarm rang, ... left the building immediately.
10 She didn't say where she was going. .... she said was that she was going away.
11 We have completely different opinions. I disagree with .... she says.
12 We all did well in the examination. .... in our class passed.
13 We all did well in the examination. .... of us passed.
14 Why are you so lazy? Why do you expect me to do .... for you?

89.2 *Write sentences with* **whole**.

1 I read the book from beginning to end. ...I read the whole book....
2 Everyone in the team played well.   The ....
3 Paul opened a box of chocolates. When he finished eating, there were no chocolates left in the box.   He ate ....
4 The police came to the house. They were looking for something. They searched everywhere, every room.   They ....
5 Ann worked from early in the morning until late in the evening.
   ....
6 Everyone in Dave and Judy's family plays tennis. Dave and Judy play, and so do all their children.   The ....
7 Jack and Jill went on holiday to the seaside for a week. It rained from the beginning of the week to the end.   It ....

Now write sentences 5 and 7 again using **all** *instead of* **whole**.

8 (5) Ann ....
9 (7) ....

89.3 *Complete these sentences using* **every** *with one of the following:*
five minutes   ~~ten minutes~~   **four hours**   **six months**   **four years**

1 The bus service is very good. There's a bus ...every ten minutes....
2 Tom is ill. He has some medicine. He has to take it ....
3 The Olympic Games take place ....
4 We live near a busy airport. A plane flies over our house ....
5 It's a good idea to have a check-up with the dentist ....

89.4 *Which is the correct alternative?*

1 I've spent ~~the whole money~~ / all the money you gave me. (all the money *is correct*)
2 Sue works every day / all days except Sunday.
3 I'm tired. I've been working hard all the day / all day.
4 It was a terrible fire. Whole building / The whole building was destroyed.
5 I've been trying to phone her all day but every time / all the time I phone her the line is engaged.
6 I don't like the weather here. It rains every time / all the time.
7 When I was on holiday, all my luggage / my whole luggage was stolen.

Each and every

A Each and every are similar in meaning. Often it is possible to use **each** or **every**:

- **Each** time (*or* **Every** time) I see you, you look different.
- There's a telephone in **each** room (*or* **every** room) of the house.

But **each** and **every** are not exactly the same. Study the difference:

We use **each** when we think of things separately, one by one.	We use **every** when we think of things as a group. The meaning is similar to **all**.
• Study **each sentence** carefully. (= study the sentences one by one)	• **Every sentence** must have a verb. (= all sentences in general)
each = ✗ + ✗ + ✗ + ✗	every = (✗✗✗✗✗✗✗✗✗✗✗)
Each is more usual for a small number:	**Every** is more usual for a large number:
• There were four books on the table. **Each** book was a different colour.	• Carol loves reading. She has read **every book** in the library. (= all the books)
• (*in a card game*) At the beginning of the game, **each** player has three cards.	• I would like to visit **every country** in the world. (= all the countries)

Each (but not **every**) can be used for two things:

- In a football match, **each team** has 11 players. (*not* 'every team')

We use **every** (not **each**) to say how often something happens:

- 'How often do you go shopping?' '**Every day**.' (*not* 'each day')
- There's a bus **every ten minutes**. (*not* 'each ten minutes')

B Compare the structures we use with **each** and **every**:

You can use **each** with a noun:
   each book   **each student**
	You can use **every** with a noun:
	   every book **every student**

You can use **each** alone (without a noun): • None of the rooms was the same. **Each** was different. (= each room) Or you can use **each one**: • **Each one** was different.	You can say **every one** (but not **every** alone): • 'Have you read all these books?' 'Yes, **every one**.'
You can say **each of** (the.../these... etc.): • Read **each of these** sentences carefully. • **Each of the** books is a different colour. *Also* **each of us/you/them**: • **Each of them** is a different colour.	You can say **every one of**... (but not 'every of...') • I've read **every one of those** books. (*not* 'every of those books') • I've read **every one of them**.

C You can also use **each** in the middle or at the end of a sentence. For example:

- The students were **each** given a book. (= Each student was given a book.)
- These oranges cost 25 pence **each**.

D **Everyone** and **every one**

Everyone (one word) is only for people (= 'everybody'). **Every one** (two words) is for things or people, and is similar to **each one** (see Section B):

- **Everyone** enjoyed the party. (= Everybody...)
- He is invited to lots of parties and he goes to **every one**. (= to **every party**)

EXERCISES

90.1 *Look at the pictures and complete the sentences with **each** or **every**.*

1 ...Each... player has three cards.
2 Carol has read ...every... book in the library.
3 .... side of a square is the same length.
4 .... seat in the theatre was taken.
5 .... apartment has a balcony.

6 There's a train to London .... hour.
7 She was wearing four rings – one on .... finger.
8 Our football team has been very successful. We've won .... game this season.

90.2 *Put in **each** or **every**.*

1 There were four books on the table. ...Each... book was a different colour.
2 The Olympic Games are held ...every... four years.
3 .... parent worries about their children.
4 In a game of tennis there are two or four players. .... player has a racket.
5 Nicola plays volleyball .... Thursday evening.
6 I understood most of what they said but not .... word.
7 The book is divided into five parts and .... of these has three sections.
8 I get paid .... four weeks.
9 We had a great weekend. I enjoyed .... minute of it.
10 I tried to phone her two or three times, but .... time there was no reply.
11 Car seat belts save lives. .... driver should wear one.
12 (*from an examination paper*) Answer all five questions. Begin your answer to .... question on a separate sheet of paper.

90.3 *Complete the sentences using **each**.*

1 The price of one of those oranges is 25 pence. Those ...oranges are 25 pence each...
2 I had ten pounds and so did Sonia. Sonia and I ....
3 One of those postcards costs 40 pence. Those ....
4 The hotel was expensive. I paid £40 and so did you. We ....

90.4 *Put in **everyone** (one word) or **every one** (two words).*

1 He's invited to a lot of parties and he goes to ...every one...
2 As soon as .... had arrived, we began the meeting.
3 I asked her lots of questions and she answered .... correctly.
4 She's very popular. .... likes her.
5 I dropped a tray of glasses. Unfortunately .... broke.

Relative clauses (1) – clauses with **who/that/which**

A Look at this example sentence:

The woman | who lives next door | is a doctor.

└── *relative clause* ──┘

A *clause* is a part of a sentence. A *relative clause* tells us which person or thing (or what kind of person or thing) the speaker means:

- The woman **who lives next door**... ('who lives next door' tells us which woman)
- People **who live in London**... ('who live in London' tells us what kind of people)

We use **who** in a relative clause when we are talking about *people* (not things). We use **who** instead of **he/she/they**:

the woman – she lives next door – is a doctor

→   The woman **who lives next door** is a doctor.

we know a lot of people – they live in London

→   We know a lot of people   **who**   **live in London.**

- An architect is someone **who designs buildings.**
- What was the name of the man **who lent you the money**?
- Anyone **who wants to do the exam** must enter before next Friday.

You can also use **that** (instead of **who**):

- The man **that lives next door** is very friendly.

But sometimes you must use **who** (*not* 'that') for people – see Unit 94.

B When we are talking about *things*, we use **that** or **which** (*not* 'who') in a relative clause:

where is the cheese? – it was in the fridge

→   Where is the cheese { **that** / **which** } was in the fridge?

- I don't like stories **that have unhappy endings.** (*or* ...stories **which** have...)
- Barbara works for a company **that makes washing machines.** (*or* ...a company **which** makes...)
- The machine **that broke down** has now been repaired. (*or*...the machine **which** broke down...)

That is more usual than **which**. But sometimes you must use **which** (*not* 'that') – see Unit 94.

C You cannot use **what** in sentences like these:

- Everything **that happened** was my fault. (*not* 'Everything what happened...')

What = 'the thing(s) that':

- **What** happened was my fault. (= the thing that happened)

D Remember that in relative clauses we use **who/that/which** *instead of* **he/she/they/it**. So we say:

- Do you know the woman **who** lives next door? (*not* '...the woman *she* lives next door')

91.1 *In this exercise you have to explain what some words mean. Choose the right meaning from the box and then write a sentence with* **who.** *Use a dictionary if necessary.*

he/she	steals from a shop ~~designs buildings~~ doesn't believe in God is not brave	he/she	buys something from a shop pays rent to live in a house or flat breaks into a house to steal things no longer works and gets money from the state

1 (an architect)   ...*An architect is someone who designs buildings.*...
2 (a burglar)   A burglar is someone ....
3 (a customer)   ....
4 (a shoplifter)   ....
5 (a coward)   ....
6 (an atheist)   ....
7 (a pensioner)   ....
8 (a tenant)   ....

91.2 *Make one sentence from two. Use* **who/that/which.**

1 A girl was injured in the accident. She is now in hospital.
   ..*The girl who was injured in the accident is now in hospital.*..
2 A man answered the phone. He told me you were away.
   The man ....
3 A waitress served us. She was very impolite and impatient.
   The ....
4 A building was destroyed in the fire. It has now been rebuilt.
   ....
5 Some people were arrested. They have now been released.
   The ....
6 A bus goes to the airport. It runs every half hour.
   ....

91.3 *Complete the sentences. Choose the most suitable ending from the box and make it into a relative clause.*

he invented the telephone	~~it makes washing machines~~
she runs away from home	it gives you the meaning of words
they are never on time	it won the race
they stole my car	it can support life
they were on the wall	it cannot be explained

1 Barbara works for a company ...*that makes washing machines.*...
2 The book is about a girl ....
3 What was the name of the horse ....?
4 The police have caught the men ....
5 Alexander Bell was the man ....
6 What's happened to the pictures ....?
7 A mystery is something ....
8 A dictionary is a book ....
9 I don't like people ....
10 It seems that Earth is the only planet ....

Relative clauses (2) – clauses with or without
who/that/which

A Look again at these example sentences from Unit 91:

- The woman who lives next door is a doctor. (*or* The woman **that** lives…)

  The woman lives next door.   who (= the woman) is the *subject*

- Where is the cheese that was in the fridge? (*or* …the cheese **which** was…)

  The cheese was in the fridge.   that (= the cheese) is the *subject*

You must use **who/that/which** when it is the subject of the relative clause. You cannot say 'The woman lives next door is a doctor' or 'Where is the cheese was in the fridge?'

B Sometimes **who/that/which** is the *object* of the verb. For example:

- The woman who I wanted to see was away on holiday.

  I wanted to see the woman.   who (= the woman) is the *object*
  I is the *subject*

- Have you found the keys that you lost?

  You lost the keys.   that (= the keys) is the *object*.
  you is the *subject*

When **who/that/which** is the object, you can leave it out. So you can say:
- **The woman I wanted to see** was away. *or* The woman **who** I wanted to see…
- Have you found **the keys you lost**? *or* …the keys **that** you lost?
- **The dress Ann bought** doesn't fit her very well. *or* The dress **that** Ann bought…
- Is there **anything I can do**? *or* …anything **that** I can do?
Note that we say:
the keys you lost (*not* 'the keys you lost *them*')   **the dress Ann bought** (*not* 'bought *it*')

C Notice the position of prepositions (**in/at/with** etc.) in relative clauses:

do you know the woman? – Tom is talking to her

→   Do you know the woman (**who/that**) **Tom is talking to** ?

the bed – I slept in it last night – wasn't very comfortable

→   The bed (**that/which**) I slept in last night wasn't very comfortable.

- Are these the keys (that/which) **you were looking for**?
- The woman (who/that) **he fell in love with** left him after a few weeks.
- The man (who/that) **I was sitting next to on the plane** talked all the time.
In all these examples, you can leave out **who/that/which**.
Note that we say:
the books you were looking for (*not* 'the books you were looking for *them*')

D You cannot use **what** in sentences like these:
- Everything (that) **they said** was true. (*not* 'Everything what they said…')
- I gave her all the money (that) **I had**. (*not* '…all the money what I had')
What = the thing(s) that:
- Did you hear **what they said**? (= the things that they said)

92.1 *In some of these sentences you don't need* **who** *or* **that***. If you don't need these words, put them in brackets like this:* (**who**) (**that**)*.*

1 The woman **who** lives next door is a doctor.   (*'who' is necessary in this sentence*)
2 Have you found the keys (**that**) you lost.   (*in this sentence you don't need* 'that')
3 The people **who** we met at the party were very friendly.
4 The people **who** work in the office are very friendly.
5 The people **who** I talked to were very friendly.
6 What have you done with the money **that** I gave you?
7 What happened to the money **that** was on the table? Did you take it?
8 It was an awful film. It was the worst film **that** I've ever seen.
9 It was an awful experience. It was the worst thing **that** has ever happened to me.

92.2 *Complete these sentences with a relative clause. Use the sentences in the box to make your relative clauses.*

we hired a car	you're going to see a film	I invited some people to the party
Ann is wearing a dress	you had to do some work	Tom recommended a hotel to us
~~you lost some keys~~	we wanted to visit a museum	

1 Have you found the keys ...**you lost?**...
2 I like the dress ....
3 The museum .... was shut when we got there.
4 What's the name of the film ....?
5 Some of the people .... couldn't come.
6 Have you finished the work ....?
7 The car .... broke down after a few miles.
8 We stayed at a hotel ....

92.3 *Complete these sentences using a relative clause with a preposition.*

we went to a party last night	you can rely on George	we were invited to a wedding
I work with a number of people	I applied for a job	you told me about a hotel
~~you were looking for some keys~~	I saw you with a man	

1 Are these the keys ...**you were looking for?**...
2 Unfortunately we couldn't go to the wedding ....
3 I enjoy my job. I like the people ....
4 What's the name of that hotel ....?
5 The party .... wasn't very enjoyable.
6 I didn't get the job ....
7 George is a good person to know. He's somebody ....
8 Who was that man .... in the restaurant?

92.4 *Put in* **that** *or* **what***. If the sentence is complete with or without* **that***, write* (**that**) – *in brackets.*

1 I gave her all the money ...(**that**)... I had.
2 They give their children everything .... they want.
3 Tell me .... you want and I'll try to get it for you.
4 Why do you blame me for everything .... goes wrong?
5 I won't be able to do much but I'll do the best .... I can.
6 I can only lend you ten pounds. It's all .... I've got.
7 I don't agree with .... you've just said.
8 I don't trust him. I don't believe anything .... he says.

Relative clauses (3) – **whose/whom/where**

A Whose

We use **whose** in relative clauses instead of **his/her/their**:

> we saw some people – their car had broken down
>
> → We saw some people **whose** car had broken down.

We use **whose** mostly for people:

- A widow is a woman **whose husband is dead.** (**her** husband is dead)
- What's the name of the man **whose car you borrowed?** (you borrowed **his** car)
- A few days ago I met someone **whose brother I went to school with.** (I went to school with **his/her** brother)

Compare **who** and **whose**:

- I met a man **who** knows you. (*he* knows you)
- I met a man **whose sister** knows you. (*his sister* knows you)

B Whom

Whom is possible instead of **who** when it is the *object* of the verb in the relative clause (like the sentences in Unit 92B):

- The woman **whom I wanted to see** was away on holiday. (I wanted to see **her**)

You can also use **whom** with a preposition (**to whom / from whom / with whom** etc.):

- The woman **with whom he fell in love** left him after a few weeks. (he fell in love **with her**)

But we do not often use **whom**. In spoken English we usually prefer **who** or **that,** or nothing (see Unit 92). So we usually say:

- The man **I saw…**   *or*   The man **who/that** I saw…
- The woman **he fell in love with…**   *or*   The woman **who/that** he fell in love with…

For **whom** see also Units 94–95.

C Where

You can use **where** in a relative clause to talk about a place:

> the hotel – we stayed there – wasn't very clean
>
> → The hotel **where** we stayed wasn't very clean.

- I recently went back to **the town where I was born.** (*or* …the town I was born in. *or* …the town **that** I was born in.)
- I would like to live in **a country where there is plenty of sunshine.**

D

We say: **the day / the year / the time** (etc.) { something happens   *or*
                                                    that something happens

- Do you still remember **the day (that) we first met?**
- **The last time (that) I saw her,** she looked very well.
- I haven't seen them since **the year (that) they got married.**

E

We say: **the reason** { something happens   *or*
                          that/why something happens

- **The reason I'm phoning you** is to invite you to a party.
  (*or* The reason **that** I'm phoning… / The reason **why** I'm phoning…)

Relative clauses (1) and (2) → **UNITS 91–92**   Relative clauses (4) and (5) → **UNITS 94–95**

EXERCISES

93.1 *You met these people at a party:*

Later you tell a friend about the people you met. Complete the sentences using **who...** *or* **whose...** .

1 I met somebody ...whose mother writes detective stories.....

2 I met a man ....

3 I met a woman ....

4 I met somebody ....

5 I met a couple ....

6 I met somebody ....

93.2 Complete the sentences. Use the sentences in the box to make relative clauses with *where*.

I want to buy some postcards	I was born in a town
Ann bought a dress in a shop	we want to have a really good meal
John is staying at a hotel	we had the car repaired at a garage

1 I recently went back to the town ...where I was born.....

2 Do you know a restaurant..?

3 Is there a shop near here ....?

4 I can't remember the name of the garage ....

5 Do you know the name of the hotel...?

6 Ann bought a dress which didn't fit her, so she took it back to the shop...........................

93.3 *Complete each sentence using* **who/whom/whose/where**.

1 What's the name of the man ...whose... car you borrowed?

2 A cemetery is a place .... people are buried.

3 A pacifist is a person .... believes that all wars are wrong.

4 An orphan is a child .... parents are dead.

5 The place .... we spent our holidays was really beautiful.

6 This school is only for children .... first language is not English.

7 I don't know the name of the woman to .... I spoke on the phone.

93.4 *Use your own ideas to complete these sentences. They are like the ones in Sections D and E.*

1 I'll always remember the day ...I first met you....

2 I'll never forget the time ....

3 The reason .... was that I didn't know your address.

4 Unfortunately I wasn't at home the evening ....

5 The reason .... is that they don't need one.

6 1989 was the year ....

Relative clauses (4) – 'extra information' clauses (1)

A

There are two types of relative clause. In these examples, the relative clauses are <u>underlined</u>. Compare:

Type 1	Type 2
● The woman <u>who lives next door</u> is a doctor. ● Barbara works for a company <u>that makes washing machines</u>. ● We stayed at the hotel <u>(that) Ann recommended to us</u>.	● My brother Jim, <u>who lives in London</u>, is a doctor. ● Colin told me about his new job, <u>which he's enjoying very much</u>. ● We stayed at the Grand Hotel, <u>which Ann recommended to us</u>.
In these examples, the relative clause tells you *which* person or thing (or *what kind* of person or thing) the speaker means: 'The woman *who lives next door*' tells us *which* woman. 'A company *that makes washing machines*' tells us *what kind* of company. 'The hotel *(that) Ann recommended*' tells us *which* hotel.	In these examples, the relative clauses do *not* tell you which person or thing the speaker means. We *already know* which thing or person is meant: 'My brother Jim', 'Colin's new job' and 'the Grand Hotel'. The relative clauses in these sentences give us *extra information* about the person or thing.
We do not use commas (,) with these clauses: ● We know a lot of people <u>who live in London</u>. (*what kind* of people)	We use commas (,) in these clauses: ● My brother Jim, <u>who lives in London</u>, is a doctor. (*extra information* about Jim)

B

In both types of relative clause we use **who** for people and **which** for things. But:

Type 1	Type 2
You can use **that**: ● Do you know anyone **who/that** speaks French and Italian? ● Barbara works for a company **which/that** makes washing machines.	You cannot use **that**: ● John, **who** (*not* 'that') speaks French and Italian, works as a tourist guide. ● Colin told me about his new job, **which** (*not* 'that') he's enjoying very much.
You can leave out **that/who/which** when it is the object (see Unit 92): ● We stayed at the hotel (that/which) Ann recommended. ● This morning I met somebody (that/who) I hadn't seen for ages. We do not often use **whom** in this type of clause (see Unit 93B).	You cannot leave out **who** or **which**: ● We stayed at the Grand Hotel, **which** Ann recommended to us. You can use **whom** (when it is the object): ● This morning I met Diane, **whom** (or **who**) I hadn't seen for ages.

In both types of relative clause you can use **whose** and **where**:

● We met some people **whose** car had broken down. ● What's the name of the place **where** you spent your holiday?	● Amy, **whose** car had broken down, was in a very bad mood. ● Mrs Bond is going to spend a few weeks in Sweden, **where** her daughter lives.

94.1 *Make one sentence from two. Use the sentence in brackets to make a relative clause (Type 2). Sometimes the clause goes in the middle of the sentence, sometimes at the end. You will need to use* **who(m)/whose/which/where**.

1 Ann is very friendly. (She lives next door.) ...Ann, who lives next door, is very friendly...
2 We stayed at the Grand Hotel. (Ann recommended it to us.)
  We stayed at the Grand Hotel, which Ann recommended to us.
3 We went to Sandra's party. (We enjoyed it very much.)
  We went to Sandra's party, ...
4 I went to see the doctor. (He told me to rest for a few days.)
  ....
5 John is one of my closest friends. (I have known him for a very long time.)
  John ....
6 Sheila is away from home a lot. (Her job involves a lot of travelling.)
  ....
7 The new stadium will be opened next month. (It can hold 90,000 people.)
  The ....
8 We often go to visit our friends in Bristol. (It is only 30 miles away.)
  ....
9 Glasgow is the largest city in Scotland. (My brother lives there.)
  ....

94.2 *Read the information and complete the sentences. Use a relative clause. Sometimes the clause tells us which thing or person (Type 1); sometimes it only gives us extra information (Type 2). Use commas where necessary.*

1 There's a woman living next door. She's a doctor.
  The woman ...who lives next door is a doctor...
2 I've got a brother called Jim. He lives in London. He's a doctor.
  My brother Jim *,* who lives in London *,* is a doctor...
3 There was a strike at the car factory. It lasted ten days. It is now over.
  The strike at the car factory ....
4 I was looking for a book this morning. I've found it now.
  I've found ....
5 London was once the largest city in the world, but the population is now falling.
  The population of London ....
6 A job was advertised. A lot of people applied for it. Few of them had the necessary
  qualifications. Few of ....
7 Margaret has a son. She showed me a photograph of him. He's a policeman.
  Margaret showed me ....

94.3 *In some of these sentences you can use* **which** *or* **that**; *in others, only* **which** *is possible. Cross out* **that** *if only* **which** *is possible. Also, put commas (,) where necessary.*

1 Jane works for a company ✓which / ✓that makes shoes. (*both possible, no commas*)
2 Colin told me about his new job **,** which / ~~that~~ he's enjoying very much. (*only* which *is possible; comma necessary*)
3 My office   which / that is on the second floor of the building   is very small.
4 The office   which / that I'm using at the moment   is very small.
5 She told me her address   which / that I wrote down on a piece of paper.
6 There are some words   which / that are very difficult to translate.
7 The sun   which / that is one of millions of stars in the universe   provides us with heat and light.

Relative clauses (5) – 'extra information' clauses (2)

A

Prepositions + **whom/which**

In 'extra information' clauses (see Unit 94 – Type 2) you can use a preposition before **whom** (for people) and **which** (for things). So you can say:

to whom / with whom / about which / for which etc.:

- Mr Carter, **to whom** I spoke on the phone last night, is very interested in our plan.
- Fortunately we had a map, **without which** we would have got lost.

In spoken English we often keep the preposition after the verb in the relative clause. When we do this, we normally use **who** (*not* 'whom') for people:

- This is Mr Carter, **who** I was telling you **about**.
- Yesterday we visited the City Museum, **which** I'd never been **to** before.

B

All of / most of etc. + **whom/which**

Study these examples:

> Mary has three brothers. All of them are married. (*2 sentences*)
> → Mary has three brothers, **all of whom** are married. (*1 sentence*)
>
> They asked me a lot of questions. I couldn't answer most of them. (*2 sentences*)
> → They asked me a lot of questions, **most of which** I couldn't answer. (*1 sentence*)

In the same way you can say:

none of / neither of / any of / either of
some of / many of / much of / (a) few of   } + **whom** (people)
both of / half of / each of / one of / two of (etc.)   } + **which** (things)

- Tom tried on three jackets, **none of which** fitted him.
- Two men, **neither of whom** I had ever seen before, came into my office.
- They've got three cars, **two of which** they never use.
- Sue has a lot of friends, **many of whom** she was at school with.

C

Which (*not* 'what')

Study this example:

| Jim passed his driving test. | This | surprised everybody. (*2 sentences*) |

| Jim passed his driving test, | which | surprised everybody. (*1 sentence*) |
—— relative clause ——

In this example, **which** = 'the fact that he passed his driving test'. You must use **which** (*not* 'what') in sentences like these:

- Sheila couldn't come to the party, **which** was a pity. (*not* '...what was a pity')
- The weather was very good, **which** we hadn't expected. (*not* '...what we hadn't expected')

For **what**, see also Units 91C and 92D.

95.1 *Make two sentences from one using a relative clause. Use the sentence in brackets to make the relative clause.*

1 Mr Carter is very interested in our plan. (I spoke to him on the phone last night.)
   ...Mr Carter, to whom I spoke on the phone last night, is very interested in our plan...
2 This is a photograph of our friends. (We went on holiday with these friends.)
   This is a photograph ....
3 The wedding took place last Friday. (Only members of the family were invited to it.)
   The wedding ....
4 Sheila finally arrived. (We had been waiting for her.)
   ....
5 We climbed to the top of the tower. (We had a beautiful view from there.)
   ....

95.2 *Write sentences with* **all of / most of** *etc.* + **whom/which**.

1 Mary has three brothers. (All of her brothers are married.)
   ...Mary has three brothers, all of whom are married...
2 We were given a lot of information. (Most of the information was useless.)
   We were given ....
3 There were a lot of people at the party. (I had met only a few of these people before.)
   ....
4 I have sent her two letters. (She has received neither of these letters.)
   ....
5 Ten people applied for the job. (None of these people were suitable.)
   ....
6 Kate has got two cars. (She hardly ever uses one of them.)
   ....
7 Norman won £50,000. (He gave half of this to his parents.)
   ....
8 Julia has two sisters. (Both of her sisters are teachers.)

95.3 *Join a sentence from Box A with a sentence from Box B to make a new sentence. Use* **which**.

A	B
1 ~~Sheila couldn't come to the party.~~	This was very nice of her.
2 Jill isn't on the phone.	This means we can't go away tomorrow.
3 Neil has passed his examinations.	This makes it difficult to contact her.
4 Our flight was delayed.	This makes it difficult to sleep.
5 Ann offered to let me stay in her house.	~~This was a pity.~~
6 The street I live in is very noisy at night.	This is good news.
7 Our car has broken down.	This meant we had to wait four hours at the airport.

1 Sheila couldn't come to the party, ...which was a pity...
2 Jill isn't ....
3 ....
4 ....
5 ....
6 ....
7 ....

-ing and -ed clauses (the woman **talking to Tom**, the boy **injured in the accident**)

A A *clause* is a part of a sentence. Some clauses begin with **-ing** or **-ed**. For example:

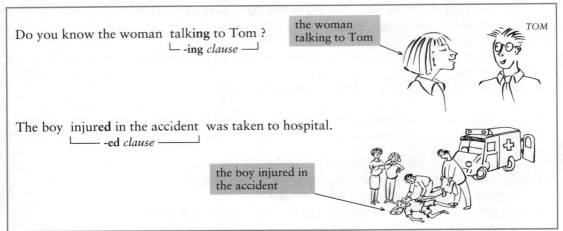

Do you know the woman talking to Tom ?
└── -ing *clause* ──┘

the woman
talking to Tom

TOM

The boy injured in the accident was taken to hospital.
└───── -ed *clause* ─────┘

the boy injured in
the accident

B We use **-ing** clauses to say what somebody (or something) is doing (or was doing) at a particular time:

- Do you know the woman **talking to Tom?** (the woman **is talking to Tom**)
- Police **investigating the crime** are looking for three men. (police **are investigating the crime**)
- Who were those people **waiting outside?** (they **were waiting**)
- I was woken up by a bell **ringing.** (a bell **was ringing**)

When you are talking about *things* (and sometimes people), you can use an **-ing** clause to say what something does all the time, not just at a particular time. For example:

- The road **joining the two villages** is very narrow. (the road **joins** the two villages)
- I live in a pleasant room **overlooking the garden.** (the room **overlooks** the garden)
- Can you think of the name of a flower **beginning with 'T'?** (the name **begins** with 'T')

C **-ed** clauses have a *passive* meaning:

- The boy **injured in the accident** was taken to hospital. (the boy **was injured** in the accident)
- Some of the people **invited to the party** can't come. (the people **have been invited** to the party)

Injured and **invited** are *past participles*. Many verbs have past participles that do *not* end in **-ed** (**made, bought, stolen** etc.):

- Most of the goods **made in this factory** are exported. (the goods **are made...**)
- The police never found the money **stolen in the robbery.** (the money **was stolen**)

You can use **left** in this way, with the meaning 'not used, still there':

- We've spent nearly all our money. We've only got a little **left.**

For irregular past participles, see Appendix 1.

D We often use **-ing** and **-ed** clauses after **there is / there was** etc.:

- **There were** some children **swimming** in the river.
- **Is there** anybody **waiting?**
- **There was** a big red car **parked** outside the house.

96.1 *Make one sentence from two. Use the information in brackets to make an* **-ing** *clause.*
Sometimes the **-ing** *clause goes in the middle of the new sentence; sometimes it goes at the end.*

1 I was woken up by a bell. (The bell was ringing.) ...I was woken up by a bell ringing...

2 I didn't talk much to the man. (The man was sitting next to me on the plane.)

....

3 The taxi broke down. (The taxi was taking us to the airport.)
The ....

4 At the end of the street there is a path. (The path leads to the river.)

....

5 A new factory has just opened in the town. (The factory employs 500 people.)

....

6 The company sent me a brochure. (The brochure contained all the information I needed.)

....

96.2 *Make one sentence from two, beginning as shown. Each time make an* **-ed** *clause.*

1 A boy was injured in the accident. He was taken to hospital.
...The boy injured in the accident was taken to hospital...

2 A window was broken in the storm last night. It has now been repaired.
The window .... repaired.

3 A number of suggestions were made at the meeting. Most of them were not very practical.
Most of the suggestions ....

4 Some paintings were stolen from the museum. They haven't been found yet.
The ....

5 A man was arrested by the police. What was his name?
What was the name ....

96.3 *Complete the sentences using one of the following verbs in the correct form:*

blow   call   ~~invite~~   live   offer   read   ~~ring~~   sit   study   work

1 I was woken up by a bell ...ringing...

2 A lot of the people ...invited... to the party cannot come.

3 Life must be very unpleasant for people .... near busy airports.

4 A few days after the interview, I received a letter .... me the job.

5 Somebody .... Jack phoned while you were out.

6 There was a tree .... down in the storm last night.

7 When I entered the waiting room it was empty except for a young man .... by
the window .... a magazine.

8 Ian has got a brother .... in a bank in London and a sister ....
economics at university in Manchester.

96.4 *Use the words in brackets to make sentences using* **there is** / **there was** *etc.*

1 That house is empty. (nobody / live / in it) ...There's nobody living in it...

2 The accident wasn't serious. (nobody / injure) ...There was nobody injured...

3 I can hear footsteps. (somebody / come) There ....

4 The train was full. (a lot of people / travel) ....

5 We were the only guests at the hotel. (nobody else / stay there)

....

6 The piece of paper was blank. (nothing / write / on it)

....

7 There are regular English courses at the college. (a course / begin / next Monday)

....

Adjectives ending in **-ing** and **-ed** (**boring/bored** etc.)

A There are many adjectives ending in **-ing** and **-ed**. For example, **boring** and **bored**. Study this example situation:

bored

boring

Jane has been doing the same job for a very long time. Every day she does exactly the same thing again and again. She doesn't enjoy it any more and would like to do something different.

Jane's job is **boring**.

Jane is **bored** (with her job).

Somebody is **bored** if something (or somebody else) is **boring**. Or, if something is **boring**, it makes you **bored**. So:
- Jane is **bored** because her job is **boring**.
- Jane's job is **boring**, so Jane is **bored**. (*not* 'Jane is boring')

If a *person* is **boring**, this means that they make other people **bored**:
- George always talks about the same things. He's really **boring**.

B Compare adjectives ending in **-ing** and **-ed**:

You can say:	You can say:
• My job is { boring. interesting. tiring. satisfying. depressing. (etc.)	• I'm **bored** with my job. • I'm not **interested** in my job any more. • I'm always **tired** when I finish work. • I'm not **satisfied** with my job. • My job makes me **depressed**. (etc.)
The **-ing** adjective tells you about the job.	The **-ed** adjective tells you how somebody feels (about the job).

Compare these examples:

interesting
- Julia thinks politics is very **interesting**.

- Did you meet anyone **interesting** at the party?

surprising
- It was quite **surprising** that he passed the examination.

disappointing
- The film was **disappointing**. I expected it to be much better.

shocking
- The news was **shocking**.

interested
- Julia is very **interested** in politics. (*not* 'interesting in politics')
- Are you **interested** in buying a car? I'm trying to sell mine.

surprised
- Everybody was **surprised** that he passed the examination.

disappointed
- I was **disappointed** with the film. I expected it to be much better.

shocked
- We were very **shocked** when we heard the news.

97.1 *Complete the sentences for each situation. Use the word given + the ending -ing or -ed.*

1 The film wasn't as good as we had expected. (**disappoint-**)
  a The film was ...**disappointing.**...
  b We were ...**disappointed**... with the film.

2 Diana teaches young children. It's a very hard job but she enjoys it. (**exhaust-**)
  a She enjoys her job but it's often ....
  b At the end of a day's work, she is often ....

3 It's been raining all day. I hate this weather. (**depress-**)
  a This weather is ....
  b This weather makes me ....
  c It's silly to get .... because of the weather.

4 Clare is going to the United States next month. She has never been there before. (**excit-**)
  a It will be an .... experience for her.
  b Going to new places is always ....
  c She is really .... about going to the United States.

97.2 *Choose the correct word.*

1 I was ~~disappointing~~ / disappointed with the film. I had expected it to be better.
2 Are you interesting / interested in football?
3 The football match was quite exciting / excited. I enjoyed it.
4 It's sometimes embarrassing / embarrassed when you have to ask people for money.
5 Do you easily get embarrassing / embarrassed?
6 I had never expected to get the job. I was really amazing / amazed when I was offered it.
7 She has really learnt very fast. She has made astonishing / astonished progress.
8 I didn't find the situation funny. I was not amusing / amused.
9 It was a really terrifying / terrified experience. Afterwards everybody was very shocking / shocked.
10 Why do you always look so boring / bored? Is your life really so boring / bored?
11 He's one of the most boring / bored people I've ever met. He never stops talking and he never says anything interesting / interested.

97.3 *Complete the sentences using one of the words in the box.*

amusing / amused	confusing / confused	exhausting / exhausted
annoying / annoyed	disgusting / disgusted	interesting / interested
boring / bored	exciting / excited	~~surprising / surprised~~

1 He works very hard. It's not ...**surprising**.... that he's always tired.
2 I've got nothing to do. I'm ....
3 The teacher's explanation was .... Most of the students didn't understand it.
4 The kitchen hadn't been cleaned for ages. It was really ....
5 I seldom visit art galleries. I'm not particularly .... in art.
6 There's no need to get .... just because I'm a few minutes late.
7 The lecture was .... I fell asleep.
8 I asked Emily if she wanted to come out with us but she wasn't ....
9 I've been working very hard all day and now I'm ....
10 I'm starting a new job next week. I'm quite .... about it.
11 Tom is very good at telling funny stories. He can be very ....
12 Liz is a very .... person. She knows a lot, she's travelled a lot and she's done lots of different things.

Adjectives: word order (a **nice new** house)
Adjectives after verbs (You **look tired**)

A Sometimes we use two or more adjectives together:
- My brother lives in a **nice new** house.
- In the kitchen there was a **beautiful large round wooden** table.

Adjectives like **new/large/round/wooden** are *fact* adjectives. They give us factual information about age, size, colour etc.

Adjectives like **nice/beautiful** are *opinion* adjectives. They tell us what somebody thinks of something or somebody.

Opinion adjectives usually go before *fact* adjectives.

	opinion	fact	
a	nice	long	summer holiday
an	interesting	young	man
	delicious	hot	vegetable soup
a	beautiful	large round wooden	table

B Sometimes we use two or more *fact* adjectives. Very often (but not always) we put *fact* adjectives in this order:

1 how big?	→	2 how old?	→	3 what colour?	→	4 where from?	→	5 what is it made of?	——→	NOUN

    a **tall young** man (1 → 2)   a **large wooden** table (1 → 5)
    big blue eyes (1 → 3)   an **old Russian** song (2 → 4)
    a **small black plastic** bag (1 → 3 → 5)   an **old white cotton** shirt (2 → 3 → 5)

Adjectives of size and length (**big/small/tall/short/long** etc.) usually go before adjectives of shape and width (**round/fat/thin/slim/wide** etc.):
    a **large round** table   a **tall thin** girl   a **long narrow** street

When there are two colour adjectives, we use **and**:
    a black **and** white dress   a red, white **and** green flag
but   a **long black** dress (*not* 'a long and black dress')

C We say 'the **first two** days', 'the **next few** weeks' , 'the **last ten** minutes' etc.:
- I didn't enjoy the **first two** days of the course. (*not* 'the two first days')
- They'll be away for the **next few** weeks. (*not* 'the few next weeks')

D We use adjectives after **be/get/become/seem**:
- **Be careful!**   • I'm **tired** and I'm **getting hungry**.
- As the film went on, it **became** more and more **boring**.
- Your friend **seems** very **nice**.

We also use adjectives to say how somebody/something looks, feels, sounds, tastes or smells:
- You **look** tired. / I **feel** tired. / She **sounds** tired.
- The dinner **smells good**.   • This tea **tastes** a bit **strange**.

But to say how somebody does something you must use an *adverb* (see Units 99–100):
- Drive **carefully**! (*not* 'Drive careful')
- Susan plays the piano very **well**. (*not* 'plays...very good')

EXERCISES

98.1 *Put the adjectives in brackets in the correct position.*

1 a beautiful table (wooden / round) ...a beautiful round wooden table...
2 an unusual ring (gold) ....
3 a new pullover (nice) ....
4 a new pullover (green) ....
5 an old house (beautiful) ....
6 black gloves (leather) ....
7 an American film (old) ....
8 a long face (thin) ....
9 big clouds (black) ....
10 a sunny day (lovely) ....
11 a wide avenue (long) ....
12 a metal box (black / small) ....
13 a big cat (fat / black) ....
14 a little village (old / lovely) ....
15 long hair (black / beautiful) ....
16 an old painting (interesting / French) ....
17 an enormous umbrella (red / yellow) ....

98.2 *Write the following in another way using* **the first... / the next... / the last...** .

1 the first day and the second day of the course ...the first two days of the course...
2 next week and the week after ...the next two weeks...
3 yesterday and the day before yesterday ....
4 the first week and the second week of September ....
5 tomorrow and a few days after that ....
6 questions 1, 2 and 3 of the examination ....
7 next year and the year after ....
8 the last day of our holiday and the two days before that ....

98.3 *Complete each sentence with a verb (in the correct form) and an adjective from the boxes.*

feel	look	~~seem~~
smell	sound	taste

awful	fine	interesting
nice	~~upset~~	wet

1 Ann ...seemed upset... this morning. Do you know what was wrong?
2 I can't eat this. I've just tried it and it ....
3 I wasn't very well yesterday but I .... today.
4 What beautiful flowers! They .... too.
5 You .... Have you been out in the rain?
6 Jim was telling me about his new job. It .... quite ....,
   much better than his old job.

98.4 *Choose the correct word.*

1 This tea tastes a bit ...strange... (strange/strangely)
2 I always feel .... when the sun is shining. (happy/happily)
3 The children were playing .... in the garden. (happy/happily)
4 The man became .... when the manager of the restaurant asked him to leave.
   (violent/violently)
5 You look ....! Are you all right? (terrible/terribly)
6 There's no point in doing a job if you don't do it .... (proper/properly)

Adjectives and adverbs (1) (**quick/quickly**)

A Look at these examples:
- Our holiday was too short – the time went very **quickly**.
- The driver of the car was **seriously** injured in the accident.

Quickly and **seriously** are *adverbs*. Many adverbs are made from an adjective + **-ly**:

adjective: quick serious careful quiet heavy bad
adverb: quick**ly** serious**ly** careful**ly** quiet**ly** heavi**ly** bad**ly**

For spelling, see Appendix 6.

Not all words ending in **-ly** are adverbs. Some *adjectives* end in **-ly** too, for example:
friendly   lively   elderly   lonely   silly   lovely

B *Adjective* or *adverb*?

Adjectives (**quick/careful** etc.) tell us about a *noun*. We use adjectives before nouns and after some verbs, especially **be**:	Adverbs (**quickly/carefully** etc.) tell us about a *verb*. An adverb tells us how somebody does something or how something happens:
• Tom is a **careful driver**. (*not* 'a carefully driver')	• Tom **drove carefully** along the narrow road. (*not* 'drove careful')
• We didn't go out because of the **heavy rain**.	• We didn't go out because it was **raining heavily**. (*not* 'raining heavy')
• Please **be quiet**.	• Please **speak quietly**. (*not* 'speak quiet')
• I was disappointed that my exam results **were** so **bad**.	• I was disappointed that I **did** so **badly** in the exam. (*not* 'did so bad')
We also use adjectives after the verbs **look/feel/sound** etc. (see Unit 98D):	
• Why do you always **look** so **serious**?	• Why do you never take me **seriously**?
Compare:	
• She speaks **perfect English**. *adjective + noun*	• She **speaks** English **perfectly**. *verb + object + adverb*
Compare these sentences with **look**:	
• Tom **looked sad** when I saw him. (= he seemed sad, his expression was sad)	• Tom **looked** at me **sadly**. (= he looked at me in a sad way)

C We also use adverbs before *adjectives* and *other adverbs*. For example:

reasonably cheap   (*adverb + adjective*)
terribly sorry   (*adverb + adjective*)
incredibly quickly   (*adverb + adverb*)

- It's a **reasonably cheap** restaurant and the food is **extremely good**.
- Oh, I'm **terribly sorry**. I didn't mean to push you. (*not* 'terrible sorry')
- Maria learns languages **incredibly quickly**.
- The examination was **surprisingly easy**.

You can also use an adverb before a *past participle* (**injured/organised/written** etc.):
- Two people were **seriously injured** in the accident. (*not* 'serious injured')
- The meeting was very **badly organised**.

99.1 *Complete the sentences with adverbs. The first letter(s) of each adverb are given.*

1 We didn't go out because it was raining **heavily.**
2 Our team lost the game because we played very **ba**........................ .
3 I had little difficulty finding a place to live. I found a flat quite **ea**........................ .
4 We had to wait for a long time but we didn't complain. We waited **pa**........................ .
5 Nobody knew George was coming to see us. He arrived **unex**........................ .
6 Mike keeps fit by playing tennis **reg**........................ .

99.2 *Put in the right word.*

1 The driver of the car was ...**seriously**... injured. (serious/seriously)
2 The driver of the car had ...**serious**.... injuries. (serious/seriously)
3 I think you behaved very .... (selfish/selfishly)
4 Rose is .... upset about losing her job. (terrible/terribly)
5 There was a .... change in the weather. (sudden/suddenly)
6 Everybody at the party was .... dressed. (colourful/colourfully)
7 Linda likes wearing .... clothes. (colourful/colourfully)
8 She fell and hurt herself quite .... (bad/badly)
9 He says he didn't do well at school because he was .... taught. (bad/badly)
10 Don't go up that ladder. It doesn't look .... (safe/safely)
11 He looked at me .... when I interrupted him. (angry/angrily)

99.3 *Complete each sentence using a word from the list. Sometimes you need the adjective* (**careful** *etc.*) *and sometimes the adverb* (**carefully** *etc.*).

careful(ly)	complete(ly)	continuous(ly)	financial(ly)	fluent(ly)
happy/happily	nervous(ly)	perfect(ly)	~~quick(ly)~~	special(ly)

1 Our holiday was too short. The time passed very ...**quickly.**...
2 Tom doesn't take risks when he's driving. He's always ....
3 Sue works .... She never seems to stop.
4 Alice and Stan are very .... married.
5 Monica's English is very .... although she makes quite a lot of mistakes.
6 I cooked this meal .... for you, so I hope you like it.
7 Everything was very quiet. There was .... silence.
8 I tried on the shoes and they fitted me ....
9 Do you usually feel .... before examinations?
10 I'd like to buy a car but it's .... impossible for me at the moment.

99.4 *Choose two words (one from each box) to complete each sentence.*

absolutely	~~reasonably~~	unusually
badly	seriously	unnecessarily
completely	slightly	

~~cheap~~	enormous	planned
changed	ill	quiet
damaged	long	

1 I thought the restaurant would be expensive but it was ...**reasonably cheap.**...
2 George's mother is .... in hospital.
3 What a big house! It's ....
4 It wasn't a serious accident. The car was only ....
5 The children are normally very lively but they're .... today.
6 When I returned home after 20 years, everything had ....
7 The film was .... It could have been much shorter.
8 A lot went wrong during our holiday because it was ....

Adjectives and adverbs (2) (**well/fast/late**, **hard/hardly**)

A   **Good/well**

Good is an *adjective*. The *adverb* is **well**:

- Your English is **good**.   *but*   You **speak** English **well**.
- Susan is a **good** pianist.   *but*   Susan **plays** the piano **well**.

We use **well** (*not* 'good') with *past participles* (**dressed/known** etc.):

well-dressed   well-known   well-educated   well-paid

But **well** is also an *adjective* with the meaning 'in good health':

- 'How are you today?'   'I'm very **well**, thanks.' (*not* 'I'm very good')

B   **Fast/hard/late**

These words are both adjectives and adverbs:

adjective	*adverb*
• Jack is a very **fast** runner.	Jack can **run** very **fast**.
• Ann is a **hard** worker.	Ann **works hard**. (*not* 'works hardly')
• The train was **late**.	I **got up late** this morning.

Lately = 'recently'

- Have you seen Tom **lately**?

C   **Hardly**

Hardly = very little, almost not. Study these examples:

- Sarah was rather unfriendly to me at the party. She **hardly** spoke to me.
  (= she spoke to me very little, almost not at all)
- George and Hilda want to get married but they've only known each other for a few days. I don't think they should get married yet. They **hardly** know each other.
  (= they know each other very little)

Hard and **hardly** are completely different. Compare:

- He tried **hard** to find a job but he had no luck. (= he tried a lot, with a lot of effort)
- I'm not surprised he didn't find a job. He **hardly** tried to find one. (= he tried very little)

We often use **hardly + any/anybody/anyone/anything/anywhere**:

There's hardly anything in the fridge.

- A: How much money have you got?
  B: **Hardly any**. (= very little, almost none)
- I'll have to go shopping. We've got **hardly any** food.
- The exam results were very bad. **Hardly anybody** in our class passed. (= very few students passed, almost nobody passed)
- She ate **hardly anything**. She wasn't feeling hungry. (= she ate very little, almost nothing)

Note the position of **hardly**. You can say:

- She ate **hardly anything**.   *or*   She **hardly** ate **anything**.
- We've got **hardly any** food.   *or*   We've **hardly** got **any** food.

We often use **can/could + hardly**. I **can hardly** do something = it's almost impossible for me to do it:

- Your writing is terrible. I **can hardly** read it. (= it is almost impossible for me to read it)
- My leg was hurting me. I **could hardly** walk.

Hardly ever = almost never

- I'm nearly always at home in the evenings. I **hardly ever** go out.

EXERCISES

100.1 *Put in* **good** *or* **well**.

1 I play tennis but I'm not very ...**good.**...
2 Your exam results were very ....
3 You did very .... in your exams.
4 The weather was very .... while
   we were on holiday.
5 I didn't sleep very .... last night.
6 How are you? Are you .... ?
7 George speaks German very ....
8 George's German is very ....
9 Our new business is going very
   .... at the moment.
10 I like your jacket. It looks .... on you.
11 I've met her a few times but I don't
   know her very ....

100.2 *Complete these sentences using* **well** + *one of the following words:*
balanced ~~**behaved**~~ **done** **dressed** **informed** **kept** **known** **paid**

1 The children were very good.   They were ...**well-behaved.**...
2 I'm surprised you haven't heard of her.   She is quite ....
3 Our neighbours' garden is neat and tidy.   It is very ....
4 You should eat different types of food.   Your diet should be ....
5 Ann knows a lot about many things.   She is quite ....
6 His clothes are always smart.   He is always ....
7 Jill has a lot of responsibility in her job but she isn't very ....
8 Congratulations on passing your examinations.   ....!

100.3 *Are the underlined words right or wrong? Correct the ones that are wrong.*

1 I'm tired because I've been working <u>hard</u>.   ...**RIGHT**...
2 I tried <u>hard</u> to remember her name but I couldn't. ....
3 This coat is practically unused. I've <u>hardly</u> worn it. ....
4 She's a good tennis player. She hits the ball <u>hardly</u>. ....
5 Don't walk so <u>fast</u>! I can't keep up with you. ....
6 Why are you walking so <u>slow</u>? Are you tired? ....

100.4 *Write sentences with* **hardly**. *Use one of the following verbs (in the correct form):*
change **hear** ~~**know**~~ **recognise** **say** **sleep** **speak**

1 George and Hilda have only met once before. They ...**hardly know**... each other.
2 You're speaking very quietly. I can .... you.
3 I'm very tired this morning. I .... last night.
4 We were so shocked when we heard the news, we could ....
5 Kate was very quiet this evening. She .... a word.
6 You look the same now as you looked 15 years ago. You've ....
7 I met Keith a few days ago. I hadn't seen him for a long time and he looks very different now.
   I .... him.

100.5 *Complete these sentences with* **hardly** + **any/anybody/anything/anywhere/ever**.

1 I'll have to go shopping. We've got ...**hardly any**... food.
2 It was a very warm day and there was .... wind.
3 'Do you know much about computers?'   'No, ...'
4 The hotel was almost empty. There was .... staying there.
5 I listen to the radio quite often but I .... watch television.
6 Our new boss is not very popular.   .... likes her.
7 It was very crowded in the room. There was .... to sit.
8 We used to be good friends but we .... see each other now.
9 It was nice driving this morning. There was .... traffic.
10 I hate this town. There's .... to do and .... to go.

So and such

A Study these examples:

● I didn't enjoy the book. The story was **so** stupid.	● I didn't enjoy the book. It was **such** a stupid story.

We use **so** + *adjective/adverb*:
  so stupid   **so quick**
  so nice   **so quickly**
	We use **such** + *noun*:
	  such a story **such people**
	We use **such** + *adjective* + *noun*:
	  such a stupid story **such nice people**
	Note that we say **such a...** (*not* 'a such...')

B **So** and **such** make the meaning of an adjective (or adverb) stronger:

● It's a lovely day, isn't it? It's **so warm**.
  (= really warm)
● He's difficult to understand because he
  speaks **so quickly**.
Compare **so** and **such** in these sentences:
● I like Tom and Ann. They are **so nice**.
	● We enjoyed our holiday. We had **such
	  a good time**. (= a really good time)
	
	● I like Tom and Ann. They are **such nice
	  people**. (*not* 'so nice people')

You can use **so...that...**:
● The book was **so good that** I couldn't
  put it down.
● I was **so tired that** I fell asleep in the
  armchair.
You can leave out **that** in sentences like this:
● I was **so tired** (that) I fell asleep.
	You can use **such...that...**:
	● It was **such a good book that** I couldn't
	  put it down.
	● It was **such lovely weather that** we
	  spent the whole day on the beach.
	
	● It was **such lovely weather** (that) we...

C We also use **so** and **such** with the meaning 'like this':

● I was surprised to find out that the house
  was built 100 years ago. I didn't realise it
  was **so old**. (as old as it is)
● I expected the weather to be much cooler.
  I didn't expect it to be **so warm**.
● I'm tired because I got up at 6 o'clock.
  I don't usually get up **so early**.
	● I didn't realise it was **such an old house**.
	● The house was so untidy. I've never seen
	  such a mess. (= a mess like this)
	
	Note the expression **no such...**:
	● You won't find the word 'blid' in an
	  English dictionary because there is **no
	  such word**. (= this word does not exist)

D

We say: **so long** *but* **such a** long **time**:
● I haven't seen her for **so long** I've
  forgotten what she looks like.
so far *but* **such a** long **way**:
● I didn't know it was **so far**.
so much, so many *but* **such a lot** (of):
● Why did you buy **so much** food?
	● I haven't seen her for **such a long time**.
	  (*not* 'a so long time')
	
	● I didn't know it was **such a long way**.
	
	● Why did you buy **such a lot** of food?

Not so...as → UNIT 106A   Such as → UNIT 116B

EXERCISES

101.1 *Put in* **so,** **such** *or* **such a.**

1 He's difficult to understand because he speaks ...**so**... quickly.
2 I like Tom and Ann. They're ...**such**... nice people.
3 It was a great holiday. We had ...**such a**... good time.
4 I was surprised that he looked .... well after his recent illness.
5 Everything is .... expensive these days, isn't it?
6 The weather is lovely, isn't it? I didn't expect it to be .... nice day.
7 I have to go. I didn't realise it was .... late.
8 He always looks good. He wears .... nice clothes.
9 It was .... boring film that I fell asleep while I was watching it.
10 I couldn't believe the news. It was .... shock.
11 I think she works too hard. She looks .... tired all the time.
12 The food at the hotel was .... awful. I've never eaten .... awful food.
13 They've got .... much money, they don't know what to do with it.
14 I didn't realise you lived .... long way from the city centre.
15 I can't decide what to do. It's .... problem.

101.2 *Make one sentence from two. Use* **so** *or* **such.**

1 ~~She worked hard.~~	You could hear it from miles away.
2 ~~It was a beautiful day.~~	You would think it was her native language.
3 I was tired.	We spent the whole day indoors.
4 We had a good time on holiday.	~~She made herself ill.~~
5 She speaks English well.	I couldn't keep my eyes open.
6 I've got a lot of things to do.	I didn't eat anything else for the rest of the day.
7 The music was loud.	~~We decided to go to the beach.~~
8 I had a big breakfast.	I don't know where to begin.
9 It was horrible weather.	We didn't want to come home.

1 ...She worked so hard she made herself ill....
2 ...It was such a beautiful day we decided to go to the beach....
3 I was ....
4 ....
5 ....
6 ....
7 ....
8 ....
9 ....

101.3 *Use your own ideas to complete these pairs of sentences.*

1 a We enjoyed our holiday. It was so ...**relaxing.**...
  b We enjoyed our holiday. We had such ...**a good time.**...
2 a I don't like London very much. It's so ....
  b I don't like London very much. It's such ....
3 a I like Ann. She's so ....
  b I like Ann. She's such ....
4 a I wouldn't like to be a teacher. It's so ....
  b I wouldn't like to be a teacher. It's such ....
5 a It's great to see you again! I haven't seen you for so ....
  b It's great to see you again! I haven't seen you for such ....

Enough and too

A The position of **enough**

Enough goes *after* adjectives and adverbs:

- He didn't get the job because he wasn't **experienced enough**. (*not* 'enough experienced')
- You won't pass the examination if you don't work **hard enough**.
- She shouldn't get married yet. She's not **old enough**.

The opposite is **too...** (**too hard** / **too old** etc.):

- You never stop working. You work **too hard**.

Enough normally goes *before* nouns:

- He didn't get the job because he didn't have **enough experience**. (*not* 'experience enough')
- I'd like to go away on holiday but I haven't got **enough money**.
- Some of us had to sit on the floor because there weren't **enough chairs**.

You can also use **enough** alone (without a noun):

- I'll lend you some money if you haven't got **enough**.

The opposite is **too much...** / **too many...**:

- We can't go away on holiday. It costs **too much** (**money**).
- There are **too many people** and not **enough chairs**.

B We say **enough/too...for** (somebody/something):

- I haven't got **enough** money **for a holiday**.
- He wasn't experienced **enough for the job**.
- This shirt is **too** big **for me**. I need a smaller size.

But we usually say **enough/too...to do something** (*not* 'for doing'). So we say:

enough money **to buy** something   **too** young **to do** something etc.

For example:

- I haven't got **enough money to go** on holiday. (*not* 'for going')
- He wasn't **experienced enough to do** the job.
- She's not **old enough to get** married.   *or*   She's **too young to get** married.
- Let's get a taxi. It's **too far to walk** home from here.
- There weren't **enough chairs** for everyone **to sit** down.
- They spoke **too quickly** for us **to understand**.

C We say:

	The food was very hot. We couldn't eat **it**.
and	The food was so hot that we couldn't eat **it**.
but	The food was **too** hot **to eat**. (*without* 'it')

Some more examples like this:

- The wallet was **too big to put** in my pocket.
  (*not* 'too big to put it')
- These boxes are **too heavy to carry**. (*not* 'too heavy to carry them')
- The water wasn't **clean enough to swim** in.

To... and for... (purpose) → **UNIT 63**   Adjective + **to...** (**difficult to understand** etc.) → **UNIT 64A**

102.1 *Complete these sentences using* **enough** *with one of the following adjectives or nouns:*

    adjectives: **big**   ~~**old**~~   **warm**   **well**

    nouns: **cups**   **milk**   **money**   **qualifications**   **room**   **time**

1 She shouldn't get married yet. She's not ....*old enough.*....
2 I'd like to buy a car but I haven't got ....
3 Have you got .... in your tea or would you like some more?
4 Are you ....? Or shall I switch on the heating?
5 It's only a small car. There isn't .... for all of you.
6 Steve didn't feel .... to go to work this morning.
7 I didn't answer all the questions in the exam. I didn't have ....
8 Do you think I've got .... to apply for the job?
9 Try this jacket on and see if it's .... for you.
10 There weren't .... for everybody to have coffee at the same time.

102.2 *Complete the answers to the questions. Use* **too** *or* **enough** *with the word in brackets.*

1	Is she going to get married?	(old) No, she's not ...*old enough to get* ...*married.*...
2	I need to talk to you about something.	(busy) Well, I'm afraid I'm .... to you now.
3	Let's go to the cinema.	(late) No, it's .... to the cinema.
4	Why don't we sit in the garden?	(warm) It's not .... in the garden.
5	Would you like to be a politician?	(nice) No, I'm .... a politician.
6	Do you want to play tennis today?	(energy) No, I haven't got .... tennis today.
7	Did you hear what he was saying?	(far away) No, we were .... what he was saying.
8	Can he read a newspaper in English?	(English) No, he doesn't know .... a newspaper.

102.3 *Make one sentence from two. Complete the new sentence using* **too** *or* **enough**.

1 We couldn't eat the food. It was too hot. ...*The food was too hot to eat.*...
2 I can't drink this coffee. It's too hot. This coffee is ....
3 Nobody could move the piano. It was too heavy.
   The piano ....
4 I don't wear this coat in winter. It isn't warm enough.
   This coat ....
5 I can't explain the situation. It is too complicated.
   The situation ....
6 Three people can't sit on this sofa. It isn't wide enough.
   This sofa ....
7 We couldn't climb over the wall. It was too high.
   The wall ....
8 You can't see some things without a microscope. They are too small.
   Some ....

Quite and rather

A
Quite = less than 'very' but more than 'a little':
- I'm surprised you haven't heard of her. She's **quite famous**. (= less than 'very famous' but more than 'a little famous')
- It's **quite cold**. You'd better wear your coat.
- Lucy lives **quite near** me, so we see each other **quite often**.

Quite goes before a/an:
   quite a nice day (*not* 'a quite nice day')   **quite an** old house   **quite a** long way

Sometimes we use **quite** + noun (without an adjective):
- I didn't expect to see them. It was **quite a surprise**.

We also use **quite** with some verbs, especially **like** and **enjoy**:
- I **quite like** tennis but it's not my favourite sport.

Quite sometimes means 'completely'. See Section C.

B
Rather is similar to **quite**. We use **rather** mainly with negative words and negative ideas:
- It's **rather cold**. You'd better wear your coat.
- 'What was the examination like?'   '**Rather difficult**, I'm afraid.'
- Let's get a taxi. It's **rather a long way** to walk.

Quite is also possible in these examples.

Often we use **quite** with a *positive* idea and **rather** with a *negative* idea:
- She's **quite intelligent** but **rather lazy**.

When we use **rather** with *positive* words (**nice/interesting** etc.), it means 'unusually' or 'surprisingly'. For example, **rather nice** = unusually nice / surprisingly nice / nicer than expected:
- These oranges are **rather nice**. Where did you get them?
- Ann didn't like the book but I thought it was **rather interesting**. (= more interesting than expected)

Rather can go before or after **a/an**. So you can say:
   a rather interesting book   *or*   **rather an** interesting book

C
Quite also means 'completely'. For example:
- 'Are you sure?'   'Yes, **quite sure**.' (= completely sure)

Quite means 'completely' with a number of adjectives, especially:

sure	right	true	clear	different	incredible	amazing
certain	wrong	safe	obvious	unnecessary	extraordinary	impossible

- She was **quite different** from what I expected. (= completely different)
- Everything they said was **quite true**. (= completely true)

We also use **quite** (= 'completely') with some verbs. For example:
- I **quite agree** with you. (= I completely agree)

Not quite = 'not completely':
- They **haven't quite finished** their dinner yet.
- I **don't quite understand** what you mean.
- 'Are you ready yet?'   '**Not quite**.' (= not completely)

EXERCISES

103.1 *Complete the sentences using* **quite** + *one of the following:*

a busy day	a good voice	a nice time	a lot of mistakes
a~~ nice day~~	a long way	a strong wind	a frightening experience

1 The weather was better than we had expected. It was ...quite a nice day...
2 Tom often sings. He's got ....
3 The bus stop wasn't very near the hotel. We had to walk ....
4 I'm tired. I've had ....
5 Our holiday was OK. We had ....
6 It's warm today but there's ....
7 I hope that never happens again. It was ....
8 She speaks English fluently but she makes ....

103.2 *Complete these sentences using the words in brackets. Each time use* **quite** *with the positive word and* **rather** *with the negative word.*

1 She's ...quite intelligent... but ...rather lazy... (intelligent / lazy)
2 The car goes .... but it's .... (well / noisy)
3 The programme was .... but ....
   (long / interesting)
4 George is .... but he's ....
   (a hard worker / slow)
5 I was .... with the hotel but Jim was ....
   (disappointed / pleased)
6 It's .... job but it's .... work.
   (a well-paid / hard)
7 Sarah lives .... us but it's .... to get to her
   house. (near / difficult)

103.3 *What does* **quite** *mean in these sentences? Tick (✔) the right meaning.*

	more than a little, less than very (Section A)	completely (Section C)
1 It's <u>quite cold</u>. You'd better wear your coat.	✔	
2 'Are you sure?' 'Yes, <u>quite sure</u>.'		✔
3 Maria's English is <u>quite good</u>.		
4 I couldn't believe it. It was <u>quite incredible</u>.		
5 The people I work with are <u>quite friendly</u>.		
6 My bedroom is <u>quite big</u>.		
7 You're <u>quite right</u>.		

103.4 *Complete these sentences using* **quite** *with one of the following:*
amazing   different   impossible   right   safe   sure   unnecessary   ~~true~~

1 I didn't believe her at first, but in fact what she said was ...quite true....
2 You won't fall. The ladder is ....
3 I'm afraid I can't do what you ask. It's ....
4 I couldn't agree with you more. You are ....
5 You can't compare the two things. They are ....
6 You needn't have done that. It was ....
7 I think I saw them go out but I'm not ....
8 I couldn't believe what had happened. It was ....

Comparison (1) – **cheaper**, **more expensive** etc.

A Look at these examples:

> How shall we travel? By car or by train?
>> Let's go by car. It's **cheaper**.
>> Don't go by train. It's **more expensive**.
> **Cheaper** and **more expensive** are *comparative* forms.

After comparatives you can use **than** (see also Unit 106):
- It's **cheaper** to go by car **than** by train.
- Going by train is **more expensive than** going by car.

B The comparative form is **-er** or **more...** .

We use **-er** for short words (one syllable):	We use **more...** for longer words (two syllables or more):
cheap → cheaper **fast**→ faster **large** → larger **thin** → thinner	**more modern** **more serious** **more expensive** **more comfortable**
We also use **-er** for two-syllable words that end in **-y** (**-y** → **-ier**):	We use **more...** for adverbs that end in **-ly**:
lucky → luckier early → earlier easy → easier pretty → prettier	**more slowly** **more seriously** **more quietly** **more carefully**
	Also: **more often** but: **earlier** (*not* 'more early')
For spelling, see Appendix 6.	

Compare these examples:

- You're **older** than me. - The exam was quite easy – **easier** than we expected. - Can you walk a bit **faster**? - I'd like to have a **bigger** car. - Last night I went to bed **earlier** than usual.	- You're **more patient** than me. - The exam was quite difficult – **more difficult** than we expected. - Can you walk a bit **more slowly**? - I'd like to have a **more reliable** car. - I don't play tennis much these days. I used to play **more often**.

You can use **-er** *or* **more...** with some two-syllable adjectives, especially:
quiet   **clever**   **narrow**   **shallow**   **simple**
- It's too noisy here. Can we go somewhere **quieter / more quiet**?

C These adjectives and adverbs have irregular comparative forms:
good/well → **better**:
- The garden looks **better** since you tidied it up.
- I know him **well** – probably **better** than anybody else.

bad/badly → **worse**:
- 'Is your headache better?'   'No, it's **worse**.'
- He did very badly in the exam – **worse** than expected.

far → **further** (*or* **farther**):
- It's a long walk from here to the station – **further** than I thought. (*or* ...**farther** than...)

Further (*but not* 'farther') can also mean 'more' or 'additional':
- Let me know if you hear any **further** news. (= any more news)

104.1 *Complete the sentences using a comparative form* (**older / more important** *etc.*).

1 It's too noisy here. Can we go somewhere ...**quieter?**..
2 This coffee is very weak. I like it a bit ....
3 The hotel was surprisingly big. I expected it to be ....
4 The hotel was surprisingly cheap. I expected it to be ....
5 The weather is too cold in this country. I'd like to live somewhere ....
6 My job is a bit boring sometimes. I'd like to do something ....
7 I was surprised how easy it was to use the computer. I thought it would be
....
8 Your work isn't very good. I'm sure you can do ....
9 Don't worry. The situation isn't so bad. It could be ....
10 I was surprised we got here so quickly. I expected the journey to take ....
11 You're talking very loudly. Can you speak a bit ....?
12 You hardly ever phone me. Why don't you phone me ....?
13 You're standing too near the camera. Can you move a bit .... away?
14 You were a bit depressed yesterday but you look .... today.

104.2 *Complete the sentences. Each time use the comparative form of one of the words in the list.*
Use **than** *where necessary.*

big	crowded	~~early~~	easily	high	important
interested	peaceful	~~reliable~~	serious	simple	thin

1 I was feeling tired last night, so I went to bed ...**earlier than**... usual.
2 I'd like to have a ...**more reliable**... car. The one I've got keeps breaking down.
3 Unfortunately her illness was .... we thought at first.
4 You look .... Have you lost weight?
5 I want a .... flat. We don't have enough space here.
6 He doesn't study very hard. He's .... in having a good time.
7 Health and happiness are .... money.
8 The instructions were very complicated. They could have been ....
9 There were a lot of people on the bus. It was .... usual.
10 I like living in the countryside. It's .... living in a town.
11 You'll find your way around the town .... if you have a good map.
12 In some parts of the country, prices are .... in others.

104.3 *Read the situations and complete the sentences. Use a comparative form* (**-er** *or* **more…**).

1 Yesterday the temperature was nine degrees. Today it's only six degrees.
  ..**It's colder today than it was yesterday.**..
2 The journey takes four hours by car and five hours by train.
  It takes ....
3 Dave and I went for a run. I ran ten kilometres. Dave stopped after eight kilometres.
  I ran ....
4 Chris and Joe both did badly in the exam. Chris got 20% but Joe only got 15%.
  Joe did ....
5 I expected my friends to arrive at about 4 o'clock. In fact they arrived at 2.30.
  My friends ....
6 You can go by bus or by train. The buses run every 30 minutes. The trains run every hour.
  The buses ....
7 We were very busy at work today. We're not usually as busy as that.
  We ....

Comparison (2)

A Before comparatives you can use:

much   **a lot**   **far** (= a lot)   **a bit**   **a little**   **slightly** (= a little)
- Let's go by car. It's **much cheaper**. (*or* It's **a lot cheaper**.)
- Don't go by train. It's **a lot more expensive**. (*or* It's **much more expensive**.)
- Could you speak **a bit more slowly**? (*or* ...speak **a little more slowly**?)
- This bag is **slightly heavier** than the other one.
- Her illness was **far more serious** than we thought at first. (*or* ...**much more serious**... *or* ...**a lot more serious**...)

B You can use **any** and **no** + comparatives (**any longer / no bigger** etc.):
- I've waited long enough. I'm not waiting **any longer**. (= not even a little longer)
- We expected their house to be very big but it's **no bigger** than ours. (*or*...it **isn't any bigger** than ours.)
- Yesterday you said you felt ill. Do you feel **any better** today?
- This hotel is better than the other one and it's **no more expensive**.

C **Harder and harder / more and more / more and more difficult** etc.

We repeat comparatives like this (...**and**...) to say that something is changing continuously:
- It's becoming **harder and harder** to find a job.
- It's becoming **more and more difficult** to find a job.
- Your English is improving. It's getting **better and better**.
- These days **more and more** people are learning English.

D **The...the better**

Study these examples:
- 'What time shall we leave?' '**The sooner the better**.' (= as soon as possible)
- 'What sort of box do you want? A big one?' 'Yes, **the bigger the better**.' (= as big as possible)
- When you're travelling, **the less luggage** you have to carry **the better**. (= it is best to have as little luggage as possible)

We also use **the...the...** (with two comparatives) to say that one thing depends on another thing:
- **The warmer** the weather, **the better** I feel. (= if the weather is warmer, I feel better)
- **The sooner** we leave, **the sooner** we will arrive.
- **The younger** you are, **the easier** it is to learn.
- **The more expensive** the hotel, **the better** the service.
- **The more** electricity you use, **the higher** your bill will be.
- **The more** I thought about the plan, **the less** I liked it.

E **Older** and **elder**

The comparative of **old** is **older**:
- Tom looks **older** than he really is.

You can use **elder** (*or* **older**) when you talk about people in a family. You can say (**my**) **elder brother/sister/son/daughter**:
- **My elder brother** is a pilot. (*or* My **older** brother...)

We say 'my **elder brother**' but we do not say that 'somebody is elder...':
- My brother is **older** than me. (*not* 'elder than me')

For **eldest**, see Unit 107D.

EXERCISES

105.1 *Use the words in brackets to complete the sentences. Use* **much / a bit** *etc. + a comparative form. Use* **than** *where necessary.*

1 Her illness was ...<u>much more serious than</u>... we thought at first. (much / serious)
2 This bag is too small. I need something .... (much / big)
3 I'm afraid the problem is .... it seems. (much / complicated)
4 You looked depressed this morning but you look ....
   now. (a bit / happy)
5 I enjoyed our visit to the museum. It was .... I expected.
   (far / interesting)
6 You're driving too fast. Could you drive ....? (a bit / slowly)
7 It's .... to learn a foreign language in the country where
   it is spoken. (a lot / easy)
8 I thought she was younger than me but in fact she's ....
   (slightly / old)

105.2 *Complete the sentences using* **any/no** *+ a comparative. Use* **than** *where necessary.*

1 I'm fed up with waiting. I'm not waiting ...<u>any longer.</u>...
2 I'm sorry I'm a bit late but I couldn't get here ....
3 This shop isn't expensive. The prices are .... anywhere else.
4 I must stop for a rest. I can't walk ....
5 The traffic isn't particularly bad today. It's .... usual.

105.3 *Complete the sentences using the structure in Section* **C** *(...and...).*

1 It's becoming ...<u>harder and harder</u>... to find a job. (hard)
2 That hole in your pullover is getting .... (big)
3 My bags seemed to get .... as I carried them. (heavy)
4 As I waited for my interview, I became .... (nervous)
5 As the day went on, the weather got .... (bad)
6 Travelling is becoming .... (expensive)
7 Since she has been in Britain, her English has got .... (good)
8 As the conversation went on, he became .... (talkative)

105.4 *These sentences are like those in Section* **D.** *Use the word(s) in brackets (in the correct form) to complete the sentences.*

1 I like warm weather. The warmer the weather, ...<u>the better I feel.</u>... (feel)
2 I didn't really like him when we first met.
   But the more I got to know him, ... (like)
3 If you're in business, you want to make a profit.
   The more goods you sell, ... (profit)
4 It's hard to concentrate when you're tired.
   The more tired you are, ... (hard)
5 She had to wait a very long time.
   The longer she waited, ... (impatient/become)

105.5 *Which is correct,* **older** *or* **elder?** *Or both of them?*

1 My <u>older / elder</u> brother is a pilot. (**older** *and* **elder** *are both correct*)
2 I'm surprised Diane is only 25. I thought she was <u>older / elder</u>.
3 Ann's younger sister is still at school. Her <u>older / elder</u> sister is a nurse.
4 Martin is <u>older / elder</u> than his brother.

Comparison (3) – **as...as / than**

A Study this example situation:

SHIRLEY   HENRY   ARTHUR

Shirley, Henry and Arthur are all millionaires. They are all very rich.
Shirley has £10 million, Henry has £8 million and Arthur has £2 million. So:

Henry is rich.
He is **richer than** Arthur.
But he isn't **as rich as** Shirley. (= Shirley is **richer than** he is)

Some more examples of **not as...** (**as**):
- Tom isn't **as old as** he looks. (= he looks **older than** he is)
- The city centre wasn't **as crowded** this morning **as** it usually is. (= it is usually **more crowded**)
- Jenny didn't do **as well** in the exam **as** she had hoped. (= she had hoped to do **better**)
- 'The weather is better today, isn't it?'   'Yes, it's **not as cold**.' (= yesterday was **colder**)
- I don't know **as many** people **as** you do. (= you know **more** people)

You can also say 'not **so**... (as)':
- It's not warm but it isn't **so** cold **as** yesterday. (= ...it isn't **as** cold **as**...)

Less... (**than**) is similar to **not as...** (**as**):
- I spent **less money** than you. (= I didn't spend as much money...)
- The city centre was **less crowded** than usual. (= it wasn't as crowded...)

B You can use **as...as** (but not 'so...as') in positive sentences and in questions:
- I'm sorry I'm late. I got here **as fast as** I could.
- There's plenty of food. You can have **as much as** you like.
- Let's walk. It's **just as quick as** taking the bus.
- Can you send me the money **as soon as possible**, please?

Also: **twice as...as**, **three times as...as** etc.:
- Petrol is **twice as expensive as** it was a few years ago.
- Their house is about **three times as big as** ours.

C We say **the same as** (*not* 'the same like'):
- Ann's salary is **the same as** mine.   *or*   Ann gets **the same** salary **as** me.
- Tom is **the same** age **as** George.
- 'What would you like to drink?'   'I'll have **the same as** you.'

D **Than me / than I am** etc.
We usually say:
- You are taller **than me**. (*not* 'than I')
- He is not as clever **as her**. (*not* 'as she')

After **than/as** it is more usual to say **me/him/her/them/us** when there is no verb. Compare:
- You are taller **than I am**.   *but*   You are taller **than me**.
- They have more money **than we have**.   *but*   They have more money **than us**.
- I can't run as fast as **he can**.   *but*   I can't run as fast **as him**.

EXERCISES

106.1 *Complete the sentences using* **as...as.**

1 I'm quite tall but you are taller.   I'm not ...as tall as you...
2 My salary is high but yours is higher.   My salary isn't ....
3 You know a bit about cars but I know more.   You don't ....
4 It's still cold but it was colder yesterday.   It isn't ....
5 I still feel a bit tired but I felt a lot more tired yesterday.
   I don't ....
6 They've lived here for quite a long time but we've lived here longer.
   They haven't ....
7 I was a bit nervous before the interview but usually I'm a lot more nervous.
   I wasn't ....

106.2 *Rewrite these sentences so that they have the same meaning.*

1 Jack is younger than he looks.   Jack isn't ...as old as he looks...
2 I didn't spend as much money as you.   You ...spent more money than me...
3 The station was nearer than I thought.   The station wasn't ....
4 The meal didn't cost as much as I expected.   The meal ....
5 I go out less than I used to.   I don't ....
6 Her hair isn't as long as it used to be.   She used to ....
7 I know them better than you do.   You don't ....
8 There were fewer people at this meeting than at the last one.
   There weren't ....

106.3 *Complete the sentences using* **as...as.** *Choose one of the following:*

bad   comfortable   ~~fast~~   long   often   quietly   soon   well   well-qualified

1 I'm sorry I'm a bit late. I got here ...as fast as... I could.
2 It was a difficult question. I answered it .... I could.
3 'How long can I stay with you?'   'You can stay .... you like.'
4 I need the information quickly, so please let me know .... possible.
5 I like to keep fit, so I go swimming .... I can.
6 I didn't want to wake anybody, so I came in .... I could.

In the following sentences use **just as...as.**

7 I'm going to sleep on the floor. It's .... sleeping in that hard bed.
8 Why did he get the job rather than me? I'm .... him.
9 At first I thought you were nice but really you're .... everybody else.

106.4 *Write sentences using* **the same as.**

1 Sally and Kate are both 22 years old.   ...Sally is the same age as Kate...
2 You and I both have dark brown hair. Your hair ....
3 I arrived at 10.25 and so did you. I ....
4 My birthday is 5 April. Tom's birthday is 5 April too. My ....

106.5 *Complete the sentences with* **than...** *or* **as...** .

1 I can't reach as high as you. You are taller ...than me...
2 He doesn't know much. I know more ....
3 I don't work particularly hard. Most people work as hard ....
4 We were very surprised. Nobody was more surprised ....
5 She's not a very good player. I'm a better player ....
6 They've been very lucky. I wish we were as lucky ....

Superlatives – **the longest / the most enjoyable** etc.

A   Study these examples:

> What is **the longest** river in the world?
> What was **the most enjoyable** holiday you've ever had?
>
> **Longest** and **most enjoyable** are *superlative* forms.

B   The superlative form is **-est** or **most...** . In general, we use **-est** for short words and **most...** for longer words. (The rules are the same as those for the comparative – see Unit 104.)

long → longest	hot → hottest	easy → easiest	hard → hardest
but **most** famous	**most** boring	**most** difficult	**most** expensive

These adjectives are irregular:

good → **best**   bad → **worst**   far → **furthest**

For spelling, see Appendix 6.

C   We normally use **the** before a superlative (**the** longest / **the** most famous etc.):
- Yesterday was **the hottest** day of the year.
- That film was really boring. It was **the most boring** film I've ever seen.
- She is a really nice person – one of **the nicest** people I know.
- Why does he always come to see me at **the worst** possible moment?

Compare:
- This hotel is **the cheapest** in town. *(superlative)*
- This hotel is **cheaper** than all the others in town. *(comparative)*

D   **Oldest** and **eldest**

The superlative of **old** is **oldest**:
- That church is **the oldest** building in the town. (*not* 'the eldest')

We use **eldest** (*or* **oldest**) when we are talking about people in a family:
- **My eldest son** is 13 years old. (*or* My **oldest** son...)
- Are you **the eldest** in your family? (*or* ...the **oldest**...)

E   After superlatives we use **in** with places (towns, buildings etc.):
- What is the longest river **in the world**? (*not* 'of the world')
- We had a lovely room. It was one of the nicest **in the hotel**. (*not* 'of the hotel')

We also use **in** for organisations and groups of people (a class / team / company etc.):
- Who is the best student **in the class**? (*not* 'of the class')

We normally use **of** for a period of time:
- What was the happiest day **of your life**?
- Yesterday was the hottest day **of the year**.

F   We often use the *present perfect* (I **have done**) after a superlative (see also Unit 10A):
- What's **the best** film **you've ever seen**?
- That was **the most delicious** meal **I've had** for a long time.

G   Sometimes we use **most** + adjective to mean 'very':
- The book you lent me was **most interesting**. (= very interesting)
- Thank you for the money. It was **most generous** of you. (= very generous)

   Comparison (**cheaper/more expensive** etc.) → **UNITS 104–106**   Elder → **UNIT 105E**

EXERCISES

107.1 *Complete the sentences. Use a superlative (-est or* **most...**) *+ a preposition.*

1 It's a very nice room. It ...**is the nicest room in**... the hotel.
2 It's a very cheap restaurant. It's .... the town.
3 It was a very happy day. It was .... my life.
4 She's a very intelligent student. She .... the class.
5 It's a very valuable painting. It .... the gallery.
6 Spring is a very busy time for me. It .... the year.

In the following sentences use **one of** *+ a superlative + a preposition.*

7 It's a very nice room. It ...**is one of the nicest rooms in**... the hotel.
8 He's a very rich man. He's one .... the world.
9 It's a very old castle. It .... Britain.
10 She's a very good player. She .... the team.
11 It was a very bad experience. It .... my life.
12 He's a very dangerous criminal. He .... the country.

107.2 *Complete the sentences. Use a superlative (-est or* **most...**) *or a comparative (-er or* **most...**).

1 We stayed at ...**the cheapest**... hotel in the town. (cheap)
2 Our hotel was ...**cheaper**... than all the others in the town. (cheap)
3 The United States is very large but Canada is .... (large)
4 What's .... river in the world? (long)
5 He was a bit depressed yesterday but he looks .... today. (happy)
6 It was an awful day. It was .... day of my life. (bad)
7 What is .... sport in your country? (popular)
8 Everest is .... mountain in the world. It is ....
than any other mountain. (high)
9 We had a great holiday. It was one of the .... holidays we've ever
had. (enjoyable)
10 I prefer this chair to the other one. It's .... (comfortable)
11 What's .... way of getting from here to the station? (quick)
12 Mr and Mrs Brown have got three daughters. .... is 14 years old.
(old)

107.3 *What do you say in these situations? Use a superlative + ...* **ever**... . *Use the words given in
brackets (in the correct form).*

1 You've just been to the cinema. The film was extremely boring. You tell your friend:
(boring/film/see) ...**That's the most boring film I've ever seen.**...
2 Your friend has just told you a joke, which you think is very funny. You say:
(funny/joke/hear) That's ....
3 You're drinking coffee with a friend. It's really good coffee. You say:
(good/coffee/taste) This ....
4 You are talking to a friend about Mary. Mary is very patient. You tell your friend about her:
(patient/person/meet) She ....
5 You have just run ten kilometres. You've never run further than this. You say to your friend:
(far/run) That ....
6 You decided to give up your job. Now you think this was a bad mistake. You say to your
friend: (bad/mistake/make) It ....
7 Your friend meets a lot of people, some of them famous. You ask your friend:
(famous/person/meet?) Who ....?

Word order (1) – verb + object; place and time

Verb + object

The *verb* and the *object* of the verb normally go together. We do *not* usually put other words between them:

	verb +	*object*	
I	like	children	very much. (*not* 'I like very much children')
Did you	see	your friends	yesterday?
Ann often	plays	tennis.	

Study these examples. Notice how the verb and the object go together each time:

- Do you **clean the house** every weekend? (*not* 'Do you clean every weekend the house?')
- Everybody **enjoyed the party** very much. (*not* 'Everybody enjoyed very much the party')
- Our guide **spoke English** fluently. (*not* '...spoke fluently English')
- I not only lost all my money – I also **lost my passport**. (*not* 'I lost also my passport')
- At the end of the street you'll **see a supermarket** on your left. (*not* '...see on your left a supermarket')

Place and *time*

Usually the *verb* and the *place* (where?) go together:
 go home   live in a city   walk to work etc.
If the verb has an *object*, the place comes after the *verb + object*:
 take somebody **home   meet** a friend **in the street**

Time (when? / how often? / how long?) normally goes after *place*:

	place +	*time*	
Tom walks	to work	every morning.	(*not* 'Tom walks every morning to work')
She has been	in Canada	since April.	
We arrived	at the airport	early.	

Study these examples. Notice how *time* goes after *place*:

- I'm going **to Paris on Monday**. (*not* 'I'm going on Monday to Paris')
- They have lived **in the same house for a long time.**
- Don't be late. Make sure you're **here by 8 o'clock.**
- Sarah gave me a lift **home after the party.**
- You really shouldn't go **to bed so late.**

It is often possible to put *time* at the beginning of the sentence:
- **On Monday** I'm going to Paris.
- **Every morning** Tom walks to work.

Some time words (for example, **always/never/often**) usually go with the verb in the middle of the sentence. See Unit 109.

108.1 *Is the word order right or wrong? Correct the ones that are wrong.*

1 Everybody enjoyed the party very much. ...RIGHT...
2 Tom walks every morning to work. ..WRONG: to work every morning...
3 Jim doesn't like very much football. ....
4 I drink three or four cups of coffee every morning. ....
5 I ate quickly my dinner and went out. ....
6 Are you going to invite to the party a lot of people? ....
7 I phoned Tom immediately after hearing the news. ....
8 Did you go late to bed last night? ....
9 Sue was here five minutes ago. Where is she now? ....
10 Did you learn a lot of things at school today? ....
11 I met on my way home a friend of mine. ....
12 I fell yesterday off my bicycle. ....

108.2 *Put the parts of the sentence in the right order.*

1 (the party / very much / everybody enjoyed) ...Everybody enjoyed the party very much...
2 (we won / easily / the game) ....
3 (quietly / the door / I closed) ....
4 (Diane / quite well / speaks / German) ....
5 (Tim / all the time / television / watches) ....
6 (again / please don't ask / that question)
    ....
7 (football / every weekend / does Ken play?)
    ....
8 (some money / I borrowed / from a friend of mine)
    ....

108.3 *Complete the sentences. Put the parts in the right order.*

1 (for a long time / have lived / in the same house)
    They ...have lived in the same house for a long time...
2 (to the bank / every Friday / go)   I ....
3 (home / did you come / so late)   Why ....?
4 (her car / drives / every day / to work)   Ann ....
5 (been / recently / to the cinema)   I haven't ....
6 (at the top of the page / your name / write)
    Please ....
7 (her name / after a few minutes / remembered)
    I ....
8 (around the town / all morning / walked)
    We ....
9 (on Saturday night / didn't see you / at the party)
    I ....
10 (some interesting books / found / in the library)
    We ....
11 (the children / yesterday / to the zoo / took)
    Sally ....
12 (opposite the park / a new hotel / are building)
    They ....

Word order (2) – adverbs with the verb

A Some adverbs (for example, **always, also, probably**) go with the verb in the middle of a sentence:
- Tom **always goes** to work by car.
- We were feeling very tired and we **were also** hungry.
- Your car **has probably been** stolen.

B Study these rules for the position of adverbs in the middle of a sentence. (They are only general rules, so there are exceptions.)

i) If the verb is one word (**goes/fell/cooked** etc.), the adverb usually goes *before* the verb:

	adverb	*verb*	
Tom	always	goes	to work by car.
I	almost	fell	as I was going down the stairs.

- I cleaned the house and **also cooked** the dinner. (*not* 'cooked also')
- Lucy **hardly ever watches** television and **rarely reads** newspapers.

Note that these adverbs (**always/often/also** etc.) go before **have to**:
- We **always have to** wait a long time for the bus. (*not* 'we have always to wait')

ii) But adverbs go *after* **am/is/are/was/were**:
- We were feeling very tired and we **were also** hungry.
- Why are you **always** late? You**'re never** on time.
- The traffic **isn't usually** as bad as it was this morning.

iii) If the verb is two or more words (**can remember / doesn't smoke / has been stolen** etc.), the adverb goes *after the first verb* (**can/doesn't/has** etc.):

	verb 1	*adverb*	*verb 2*	
I	can	never	remember	his name.
Ann	doesn't	usually	smoke.	
	Are you	definitely	going	to the party tomorrow?
Your car	has	probably	been	stolen.

- My parents **have always lived** in London.
- Jack can't cook. He **can't even boil** an egg.
- The house **was only** built a year ago and it**'s already falling** down.

Note that **probably** goes before the negative. So we say:
- I **probably** won't see you. *or* I will **probably not** see you. (*but not* 'I won't probably…')

C We also use **all** and **both** in these positions:
- We **all felt** ill after the meal. (*not* 'we felt all ill')
- My parents **are both** teachers. (*not* 'my parents both are teachers')
- Sarah and Jane **have both applied** for the job.
- We **are all going** out this evening.

D Sometimes we use **is/will/did** etc. instead of repeating part of a sentence (see Unit 50A). Note the position of **always/never** etc. in these sentences:
- He always says he won't be late but he **always is.** (= he **is always** late)
- I've never done it and I **never will.** (= I **will never** do it)

We normally put **always/never** etc. *before* the verb in sentences like these.

109.1 *Are the <u>underlined</u> words in the right position or not? Correct the sentences that are wrong.*

1 Tom goes <u>always</u> to work by car. ...WRONG: Tom always goes...
2 I cleaned the house and <u>also</u> cooked the dinner. ...RIGHT...
3 I have <u>usually</u> a shower when I get up. ....
4 We <u>soon</u> found the solution to the problem. ....
5 Steve gets <u>hardly ever</u> angry. ....
6 I did some shopping and I went <u>also</u> to the bank. ....
7 Jane has <u>always</u> to hurry in the morning because she gets up so late. ....
8 We <u>all</u> were tired so we <u>all</u> fell asleep. ....
9 She <u>always</u> says she'll phone me but she <u>never</u> does. ....

109.2 *Rewrite the sentences to include the word in brackets.*

1 Ann doesn't drink tea. (often) ...Ann doesn't often drink tea...
2 We were on holiday. (all) ....
3 We were staying at the same hotel. (all) ....
4 We enjoyed ourselves. (all) ....
5 Catherine is very generous. (always) ....
6 I don't have to work on Saturdays. (usually)
   I ....
7 Do you watch television in the evenings? (always)
   ....
8 Martin is learning French. He is learning Italian. (also)
   Martin is learning French. He ....
9 That hotel is very expensive. (probably) ....
10 It costs a lot to stay there. (probably) ....
11 I can help you. (probably) ....
12 I can't help you. (probably) ....

109.3 *Complete the sentences. Use the words in brackets in the correct order.*

1 I ...can never remember... her name. (remember / never / can)
2 I .... sugar in coffee. (take / usually)
3 I .... hungry when I get home from work. (am / usually)
4 'Where's Jim?' 'He .... home early.' (gone / has / probably)
5 Mark and Diane .... in Manchester. (both / were / born)
6 Liz is a good pianist. She .... very well. (sing / also / can)
7 Our car .... down. (often / breaks)
8 They live in the same street as me but I .... to them.
   (never / have / spoken)
9 We .... a long time for the bus. (have / always / to wait)
10 My sight isn't very good. I .... with glasses. (read / can / only)
11 I .... early tomorrow. (probably / leaving / will / be)
12 I'm afraid I .... able to come to the party. (probably / be / won't)
13 It's difficult to contact Sue. She .... at home when I
   phone her. (is / hardly ever)
14 We .... in the same place. We haven't moved.
   (still / are / living)
15 If we hadn't taken the same train, we .... each other.
   (never / met / would / have)
16 'Are you tired?' 'Yes, I .... at this time of day.' (am / always)

Still, yet and already   Any more / any longer / no longer

A   **Still**

We use **still** to say that a situation or action is continuing. It hasn't changed or stopped:

- It's 10 o'clock and Tom is **still** in bed.
- When I went to bed, Jane was **still** working.
- Do you **still** want to go to the party or have you changed your mind?

Still usually goes in the middle of the sentence with the verb. See Unit 109.

B   **Any more / any longer / no longer**

We use **not...any more** or **not...any longer** to say that a situation has changed. **Any more** and **any longer** go at the end of a sentence:

- Ann doesn't work here **any more** (*or* any longer). She left last month.
  (*not* 'Ann doesn't still work here')
- We used to be good friends but we are**n't any more** (*or* any longer).

You can also use **no longer**. **No longer** goes in the middle of the sentence:

- Ann **no longer** works here.

Note that we do not normally use **no more** in this way:

- We are **no longer** friends. (*not* 'We are no more friends')

Compare **still** and **not...any more**:

- Sheila **still** works here but Ann doesn't work here **any more**.

C   **Yet**

Yet = 'until now'. We use **yet** mainly in negative sentences (I have**n't** finished **yet**) and questions (**Have you** finished **yet**?). **Yet** shows that the speaker is expecting something to happen. **Yet** usually goes at the end of a sentence:

- It's 10 o'clock and Tom has**n't** got up **yet**.
- I'm hungry. Is dinner ready **yet**?
- We do**n't** know where we're going for our holidays **yet**.

We often use **yet** with the *present perfect* (**Have you finished yet?**). See also Unit 7C.

Compare **yet** and **still**:

- Jack lost his job a year ago and **is still** unemployed.
  Jack lost his job a year ago and **hasn't found** another job **yet**.
- Is it **still** raining?
  Has it **stopped** raining **yet**?

Still is also possible in *negative* sentences (before the negative):

- She said she would be here an hour ago and she **still** hasn't come.

This is similar to 'she hasn't come **yet**'. But **still... not** shows a stronger feeling of surprise or impatience. Compare:

- I wrote to him last week. He has**n't** replied **yet**. (but I expect he will reply soon)
- I wrote to him months ago and he **still** hasn't replied. (he should have replied before now)

D   **Already**

We use **already** to say that something happened sooner than expected. **Already** usually goes in the middle of a sentence (see Unit 109):

- 'When is Sue going on holiday?'   'She has **already** gone.' (= sooner than you expected)
- Shall I tell Liz the news or does she **already** know?
- I've only just had lunch and I'm **already** hungry.

Present perfect + **already/yet** → **UNIT 7C**   Word order → **UNIT 109**

110.1 *Compare what Paul said a few years ago with what he says now. Some things are the same as before and some things have changed.*

Paul a few
years ago

beard

> I travel a lot.
>   I work in a shop.
> I write poems.
>   I want to be a teacher.
> I'm interested in politics.
>   I'm single.
> I go fishing a lot.

Paul now

> I travel a lot.
>   I work in a hospital.
> I gave up writing poems.
>   I want to be a teacher.
> I'm not interested in politics.
>   I'm single.
> I haven't been fishing for years.

Write sentences about Paul using **still** *and* **not…any more.**

1 (travel) ...He still travels a lot.....
2 (shop) He doesn't work in a shop any more.
3 (poems) He ....
4 (teacher) ....
5 (politics) ....
6 (single) ....
7 (fishing) ....
8 (beard) ....

Now write three sentences about Paul using **no longer.**

9 ...He no longer works in a shop.....
10 He ....
11 ....
12 ....

110.2 *For each sentence (with* **still***) write a sentence with a similar meaning using* **not…yet** + *one of the following verbs:*

decide   find   finish   go   ~~stop~~   take off   wake up

1 It's still raining. ...It hasn't stopped raining yet.....
2 George is still here. He ....
3 They're still having their dinner. They ....
4 The children are still asleep. ....
5 Ann is still looking for a job. ....
6 I'm still wondering what to do. ....
7 The plane is still waiting on the runway. ....

110.3 *In this exercise you have to put in* **still, yet, already** *or* **not…any more** *in the* <u>underlined</u> *sentence (or part of a sentence). Study the examples carefully.*

1 Jack lost his job a year ago and <u>he is unemployed</u>. ...he is still unemployed.....
2 Do you want me to tell Liz the news or <u>does she know</u>? ...does she already know.....
3 I'm hungry. <u>Is dinner ready</u>? ...Is dinner ready yet?.....
4 I was hungry earlier but <u>I'm not hungry</u>. ...I'm not hungry any more.....
5 Can we wait a few minutes? <u>I don't want to go out</u>. ....
6 Jill used to work at the airport but <u>she doesn't work there</u>. ....
7 I used to live in Amsterdam. <u>I have a lot of friends there</u>. ....
8 'Shall I introduce you to Jim?' 'There's no need. <u>We've met</u>.' ....
9 <u>Do you live in the same house</u> or have you moved? ....
10 Would you like to eat with us or <u>have you eaten</u>? ....
11 'Where's John?' '<u>He isn't here</u>. He'll be here soon.' ....
12 Tim said he would be here at 8.30. It's 9 o'clock now and <u>he isn't here</u>. ....
13 Do you want to join the club or <u>are you a member</u>? ....
14 It happened a long time ago but <u>I can remember it very clearly</u>. ....
15 I've put on weight. <u>These trousers don't fit me</u>. ....
16 '<u>Have you finished with the paper</u>?' 'No, <u>I'm reading it</u>.'
....

Even

A Study this example situation:

> Tina loves watching television. She has a TV set in every room of the house – **even** the bathroom.
>
> We use **even** to say that something is unusual or surprising. It not usual to have a TV set in the bathroom.

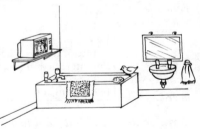

Some more examples:
- These photographs aren't very good. **Even I** could take better photographs than these. (and I'm certainly not a good photographer)
- He always wears a coat – **even in hot weather**.
- Nobody would lend her the money – **not even her best friend.**   *or*   **Not even** her best friend would lend her the money.

B Very often we use **even** with the verb in the middle of a sentence (see Unit 109):
- Sue has travelled all over the world. She has **even** been to the Antarctic. (It's especially unusual to go to the Antarctic, so she must have travelled a lot.)
- They are very rich. They **even** have their own private jet.

Study these examples with **not even**:
- I can't cook. I **can't even** boil an egg. (and boiling an egg is very easy)
- They weren't very friendly to us. They did**n't even** say hello.
- Jenny is very fit. She's just run five miles and she's **not even** out of breath.

C You can use **even** + *a comparative* (**cheaper / more expensive** etc.):
- I got up very early but John got up **even earlier**.
- I knew I didn't have much money but I've got **even less** than I thought.
- We were surprised to get a letter from her. We were **even more surprised** when she came to see us a few days later.

D **Even though / even when / even if**

You can use **even** + **though / when / if** to join sentences. Note that you cannot use **even** alone in the following examples:
- **Even though** she can't drive, she has bought a car. (*not* 'Even she can't drive…')
- He never shouts, **even when** he's angry.
- I'll probably see you tomorrow. But **even if** I don't see you tomorrow, we're sure to see each other before the weekend. (*not* 'even I don't see you')

Compare **even if** and **if**:
- We're going to the beach tomorrow. It doesn't matter what the weather is like. We're going to the beach **even if** it's raining.
- We hope to go to the beach tomorrow, but we won't go **if** it's raining.

EXERCISES

111.1 *Sharon, Linda and Angela are three friends who went on holiday together. Use the information given about them to complete the sentences using* **even** *or* **not even**.

Sharon		Linda		Angela	
is usually on time		isn't very keen on art		is almost always late	
is usually happy		is usually miserable		is a keen photographer	
likes getting up early		usually hates hotels		loves staying at hotels	
is very interested in art		hasn't got a camera		isn't very good at getting up	

1 They stayed at a hotel. Everybody liked it, ...*even Linda.*....
2 They arranged to meet. They all arrived on time, ...
3 They went to an art gallery. Nobody enjoyed it, ...
4 Yesterday they had to get up early. They all managed to do this, ...
5 They were together yesterday. They were all in a good mood, ...
6 None of them took any photographs, ...

111.2 *Make sentences with* **even**. *Use the words in brackets.*

1 She has been all over the world. (the Antarctic) ...*She has even been to the Antarctic.*...
2 She has to work every day. (on Sundays) ....
3 They painted the whole room. (the floor) They ....
4 You could hear the noise from a long way away. (from the next street)
   You ....
5 They have the windows open all the time. (when it's freezing)
   ....

In the following sentences you have to use **not...even**.

6 They didn't say anything to us. (hello) ...*They didn't even say hello.*...
7 I can't remember anything about her. (her name) I ....
8 There isn't anything to do in this town. (a cinema) ....
9 He didn't tell anybody where he was going. (his wife) ....
   ....

111.3 *Complete these sentences using* **even** *+ a comparative.*

1 It was very hot yesterday but today it's ...*even hotter.*...
2 The church is 500 years old but the house next to it is ....
3 That's a very good idea but I've got an .... one.
4 The first question was very difficult to answer. The second one was ....
5 I did very badly in the examination but most of my friends did ....
6 Neither of us was hungry. I ate very little and my friend ate ....

111.4 *Put in* **if**, **even**, **even if** *or* **even though**.

1 ...*Even though*... she can't drive, she has bought a car.
2 The bus leaves in five minutes but we can still catch it .... we run.
3 The bus leaves in two minutes. We won't catch it now .... we run.
4 His Spanish isn't very good – .... after three years in Spain.
5 His Spanish isn't very good .... he's lived in Spain for three years.
6 .... with the heating on, it was very cold in the house.
7 .... I was very tired, I couldn't sleep.
8 I won't forgive them for what they said, ... they apologise.
9 .... I hadn't eaten anything for 24 hours, I wasn't hungry.

Although / though / even though   In spite of / despite

A Study this example situation:

Last year Jack and Jill spent their holidays by the sea.
It rained a lot but they enjoyed themselves.
You can say:

Although it rained a lot, they enjoyed themselves.
(= It rained a lot *but* they...)
or
In spite of } the rain, they enjoyed themselves.
Despite

B After **although** we use a *subject + verb*:
- **Although it rained** a lot, we enjoyed our holiday.
- I didn't get the job **although I had** all the necessary qualifications.

Compare the meaning of **although** and **because**:
- We went out **although** it was raining.
- We didn't go out **because** it was raining.

C After **in spite of** or **despite**, we use a *noun*, a *pronoun* (**this/that/what** etc.) or -ing:
- **In spite of the rain**, we enjoyed our holiday.
- I didn't get the job **in spite of having** all the necessary qualifications.
- She wasn't well, but **in spite of this** she went to work.
- **In spite of what** I said yesterday, I still love you.

Despite is the same as **in spite of**. Note that we say 'in spite **of**', but **despite** (without 'of'):
- She wasn't well, but **despite this** she went to work. (*not* 'despite of this')

You can say '**in spite of the fact (that)**...' and '**despite the fact (that)**...':
- I didn't get the job { **in spite of the fact** (that)
  despite the fact (that) } I had all the necessary qualifications.

Compare **in spite of** and **because of**:
- We went out **in spite of the rain**. (*or* ...**despite the rain**.)
- We didn't go out **because of the rain**.

D Compare **although** and **in spite of / despite**:
- **Although the traffic was** bad,
  In spite of the traffic, } I arrived on time. (*not* 'in spite of the traffic was bad')
- I couldn't sleep { **although I was** very tired. (*not* 'despite I was tired')
  despite being very tired.

E Sometimes we use **though** instead of **although**:
- I didn't get the job **though** I had all the necessary qualifications.

In spoken English we often use **though** at the end of a sentence:
- The house isn't very nice. I like the garden **though**. (= but I like the garden)
- I see him every day. I've never spoken to him **though**. (= but I've never spoken to him)

Even though (but *not* 'even' alone) is a stronger form of **although**:
- **Even though** I was really tired, I couldn't sleep. (*not* 'Even I was really tired...')

112.1 *Complete the sentences. Use* **although** + *a sentence from the box.*

I didn't speak the language	~~he has a very important job~~
I had never seen her before	we don't like them very much
it was quite cold	the heating was on
I'd met her twice before	we've known each other for a long time

1 ...Although he has a very important job..., he isn't particularly well-paid.
2 ...., I recognised her from a photograph.
3 She wasn't wearing a coat ....
4 We thought we'd better invite them to the party ....
5 ...., I managed to make myself understood.
6 ...., the room wasn't warm.
7 I didn't recognise her ....
8 We're not very good friends ....

112.2 *Complete the sentences with* **although / in spite of / because / because of.**

1 ...Although... it rained a lot, we enjoyed our holiday.
2 a .... all our careful plans, a lot of things went wrong.
   b .... we had planned everything carefully, a lot of things went wrong.
3 a I went home early .... I was feeling unwell.
   b I went to work the next day .... I was still feeling unwell.
4 a She only accepted the job .... the salary, which was very high.
   b She accepted the job .... the salary, which was rather low.
5 a I managed to get to sleep .... there was a lot of noise.
   b I couldn't get to sleep .... the noise.

Use your own ideas to complete the following sentences:
6 a He passed the exam although ....
   b He passed the exam because ....
7 a I didn't eat anything although ....
   b I didn't eat anything in spite of ....

112.3 *Make one sentence from two. Use the word(s) in brackets in your sentences.*

1 I couldn't sleep. I was tired. (despite) ...I couldn't sleep despite being tired...
2 They have very little money. They are happy. (in spite of)
   In spite of ....
3 My foot was injured. I managed to walk to the nearest village. (although)
   ....
4 I enjoyed the film. The story was silly. (in spite of)
   ....
5 We live in the same street. We hardly ever see each other. (despite)
   ....
6 I got very wet in the rain. I had an umbrella. (even though)
   ....

112.4 *Use the words in brackets to make a sentence with* **though** *at the end.*

1 The house isn't very nice.   (like / garden) ...I like the garden though...
2 It's quite warm.   (a bit windy) ....
3 We didn't like the food.   (ate) ....
4 Liz is very nice.   (don't like / husband)   I ....

225

In case

Study this example situation:

Geoff is a football referee. He always wears two watches during a game because it is possible that one watch will stop.

He wears two watches **in case one of them stops.**

In case one of them stops = 'because it is possible one of them will stop'.

Some more examples of **in case:**
- Ann might phone tonight. I don't want to go out **in case she phones.** (= because it is possible she will phone)
- I'll draw a map for you **in case you can't find our house.** (= because it is possible you won't be able to find it)

We use **just in case** for a smaller possibility:
- I don't think it will rain but I'll take an umbrella **just in case.** (= **just in case** it rains)

Do not use **will** after **in case.** Use a present tense for the future (see also Unit 25):
- I don't want to go out tonight **in case** Ann **phones.** (*not* 'in case Ann will phone')

In case is not the same as **if.** We use **in case** to say *why* somebody does (or doesn't do) something. You do something *now* **in case** something happens *later*. Compare:

in case	if
• We'll buy some more food **in case** Tom comes. (= Perhaps Tom will come; we'll buy some more food now, whether he comes or not; then we'll *already* have the food *if* he comes.)	• We'll buy some more food **if** Tom comes. (= Perhaps Tom will come; if he comes, we'll buy some more food; if he doesn't come, we won't buy any more food.)
• I'll give you my phone number **in case** you need to contact me.	• You can phone me at the hotel **if** you need to contact me.
• You should insure your bicycle **in case** it is stolen.	• You should inform the police **if** your bicycle is stolen.

You can use **in case** (+ *past*) to say why somebody did something:
- We bought some more food **in case Tom came.** (= because it was possible that Tom would come)
- I drew a map for Sarah **in case she couldn't find the house.**
- We rang the bell again **in case they hadn't heard it the first time.**

'In case of...' is not the same as 'in case'. **In case of...** = 'if there is...' (especially in notices etc.):
- **In case of fire,** please leave the building as quickly as possible. (= if there is a fire)
- **In case of emergency,** telephone this number. (= if there is an emergency)

113.1 *Barbara is going for a long walk in the country. She is going to take these things with her:*
~~some chocolate~~   a map   an umbrella   her camera   some water   a towel

She has decided to take these things because:
perhaps she'll want to have a swim   it's possible she'll get lost   ~~she might get hungry~~
she might want to take some photographs   perhaps she'll get thirsty   perhaps it will rain

Write sentences with **in case** *saying why Barbara has decided to take these things with her.*

1   She's going to take some chocolate in case she gets hungry.
2   She's going to take a map in case ....
3   She's going to ....
4   ....
5   ....
6   ....

113.2 *What do you say in these situations? Use* **in case**.

1   It's possible that Mary will need to contact you, so you give her your phone number.
    You say: Here's my phone number ....
2   A friend of yours is going away for a long time. Maybe you won't see her again before she
    goes, so you decide to say goodbye now.
    You say: I'll say ....
3   You are shopping in a supermarket with a friend. You think you have everything you need
    but perhaps you've forgotten something. Your friend has the list. You ask him to check it.
    You say: Can you ....

113.3 *Write sentences with* **in case**.

1   There was a possibility that Ann would phone. So I didn't go out.
    I didn't go out in case Ann phoned.
2   John thought that he might forget the name of the book. So he wrote it down.
    He wrote down ....
3   I thought my parents might be worried about me. So I phoned them.
    I phoned ....
4   I wrote a letter to Jane but I didn't receive a reply. So I wrote to her again because I thought
    that perhaps she hadn't received my first letter.
    I ....
5   I met some people when I was on holiday in France. They said they might come to London
    one day. I live in London, so I gave them my address.
    I ....

113.4 *Put in* **in case** *or* **if**.

1   Ann might phone this evening. I don't want to go out ...in case... she phones.
2   You should tell the police ...if... your bicycle is stolen.
3   I hope you'll come to London sometime.   .... you come, you can stay with us.
4   This letter is for Susan. Can you give it to her .... you see her?
5   Write your name and address on your bag .... you lose it.
6   Go to the lost property office .... you lose your bag.
7   The burglar alarm will ring .... somebody tries to break into the house.
8   I've just painted the door. I'll put a WET PAINT notice next to it ....
    somebody doesn't realise it's just been painted.
9   I was advised to arrange insurance .... I needed medical treatment while I was
    abroad.

Unless   As long as and provided/providing

A   **Unless**

Study this example situation:

The club is for members only.

You can't go in **unless you are a member**.

This means:
'You can't go in *except if* you are a member.' *or*
'You can go in *only if* you are a member.'

Unless = 'except if'

Some more examples of **unless**:
- I'll see you tomorrow **unless I have to work late**. (= except if I have to work late)
- Don't tell Sue what I said **unless she asks you**. (= except if she asks you)
- 'Shall I tell Sue what you said?'   '**Not unless** she asks you.' (= only if she asks you)
- I don't like fish. I wouldn't eat it **unless I was extremely hungry**. (= except if I was extremely hungry)

We often use **unless** in warnings:
- We'll be late **unless we hurry**. (= except if we hurry)
- **Unless you work much harder**, you won't pass the exam.
- I was told I wouldn't pass the exam **unless I worked harder**.

Instead of **unless** it is often possible to say **if...not**:
- Don't tell Sue what I said **if** she does**n't** ask you.
- We'll be late **if** we don**'t** hurry.

B   **As long as** etc.

> **as long as** *or* **so long as**
> **provided** (that) *or* **providing** (that)

All these expressions mean 'if' or 'on condition that'.

For example:
- You can use my car { **as long as** / **so long as** } you drive carefully.

  (= you can use my car but you must drive carefully – this is a condition)
- Travelling by car is convenient { **provided (that)** / **providing (that)** } you have somewhere to park.

  (= but only if you have somewhere to park)
- **Providing (that)** / **Provided (that)** she studies hard, she'll pass her exams.

  (= she must study hard – if she does this, she will pass)

C   When you are talking about the future, do *not* use **will** after **unless / as long as / provided / providing**. Use a *present* tense (see also Unit 25):
- We'll be late **unless we hurry**. (*not* 'unless we will hurry')
- **Providing** she **studies** hard, she will pass the exam. (*not* 'providing she will study')

EXERCISES

114.1 *Write a new sentence with the same meaning. Use* **unless** *in your sentence.*

1 You must work much harder or you won't pass the exam.
...**You won't pass the exam unless you work much harder.**...

2 Listen carefully or you won't know what to do.
You won't know what to do ....

3 She must apologise to me or I'll never speak to her again.
I'll...

4 You have to speak very slowly or he won't be able to understand you.
....

5 The company must offer me more money or I'm going to look for another job.
....

114.2 *Write a new sentence with the same meaning. Use* **unless** *in your sentence.*

1 You are allowed into the club only if you're a member.
...**You aren't allowed into the club unless you're a member.**...

2 I'm going to the party only if you go too.
I'm not going ....

3 The dog will attack you only if you move suddenly.
....

4 He'll speak to you only if you ask him a question.
....

5 The doctor will see you today only if it's an emergency.
....

114.3 *Choose the correct word or expression for each sentence.*

1 You can use my car ~~unless~~ / as long as you drive carefully. (**as long as** *is correct*)
2 I'm playing tennis tomorrow unless / providing it's raining.
3 I'm playing tennis tomorrow unless / providing it's not raining.
4 I don't mind if you come in late unless / as long as you come in quietly.
5 I'm going now unless / provided you want me to stay.
6 I don't watch television unless / as long as I've got nothing else to do.
7 Children are allowed to use the swimming pool unless / provided they are with an adult.
8 Unless / provided they are with an adult, children are not allowed to use the swimming pool.
9 We can sit here in the corner unless / as long as you'd rather sit over there by the window.
10 A: Our holiday cost a lot of money.
   B: Did it? Well, that doesn't matter unless / as long as you enjoyed yourselves.

114.4 *Use your own ideas to complete these sentences.*

1 We'll be late unless ...**we hurry.**...
2 I like hot weather unless ....
3 I like hot weather provided ....
4 Kate reads a newspaper every day as long as ....
5 I don't mind walking home as long as ....
6 I like to walk to work in the morning unless ....
7 We can meet tomorrow unless ....
8 You can borrow the money providing ....
9 You won't achieve anything unless ....

As (reason and time)

A

As *(reason)*

As sometimes means 'because':

- **As** it was a public holiday, all the shops were shut. (= because it was a public holiday)
- **As** they live near us, we see them quite often.
- We watched television all evening **as** we had nothing better to do.

We also use **as** to say that two things happened at the same time. See Section **B**.

B

As *(time)*

You can use **as** when two things happen at the same time:

- I watched her **as** she opened the letter. ('I watched' and 'she opened' at the same time)
- **As** they walked along the street, they looked in the shop windows.
- Can you turn off the light **as** you go out, please? (= on your way out of the room)

Or you can say that something happened **as** you were doing something else (= in the middle of doing something else):

- Jill slipped **as she was getting off the bus.**
- The thief was seen **as he was climbing over the wall.**

Most often we use **as** when two *short* actions happen at the same time:

- George arrived **as** Sue left. (= he arrived and Sue left at the same time)
- We all waved goodbye to Liz **as** she drove away in her car.

GEORGE   SUE

But we also use **as** when two things happen together over a longer period of time:

- **As the day went on,** the weather got worse.
- I began to enjoy the job more **as I got used to it.**

You can also use **just as** (= exactly at that moment):

- **Just as** I sat down, the phone rang.
- **Just as we were going out,** it started to rain.
- I had to leave **just as the conversation was getting interesting.**

For the *past continuous* (**was getting / were going** etc.) see Unit 6.

C

As, when and **while**

We use **as** only if two things happen *at the same time*. We use **when** (*not* 'as') if one thing happens after another. Compare **when** and **as**:

- **When** I got home, I had a bath. (*not* 'as I got home')
- **As** I walked into the room, the phone started ringing. (= at the same time)

We use **as** (*time*) for actions and happenings. **As** + a *situation* (not an action) usually means 'because' (see Section **A**):

- **As we were asleep,** we didn't hear the doorbell. (= because we were asleep)
- **As they live near me,** I see them quite often. (= because they live near me)

You cannot use **as** for *time* in sentences like this. You have to use **while** or **when**:

- The doorbell rang **while** we were asleep. (*not* 'as we were asleep')
- Angela got married **when** she was 23. (*not* 'as she was 23')

115.1 *What does* **as** *mean in these sentences?*

	because	at the same time as
1 As they live near us, we see them quite often.	✔	
2 Jill slipped **as** she was getting off the bus.		✔
3 **As** I was tired, I went to bed early.		
4 Unfortunately, **as** I was parking the car, I hit the car behind.		
5 **As** we climbed the hill, we got more and more tired.		
6 We decided to go out to eat **as** we had no food at home.		
7 **As** we don't use the car very often, we've decided to sell it.		

115.2 *(Section A) Join a sentence from List A with one from List B. Begin each sentence with* **As.**

A 1 ~~yesterday was a public holiday~~
2 it was a nice day
3 we didn't want to wake anybody up
4 the door was open
5 none of us had a watch

B I walked in
we came in very quietly
~~all the shops were shut~~
we didn't know what time it was
we went for a walk by the sea

1 *As yesterday was a public holiday, all the shops were shut.*
2 ....
3 ....
4 ....
5 ....

115.3 *(Section B) Use* **as** *to join a sentence from List A with one from List B.*

A 1 ~~we all waved goodbye to Liz~~
2 we all smiled
3 I burnt myself
4 the crowd cheered
5 a dog ran out in front of the car

B we were driving along the road
I was taking a hot dish out of the oven
~~she drove away in her car~~
we posed for the photograph
the two teams ran onto the field

1 *We all waved goodbye to Liz as she drove away in her car.*
2 ....
3 ....
4 ....
5 ....

115.4 *Put in* **as** *or* **when.** *Sometimes you can use either* **as** *or* **when.**

1 Angela got married ...**when**... she was 23.
2 My camera was stolen .... I was on holiday.
3 He dropped the glass .... he was taking it out of the cupboard.
4 .... I left school, I went to work in a shop.
5 The train slowed down .... it approached the station.
6 I used to live near the sea .... I was a child.

115.5 *Use your own ideas to complete these sentences.*

1 I saw you as ....
2 It began to rain just as ....
3 As I didn't have enough money for a taxi, ...
4 Just as I took the photograph, ...

Like and as

A Like = 'similar to', 'the same as'. Note that you can*not* use **as** in this way:
- What a beautiful house! It's **like a palace**. (*not* 'as a palace')
- 'What does Sandra do?'   'She's a teacher, **like me**.' (*not* 'as me')
- Be careful! The floor has been polished. It's **like walking on ice**. (*not* 'as walking')
- It's raining again. I hate weather **like this**. (*not* 'as this')

In these sentences, **like** is a *preposition*. So it is followed by a *noun* (like **a palace**), a *pronoun* (like **me** / like **this**) or *-ing* (like walk**ing**).

You can also say '**like** (somebody/something) do**ing** something':
- 'What's that noise?'   'It sounds **like a baby** crying.'

B Sometimes **like** = 'for example':
- Some sports, **like motor racing**, can be dangerous.

You can also use **such as** (= for example):
- Some sports, **such as** motor racing, can be dangerous.

C We use **as** (*not* 'like') before a *subject + verb*:
- I didn't move anything. I left everything **as I found it**.
- They did **as they promised**. (= They did what they promised.)

Compare **like** and **as** in these sentences:
- You should have done it **like this**. (like + *pronoun*)
- You should have done it **as I showed you**. (as + *subject + verb*)

We also say **as you know / as I said / as she expected / as I thought** etc.:
- **As you know**, it's Tom's birthday next week. (= you know this already)
- Jane failed her driving test, **as she expected**. (= she expected this before)

Note that we say **as usual / as always**:
- You're late **as usual**.

D As can also be a *preposition* but the meaning is different from **like**. Compare:

as	like
• Brenda Casey is the manager of a company. **As the manager**, she has to make many important decisions. ('**As the manager**' = in her position as the manager)	• Mary Stone is the assistant manager. **Like the manager** (Brenda Casey), she also has to make important decisions. ('**Like the manager**' = similar to the manager)
• During the war this hotel was used **as a hospital**. (so it really was a hospital)	• Everyone is ill at home. Our house is **like a hospital**. (it isn't really a hospital)

As (*preposition*) = 'in the position of', 'in the form of' etc.:
- A few years ago I worked **as a bus driver**. (*not* 'like a bus driver')
- We've got a garage but we haven't got a car, so we use the garage **as a workshop**.
- Many English words (for example, 'work' and 'rain') can be used **as verbs or nouns**.
- London is all right **as a place to visit**, but I wouldn't like to live there.
- The news of her death came **as a great shock**.

We say **regard...as**:
- I regard her **as my best friend**.

EXERCISES

116.1 *(Sections A, B and C) Put in* **like** *or* **as.**

1 It's raining again. I hate weather ...**like**... this.
2 Jane failed her driving test ...**as**... she expected.
3 Do you think Carol looks .... her mother?
4 He really gets on my nerves. I can't stand people .... him.
5 Why didn't you do it .... I told you to do it?
6 'What does Bill do?' 'He's a student, ... most of his friends.'
7 Why do you never listen? Talking to you is .... talking to the wall.
8 .... I said yesterday, I'm thinking of changing my job.
9 Tom's idea seemed a good one, so we did .... he suggested.
10 It's a difficult problem. I never know what to do in situations .... this.
11 I'll phone you tomorrow .... usual, OK?
12 This tea is awful. It tastes .... water.
13 Suddenly there was a terrible noise. It was .... a bomb exploding.
14 She's a very good swimmer. She swims .... a fish.
15 I'm afraid I can't meet you on Sunday .... we arranged.
16 We met Keith last night. He was very cheerful, ... always.

116.2 *(Sections A and D) Complete the sentences using* **like** *or* **as** *+ one of the following:*

a beginner	blocks of ice	~~a palace~~	a birthday present	a problem
a child	a church	winter	a tourist guide	

1 This house is beautiful. It's ...**like a palace.**...
2 Margaret once had a part-time job ....
3 My feet are really cold. They're ....
4 I've been learning Spanish for a few years but I still speak ....
5 I wonder what that building with the tower is. It looks ....
6 My brother gave me this watch .... a long time ago.
7 It's true that we disagree about some things but I don't regard this ....
8 It's very cold for the middle of summer. It's ....
9 He's 22 years old but he sometimes behaves ....

116.3 *(All sections) Put in* **like** *or* **as.**

1 Your English is very fluent. I wish I could speak .... you.
2 Don't take my advice if you don't want to. You can do .... you like.
3 You waste too much time doing things .... sitting in cafés all day.
4 I wish I had a car .... yours.
5 There's no need to change your clothes. You can go out .... you are.
6 My neighbour's house is full of interesting things. It's .... a museum.
7 I think I preferred this room .... it was, before we decorated it.
8 When we asked Sue to help us, she agreed immediately, ... I knew she would.
9 Sharon has been working .... a waitress for the last two months.
10 While we were on holiday, we spent most of our time doing energetic things ....
   sailing, water skiing and swimming.
11 You're different from the other people I know. I don't know anyone .... you.
12 We don't need all the bedrooms in the house, so we use one of them .... a study.
13 .... her father, Catherine has a very good voice.
14 The news that Sue and Jim were getting married came .... a complete surprise to me.
15 At the moment I've got a temporary job in a bookshop. It's OK .... a temporary job
   but I wouldn't like to do it permanently.

As if

A

You can use **as if** to say how somebody or something **looks/sounds/feels** etc.:
- That house **looks as if** it's going to fall down.
- Ann **sounded as if** she had a cold, didn't she?
- I've just come back from holiday but I feel tired and depressed. I don't **feel as if** I've just had a holiday.

Compare:
- You look **tired**. (**look** + *adjective*)
  You look **as if you haven't slept**. (**look** + **as if** + *subject* + *verb*)
- Tom sounded **worried**. (**sound** + *adjective*)
  Tom sounded **as if he was worried**. (**sound** + **as if** + *subject* + *verb*)

You can use **as though** instead of **as if**:
- Ann sounds **as though** she's got a cold. (= ...**as if** she's got a cold.)

B

You can also say **It looks/sounds/smells as if** (*or* **as though**):
- Sandra is very late, isn't she? **It looks as if** she isn't coming.
- We took an umbrella with us because **it looked as if** it was going to rain.
- Do you hear that music next door? **It sounds as if** they're having a party.
- **It smells as though** someone has been smoking in here.

> It sounds as if they're having a party next door.

After **It looks/sounds/smells**, many people use **like** instead of **as if / as though**:
- It looks **like** Sandra isn't coming.

C

You can use **as if** with other verbs to say how somebody does something:
- He **ran as if** he was running for his life.
- After the interruption, the speaker **carried on talking as if** nothing had happened.
- When I told them my plan, they **looked at me as if** I was mad.

D

After **as if** we sometimes use the *past* when we are talking about the *present*. For example:
- I don't like Norma. She talks as if she **knew** everything.

The meaning is *not* past in this sentence. We use the past ('as if she **knew**') because the idea is *not real*: Norma does *not* know everything. We use the past in the same way with **if** and **wish** (see Unit 38).

Some more examples:
- She's always asking me to do things for her – **as if I didn't** have enough to do. (I *do* have enough to do)
- Harry's only 40. Why do you talk about him **as if he was** an old man? (he isn't an old man)

When you use the past in this way, you can use **were** instead of **was**:
- Why do you talk about him as if **he were** an old man?
- They treat me **as if I were** (*or* **was**) their own son. (I'm not their son)

117.1 *Use the sentences in the box to make sentences with* **as if.**

it has just been cut	I'm going to be sick	he hadn't eaten for a week
she was enjoying it	she had hurt her leg	he meant what he was saying
~~he needs a good rest~~	she didn't want to come	

1 Mark looks very tired. He looks ...*as if he needs a good rest.*...
2 Sue was walking with difficulty. She looked ....
3 I don't think he was joking. He looked ....
4 The grass is very short. It looks ....
5 Peter was extremely hungry and ate his dinner very quickly.
   He ate ....
6 Carol had a bored expression on her face during the concert.
   She didn't look ....
7 I've just eaten too many chocolates. Now I'm feeling ill.
   I feel ....
8 I phoned Emma and invited her to the party but she wasn't very enthusiastic about it.
   She sounded ....

117.2 *What do you say in these situations? Use* **You look / You sound / I feel as if...** *. Use the words in brackets to make your sentence.*

1 You meet Bill. He has a black eye and some plasters on his face.
   You say to him: ...*You look as if you've been in a fight.*... (be / a fight)
2 Christine comes into the room. She looks absolutely terrified.
   You say to her: What's the matter? You .... (see / a ghost)
3 Sarah is talking to you on the phone about her new job and she sounds very happy about it.
   You say to her: .... (enjoy / it)
4 You have just run one kilometre. You are absolutely exhausted.
   You say to a friend: I .... (run / a marathon)

117.3 *Make sentences beginning* **It looks as if... / It sounds as if...** *.*

you had a good time	there's been an accident	they are having an argument
it's going to rain	~~she isn't coming~~	we'll have to walk

1 Sandra said she would be here an hour ago. *You say:* ...*It looks as if she isn't coming.*...
2 The sky is full of black clouds. *You say:* It ....
3 You hear two people shouting at each other next door.
   You say: ....
4 You see an ambulance, some policemen and two damaged cars at the side of the road.
   You say: ....
5 You and a friend have just missed the last bus home.
   You say: ....
6 Sue and Dave have just been telling you about all the interesting things they did while they
   were on holiday. *You say:* ....

117.4 *These sentences are like the ones in Section D. Complete each sentence using* **as if.**

1 Brian is a terrible driver. He drives ...*as if he were*... the only driver on the road.
2 I'm 20 years old, so please don't talk to me .... a child.
3 Steve has only met Nicola once but he talks about her .... a close friend.
4 It was a long time ago that we first met but I remember it .... yesterday.

For, during and while

A   **For** and **during**

We use **for** + a period of time to say *how long* something goes on:

   for **two hours**   for **a week**   for **ages**

For example:

- We watched television **for two hours** last night.
- Victoria is going away **for a week** in September.
- Where have you been? I've been waiting **for ages**.
- Are you going away **for the weekend?**

We use **during** + *noun* to say *when* something happens (*not* how long):

   during **the film**   during **our holiday**   during **the night**

For example:

- I fell asleep **during the film**.
- We met a lot of people **during our holiday**.
- The ground is wet. It must have rained **during the night**.

With a 'time word' (for example, **the morning / the afternoon / the summer**), you can usually say **in** or **during**:

- It must have rained **in the night**. (*or* ...**during the night**.)
- I'll phone you sometime **during the afternoon**. (*or* ...**in the afternoon**.)

You cannot use **during** to say *how long* something goes on:

- It rained **for** three days without stopping. (*not* 'during three days')

Compare **during** and **for**:

- I fell asleep **during the film**. I was asleep **for half an hour**.

B   **During** and **while**

Compare:

We use **during** + *noun*:	We use **while** + *subject* + *verb*:
noun	*subject* + *verb*
- I fell asleep **during the film**.	- I fell asleep **while I was watching** television.
Compare **during** and **while** in these examples:	
- We met a lot of interesting people **during our holiday**.	- We met a lot of interesting people **while we were on holiday**.
- Robert suddenly began to feel ill **during the examination**.	- Robert suddenly began to feel ill **while he was doing** the examination.

Some more examples of **while**:

- We saw Amanda **while we were waiting** for the bus.
- **While you were** out, there was a phone call for you.
- Christopher read a book **while I watched** television.

When you are talking about the future, use the *present* (*not* 'will') after **while**:

- I'll be in London next week. I hope to see Tom **while I'm** there. (*not* 'while I will be there')
- What are you going to do **while you are** waiting? (*not* 'while you will be waiting')

See also Unit 25.

EXERCISES

118.1 *Put in* **for** *or* **during**.

1 It rained ...**for**... three days without stopping.
2 I fell asleep ...**during**.... the film.
3 I went to the theatre last night. I met Lucy .... the interval.
4 Martin hasn't lived in Britain all his life. He lived in Brazil .... four years.
5 Production at the factory was seriously affected .... the strike.
6 I felt really ill last week. I could hardly eat anything .... three days.
7 I waited for you .... half an hour and decided that you weren't coming.
8 Sue was very angry with me. She didn't speak to me .... a week.
9 We usually go out at weekends, but we don't often go out .... the week.
10 Jack started a new job a few weeks ago. Before that he was out of work .... six months.
11 I need a change. I think I'll go away .... a few days.
12 The President gave a long speech. She spoke .... two hours.
13 We were hungry when we arrived. We hadn't had anything to eat .... the journey.
14 We were hungry when we arrived. We hadn't had anything to eat .... eight hours.

118.2 *Put in* **during** *or* **while**.

1 We met a lot of people ...**while**... we were on holiday.
2 We met a lot of people ...**during**... our holiday.
3 I met Mike .... I was shopping.
4 .... we were in Paris, we stayed at a very comfortable hotel.
5 .... our stay in Paris, we visited a lot of museums and galleries.
6 The phone rang three times .... we were having dinner.
7 The phone rang three times .... the night.
8 I had been away for many years. .... that time, many things had changed.
9 What did they say about me .... I was out of the room?
10 Jack read a lot of books and magazines .... he was ill.
11 I went out for dinner last night. Unfortunately, I began to feel ill .... the meal and had to go home.
12 Please don't interrupt me .... I'm speaking.
13 There were many interruptions .... the President's speech.
14 Can you lay the table .... I get the dinner ready?
15 We were hungry when we arrived. We hadn't had anything to eat .... we were travelling.

118.3 *Use your own ideas to complete these sentences.*

1 I fell asleep while ...**I was watching television.**...
2 I fell asleep during ...**the film.**...
3 I hurt my arm while ....
4 Can you wait here while ....?
5 Most of the students looked bored during ....
6 I was asked a lot of questions during ....
7 Don't open the car door while ....
8 The lights suddenly went out during ....
9 It started to rain during ....
10 It started to rain while ....

By and until   By the time...

A

By (+ *a time*) = 'not later than':
- I posted the letter today, so they should receive it **by Monday**. (= on or before Monday, not later than Monday)
- We'd better hurry. We have to be at home **by 5 o'clock**. (= at or before 5 o'clock, not later than 5 o'clock)
- Where's Sue? She should be here **by now**. (= now or before now – so she should have arrived already)

This cheese should be used **by 14 August**.

You cannot use **until** with this meaning:
- Tell me **by Friday** whether or not you can come to the party. (*not* 'Tell me until Friday')

B

We use **until** (*or* **till**) to say *how long* a situation continues:
- 'Shall we go now?'   'No, let's **wait until** (*or* **till**) it stops raining.'
- I couldn't get up this morning. { I **stayed in bed until** half past ten.
                                    I **didn't get up until** half past ten.

Compare **until** and **by**:

until	by
Something *continues* **until** a time in the future:	Something *happens* **by** a time in the future:
• Fred **will be away until** Monday. (so he'll be back *on* Monday)	• Fred **will be back by** Monday. (= he'll be back not later than Monday)
• I'll be working until 11.30. (so I'll stop working *at* 11.30)	• I'll have finished my work by 11.30. (I'll finish my work not later than 11.30)

C

You can say '**by the time** something happens'. Study these examples:
- It's not worth going shopping now. **By the time we get to the shops**, they will be closed. (= the shops will close between now and the time we get there)
- (*from a letter*) I'm flying to the United States this evening. So **by the time you receive this letter**, I'll be in New York. (= I will arrive in New York between now and the time you receive this letter)
- Hurry up! **By the time we get to the cinema**, the film will already have started.

You can say '**by the time** something happened' (for the *past*):
- Jane's car broke down on the way to the party last night. **By the time she arrived**, most of the other guests had gone. (= it took her a long time to get to the party and most of the guests went home during this time)
- I had a lot of work to do yesterday evening. I was very tired **by the time I finished**. (= it took me a long time to do the work and I became more and more tired during this time)
- We went to the cinema last night. It took us a long time to find somewhere to park the car. **By the time we got to the cinema**, the film had already started.

Also **by then** *or* **by that time**:
- Jane finally arrived at the party at midnight, but **by then** (*or* **by that time**), most of the guests had gone.

119.1 *Make sentences with* **by.**

1 I have to be at home not later than 5 o'clock. ....I have to be at home by 5 o'clock.

2 I have to be at the airport not later than 10.30. I have to be at the airport ....

3 Let me know not later than Saturday whether you can come to the party.
   Let me know ....

4 Please make sure that you're here not later than 2 o'clock.
   Please ....

5 If we leave now, we should arrive not later than lunchtime.
   ....

119.2 *Put in* **by** *or* **until.**

1 Fred has gone away. He'll be away ....until... Monday.

2 Sorry, but I must go. I have to be at home ....by.... 5 o'clock.

3 I've been offered a job. I haven't decided yet whether to accept it or not. I have to decide
   .... Thursday.

4 I think I'll wait .... Thursday before making a decision.

5 It's too late to go shopping. The shops are only open .... 5.30. They'll be
   closed .... now.

6 I'd better pay the phone bill. It has to be paid .... tomorrow.

7 Don't pay the bill today. Wait .... tomorrow.

8 A: Have you finished redecorating your house?
   B: Not yet. We hope to finish .... the end of the week.

9 A: I'm going out now. I'll be back at 4.30. Will you still be here?
   B: I don't think so. I'll probably have gone out .... then.

10 I'm moving into my new flat next week. I'm staying with a friend .... then.

11 I've got a lot of work to do. .... the time I finish, it will be time to go to bed.

12 If you want to do the exam, you should enter .... 3 April.

119.3 *Use your own ideas to complete these sentences. Use* **by** *or* **until.**

1 Fred is away at the moment. He'll be away ....until Monday.

2 Fred is away at the moment. He'll be back ....by Monday.

3 I'm just going out. I won't be very long. Wait here ....

4 I'm going shopping. It's 4.30 now. I won't be very long. I'll be back ....

5 If you want to apply for the job, your application must be received ....

6 Last night I watched TV ....

119.4 *Read the situations and complete the sentences using* **By the time... .**

1 Jane was invited to a party but she got there much later than she intended.
   ..By the time she got to the party.. , most of the other guests had gone.

2 I had to catch a train but it took me longer than expected to get to the station.
   .... , my train had already gone.

3 I saw two men who looked as if they were trying to steal a car. I called the police but it was
   some time before they arrived.
   .... , the two men had disappeared.

4 A man escaped from prison last night. It was a long time before the guards discovered what
   had happened.
   .... , the escaped prisoner was miles away.

5 I intended to go shopping after finishing my work. But I finished my work much later than
   expected. .... , it was too late to go shopping.

At/on/in (time)

A Compare **at**, **on** and **in**:
- They arrived **at 5 o'clock**.
- They arrived **on Friday**.
- They arrived **in October**. / They arrived **in 1968**.

We use:

at for the time of day: **at 5 o'clock**   **at 11.45**   **at midnight**   **at lunchtime**   **at sunset** etc.
on for days and dates: **on Friday / on Fridays**   **on 12 March 1991**   **on Christmas Day**   **on my birthday**

in for longer periods (for example, months/years/seasons):
  in October   **in 1968**   **in the 18th century**   **in the past**
  in (the) winter   **in the 1970s**   **in the Middle Ages**   **in (the) future**

B We use **at** in these expressions:

at night	• I don't like going out **at night**.
at the weekend / at weekends	• Will you be here **at the weekend**?
at Christmas / at Easter	• Do you give each other presents **at Christmas**?
(*but* **on** Christmas Day)	
at the moment / at present	• Mr Benn is busy **at the moment / at present**.
at the same time	• Liz and I arrived **at the same time**.

Note that we usually ask '**What time…?**' (*not usually* 'At what time…?'):
- **What time** are you going out this evening?

C We say:
  in the morning(s)   **in the afternoon(s)**   **in the evening(s)**
- I'll see you **in the morning**.   • Do you work **in the evenings**?

but:
  on Friday morning(s)   **on Sunday** afternoon(s)   **on Monday** evening(s) etc.
- I'll be at home **on Friday morning**.   • Do you usually go out **on Saturday evenings**?

D We do *not* use **at/on/in** before **last/next/this/every**:
- I'll see you **next Friday**. (*not* 'on next Friday')
- They got married **last March**.

E **In a few minutes / in six months** etc. = a time in the future
- The train will be leaving **in a few minutes**. (= a few minutes from now)
- Jack has gone away. He'll be back **in a week**. (= a week from now)
- She'll be here **in a moment**. (= a moment from now)

You can also say 'in six months' time', 'in a week's time' etc.:
- They're getting married **in six months' time**. (*or* …**in six months**.)

We also use **in…** to say how long it takes to do something:
- I learnt to drive **in four weeks**. (= it took me four weeks to learn)

On/In time, at/in the end → UNIT 121   In/at/on (place) → UNITS 122–124   On/in/at (other meanings) → UNIT 126

120.1 *Complete the sentences. Each time use* **at, on** *or* **in** + *one of the following:*

the evening	about 20 minutes	~~1492~~	Christmas
the moment	21 July 1969	the 1920s	the same time
Sundays	the Middle Ages	11 seconds	night

1 Columbus made his first voyage from Europe to America ...in 1492.

2 In Britain most people do not work ....

3 If the sky is clear, you can see the stars ....

4 After working hard during the day, I like to relax ....

5 The first man walked on the moon ....

6 It's difficult to listen if everyone is speaking ....

7 Jazz became popular in the United States ....

8 I'm just going out to the shop. I'll be back ....

9 *(on the phone)* 'Can I speak to Clare?'   'I'm afraid she's not here ....,'

10 In Britain people send each other cards ....

11 Many of Europe's great cathedrals were built ....

12 Bob is a very fast runner. He can run 100 metres ....

120.2 *Put in* **at, on** *or* **in** *where necessary. Leave an empty space (–) if no preposition is necessary.*

1 a I'll see you ...on... Friday.
   b I'll see you ...–... next Friday.
      (no preposition)

2 a What are you doing .... Saturday?
   b What are you doing .... the weekend?

3 a They often go out .... the evenings.
   b They often go out .... Sunday evenings.

4 a Do you work .... Wednesdays?
   b Do you work .... every Wednesday?

5 a We usually have a holiday .... the summer.
   b We often have a short holiday .... Christmas.

6 a Pauline got married .... 1991.
   b Pauline got married .... 18 May 1991.
   c Chris is getting married .... this year.

120.3 *Put in* **at, on** *or* **in.**

1 Mozart was born in Salzburg .... 1756.

2 I haven't seen Kate for a few days. I last saw her .... Tuesday.

3 The price of electricity is going up .... October.

4 I've been invited to a wedding .... 14 February.

5 Hurry up! We've got to go .... five minutes.

6 I'm busy just now but I'll be with you .... a moment.

7 Jenny's brother is an engineer but he's out of work .... the moment.

8 There are usually a lot of parties .... New Year's Eve.

9 I hope the weather will be nice .... the weekend.

10 .... Saturday night I went to bed .... 11 o'clock.

11 I don't like travelling .... night.

12 We travelled overnight to Paris and arrived .... 5 o'clock .... the morning.

13 The course begins .... 7 January and ends sometime .... April.

14 It was quite a short book and easy to read. I read it .... a day.

15 I might not be at home .... Tuesday morning but I'll probably be there .... the afternoon.

16 My car is being repaired at the garage. It will be ready .... two hours.

17 The telephone and the doorbell rang .... the same time.

18 Mary and Henry always go out for a meal .... their wedding anniversary.

19 Henry is 63. He'll be retiring from his job .... two years' time.

On time / in time   At the end / in the end

A   On time and in time

On time = punctual, not late. If something happens **on time**, it happens at the time which was planned:

- The 11.45 train left **on time**. (= it left at 11.45)
- 'I'll meet you at 7.30.'   'OK, but please be **on time**.' (= don't be late, be there at 7.30)
- The conference was very well organised. Everything began and finished **on time**.

The opposite of **on time** is **late**:

- Be **on time**. Don't be **late**.

In time (for something / to do something) = soon enough
- Will you be home **in time** for dinner? (= soon enough for dinner)
- I've sent Jill her birthday present. I hope it arrives **in time** (for her birthday). (= soon enough for her birthday)
- I must hurry. I want to get home **in time to see** the football match on television. (= soon enough to see the football match)

The opposite of **in time** is **too late**:
- I got home **too late** to see the football match.

You can say **just in time** (= almost too late):
- We got to the station **just in time** to catch the train.
- A child ran across the road in front of the car, but I managed to stop **just in time**.

B   At the end and in the end

At the end (of something) = at the time when something ends. For example:

at the end of **the month**	at the end of **January**	at the end of **the match**
at the end of **the film**	at the end of **the course**	at the end of **the concert**

- I'm going away **at the end of January / at the end of the month**.
- **At the end of the concert**, there was great applause.
- All the players shook hands **at the end of the match**.

You can*not* say '**in the end** of *something*'. So you can*not* say 'in the end of January' or 'in the end of the concert'.

The opposite of **at the end** is **at the beginning**:
    at the beginning of January   at the beginning of the concert

---

In the end = finally
We use **in the end** when we say what the final result of a situation was:
- We had a lot of problems with our car. **In the end** we sold it and bought another one. (= finally we sold it)
- He got more and more angry. **In the end** he just walked out of the room.
- Jim couldn't decide where to go for his holidays. He didn't go anywhere **in the end**.

The opposite of **in the end** is usually **at first**:
- **At first** we didn't like each other very much, but **in the end** we became good friends.

121.1 *Complete the sentences with* **on time** *or* **in time**.

1　The bus was late this morning but it's usually ...**on time.**..
2　The film was supposed to start at 8.30 but it didn't begin ....
3　I like to get up .... to have a big breakfast before going to work.
4　We want to start the meeting .... , so please don't be late.
5　I've just washed this shirt. I want to wear it this evening, so I hope it will be dry
　 ....
6　The train service isn't very good. The trains are rarely ....
7　I nearly missed my flight this morning. I got to the airport just ....
8　I nearly forgot that it was Joe's birthday. Fortunately I remembered ....
9　Why are you never ....? You always keep everybody waiting.

121.2 *Read the situations and make sentences using* **just in time**.

1　A child ran across the road in front of your car. You saw the child at the last moment.
　 (manage / stop) ...**I managed to stop just in time.**..
2　You were walking home without an umbrella. Just after you got home, it started to rain very
　 heavily.　(get / home) ....
3　Tim was going to sit on the chair you had just painted. You said, 'Don't sit in that chair!', so
　 he didn't.　(stop / him) I ....
4　You went to the cinema. You were a bit late and you thought you would miss the beginning
　 of the film. But the film began just as you sat down in the cinema.　(get / cinema / beginning
　 of the film) ....

121.3 *Complete the sentences using* **at the end** + *one of the following:*
the course　　the interview　　~~the match~~　　the month　　the race

1　All the players shook hands ...**at the end of the match.**..
2　I normally get paid ....
3　The students had a party ....
4　Two of the runners collapsed ....
5　To my surprise I was offered the job ....

121.4 *Write sentences with* **In the end**. *Use the verb in brackets.*

1　We had a lot of problems with our car.　(sell) ...**In the end we sold it.**..
2　Judy got more and more fed up with her job.　(resign) ....
3　I tried to learn German but I found it too difficult.　(give up) ....
4　We couldn't decide whether to go to the party or not.　(not / go)
　 ....

121.5 *Put in* **at** *or* **in**.

1　I'm going away ...**at**... the end of the month.
2　It took me a long time to find a job.　.................. the end I got a job in a hotel.
3　Are you going away .... the beginning of August or .... the end?
4　I couldn't decide what to buy Mary for her birthday. I didn't buy her anything .... the
　 end.
5　We waited ages for a taxi. We gave up .... the end and walked home.
6　I'll be moving to a new address .... the end of September.
7　At first Helen didn't want to go to the theatre but she came with us .... the end.
8　I'm going away .... the end of this week.
9　'I didn't know what to do.'　'Yes, you were in a difficult position. What did you do
　 .... the end?'

In/at/on (place) (1)

A **In** Study these examples:

in a room
in a building
in a box

in a garden
in a town/city
in a country

- There's no one **in the room** / **in the building** / **in the garden**.
- What have you got **in your hand** / **in your mouth**?
- When we were **in Italy**, we spent a few days **in Venice**. (*not* 'at Venice')
- I have a friend who lives **in a small village** in the mountains.
- Look at those people swimming **in the pool** / **in the sea** / **in the river**.

B **At** Study these examples:

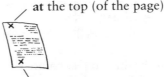

at the top (of the page)

at the bus stop
at the door
at the window

at the bottom (of the page)

at the end
of the street

- Who is that man standing **at the bus stop** / **at the door** / **at the window**?
- Turn left **at the traffic lights** / **at the church** / **at the roundabout**.
- Write your name **at the top** / **at the bottom** of the page.
- Angela's house is the white one **at the end** of the street.
- When you leave the hotel, please leave your key **at reception**.

C **On** Study these examples:

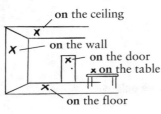

on the ceiling

on the wall

on the door

on the table

on the floor

on her nose

on a page

on an island

- I sat **on the floor** / **on the ground** / **on the grass** / **on a chair** / **on the beach**.
- There's a dirty mark **on the wall** / **on the ceiling** / **on your nose** / **on your shirt**.
- Have you seen the notice **on the notice board** / **on the door**?
- You'll find details of TV programmes **on page seven** (of the newspaper).

D Compare **in** and **at**:
- There were a lot of people **in the shop**. It was very crowded.

but Go along this road, then turn left **at the shop**. (*somebody giving directions*)

Compare **in** and **on**:
- There is some water **in the bottle**.

but There is a label **on the bottle**.

in the bottle

on the bottle

Compare **at** and **on**:
- There is somebody **at the door**. Shall I go and see who it is?

but There is a notice **on the door**. It says 'Do not disturb'.

122.1 *Answer the questions about the pictures. Use* **in, at** *or* **on** *with the words below the pictures.*

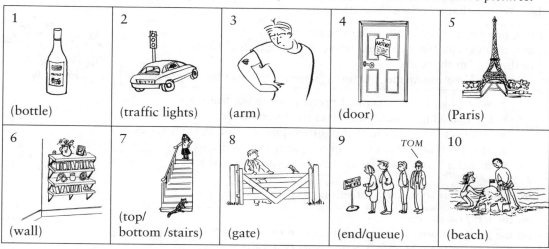

1	2	3	4	5
(bottle)	(traffic lights)	(arm)	(door)	(Paris)

6	7	8	9	10
(wall)	(top/ bottom /stairs)	(gate)	(end/queue)	(beach)

1 Where's the label? ...**On the bottle.**...
2 Where is the car waiting? ....
....
3 Where's the fly? ....
4 a Where's the notice? ....
b Where's the key? ....
5 Where's the Eiffel Tower? ....
6 Where are the shelves? ....

7 a Where's the woman standing? ....
....
b And the cat? ....
8 a Where's the man standing? ....
b Where's the bird? ....
9 Where's Tom standing? ....
....
10 Where are the children playing? ....

122.2 *Complete the sentences. Use* **in, at** *or* **on** *+ one of the following:*

the window   your coffee   the mountains   that tree
my guitar   ~~the river~~   the island   the next garage

1 Look at those people swimming ...**in the river.**...
2 One of the strings .... is broken.
3 There's something wrong with the car. We'd better stop ....
4 Would you like sugar ....?
5 The leaves .... are a beautiful colour.
6 Last year we had a wonderful skiing holiday ....
7 There's nobody living .... It's uninhabited.
8 He spends most of the day sitting .... and looking outside.

122.3 *Complete the sentences with* **in, at** *or* **on.**

1 Write your name ...**at**... the top of the page.
2 I like that picture hanging .... the wall .... the kitchen.
3 There was an accident .... the crossroads this morning.
4 I wasn't sure whether I had come to the right office. There was no name .... the door.
5 .... the end of the street there is a path leading to the river.
6 You'll find the sports results .... the back page of the newspaper.
7 I wouldn't like an office job. I couldn't spend the whole day sitting .... a desk.
8 My brother lives .... a small village .... the south-west of England.
9 The man the police are looking for has a scar .... his right cheek.
10 The headquarters of the company are .... Milan.
11 Nicola was wearing a silver ring .... her little finger.

In/at/on (place) (2)

A **In**   We say that somebody/something is:

> in a line / in a row / in a queue / in a street
> in a photograph / in a picture / (look at yourself) in a mirror
> in the sky / in the world
> in a book / in a newspaper / in a magazine / in a letter (*but* 'on a page')

in a row

- When I go to the cinema, I prefer to sit **in the front row.**
- I live **in King Street.** Sarah lives **in Queen Street.**
- Who is the woman **in that photograph?** (*not* 'on that photograph')
- Have you seen this article **in the paper** (= newspaper)?
- It was a lovely day. There wasn't a cloud **in the sky.**

B **On**   We say that somebody/something is:

> on the left / on the right
> on the ground floor / on the first floor / on the second floor etc.
> on a map / on the menu (in a restaurant) / on a list
> on a farm

- In Britain we drive **on the left.** (*or* ...**on the left-hand side.**)
- Our flat is **on the second floor** of the building.
- Here's a shopping list. Don't buy anything that's not **on the list.**
- Have you ever worked **on a farm?**

We say that a place is **on a river / on a road / on the coast:**
- London is **on the river Thames.**
- Portsmouth is **on the south coast** of England.

We say that a place is **on the way** to another place:
- We stopped at a small village **on the way** to London.

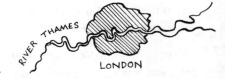

C **The corner**
We say '**in the corner** of a **room**', but '**at the corner**
(*or* **on the corner**) of a **street**':
- The television is **in the corner** of the room.
- There is a public telephone **at/on the corner**
  of the street.

in the corner   at/on the corner

D **The front** and **the back**
We say **in the front / in the back** of **a car:**
- I was sitting **in the back** (of the car) when we crashed.

but
at the front / at the back of **a building / cinema / group of people** etc.:
- The garden is **at the back of the house.**
- Let's sit **at the front** (of the cinema). (*but* '**in the
  front row**' – see Section **A**)
- I was standing **at the back,** so I couldn't see very well.

Also
on the front / on the back of **a letter / piece of paper** etc.:
- Write your name **on the back of this envelope.**

at the back

at the front

123.1 *Answer the questions about the pictures. Use* **in, at** *or* **on** *with the words below the pictures.*

1 SUE	2	3	4	5
(queue)	(second floor)	(corner)	(corner)	(back/car)

6	7	8	9	10 KATE
(mirror)	(front) ANN	(back row)	(left/right)	(farm)

1 What's Sue doing?
  She's standing ...in a queue....
2 Sue lives in this building. Where's her
  flat exactly? ....
3 Where is the woman standing?
  ....
4 Where is the man standing?
  ....
5 Where's the dog? ....

6 What's the man doing?
  He's looking ....
7 Ann is in this group of people. Where is
  she? ....
8 Tom is at the cinema. Where is he sitting?
  ....
9 a Where's the post office? ....
  b And the bank? ....
10 Where does Kate work? ....

123.2 *Complete the sentences. Use* **in, at** *or* **on** + *one of the following:*

the west coast	the world	the front row	the right
the back of the envelope	~~the sky~~	the back of the class	my way to work

1 It was a lovely day. There wasn't a cloud ...in the sky...
2 In most countries people drive ....
3 What is the tallest building ....?
4 I usually buy a newspaper .... in the morning.
5 San Francisco is .... of the United States.
6 We went to the theatre last night. We had seats ....
7 I couldn't hear the teacher very well. She spoke quietly and I was sitting ....
8 When you send a letter, it is a good idea to write your name and address ....

123.3 *Complete the sentences with* **in, at** *or* **on**.

1 It can be dangerous when children play .... the street.
2 If you walk to the end of the street, you'll see a small shop .... the corner.
3 Is Tom .... this photograph? I can't find him.
4 My office is .... the first floor. It's .... the left as you come out of the lift.
5 We normally use the front entrance but there's another entrance .... the back.
6 A: Is there anything interesting .... the paper today?
  B: Well, there's an unusual photograph .... the back page.
7 I love to look up at the stars .... the sky at night.
8 *(in a restaurant)* 'Where shall we sit?' 'Over there, ... the corner.'
9 When I'm a passenger in a car, I prefer to sit .... the front.
10 It's a very small village. You probably won't find it .... your map.
11 Paris is .... the river Seine.

In/at/on (place) (3)

A

In bed / at home etc.

We say that somebody is **in bed / in hospital / in prison**:

- Mark isn't up yet. He's still **in bed**.
- Kay's mother is **in hospital**.

We say that somebody is **at home / at work / at school / at university / at college**:

- I'll be **at work** until 5.30 but I'll be **at home** all evening.
- Julia is studying chemistry **at university**.

Also **at sea** (= on a voyage). Compare **at sea** and **in the sea**:

- It was a long voyage. We were **at sea** for 30 days.
- I love swimming **in the sea**.

B

At a party / at a concert etc.

We say that somebody is **at** an *event* (**at a party / at a conference** etc.):

- Were there many people **at the party / at the meeting**?
- I saw Jack **at a football match / at a concert** last Saturday.

C

In and **at** for buildings

You can often use **in** or **at** with buildings. For example, you can eat **in a restaurant** or **at a restaurant**. We usually say **at** when we say *where an event takes place* (for example, a concert, a film, a party, a meeting, a sports event):

- We went to a concert **at the Royal Festival Hall**.
- The meeting took place **at the company's headquarters**.
- The film I want to see is showing **at the Odeon** (cinema).

We say **at the station / at the airport**:

- Don't meet me **at the station**. I can get a taxi.

We say **at** somebody's house:

- I was **at Judy's house** last night.   *or*   I was **at Judy's** last night.

Also: **at the doctor's, at the hairdresser's** etc.

We use **in** when we are thinking about the building itself:

- The rooms **in Judy's house** are very small. (*not* 'at Judy's house')
- I enjoyed the film but it was very cold **in the cinema**. (*not* 'at the cinema')

D

In and **at** for towns etc.

We normally use **in** with cities, towns and villages:

- Tom's parents live **in Nottingham**. (*not* 'at Nottingham')
- The Louvre is a famous art museum **in Paris**. (*not* 'at Paris')

But you can use **at** *or* **in** when you think of the place as *a point or station on a journey*:

- Do you know if this train stops **at** (*or* **in**) **Nottingham**? (= at Nottingham station)
- We stopped **at** (*or* **in**) a small **village** on the way to London.

E

On a bus / in a car etc.

We usually say **on a bus / on a train / on a plane / on a ship**   *but*   **in a car / in a taxi**:

- **The bus** was very full. There were too many people **on it**.
- George arrived **in a taxi**.

We say **on a bicycle / on a motorcycle / on a horse**:

- Mary passed me **on her bicycle**.

For **by bus / by car / by bicycle** etc., see Unit 127.

124.1 *Complete the sentences about the pictures. Use* **in**, **at** *or* **on** *with the words below the pictures.*

1 CAR HIRE / LONDON AIRPORT (the airport)	2 DAVE (a train)	3 CONFERENCE TESSA (a conference)	4 MARTIN (hospital)
5 JUDY (the hairdresser)	6 MARY (her bicycle)	7 (New York)	8 THE NATIONAL THEATRE (the National Theatre)

1 You can hire a car ...**at the airport.**.........
2 Dave is ....
3 Tessa is ....
4 Martin is ....

5 Judy is ....
6 I saw Mary ....
7 We spent a few days ....
8 We saw a play ....

124.2 *Complete the sentences. Use* **in**, **at** *or* **on** + *one of the following:*

sea	hospital	bed	~~the station~~	the cinema
the plane	school	prison	the airport	the Sports Centre

1 My train arrives at 11.30. Can you meet me ...**at the station?**...
2 I didn't feel very well when I woke up, so I stayed ....
3 I think I'd like to see a film. What's on .... this week?
4 Some people are .... for crimes that they did not commit.
5 'What does your sister do? Has she got a job?'   'No, she's still ....'
6 I play basketball .... on Friday evenings.
7 A friend of mine was injured in an accident a few days ago. She's still ....
8 Our flight was delayed. We had to wait .... for four hours.
9 I enjoyed the flight but the food .... wasn't very nice.
10 Bill works on ships. He is away .... most of the time.

124.3 *Complete these sentences with* **in**, **at** *or* **on**.

1 I didn't see you .... the party on Saturday. Where were you?
2 It was a very slow train. It stopped .... every station.
3 I don't know where my umbrella is. Perhaps I left it .... the bus.
4 Shall we travel .... your car or mine?
5 The exhibition .... the Museum of Modern Art finished on Saturday.
6 We stayed .... a very nice hotel when we were .... Amsterdam.
7 There were fifty rooms .... the hotel.
8 Tom is ill. He wasn't .... work today. He was .... home .... bed.
9 I wasn't in when you phoned. I was .... my sister's house.
10 It's always too hot .... my sister's house. The heating is always on too high.
11 I haven't seen Kate for some time. I last saw her .... Dave's wedding.
12 Paul lives .... London. He's a student .... London University.

A

We say **go/come/travel** (etc.) **to** a place or event. For example:

go to America	**go to** bed	**take** (somebody) **to** hospital
return to Italy	**go to** the bank	**come to** my house
drive to the airport	**go to** a concert	**be sent to** prison

- When are your friends **returning to** Italy? (*not* 'returning in Italy')
- After the accident three people were **taken to hospital.**

In the same way we say: **on my way to…** / **a journey to…** / **a trip to…** / **welcome to…** etc.:

- **Welcome to** our country! (*not* 'welcome in')

Compare **to** (for *movement*) and **in/at** (for *position*):

- They are **going to** France.   *but*   They **live in** France.
- Can you **come to** the party?   *but*   I'll **see you at** the party.

B

Been to

We usually say 'I've **been to** a place':

- I've **been to Italy** four times but I've never **been to Rome.**
- Ann has never **been to a football match** in her life.
- Jack has got some money. He has just **been to the bank.**

C

Get and **arrive**

We say '**get to** a place':

- What time did they **get to London** / **get to work** / **get to the party?**

But we say '**arrive in…**' or '**arrive at…**' (*not* 'arrive to').
We say '**arrive in** a country or town/city':

- When did they **arrive in Britain** / **arrive in London?**

For other places (buildings etc.) or events, we say '**arrive at**':

- What time did they **arrive at the hotel** / **arrive at the party** / **arrive at work?**

D

Home

We do not say 'to home'. We say **go home** / **come home** / **get home** / **arrive home** / **on the way home** etc. (no preposition):

- I'm tired. Let's **go home.** (*not* 'go to home')
- I met Caroline **on my way home.**

But we say '**be at** home', '**stay at** home', 'do something **at** home' etc. See Units 73C and 124A.

E

Into

'**Go into…**', '**get into…**' etc. = 'enter' (a room / a building / a car etc.):

- She **got into** the car and drove away.
- A bird **flew into** the kitchen through the window.

We sometimes use **in** (instead of **into**):

- Don't wait outside. **Come in the house.** (*or* **Come into** the house.)

Note that we say '**enter** a building / **enter** a room' etc. (*not* 'enter into')

The opposite of **into** is **out of**:

- She **got out of** the car and **went into** a shop.

Note that we usually say '**get on/off** a bus / a train / a plane':

- She **got on the bus** and I never saw her again.

125.1 *Put in* **to/at/in/into** *where necessary. If no preposition is necessary leave an empty space (–).*

1 Three people were taken ...**to**... hospital after the accident.
2 I met Caroline on my way ...**–**... home. (*no preposition*)
3 We left our luggage .... the station and went to find something to eat.
4 Shall we take a taxi .... the station or shall we walk?
5 I must go .... the bank today to change some money.
6 The river Rhine flows .... the North Sea.
7 I'm tired. As soon as I get .... home, I'm going .... bed.
8 'Have you got your camera?'   'No, I left it .... home.'
9 Marcel is French. He has just returned .... France after two years .... Brazil.
10 Are you going .... Linda's party next week?
11 Carl was born .... Chicago but his family moved .... New York when he was three. He still lives .... New York.
12 Have you ever been .... China?
13 I had lost my key but I managed to climb .... the house through a window.
14 We got stuck in a traffic jam on our way .... the airport.
15 We had lunch .... the airport while we were waiting for our plane.
16 Welcome .... the hotel. We hope you enjoy your stay here.
17 *What do you say to someone visiting your town or country?* Welcome ....!

125.2 *Have you been to these places? If so, how many times? Choose three of the places and write a sentence using* **been to.**

Athens   Australia   Ireland   London   Paris   Rome   Sweden   the United States

1 (*example answers*) ...**I've never been to Australia. / I've been to Australia three times.**
2 ....
3 ....
4 ....

125.3 *Put in* **to/at/in** *where necessary. If no preposition is necessary leave an empty space (–).*

1 What time does this train get ...**to**... London?
2 What time does this train arrive .... London?
3 What time did you get .... home last night?
4 What time do you usually arrive .... work in the morning?
5 When we got .... the cinema, there was a long queue outside.
6 I arrived .... home feeling very tired.

125.4 *Write sentences using* **get into / out of / on / off.**

1 You were walking home. A friend passed you in her car. She saw you, stopped and offered you a lift. She opened the door. What did you do? ...**I got into the car.**...
2 You were waiting for the bus. At last your bus came. The doors opened. What did you do then? I ....
3 You drove home in your car. You arrived at your house and parked the car. What did you do then? ....
4 You were travelling by train to Manchester. When the train got to Manchester, what did you do? ....
5 You needed a taxi. After a few minutes a taxi stopped for you. You opened the door. What did you do then? ....
6 You were travelling by air. At the end of your flight the plane landed at the airport and stopped. The doors were opened, you took your bag and stood up. What did you do then?
....

On/in/at (other uses)

A

On holiday etc.

(be/go) **on holiday / on business / on a trip / on a tour / on a cruise** etc.:
- Tom's away at the moment. He's **on holiday** in France. (*not* 'in holiday')
- Did you go to Germany **on business** or **on holiday**?
- One day I'd like to go **on a world tour**.

Note that you can also say: 'go to a place **for a** holiday / **for my** holiday(s)':
- Tom has gone to France **for a holiday**. (*not* 'for holiday')
- Where are you going **for your holidays** next summer?

B

Other expressions with **on**

on television / on the radio:
- I didn't watch the news **on television**, but I heard it **on the radio**.

on the phone/telephone:
- You can't phone me. I'm not **on the phone**. (= I haven't got a phone.)
- I've never met her but I've spoken to her **on the phone**.

(be/go) **on strike / on a diet:**
- There are no trains today. The railway workers are **on strike**.
- I've put on a lot of weight. I'll have to go **on a diet**.

(be) **on fire:**
- Look! That car is **on fire**!

on the whole (= in general):
- Sometimes I have problems at work but **on the whole** I enjoy my job.

on purpose (= intentionally):
- I'm sorry. I didn't mean to annoy you. I didn't do it **on purpose**.

But: **by** mistake / **by** chance / **by** accident (see Unit 127).

C

Expressions with **in**

in the rain / in the sun (= sunshine) **/ in the shade / in the dark / in bad weather** etc.:
- We sat **in the shade**. It was too hot to sit **in the sun**.
- Don't go out **in the rain**. Wait until it stops.

(write) **in ink / in biro / in pencil:**
- When you do the exam, you're not allowed to write **in pencil**.

Also: **in words, in figures, in BLOCK LETTERS** etc.:
- Please fill in the form **in block letters**.

(pay) **in cash:**
- I paid the bill **in cash**.   *but*   I paid **by** cheque / **by** credit card (see Unit 127).

(be/fall) **in love (with** somebody):
- Have you ever been **in love with** anybody?

in (my) opinion:
- **In my opinion**, the film wasn't very good.

D

At the age of... etc.

We say: **at the age of... / at a speed of... / at a temperature of...** etc. For example:
- Jill left school **at 16**.   *or*   ...**at the age of 16**.
- The train was travelling **at 120 miles an hour**.   *or*   ...**at a speed** of 120 miles an hour.
- Water boils **at 100 degrees celsius**.

126.1 *Complete the sentences using* **on** + *one of the following:*

business	strike	a tour	the whole	television
~~fire~~	holiday	a diet	the phone	purpose

1 Look! That car is ...*on fire*...! Somebody call the fire brigade.
2 It's difficult to contact Sarah because she's not ....
3 Workers at the factory have gone .... for better pay and conditions.
4 Soon after we arrived, we were taken .... of the city.
5 A: I'm going .... next week.
   B: Are you? Where are you going? Somewhere nice?
6 I feel lazy this evening. Is there anything worth watching ....?
7 I'm sorry. It was an accident. I didn't do it ....
8 George has put on a lot of weight recently. I think he should go ....
9 Jane's job involves a lot of travelling. She often has to go away ....
10 A: How did your exams go?
    B: Well, there were some difficult questions but .... they were OK.

126.2 *Complete the sentences using* **in** + *one of the following:*

block letters	cash	my opinion	the shade	cold weather	love	pencil

1 He likes to keep warm, so he doesn't go out much ....
2 Diane never uses a pen. She always writes ....
3 They fell .... with each other almost immediately and were married in a few weeks.
4 Please write your address clearly, preferably ....
5 I don't like the sun. I prefer to sit ....
6 Ann thought the restaurant was OK, but .... it wasn't very good.
7 I hardly ever use a credit card or cheques. I prefer to pay for things ....

126.3 *Put in the correct preposition:* **on, in, at,** *or* **for.**

1 Water boils ...*at*... 100 degrees celsius.
2 When I was 14, I went .... a trip to France organised by my school.
3 I wouldn't like his job. He spends most of his time talking .... the phone.
4 Julia's grandmother died recently .... the age of 79.
5 Can you turn the light on, please? I don't want to sit .... the dark.
6 We didn't go .... holiday last year. We stayed at home.
7 I'm going to Scotland .... a short holiday next month.
8 I won't be here next week. I'll be .... holiday.
9 He got married .... 17, which is rather young to get married.
10 There was an interesting programme .... the radio this morning.
11 .... my opinion, violent films should not be shown .... television.
12 I wouldn't like to go .... a cruise. I think I'd get bored.
13 I mustn't eat too much. I'm supposed to be .... a diet.
14 In Britain, children start school .... the age of five.
15 There was panic when people realised that the building was .... fire.
16 The Earth travels round the Sun .... a speed of 107,000 kilometres an hour.
17 'Did you enjoy your holiday?' 'Not every minute, but .... the whole, yes.'
18 When you write a cheque, you have to write the amount .... words and figures.

By

We use **by** in a number of different ways:

A

We use **by...** in many expressions to say *how* we do something. For example, you can:
send something **by post**   do something **by hand**
pay **by cheque / by credit card** (*but* pay **in cash**)
or something can happen **by mistake / by accident / by chance** (*but* do something **on purpose**):
- Did you pay **by cheque** or **in cash**?
- We hadn't arranged to meet. We met **by chance**.

In these expressions we use **by** + *noun* without 'a' or 'the'. We say **by chance / by cheque** etc. (*not* 'by a chance / by a cheque').

B

In the same way we use **by...** to say how somebody travels:
by car / by train / by plane / by boat / by ship / by bus / by bicycle etc.
and   **by road / by rail / by air / by sea / by underground**
- Liz usually goes to work **by bus**.   • Do you prefer to travel **by air** or **by train**?

But we say '**on foot**':
- Did you come here **by car** or **on foot**?

You cannot use **by** if you say '**my car**' / '**the train**' / '**a taxi**' etc. We use **by** + *noun* without 'a/the/my' etc. We say:
by car   *but*   **in my** car (*not* 'by my car')
by train   *but*   **on the** train (*not* 'by the train')

We use **in** for cars and taxis:
- They didn't come **in their car**. They came **in a taxi**.

We use **on** for bicycles and public transport (buses, trains etc.):
- We travelled **on the 6.45 train**.

C

We say 'something is done **by** somebody/something' (*passive* – see Units 41–43):
- Have you ever been bitten **by a dog**?
- The programme was watched **by millions of people**.

Compare **by** and **with**:
- The door must have been opened **with a key**. (*not* 'by a key')
  (= somebody used a key to open it)
- The door must have been opened **by somebody** with a key.

We say 'a play **by** Shakespeare', 'a painting **by** Rembrandt', 'a novel **by** Tolstoy' etc.
- Have you read any books **by Agatha Christie**?

D

By also means next to / beside:
- Come and sit **by me**. (= beside me)
- 'Where's the light switch?' '**By the door**.'

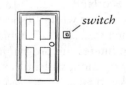

switch

E

Note the following use of **by...**:
- Clare's salary has just gone up **from £1,000 a month to £1,100**. So it has increased **by £100** / **by ten per cent**.
- John and Roger had a race over 100 metres. Roger won **by about five metres**.

New salary   £1,100
increased BY £100
Old salary   £1,000

By -ing → **UNIT 59B**   By myself → **UNIT 81C**   By (time) → **UNIT 119**

EXERCISES

127.1 *Complete the sentences using* **by** + *one of the following:*

~~chance~~   chance   cheque   hand   mistake   satellite

1 We hadn't arranged to meet. We met .....**by chance.**.....
2 I didn't intend to take your umbrella. I took it ....
3 I didn't put the pullover in the washing machine. I washed it ....
4 If you haven't got any cash, you can pay ....
5 The two cities were connected .... for a television programme.
6 I never suspected anything. It was only .... that I found out what had happened.

127.2 *Put in* **by, in** *or* **on.**

1 Liz usually goes to work ....**by**.... bus.
2 I saw Jane this morning. She was .... the bus.
3 How did you get here? Did you come .... train?
4 How did you get here? Did you come .... the train?
5 I decided not to go .... car. I went .... my bike instead.
6 I didn't feel like walking home, so I came home .... a taxi.
7 Sorry we're late. We missed the bus, so we had to come .... foot.
8 How long does it take to cross the Atlantic .... sea?

127.3 *Write three sentences like the examples. Write about a book, a song, a painting, a film etc.*

1 ..'War and Peace' is a book by Tolstoy...
2 ..'Romeo and Juliet' is a play by Shakespeare...
3 ....
4 ....
5 ....

127.4 *Put in the correct preposition:* **by, in, on** *or* **with.**

1 Who is that man standing .... the window?
2 I managed to put the fire out .... a fire extinguisher.
3 The plane was badly damaged .... lightning.
4 These photographs were taken .... a friend of mine.
5 These photographs were taken .... a very good camera.
6 I don't mind going .... car but I don't want to go .... your car.
7 Shall we get a taxi or shall we go .... foot?
8 What's that music? I know it's .... Beethoven but I can't remember what it's called.
9 There was a small table .... the bed .... a lamp and a clock .... it.
10 Our team lost the game only because of a mistake .... one of our players.

127.5 *Complete the sentences using* **by.**

1 Clare's salary was £1,000 a month. Now it is £1,100.
   Her salary ...**has increased by £100 a month.**...
2 My daily newspaper used to cost 50 pence. From today it costs 60 pence.
   The price has gone up ....
3 There was an election. Helen got 25 votes and Norman got 23.
   Helen won ....
4 I went to Kate's house to see her but she had gone out five minutes before I arrived.
   I missed ....

Noun + preposition (reason **for**, cause **of** etc.)

A   *Noun + for…*

> a **cheque FOR** (a sum of money):
> - They sent me **a cheque for** £75.
>
> a **demand FOR** / a **need FOR**…:
> - The firm closed down because there wasn't enough **demand for** its product.
> - There's no excuse for behaviour like that. There's no **need for** it.
>
> a **reason FOR**…:
> - The train was late but nobody knew the **reason** for the delay. (*not* 'reason of')

B   *Noun + of…*

> an **advantage** / a **disadvantage OF**…:
> - The **advantage of living alone** is that you can do what you like.
>   *but* we usually say: '**there is an advantage in** (*or* **to**) doing something':
> - **There are** many advantages **in** (*or* **to**) living alone.
>
> a **cause OF**…:
> - Nobody knows what the **cause of** the explosion was.
>
> a **photograph** / a **picture** / a **map** / a **plan** / a **drawing** (etc.) **OF**…:
> - She showed me some **photographs of** her family.
> - I had a **map of** the town, so I was able to find my way around.

C   *Noun + in…*

> an **increase** / a **decrease** / a **rise** / a **fall IN** (prices etc.):
> - There has been an **increase in** the number of road accidents recently.
> - Last year was a bad year for the company. There was a big **fall in** sales.

D   *Noun + to…*

> **damage TO**…:
> - The accident was my fault, so I had to pay for the **damage to** the other car.
>
> an **invitation TO**… (a party / a wedding etc.):
> - Did you get an **invitation to** the party?
>
> a **solution TO** (a problem) / a **key TO** (a door) / an **answer TO** (a question) / a **reply TO** (a letter) / a **reaction TO**…:
> - Do you think we'll find a **solution to** the problem? (*not* 'a solution of the problem')
> - I was surprised at her **reaction to** my suggestion.
>
> an **attitude TO**… (*or* **TOWARDS**…):
> - His **attitude to** his job is very negative.   *or*   His **attitude towards** his job…

E   *Noun + with… / between…*

> a **relationship** / a **connection** / **contact WITH**…:
> - Do you have a good **relationship with** your parents?
> - The police want to question a man in **connection with** the robbery.
>
> *but:* a **relationship** / a **connection** / **contact** / a **difference BETWEEN** two things or people:
> - The police believe that there is no **connection between** the two crimes.
> - There are some **differences between** British and American English.

128.1 *Complete the second sentence so that it has the same meaning as the first.*

1 What caused the explosion? What was the cause ...of the explosion?...
2 We're trying to solve the problem. We're trying to find a solution ....
3 Sue gets on well with her brother. Sue has a good relationship ....
4 Prices have gone up a lot. There has been a big increase ....
5 I don't know how to answer your question. I can't think of an answer ....
6 I don't think that a new road is necessary.
  I don't think there is any need ....
7 The number of people without jobs fell last month.
  Last month there was a fall ....
8 Nobody wants to buy shoes like these any more.
  There is no demand ....
9 In what way is your job different from mine?
  What is the difference ....?

128.2 *Complete the sentences using one of the following nouns + the correct preposition.*

cause	connection	invitation	~~map~~	reason
damage	contact	key	pictures	reply

1 On the wall there were some pictures and a ...map of... the world.
2 Thank you for the .... your party next week.
3 Since she left home two years ago, she has had little .... her family.
4 I can't open this door. Have you got a .... the other door?
5 The .... the fire at the hotel last night is still unknown.
6 I wrote to Jim last week, but I still haven't received a .... my letter.
7 The two companies are completely independent. There is no .... them.
8 Jane showed me some old .... the city as it looked 100 years ago.
9 Carol has decided to give up her job. I don't know her .... doing this.
10 It wasn't a bad accident. The .... the car wasn't serious.

128.3 *Complete the sentences with the correct preposition.*

1 There are some differences ...between... British and American English.
2 Everything can be explained. There's a reason .... everything.
3 If I give you the camera, can you take a photograph .... me?
4 Money isn't the solution .... every problem.
5 There has been an increase .... the amount of traffic using this road.
6 When I opened the envelope, I was delighted to find a cheque .... £500.
7 The advantage .... having a car is that you don't have to rely on public transport.
8 There are many advantages .... being able to speak a foreign language.
9 When Paul left home, his attitude .... his parents seemed to change.
10 Bill and I used to be good friends but I don't have much contact .... him now.
11 There has been a sharp rise .... the cost of living in the past few years.
12 I'm sorry I haven't written to you for so long. The reason .... this is that I've been ill.
13 What was Emma's reaction .... the news?
14 Ken showed me a photograph .... the house where he lived as a child.
15 The company has rejected the workers' demands .... a rise .... pay.
16 What was the answer .... question 3 in the test?
17 The fact that Jane was offered a job has no connection .... the fact that her cousin is
  the managing director.

Adjective + preposition (1)

A It was **nice of** you to...

> **nice / kind / good / generous / polite / silly / stupid** etc. **OF** somebody (to do something):
> - Thank you. It was very **nice/kind of you** to help me.
> - It is **stupid of her** to go out without a coat in such cold weather.
>
> *but* (be) **nice / kind / good / generous / polite / friendly / cruel** etc. **TO** somebody:
> - They have always been very **nice / kind to** me. (*not* 'with me')
> - Why were you so **unfriendly to** Tessa?

B *Adjective +* **about / with**

> **angry / annoyed / furious** { **ABOUT** something
> { **WITH** somebody **FOR** doing something
> - It's stupid to get **angry about** things that don't matter.
> - Are you **annoyed with** me **for** being late?
>
> **excited / worried / upset / nervous / happy** etc. **ABOUT** something:
> - Are you **excited about** going on holiday next week?
> - Carol is **upset about** not being invited to the party.
>
> **delighted / pleased / satisfied / disappointed WITH** something:
> - I was **delighted with** the present you gave me.
> - Were you **disappointed with** your exam results?

C *Adjective +* **at / by / with**

> **surprised / shocked / amazed / astonished AT / BY** something:
> - Everybody was **surprised at** (*or* **by**) the news.
> - I hope you weren't **shocked by** (*or* **at**) what I said.
>
> **impressed WITH / BY** somebody/something:
> - I'm very **impressed with** (*or* **by**) her English. It's very good.
>
> **fed up / bored WITH** something:
> - I don't enjoy my job any more. I'm **fed up with** it. / I'm **bored with** it.

D **sorry about / for**

> **sorry ABOUT** something:
> - I'm **sorry about** the noise last night. We were having a party.
>
> *but usually* **sorry FOR doing** something:
> - I'm **sorry for shouting** at you yesterday.
>
> You can also say 'I'm sorry I (did something)':
> - I'm **sorry I shouted** at you yesterday.
>
> We say 'to **feel** / to **be** sorry **FOR** somebody':
> - I **feel sorry for** George. He has a lot of problems.

Preposition + **-ing** → **UNIT 59**   Adjective + **to...** → **UNIT 64**   Adjective + preposition (2) → **UNIT 130**

129.1 *Write sentences using* **nice of…, kind of…** *etc.*

1	I went out in the cold without a coat.	(silly)	**That was silly of you.**
2	Sue offered to drive me to the airport.	(nice)	That was .... her.
3	I needed money and Ian gave me some.	(generous)	That ....
4	They didn't invite us to their party.	(not very nice)	
			That wasn't ....
5	Can I help you with your luggage?	(very kind)	.... you.
6	Kevin didn't thank me for the present.	(not very polite)	
			....
7	They've had an argument and now they refuse to speak to each other.	(a bit childish)	
			....

129.2 *Complete the sentences using one of the following adjectives + the correct preposition:*

annoyed   annoyed   astonished   bored   ~~excited~~   impressed   kind   sorry

1 We're all ...**excited about**... going on holiday next week.
2 Thank you for all your help. You've been very .... me.
3 I wouldn't like to be in her position. I feel .... her.
4 What have I done wrong? Why are you .... me?
5 Why do you always get so .... little things?
6 I wasn't very .... the service in the restaurant. We had to wait ages before our food arrived.
7 John isn't happy at college. He says he's .... the course he's doing.
8 I had never seen so many people before. I was .... the crowds.

129.3 *Put in the correct preposition.*

1 I was delighted ...**with**... the present you gave me.
2 It was very nice .... you to do my shopping for me. Thank you very much.
3 Why are you always so rude .... your parents? Can't you be nice .... them?
4 It was a bit careless .... you to leave the door unlocked when you went out.
5 They didn't reply to our letter, which wasn't very polite .... them.
6 We always have the same food every day. I'm fed up .... it.
7 I can't understand people who are cruel .... animals.
8 We enjoyed our holiday, but we were a bit disappointed .... the hotel.
9 I was surprised .... the way he behaved. It was completely out of character.
10 I've been trying to learn Spanish but I'm not very satisfied .... my progress.
11 Linda doesn't look very well. I'm worried .... her.
12 Are you angry .... what happened?
13 I'm sorry .... what I said. I hope you're not angry .... me.
14 The people next door are furious .... us .... making so much noise last night.
15 Jill starts her new job next week. She's quite excited .... it.
16 I'm sorry .... the smell of paint in this room. I've just decorated it.
17 I was shocked .... what I saw. I'd never seen anything like it before.
18 The man we interviewed for the job was intelligent but we weren't very impressed .... his appearance.
19 Are you still upset .... what I said to you yesterday?
20 He said he was sorry .... the situation but there was nothing he could do.
21 I felt sorry .... the children when we went on holiday. It rained every day and they had to spend most of the time indoors.

Adjective + preposition (2)

A *Adjective +* **of** (1)

> **afraid / frightened / terrified / scared OF**…:
> - 'Are you **afraid of** dogs?'   'Yes, I'm **terrified of** them.'
>
> **fond / proud / ashamed / jealous / envious OF**…:
> - Why are you always so **jealous of** other people?
>
> **suspicious / critical / tolerant OF**…:
> - He didn't trust me. He was **suspicious of** my intentions.

B *Adjective +* **of** (2)

> **aware / conscious OF**…:
> - 'Did you know he was married?'   'No, I wasn't **aware of** that.'
>
> **capable / incapable OF**…:
> - I'm sure you are **capable of** passing the examination.
>
> **full OF**… / **short OF**…:
> - The letter I wrote was **full of** mistakes. (*not* 'full with')
> - I'm a bit **short of** money. Can you lend me some?
>
> **typical OF**…:
> - He's late again. It's **typical of** him to keep everybody waiting.
>
> **tired OF**…:
> - Come on, let's go! I'm **tired of** waiting. (= I've had enough of waiting)
>
> **certain / sure OF** *or* **ABOUT**…:
> - I think she's arriving this evening but I'm not **sure of** that. (*or* …**sure about** that.)

C *Adjective +* **at** / **to** / **from** / **in** / **on** / **with** / **for**

> **good / bad / excellent / brilliant / hopeless** (etc.) **AT**…:
> - I'm not very **good at** repairing things. (*not* 'good in repairing things')
>
> **married / engaged TO**…:
> - Linda is **married to** an American. (*not* 'married with')
>
> *but* - Linda is married **with three children**. (= she is married and has three children)
>
> **similar TO**…:
> - Your writing is **similar to** mine.
>
> **different FROM** (*or* **TO**)…:
> - The film was **different from** what I'd expected. (*or* …**different to** what I'd expected.)
>
> **interested IN**…:
> - Are you **interested in** art?
>
> **keen ON**…:
> - We stayed at home because Cathy wasn't very **keen on** going out.
>
> **dependent ON**… (*but* '**independent OF**…'):
> - I don't want to be **dependent on** anybody.
>
> **crowded WITH** (people etc.):
> - The city centre was **crowded with** tourists. (*but* '**full of** tourists')
>
> **famous FOR**…:
> - The Italian city of Florence is **famous for** its art treasures.
>
> **responsible FOR**…:
> - Who was **responsible for** all that noise last night?

Preposition + -ing → UNIT 59   **Afraid of… / to…** → UNIT 65A   Adjective + preposition (1) → UNIT 129
American English → APPENDIX 7

130.1 *Complete the second sentence so that it has the same meaning as the first one.*

1 There were lots of tourists in the city centre.   The city centre was crowded ..**with tourists.**..
2 There was a lot of furniture in the room.   The room was full ....
3 I don't like sport very much.   I'm not very keen ....
4 We haven't got enough time.   We're a bit short ....
5 I'm not a very good tennis player.   I'm not very good ....
6 Catherine's husband is Russian.   Catherine is married ....
7 I don't trust Robert.   I'm suspicious ....
8 My problem is not the same as yours.   My problem is different ....

130.2 *Complete the sentences with one of the following adjectives + the correct preposition:*
afraid   different   interested   proud   responsible   similar   ~~sure~~

1 I think she's arriving this evening but I'm not ..**sure of**.. that.
2 Your camera is .... mine but it isn't exactly the same.
3 Don't worry. I'll look after you. There's nothing to be ....
4 'Do you want to watch the news on television?'   'No, I'm not .... the news.'
5 The editor is the person who is .... what appears in a newspaper.
6 Mrs Davis is a very keen gardener. She's very .... her garden and loves showing it to visitors.
7 I was surprised when I met her for the first time. She was .... what I expected.

130.3 *Put in the correct preposition.*

1 The letter I wrote was full ..**of**.. mistakes.
2 My home town is not especially interesting. It's not famous .... anything.
3 Kate is very fond .... her younger brother.
4 I don't like going up ladders. I'm afraid .... heights.
5 You look bored. You don't seem interested .... what I'm saying.
6 Did you know that Liz is engaged .... a friend of mine?
7 I'm not ashamed .... what I did. In fact I'm quite proud .... it.
8 I suggested we should all go out for a meal but nobody else was keen .... the idea.
9 These days everybody is aware .... the dangers of smoking.
10 The station platform was crowded .... people waiting for the train.
11 She's much more successful than I am. Sometimes I feel a bit jealous .... her.
12 I'm tired .... doing the same thing every day. I need a change.
13 Do you know anyone who might be interested .... buying an old car?
14 We've got plenty to eat. The fridge is full .... food.
15 She is a very honest person. I don't think she is capable .... telling a lie.
16 I'm not surprised she changed her mind at the last moment. That's typical .... her.
17 Our house is similar .... yours. Perhaps yours is a bit larger.
18 John has no money of his own. He's totally dependent .... his parents.

130.4 *Write sentences about yourself. Are you good at these things or not? Use:*
brilliant   very good   quite good   not very good   hopeless

1 (repairing things) ..**I'm not very good at repairing things.**..
2 (telling jokes) ....
3 (mathematics) ....
4 (remembering names) ....

Verb + preposition (1) **at** and **to**

A *Verb +* **at**

> **look / have a look / stare / glance** (etc.) **AT…:**
> - Why are you **looking at** me like that?
>
> **laugh / smile AT…:**
> - I look stupid with this haircut. Everybody will **laugh at** me.
>
> **aim / point** (something) **AT…**, **shoot / fire** (a gun) **AT…** (= 'in the direction of'):
> - Don't **point** that knife **at** me. It's dangerous.
> - We saw some people with guns **shooting at** birds.

B *Verb +* **to**

> **talk / speak TO** (somebody) ('with' is also possible but less usual):
> - Who was that man you were **talking to**?   • Can I **speak to** Jane, please?
>
> **listen TO…:**
> - We spent the evening **listening to** music. (*not* 'listening music')
>
> **write** (a letter) **TO…:**
> - Sorry I haven't **written to** you for such a long time.
>
> *but* **phone/telephone** somebody (no preposition):
> - Did you **phone your father** yesterday? (*not* 'phone to your father')
>
> **invite** (somebody) **TO** (a party / a wedding etc.):
> - They only **invited** a few people **to** their wedding.

C Some verbs can be followed by **at** or **to,** with a difference of meaning. For example:

> **shout AT** somebody (*when you are angry*):
> - She got very angry and started **shouting at** me.
>
> **shout TO** somebody (*so that they can hear you*):
> - She **shouted to** me from the other side of the street.
>
> **throw** something **AT** somebody/something (*in order to hit them*):
> - Somebody **threw** an egg **at** the minister.
>
> **throw** something **TO** somebody (*for somebody to catch*):
> - Judy shouted 'Catch!' and **threw** the keys **to** me from the window.

D Explain / describe / apologise

> We say **explain** something (**TO** somebody):
> - Can you **explain** this word **to** me? (*not* 'explain me this word')
>
> *also:* 'explain (to somebody) **that / what / how / why…**':
> - I **explained to them what** I wanted them to do. (*not* 'I explained them')
>
> **Describe** is similar:
> - Let me **describe to you what** I saw.
>
> Note that we say 'apologise TO somebody (for…)':
> - He **apologised to** me. (*not* 'He apologised me')
>
> *but* '**thank** somebody (for something)', '**ask** somebody (for something)':
> - He **asked** me for money. (*not* 'He asked to me')

EXERCISES

131.1 *Complete the sentences. Choose one of the following verbs (in the correct form) + the correct preposition:*

~~explain~~   invite   ~~laugh~~   listen   point   glance   speak   throw   throw   write

1 I look stupid with this haircut. Everybody will ...laugh at... me.
2 I don't understand what this means. Can you ...explain... it ..to.. me?
3 I .... my watch to see what the time was.
4 We've been .... the party but unfortunately we can't go.
5 Please .... me! I've got something important to tell you.
6 Don't .... stones .... the birds! It's cruel.
7 If you don't want to eat that sandwich, ... it .... the birds. They'll eat it.
8 Sally and Kevin had an argument and now they're not .... one another.
9 I .... Joanna last week but she hasn't replied to my letter yet.
10 Be careful with those scissors! Don't .... them .... me!

131.2 *Put in* to *or* at *where necessary.*

1 They only invited a few people ..to.. their wedding.
2 Look .... these flowers. Aren't they pretty?
3 Please don't shout .... me! Be nice to me!
4 I saw Sue as I was cycling along the road. I shouted .... her but she didn't hear me.
5 Don't listen .... what he says. He doesn't know what he's talking about.
6 Can I speak .... you for a moment? There's something I want to ask you.
7 Do you think I could have a look .... your newspaper, please?
8 I'm a bit lonely. I need somebody to talk ....
9 She was so angry she threw a chair .... me.
10 The woman sitting opposite me on the train kept staring .... me.

131.3 *You ask somebody to explain some things that you don't understand. Write sentences using* **explain** (something) **to me** *or* **explain to me** (how/what... *etc.*).

1 (I don't understand this word.)   ...Can you explain this word to me?...
2 (I don't understand what you mean.)   ...Can you explain to me what you mean?...
3 (I don't understand this question.)   Can you explain ....
4 (I don't understand the system.)   Can ....
5 (I don't understand how this machine works.)
   ....
6 (I don't understand what your problem is.)
   ....

131.4 *Put in* to *where necessary. If the sentence is already complete, leave an empty space (–).*

1 I know who she is but I've never spoken ...to... her.
2 George won't be able to help you, so there's no point in asking ..–.. him.
3 I like to listen .... the radio while I'm having breakfast.
4 We'd better phone .... the restaurant to reserve a table.
5 I apologised .... Bridget for the misunderstanding.
6 Don't forget to write .... me while you're away.
7 I thanked .... everybody for all the help they had given me.
8 I explained .... everybody what they had to do.
9 Mike described .... me how the accident happened.
10 I'd like to ask .... you some questions.

Verb + preposition (2) **about/for/of/after**

Verb + **about**

> **talk ABOUT...** / **read ABOUT...** / **tell** somebody **ABOUT...** / **have a discussion ABOUT...:**
> - We **talked about** a lot of things at the meeting.
>
> *but* '**discuss** something' (no preposition):
> - We **discussed** a lot of things at the meeting. (*not* 'discussed about')
>
> *also:* '**do** something **ABOUT** something' (= do something to improve a bad situation):
> - If you're worried about the problem, you should **do** something **about** it.

Care about, **care for** and **take care of**

> **care ABOUT** somebody/something (= think that somebody/something is important):
> - He's very selfish. He doesn't **care about** other people.
>
> We say '**care what/where/how**' (etc.) (without 'about'):
> - You can do what you like. I don't **care what** you do.
>
> **care FOR** somebody/something:
>   i) = like something (usually in questions and negative sentences):
> - Would you **care for** a cup of coffee? (= Would you like...?)
> - I don't **care for** very hot weather. (= I don't like...)
>   ii) = look after somebody:
> - Albert is 85 and lives alone. He needs somebody to **care for** him.
>
> **take care OF...** (= look after):
> - Have a nice holiday. **Take care of** yourself! (= look after yourself)

Verb + **for**

> **ask** (somebody) **FOR...:**
> - I wrote to the company **asking** them **for** more information about the job.
>
> *but* • I **asked** her **a question.** / They **asked** me **the way** to the station. (no preposition)
> **apply** (**TO** a person, a company etc.) **FOR** (a job etc.):
> - I think this job would suit you. Why don't you **apply for** it?
>
> **wait FOR...** / **wait FOR** something to happen:
> - Don't **wait for** me. I'll join you later.
> - I'm not going out yet. I'm **waiting for** the rain to stop.
>
> **search** (a person / a place / a bag etc.) **FOR...:**
> - I've **searched** (the house) **for** my keys but I still can't find them.
>
> **leave** (a place) **FOR** (another place):
> - I haven't seen her since she **left** (home) **for** work this morning. (*not* 'left to work')

Look for and **look after**

> **look FOR...** (= search for, try to find):
> - I've lost my keys. Can you help me to **look for** them?
>
> **look AFTER...** (= take care of):
> - Albert is 85 and lives alone. He needs somebody to **look after** him. (*not* 'look for')
> - You can borrow this book if you promise to **look after** it.

132.1 *Put in the correct preposition. If no preposition is needed, leave the space empty (–).*

1 I'm not going out yet. I'm waiting ...**for**... the rain to stop.
2 You're always asking me .... money. Ask somebody else for a change.
3 I've applied .... a job at the factory. I don't know if I'll get it.
4 If I want a job at the factory, who do I apply .... ?
5 I've searched everywhere .... John but I haven't been able to find him.
6 I don't want to talk .... what happened last night. Let's forget it.
7 I don't want to discuss .... what happened last night. Let's forget it.
8 We had an interesting discussion .... the problem but we didn't reach a decision.
9 We discussed .... the problem but we didn't reach a decision.
10 I don't want to go out yet. I'm waiting .... the post to arrive.
11 Keith and Sonia are touring Europe. They're in Rome at the moment, but tomorrow they leave .... Venice.
12 The roof of the house is in very bad condition. I think we ought to do something .... it.
13 We waited .... Jim for half an hour but he never came.
14 Tomorrow morning I have to catch a plane. I'm leaving my house .... the airport at 7.30.

132.2 *Complete the sentences with one of the following verbs (in the correct form) + preposition:*

apply   ask   do   leave   look   ~~search~~   talk   wait

1 Police are ...**searching for**... the man who escaped from prison.
2 We're still .... a reply to our letter. We haven't heard anything yet.
3 George likes his job but he doesn't .... it much.
4 When I'd finished my meal, I .... the waiter .... the bill.
5 Kate is unemployed. She has .... several jobs but she hasn't had any luck.
6 If something is wrong, why don't you .... something .... it?
7 Linda's car is very old but it's in excellent condition. She .... it well.
8 Diane is from Boston but now she lives in Paris. She .... Boston .... Paris when she was 19.

132.3 *Put in the correct preposition after* **care**. *If no preposition is needed, leave the space empty (–).*

1 He's very selfish. He doesn't care ...**about**... other people.
2 Are you hungry? Would you care .... something to eat?
3 She doesn't care .... the examination. She's not worried whether she passes or fails.
4 Please let me borrow your camera. I promise I'll take good care .... it.
5 'Do you like this coat?' 'Not really. I don't care .... the colour.'
6 Don't worry about arranging our holiday. I'll take care .... that.
7 I want to have a good holiday. I don't care .... the cost.
8 I want to have a good holiday. I don't care .... how much it costs.

132.4 *Complete the sentences with* **look for** *or* **look after**. *Use the correct form of* **look**.

1 I ...**looked for**... my keys but I couldn't find them anywhere.
2 Kate is .... a job. I hope she finds one soon.
3 Who .... you when you were ill?
4 I'm .... Elizabeth. Have you seen her?
5 All the car parks were full, so we had to .... somewhere to park.
6 A baby-sitter is somebody who .... other people's children.

Verb + preposition (3) **about** and **of**

Some verbs can be followed by **about** or **of**, usually with a difference of meaning:

A

> **dream ABOUT...:**
> * I **dreamt about** you last night. (when I was asleep)
>
> **dream OF** being something / doing something (= imagine):
> * I often **dream of** being rich.
> * 'Don't tell anyone what I said.'   'No, I **wouldn't dream of** it.' (= I would never do it)

B

> **hear ABOUT...** (= be told about something):
> * Did you **hear about** the fight in the club on Saturday night?
>
> **hear OF...** (= know that somebody/something exists):
> * 'Who is Tom Madely?'   'I've no idea. I've never **heard of** him.' (*not* 'heard from him')
>
> *Also:* **hear FROM...** (= receive a letter or phone call from somebody):
> * 'Have you **heard from** Jane recently?'   'Yes, I got a letter from her a few days ago.'

C

> **think ABOUT...** and **think OF...**
> When you **think ABOUT** something, you *consider* it, you *concentrate your mind* on it:
> * You look serious. What are you **thinking about**?
> * 'Will you lend me the money?'   'I'll **think about** it.'
>
> When you **think OF** something, the idea *comes* to your mind:
> * He told me his name but I can't **think of** it now. (*not* 'think about it')
> * That's a good idea. Why didn't I **think of** that? (*not* 'think about that')
>
> We also use **think of** when we ask or give an opinion:
> * 'What did you **think of** the film?'   'I didn't **think** much **of** it.'
>
> The difference is sometimes very small. Often you can use **of** or **about**:
> * When I'm alone, I often **think of** (*or* about) you.
>
> You can say '**think of** *or* **think about** doing something' (for possible future actions):
> * My sister is **thinking of** (*or* about) going to Canada. (= she is considering it)

D

> **remind** somebody **ABOUT...** (= tell somebody not to forget):
> * I'm glad you **reminded** me **about** the meeting. I had completely forgotten it.
>
> **remind** somebody **OF...** (= cause somebody to remember):
> * This house **reminds** me **of** the one I lived in when I was a child.
> * Look at this photograph of Richard. Who does he **remind** you **of**?

E

> **complain (TO** somebody) **ABOUT...** (= say that you are not satisfied):
> * We **complained to** the manager of the restaurant **about** the food.
>
> **complain OF** a pain, an illness etc. (= say that you have a pain etc.):
> * We called the doctor because George was **complaining of** a pain in his stomach.

F

> **warn** somebody **OF/ABOUT** *a danger, something bad which might happen*:
> * Everybody has been **warned of/about** the dangers of smoking.
>
> **warn** somebody **ABOUT** *somebody/something which is dangerous, unusual* etc.:
> * I knew he was a strange person. I had been **warned about** him. (*not* 'warned of him')
> * Vicky **warned** us **about** the traffic. She said it would be bad.

133.1 *Put in the correct preposition.*

1 Did you hear ...**about**... what happened at the party on Saturday?
2 'I had a strange dream last night.'   'Did you? What did you dream ....?'
3 Our neighbours complained .... us .... the noise we made last night.
4 Ken was complaining .... pains in his chest, so he went to the doctor.
5 I love this music. It reminds me .... a warm day in spring.
6 He loves his job. He thinks .... his job all the time, he dreams .... it, he talks .... it and I'm fed up with hearing .... it.
7 I tried to remember the name of the book but I couldn't think .... it.
8 Janet warned me .... the water. She said it wasn't safe to drink.
9 We warned our children .... the dangers of playing in the street.

133.2 *Complete the sentences using one of the following verbs (in the correct form) + the correct preposition:* **complain   dream   hear   remind   remind   ~~think~~   think   warn**

1 That's a good idea. Why didn't I ...**think of**... that?
2 Bill is never satisfied. He is always .... something.
3 I can't make a decision yet. I need time to .... your proposal.
4 Before you go into the house, I must .... you .... the dog. He is very aggressive sometimes, so be careful.
5 She's not a well-known singer. Not many people have .... her.
6 A: You wouldn't go away without telling me, would you?
   B: Of course not. I wouldn't .... it.
7 I would have forgotten my appointment if Jane hadn't .... me .... it.
8 Do you see that man over there? Does he .... you .... anybody you know?

133.3 *Complete the sentences using* **hear** *or* **heard** *+ the correct preposition* (**about/of/from**).

1 I've never ...**heard of**... Tom Madely. Who is he?
2 'Did you .... the accident last night?'   'Yes, Vicky told me.'
3 Jill used to write to me quite often but I haven't .... her for ages now.
4 A: Have you .... a writer called William Hudson?
   B: No, I don't think so. What sort of writer is he?
5 Thank you for your letter. It was good to .... you again.
6 'Do you want to .... our holiday?'   'Not now. Tell me later.'
7 I live in a very small town in the north of England. You've probably never .... it.

133.4 *Complete the sentences using* **think about** *or* **think of.** *Use the correct form of* **think.**

1 You look serious. What are you ...**thinking about?**...
2 I like to have time to make decisions. I like to .... things carefully.
3 He's a very selfish person. He only .... himself.
4 I don't know what to get Ann for her birthday. Can you .... anything?
5 A: I've finished reading the book you lent me.
   B: Have you? What did you .... it? Did you like it?
6 We're .... going out for a meal this evening. Would you like to come?
7 I don't really want to go out with Ian tonight. I'll have to .... an excuse.
8 Carol is rather homesick. She's always .... her family back home.
9 When I was offered the job, I didn't accept immediately. I went away and .... it for a while. In the end I decided to take the job.
10 I don't .... much .... this coffee. It's like water.

Verb + preposition (4) **of/for/from/on**

A *Verb +* **of**

> **accuse / suspect** somebody **OF**...:
> - Sue **accused** me **of** being selfish.
> - Three students were **suspected of** cheating in the examination.
>
> **approve OF**...:
> - His parents don't **approve of** what he does, but they can't stop him.
>
> **die OF** (an illness):
> - 'What did he **die of**?'   'A heart attack.'
>
> **consist OF**...:
> - We had an enormous meal. It **consisted of** seven courses.

B *Verb +* **for**

> **pay** (somebody) **FOR**...:
> - I didn't have enough money to **pay** (the waiter) **for** the meal. (*not* 'pay the meal')
>
> *but* '**pay** a bill / a fine / a tax / a fare / rent / a sum of money etc. (*no* preposition):
> - I didn't have enough money to **pay my telephone bill**.
>
> **thank / forgive** somebody **FOR**...:
> - I'll never **forgive** them **for** what they did.
>
> **apologise** (**to** somebody) **FOR**...:
> - When I realised I was wrong, I **apologised** (to them) **for** my mistake.
>
> **blame** somebody/something **FOR**...:
> - Everybody **blamed** me **for** the accident.
>
> *also:* 'somebody is **to blame for**...':
> - Everybody said that I was **to blame for** the accident.
>
> *also:* **blame** something **ON**...:
> - Everybody **blamed** the accident **on** me.

C *Verb +* **from**

> **suffer FROM** (an illness etc.):
> - The number of people **suffering from** heart disease has increased.
>
> **protect** somebody/something **FROM** (*or* **AGAINST**)...:
> - Sun oil can **protect** the skin **from** the sun. (*or* ...**against** the sun.)

D *Verb +* **on**

> **depend ON**... / **rely ON**...:
> - 'What time will you arrive?'   'I don't know. It **depends on** the traffic.'
> - You can **rely on** Jill. She always keeps her promises.
>
> You can use **depend** + **when/where/how** etc. (question words) with or without **on**:
> - 'Are you going to buy it?'   'It **depends how** much it is.' (*or* depends **on** how much)
>
> **live ON** (money/food):
> - George's salary is very low. It isn't enough to **live on**.
>
> **congratulate** (someone) **ON**... / **compliment** (somebody) **ON**...:
> - I **congratulated** her **on** her success in the exam.

EXERCISES

134.1 *Complete the second sentence so that it means the same as the first.*

1 Sue said I was selfish. Sue accused me ...of being selfish...

2 The misunderstanding was my fault, so I apologised.
I apologised ....

3 She won the tournament, so I congratulated her.
I congratulated her ....

4 He has enemies but he has a bodyguard to protect him.
He has a bodyguard to protect him ....

5 There are 11 players in a football team.
A football team consists ....

6 She eats only bread and eggs. She lives ....

Complete the second sentence using **for** *or* **on**. *(These sentences all have* **blame**.*)*

7 Kay said that what happened was Jim's fault. Kay blamed Jim ...for what happened...

8 You always say everything is my fault. You always blame me ....

9 Do you think the economic crisis is the fault of the government?
Do you blame the government ....

10 I think the increase in violent crime is because of television.
I blame the increase in ....

Now rewrite sentences 9 and 10 using ...**to blame for**... .

11 (9) Do you think the government ....

12 (10) I think that ....

134.2 *Complete the sentences using one of the following verbs (in the correct form) + the correct preposition:*

accuse   apologise   ~~approve~~   congratulate   depend   live   pay

1 His parents don't ...approve of... what he does, but they can't stop him.

2 When you went to the theatre with Paul, who .... the tickets?

3 It's not very pleasant when you are .... something you didn't do.

4 'Are you playing tennis tomorrow?' 'I hope so. It .... the weather.'

5 Things are very cheap there. You can .... very little money.

6 When I saw Dave, I .... him .... passing his driving test.

7 You were very rude to Fiona. Don't you think you should .... her?

134.3 *Put in the correct preposition. If no preposition is necessary, leave the space empty (–).*

1 Three students were suspected ...of... cheating in the examination.

2 Sally is often not well. She suffers .... very bad headaches.

3 You know that you can rely .... me if you ever need any help.

4 It is terrible that some people are dying .... hunger while others eat too much.

5 Are you going to apologise .... what you did?

6 The accident was my fault, so I had to pay .... the damage.

7 I didn't have enough money to pay .... the bill.

8 I complimented her .... her English. She spoke fluently and made very few mistakes.

9 She hasn't got a job. She depends .... her parents for money.

10 I don't know whether I'll go out tonight. It depends .... how I feel.

11 They wore warm clothes to protect themselves .... the cold.

12 The apartment consists .... three rooms, a kitchen and bathroom.

Verb + preposition (5) **in/into/with/to/on**

A *Verb* + **in**

> **believe IN…:**
> - Do you **believe in** God? (= do you believe that God exists?)
> - I **believe in** saying what I think. (= I believe it is right to say what I think)
>
> **specialise IN…:**
> - Helen is a lawyer. She **specialises in** company law.
>
> **succeed IN…:**
> - I hope you **succeed in** finding the job you want.

B *Verb* + **into**

> **break INTO…:**
> - Our house was **broken into** a few days ago but nothing was stolen.
>
> **crash / drive / bump / run INTO…:**
> - He lost control of the car and **crashed into** a wall.
>
> **divide / cut / split something INTO (two or more parts):**
> - The book is **divided into** three parts.
> - **Cut** the meat **into** small pieces before frying it.
>
> **translate (a book etc.) FROM one language INTO another:**
> - George Orwell's books have been **translated into** many languages.

C *Verb* + **with**

> **collide WITH…:**
> - There was an accident this morning. A bus **collided with** a car. (*but* '**crashed into**')
>
> **fill something WITH… (but full of… – see Unit 130B):**
> - Take this saucepan and **fill** it **with** water.
>
> **provide / supply somebody WITH…:**
> - The school **provides** all its students **with** books.

D *Verb* + **to**

> **happen TO…:**
> - What **happened to** that gold watch you used to have? (= where is it now?)
>
> **prefer one thing/person TO another:**
> - I **prefer** tea **to** coffee.

E *Verb* + **on**

> **concentrate ON…:**
> - Don't look out of the window. **Concentrate on** your work.
>
> **insist ON…:**
> - I wanted to go alone but they **insisted on** coming with me.
>
> **spend (money) ON…:**
> - How much money do you **spend on** food each week?

135.1 *Complete the second sentence so that it means the same as the first.*

1 There was a collision between a bus and a car.   A bus collided ...*with a car.*...
2 I don't mind big cities but I prefer small towns.
   I prefer ....
3 I got all the information I needed from Jill.
   Jill provided me ....
4 This morning I bought a pair of shoes which cost £60.
   This morning I spent ....

135.2 *Complete the sentences using one of the following verbs (in the correct form) + the correct preposition:*

believe   concentrate   divide   drive   fill   happen   ~~insist~~   succeed

1 I wanted to go alone but Sue ...*insisted on*... coming with me.
2 I haven't seen Harry for ages. I wonder what has .... him.
3 I was driving along when the car in front of me stopped suddenly. Unfortunately, I couldn't
   stop in time and .... the back of it.
4 It's a very large house. It's .... four flats.
5 I don't .... ghosts. I think people only imagine that they see them.
6 Steve gave me an empty bucket and told me to .... it .... water.
7 Don't try and do two things together. .... one thing at a time.
8 It wasn't easy but in the end we .... finding a solution to the problem.

135.3 *Put in the correct preposition.*

1 The school provides all its students ...*with*... books.
2 A strange thing happened .... me a few days ago.
3 Mark decided to give up sport so that he could concentrate .... his studies.
4 I don't believe .... working very hard. It's not worth it.
5 My present job isn't wonderful, but I prefer it .... what I did before.
6 I hope you succeed .... getting what you want.
7 As I was coming out of the room, I collided .... somebody who was coming in.
8 There was an awful noise as the car crashed .... a tree.
9 Jim is a photographer. He specialises .... sports photography.
10 Do you spend much money .... clothes?
11 The country is divided .... six regions.
12 I prefer travelling by train .... driving. It's much more pleasant.
13 Somebody broke .... my car and stole the radio.
14 I felt quite cold but Peter insisted .... having the window open.
15 Some words are difficult to translate .... one language .... another.
16 What happened .... the money I lent you? What did you spend it ....?
17 The teacher decided to split the class .... four groups.
18 I filled the tank but unfortunately I filled it .... the wrong kind of petrol.

135.4 *Use your own ideas to complete these sentences. Use a preposition.*

1 I wanted to go out alone but my friend insisted ...*on coming with me.*...
2 I spend quite a lot of money ....
3 I saw the accident. The car crashed ....
4 Sarah prefers basketball ....
5 Shakespeare's plays have been translated ....

Phrasal verbs (**get up** / **break down** / **fill in** etc.)

A We often use verbs with the following words:

in	on	up	away	round	about	over	by
out	off	down	back	through	along	forward	

So you can say **put out** / **get on** / **take off** / **run away** etc. These verbs are *phrasal verbs*.

We often use **out/off/up** etc. with verbs of movement. For example:

get on	●	The bus was full. We couldn't **get on**.
drive off	●	A woman got into the car and **drove off**.
come back	●	Sally is leaving tomorrow and **coming back** on Saturday.
turn round	●	When I touched him on the shoulder, he **turned round**.

But often the second word (**out/off/up** etc.) gives a special meaning to the verb. For example:

break down	●	Sorry I'm late. The car **broke down**. (= the engine stopped working)
look out	●	**Look out!** There's a car coming. (= be careful)
take off	●	It was my first flight. I was nervous as the plane **took off**. (= went into the air)
get up	●	I was very tired this morning. I couldn't **get up**. (= get out of bed)
get on	●	How was the exam? How did you **get on**? (= how did you do?)
get by	●	My French isn't very good but it's enough to **get by**. (= to manage)

B Sometimes a phrasal verb is followed by a *preposition*. For example:

phrasal verb	*preposition*		
run away	**from**	●	Why did you **run away from** me?
keep up	**with**	●	You're walking too fast. I can't **keep up with** you.
look forward	**to**	●	Are you **looking forward to** your holiday?
cut down	**on**	●	Jack is trying to **cut down on** smoking. (= reduce smoking)

C Sometimes a phrasal verb has an *object*. Usually there are two possible positions for the object. So you can say:

            object   *object*

I **turned off** the light. *or* I **turned** the light **off**.

If the object is a *pronoun* (**it/them/me/him** etc.), only one position is possible:

                I **turned**   **it**   **off**. (*not* 'I turned off it')

Some more examples:

● Could you { **fill in** this form? / **fill** this form **in**?

but   They gave me a form and told me to **fill it in**. (*not* 'fill in it')

● The police got into the house by { **breaking down** the door. / **breaking** the door **down**.

but   The door wasn't locked. Why did the police **break it down**? (*not* 'break down it')

● I think I'll { **throw away** these newspapers. / **throw** these newspapers **away**.

but   Do you want these newspapers or shall I **throw them away**? (*not* 'throw away them')

● Don't { **wake up** the baby. / **wake** the baby **up**.

but   The baby is asleep. Don't **wake her up**. (*not* 'wake up her')

EXERCISES

136.1 *Complete the sentences using one of these phrasal verbs (in the correct form):*

~~break down~~
clear up (= become brighter – *for weather*)
close down (= go out of business)
doze off (= fall asleep)

drop out (= stop taking part in something)
move in (= start living in a house etc.)
show off (= show how clever you are)
turn up (= appear/arrive)

1 Sorry I'm late. The car ....*broke down*.... on the way here.
2 I arranged to meet Jane after work last night but she didn't ....
3 'We've bought a new house.' 'Oh, have you? When are you ....?'
4 There used to be a shop at the end of the street but it .... a year ago.
5 I ran in a marathon last week but I wasn't fit enough. I .... after 15 kilometres.
6 We all know how wonderful you are. There's no need to ....
7 I was very tired. I sat in an armchair and ....
8 The weather is horrible at the moment, isn't it? I hope it .... later.

136.2 *Complete the sentences using a word from List A and a word from List B. You need to use some words more than once.*

A: away   back   forward   on   out   up   B: at   of   to   with

1 You're walking too fast. I can't keep ...*up with*... you.
2 My holidays are nearly over. Next week I'll be .... work.
3 We've nearly run .... money. We've got very little left.
4 Martin isn't very happy in his job because he doesn't get .... his boss.
5 I love to look .... the stars in the sky at night.
6 Are you looking .... the party next week?
7 There was a bank robbery last week. The robbers got .... £30,000.

136.3 *Complete the sentences using one of these verbs (in the correct form)* + it/them/her/you:

cross out   give away   make up   turn down (= refuse)
~~fill in~~   give back   show round   see off (= see somebody leave)

1 They gave me a form and told me to ...*fill it in*...
2 If you make a mistake on the form, just ....
3 The story she told you wasn't true. She ....
4 I don't like people who borrow things and don't ....
5 Katy is going to Australia tomorrow. I'm going to the airport to ....
6 I had a lot of books that I didn't want to keep, so I .... to a friend.
7 Would you like to see the factory? Would you like me to ....?
8 Sue was offered a job as a translator but she ....

136.4 *Complete the sentences. Use the word in brackets (away/up etc.) with one of the following:*

~~that box~~   your cigarette   a jacket   the television   a word   ~~it~~   it   it   them   him

1 Don't throw ...*away that box (OR that box away)*... I want to keep it.   (away)
2 'Do you want this box?' 'No, you can throw ...*it away*....'   (away)
3 Shhh! The children are asleep. Don't wake .... (up)
4 We can turn .... Nobody is watching it.   (off)
5 Tom got very angry and started shouting. I tried to calm .... (down)
6 I tried .... in the shop but I didn't buy it.   (on)
7 Please put .... This is a no-smoking area.   (out)
8 It was only a small fire. I was able to put .... quite easily.   (out)
9 You can look .... in a dictionary if you don't know what it means.   (up)
10 You're doing very well. Keep ....!   (up)

APPENDIX 1
Regular and irregular verbs

1.1 *Regular verbs*
If a verb is regular, the past simple and past participle end in **-ed**. For example:

infinitive	clean	finish	use	paint	stop	carry
past simple *past participle* }	cleaned	finished	used	painted	stopped	carried

For spelling rules, see Appendix 6.

For the *past simple* (I **cleaned** / they **finished** / she **carried** etc.), see Unit 5.

We use the *past participle* to make the perfect tenses and for all the passive forms.
Perfect tenses (**have/has/had** cleaned):
- I **have cleaned** the windows. (*present perfect* – see Units 7–8)
- They were still working. They **hadn't finished**. (*past perfect* – see Unit 15)

Passive (**is** cleaned / **was** cleaned etc.):
- He **was carried** out of the room. (*past simple passive*)
- This gate **has** just **been painted**. (*present perfect passive*) } see Units 41–43

1.2 *Irregular verbs*
When the past simple / past participle do *not* end in **-ed** (for example, **I saw / I have seen**), the verb is *irregular*.

With some irregular verbs, all three forms (*infinitive*, *past simple* and *past participle*) are the same. For example, **hit**:
- Don't **hit** me. (*infinitive*)
- Somebody **hit** me as I came into the room. (*past simple*)
- I've never **hit** anybody in my life. (*past participle – present perfect*)
- George was **hit** on the head by a stone. (*past participle – passive*)

With other irregular verbs, the past simple is the same as the past participle (but different from the infinitive). For example, **tell → told**:
- Can you **tell** me what to do? (*infinitive*)
- She **told** me to come back the next day. (*past simple*)
- Have you **told** anybody about your new job? (*past participle – present perfect*)
- I was **told** to come back the next day. (*past participle – passive*)

With other irregular verbs, all three forms are different. For example, **wake → woke/woken**:
- I'll **wake** you up. (*infinitive*)
- I **woke** up in the middle of the night. (*past simple*)
- The baby has **woken** up. (*past participle – present perfect*)
- I was **woken** up by a loud noise. (*past participle – passive*)

1.3 The following verbs can be *regular* or *irregular*:

burn	→	burned *or* burnt	**smell**	→	smelled *or* smelt
dream	→	dreamed *or* dreamt [dremt]*	**spell**	→	spelled *or* spelt
lean	→	leaned *or* leant [lent]*	**spill**	→	spilled *or* spilt
learn	→	learned *or* learnt	**spoil**	→	spoiled *or* spoilt

* pronunciation

So you can say:
- I **leant** out of the window.   *or*   I **leaned** out of the window.
- The dinner has been **spoilt**.   *or*   The dinner has been **spoiled**.

In British English the irregular form (**burnt/learnt** etc.) is more usual.
For American English, see Appendix 7.

1.4 List of irregular verbs

infinitive	past simple	past participle
be	was/were	been
beat	beat	beaten
become	became	become
begin	began	begun
bend	bent	bent
bet	bet	bet
bite	bit	bitten
blow	blew	blown
break	broke	broken
bring	brought	brought
broadcast	broadcast	broadcast
build	built	built
burst	burst	burst
buy	bought	bought
catch	caught	caught
choose	chose	chosen
come	came	come
cost	cost	cost
creep	crept	crept
cut	cut	cut
deal	dealt	dealt
dig	dug	dug
do	did	done
draw	drew	drawn
drink	drank	drunk
drive	drove	driven
eat	ate	eaten
fall	fell	fallen
feed	fed	fed
feel	felt	felt
fight	fought	fought
find	found	found
flee	fled	fled
fly	flew	flown
forbid	forbade	forbidden
forget	forgot	forgotten
forgive	forgave	forgiven
freeze	froze	frozen
get	got	got
give	gave	given
go	went	gone
grow	grew	grown
hang	hung	hung
have	had	had
hear	heard	heard
hide	hid	hidden
hit	hit	hit
hold	held	held
hurt	hurt	hurt
keep	kept	kept
kneel	knelt	knelt
know	knew	known
lay	laid	laid
lead	led	led
leave	left	left
lend	lent	lent
let	let	let
lie	lay	lain

infinitive	past simple	past participle
light	lit	lit
lose	lost	lost
make	made	made
mean	meant	meant
meet	met	met
pay	paid	paid
put	put	put
read	read [red]*	read [red]*
ride	rode	ridden
ring	rang	rung
rise	rose	risen
run	ran	run
say	said	said
see	saw	seen
seek	sought	sought
sell	sold	sold
send	sent	sent
set	set	set
sew	sewed	sewn/sewed
shake	shook	shaken
shine	shone	shone
shoot	shot	shot
show	showed	shown/showed
shrink	shrank	shrunk
shut	shut	shut
sing	sang	sung
sink	sank	sunk
sit	sat	sat
sleep	slept	slept
slide	slid	slid
speak	spoke	spoken
spend	spent	spent
spit	spat	spat
split	split	split
spread	spread	spread
spring	sprang	sprung
stand	stood	stood
steal	stole	stolen
stick	stuck	stuck
sting	stung	stung
stink	stank	stunk
strike	struck	struck
swear	swore	sworn
sweep	swept	swept
swim	swam	swum
swing	swung	swung
take	took	taken
teach	taught	taught
tear	tore	torn
tell	told	told
think	thought	thought
throw	threw	thrown
understand	understood	understood
wake	woke	woken
wear	wore	worn
weep	wept	wept
win	won	won
write	wrote	written

* pronunciation

Present and past tenses

	simple	continuous
present	**I do** *present simple* (⇒ Units 2–4) ● Ann often **plays** tennis. ● I **work** in a bank but I **don't enjoy** it very much. ● **Do** you **like** parties? ● It **doesn't rain** much in summer.	**I am doing** *present continuous* (⇒ Units 1, 3–4) ● 'Where's Ann?' 'She**'s playing** tennis.' ● Please don't disturb me now. I**'m working**. ● Hello. **Are** you **enjoying** the party? ● It **isn't raining** at the moment.
present perfect	**I have done** *present perfect simple* (⇒ Units 7–8, 10–14) ● Ann **has played** tennis many times. ● I**'ve lost** my key. **Have** you **seen** it anywhere? ● How long **have** they **known** each other? ● 'Is it still raining?' 'No, it **has stopped**.' ● The house is dirty. We **haven't cleaned** it for weeks.	**I have been doing** *present perfect continuous* (⇒ Units 9–11) ● Ann is very tired. She **has been playing** tennis. ● You're out of breath. **Have** you **been running**? ● How long **have** they **been learning** English? ● It's still raining. It **has been raining** all day. ● I **haven't been feeling** well recently. Perhaps I should go to the doctor.
past	**I did** *past simple* (⇒ Units 5–6, 13–14) ● Ann **played** tennis yesterday afternoon. ● I **lost** my key a few days ago. ● There was a film on TV last night but we **didn't watch** it. ● What **did** you **do** when you finished work yesterday?	**I was doing** *past continuous* (⇒ Unit 6) ● I saw Ann in the park yesterday. She **was playing** tennis. ● I dropped my key when I **was trying** to open the door. ● The television was on but we **weren't watching** it. ● What **were** you **doing** at this time yesterday?
past perfect	**I had done** *past perfect* (⇒ Unit 15) ● It wasn't her first game of tennis. She **had played** many times before. ● I couldn't get into the house because I **had lost** my key. ● The house was dirty because we **hadn't cleaned** it for weeks.	**I had been doing** *past perfect continuous* (⇒ Unit 16) ● Ann was tired yesterday evening because she **had been playing** tennis in the afternoon. ● George decided to go to the doctor because he **hadn't been feeling** well.

For the passive, see Units 41–43.

The future

3.1 *List of future forms*

• I'm **leaving** tomorrow.	*present continuous*	(⇒ Unit 19A)
• My train **leaves** at 9.30.	*present simple*	(⇒ Unit 19B)
• I'm **going to leave** tomorrow.	**(be) going to**	(⇒ Units 20, 23)
• I'll **leave** tomorrow.	**will**	(⇒ Units 21–23)
• I'll **be leaving** tomorrow.	*future continuous*	(⇒ Unit 24)
• I'll **have left** by this time tomorrow.	*future perfect*	(⇒ Unit 24)
• I hope to see you **before I leave** tomorrow.	*present simple*	(⇒ Unit 25)

3.2 *Future actions*

We use the present continuous (**I'm doing**) for arrangements:
- **I'm leaving** tomorrow. I've got my plane ticket. (already planned and arranged)
- 'When **are** they **getting** married?' 'Next month.'

We use the present simple (**I leave / it leaves** etc.) for timetables, programmes etc.:
- My train **leaves** at 9.30. (according to the timetable)
- What time **does** the film **begin**?

We use (**be**) **going to**… to say what somebody has already decided to do:
- I've decided not to stay here any longer. **I'm going to leave** tomorrow. (*or* **I'm leaving** tomorrow.)
- **Are** you **going to watch** the film on television tonight?

We use **will** (**'ll**) when we decide or agree to do something at the time of speaking:
- A: I don't want you to stay here any longer.
  B: OK. **I'll leave** tomorrow. (B decides this at the time of speaking)
- That bag looks heavy. **I'll help** you with it.
- I promise I **won't tell** anybody what happened. (**won't** = **will not**)

3.3 *Future happenings and situations*

Most often we use **will** to talk about future happenings or situations ('something **will happen**'):
- I don't think John is happy in his job. I think he**'ll leave** soon.
- This time next year I**'ll be** in Japan. Where **will** you **be**?

We use (**be**) **going to** when the situation *now* shows what **is going to happen** *in the future*:
- Look at those black clouds. It**'s going to rain**. (you can see the clouds *now*)

3.4 *Future continuous and future perfect*

Will be (**do**)**ing** = will be in the middle of (doing something):
- This time next week I'll be on holiday. **I'll be lying** on a beach and **swimming** in the sea.

We also use **will be -ing** for future actions (see Unit 24C):
- What time **will** you **be leaving** tomorrow?

We use **will have** (**done**) to say that something will already be complete before a time in the future:
- I won't be here this time tomorrow. **I'll have** already **left**.

3.5 We use the *present* (*not* 'will') after **when/if/while/before** etc. (see Unit 25):
- I hope to see you **before I leave** tomorrow. (*not* 'before I will leave')
- You must come and see us **when** you **are** in England again. (*not* 'when you will be')
- If we **don't hurry**, we'll be late.

Modal verbs (**can/could/will/would** etc.)

This appendix is a summary of *modal verbs* (**can/could/will/would** etc.). For more information, see Units 21–40.

4.1 Compare **can/could** etc. for actions:

can **could**	● I **can go** out tonight. (= there is nothing to stop me) ● I **can't go** out tonight. ● I **could go** out tonight. (but I'm not very keen) ● I **couldn't go** out last night. (= I wasn't able)
can *or* **may**	● **Can** / **May** } I **go** out tonight? (= do you allow me to go out?)
will/won't **would**	● I think **I'll go** out tonight. ● I promise I **won't go** out. ● I **would go** out tonight but I've got too much to do. ● I promised I **wouldn't go** out.
shall	● **Shall I go** out tonight? (= do you think it is a good idea?)
should *or* **ought to**	● I { **should** / **ought to** } **go** out tonight. (= it would be a good thing to do)
must **needn't**	● I **must go** out tonight. (= it is necessary) ● I **mustn't go** out tonight. (= it is necessary that I *do not go* out) ● I **needn't go** out tonight. (= it is *not necessary* that I *go* out)

Compare **could have… / would have…** etc.:

could **would** **should** *or* **ought to** **needn't**	● I **could have gone** out last night but I decided to stay at home. ● I **would have gone** out last night but I had too much to do. ● I { **should** / **ought to** } **have gone** out last night. I'm sorry I didn't. ● I **needn't have gone** out last night. (= I went out but it was not necessary)

4.2 We use **will/would/may** etc. to say whether something is possible, impossible, probable, certain etc. Compare:

will **would**	● 'What time **will** she **be** here?' 'She'll **be** here soon.' ● She **would be** here now but she has been delayed.
should *or* **ought to**	● She { **should** / **ought to** } **be** here soon. (= I expect she will be here soon)
may *or* **might** *or* **could**	● She { **may** / **might** / **could** } **be** here now. I'm not sure. (= it's possible that she is here)
must **can't**	● She **must be** here. I saw her come in. (= I'm sure – there is no other possibility) ● She **can't** possibly **be** here. I know for certain that she's away on holiday.

Compare **would have… / should have…** etc.:

will **would**	● She **will have arrived** by now. ● She **would have arrived** earlier but she was delayed.
should *or* **ought to**	● I wonder where she is. She { **should** / **ought to** } **have arrived** by now.
may *or* **might** *or* **could**	● She { **may** / **might** / **could** } **have arrived**. I'm not sure. (= it's possible that she has arrived)
must **can't**	● She **must have arrived** by now. (I'm sure – there is no other possibility) ● She **can't** possibly **have arrived** yet. It's much too early. (= it's impossible)

Short forms (**I'm** / **you've** / **didn't** etc.)

5.1 In spoken English we usually say **I'm** / **you've** / **didn't** etc. (*short forms*) rather than **I am** / **you have** / **did not** etc. We also use short forms in *informal* written English (for example, in letters to friends).

When we write short forms, we use an *apostrophe* (') for the missing letter(s):

    I'm = I am   you've = you **have**   didn't = did **not**

5.2 List of short forms of auxiliary verbs

'm = am	I'm						
's = is *or* has		he's	she's	it's			
're = are					you're	we're	they're
've = have	I've				you've	we've	they've
'll = will	I'll	he'll	she'll		you'll	we'll	they'll
'd = would *or* had	I'd	he'd	she'd		you'd	we'd	they'd

's can be **is** or **has**:
- She's ill. (= She **is** ill.)
- She's gone away. (= She **has** gone away.)

but **let's** = let us:
- Let's go now. (= Let **us** go)

'd can be **would** or **had**:
- I'd see a doctor if I were you. (= I **would** see)
- I'd never seen her before. (= I **had** never seen)

We use some of these short forms (especially 's) after question words (**who/what** etc.) and after **that/there/here**:

    who's what's where's how's that's there's here's who'll there'll who'd
- **Who's** that woman over there? (= who **is**)
- **What's** happened? (= what **has**)
- Do you think **there'll** be many people at the party? (= there **will**)

You can also use short forms (especially 's) after a noun:
- **John's** going out tonight. (= John **is**)
- **My friend's** just got married. (= My friend **has**)

You cannot use 'm / 's / 're / 've / 'll / 'd *at the end of a sentence* (because the verb is stressed in this position):
- 'Are you tired?' 'Yes, I **am**.' (*not* 'Yes, I'm.')
- Do you know where she **is**? (*not* 'Do you know where she's?')

5.3 Negative short forms

isn't	(= is not)	**haven't**	(= have not)	**shan't**	(= shall not)
aren't	(= are not)	**hasn't**	(= has not)	**shouldn't**	(= should not)
wasn't	(= was not)	**hadn't**	(= had not)	**mightn't**	(= might not)
weren't	(= were not)	**can't**	(= cannot)	**mustn't**	(= must not)
don't	(= do not)	**couldn't**	(= could not)	**needn't**	(= need not)
doesn't	(= does not)	**won't**	(= will not)	**daren't**	(= dare not)
didn't	(= did not)	**wouldn't**	(= would not)		

Negative short forms for **is** and **are** can be:

    he **isn't** / she **isn't** / it **isn't**   *or*   he's **not** / she's **not** / it's **not**
    you **aren't** / we **aren't** / they **aren't** *or*   you're **not** / we're **not** / they're **not**

APPENDIX 6
Spelling

6.1 Nouns, verbs and adjectives can have the following endings:

noun + -s/-es (*plural*)	books	ideas	matches
verb + -s/-es (after **he/she/it**)	works	enjoys	washes
verb + -ing	working	enjoying	washing
verb + -ed	worked	enjoyed	washed
adjective + -er (*comparative*)	cheaper	quicker	brighter
adjective + -est (*superlative*)	cheapest	quickest	brightest
adjective + -ly (*adverb*)	cheaply	quickly	brightly

When we use these endings, there are sometimes changes in spelling. These changes are listed below.

6.2 Nouns and verbs + -s/-es
The ending is -es when the word ends in -s/-ss/-sh/-ch/-x:

    match/matches   bus/buses   box/boxes
    wash/washes   miss/misses   search/searches

Note also:

    potato/potatoes   tomato/tomatoes
    do/does   go/goes

6.3 Words ending in -y (baby, carry, easy etc.)

If a word ends in a *consonant** + **y** (-**by**/-**ry**/-**sy**/-**vy** etc.):

y changes to **ie** before the ending -s:
    baby/babies   lorry/lorries   country/countries   secretary/secretaries
    hurry/hurries   study/studies   apply/applies   try/tries

y changes to **i** before the ending -ed:
    hurry/hurried   study/studied   apply/applied   try/tried

y changes to **i** before the endings -er and -est:
    easy/easier/easiest   heavy/heavier/heaviest   lucky/luckier/luckiest

y changes to **i** before the ending -ly:
    easy/easily   heavy/heavily   temporary/temporarily

y does *not* change before -ing:
    hurrying   studying   applying   trying
y does *not* change if the word ends in a *vowel** + **y** (-**ay**/-**ey**/-**oy**/-**uy**):
    play/plays/played   enjoy/enjoys/enjoyed   buy/buys   monkey/monkeys
An exception is: **day/daily**
Note also: **pay/paid**   **lay/laid**   **say/said**

6.4 Verbs ending in -ie (**die, lie, tie**)
If a verb ends in -ie, **ie** changes to **y** before the ending -ing:
    die/dying   lie/lying   tie/tying

---

* **a e i o u** are *vowel* letters. The other letters (**b c d f g** etc.) are *consonant* letters.

6.5 Words ending in **-e** (hope, dance, wide etc.)

Verbs

If a verb ends in **-e**, we leave out **e** before the ending **-ing**:
 hope/hoping smile/smiling dance/dancing confuse/confusing
Exceptions are: **be/being**
   and verbs ending in **-ee**:   see/seeing   agree/agreeing

If a verb ends in **-e**, we add **-d** for the *past* (of regular verbs):
 hope/hoped smile/smiled dance/danced confuse/confused

Adjectives and adverbs

If an adjective ends in **-e**, we add **-r** and **-st** for the *comparative* and *superlative*:
 wide/wider/widest   late/later/latest   large/larger/largest

If an adjective ends in **-e**, we *keep* **e** before the adverb ending **-ly**:
 polite/politely   extreme/extremely   absolute/absolutely

If an adjective ends in **-le** (simple, terrible etc.), the adverb ending is **-ply**, **-bly** etc.:
 simple/simply   terrible/terribly   reasonable/reasonably

6.6 Doubling consonants (**stop/stopping/stopped, wet/wetter/wettest** etc.)

Sometimes a word ends in *vowel + consonant*. For example:
stop   plan   wet   thin   slip   prefer   regret

Before the endings **-ing/-ed/-er/-est**, we double the consonant at the end. So **p → pp, n → nn** etc. For example:

stop	p	→ **pp**	stopping	stopped
plan	n	→ **nn**	planning	planned
rub	b	→ **bb**	rubbing	rubbed
big	g	→ **gg**	bigger	biggest
wet	t	→ **tt**	wetter	wettest
thin	n	→ **nn**	thinner	thinnest

If the word has more than one syllable (**prefer, begin** etc.), we double the consonant at the end *only if the final syllable is stressed*:
 preFER / preferring / preferred   perMIT / permitting / permitted
 reGRET / regretting / regretted   beGIN / beginning

If the final syllable is *not* stressed, we do *not* double the final consonant:
 VISit / visiting / visited   deVELop / developing / developed
 HAPpen / happening / happened   reMEMber / remembering / remembered

In British English, verbs ending in **-l** have **-ll-** before **-ing** and **-ed** whether the final syllable is stressed or not:
 travel / travelling / travelled   cancel / cancelling / cancelled
For American spelling, see Appendix 7.

Note that:
we do *not* double the final consonant if the word ends in *two* consonants (**-rt**, **-lp**, **-ng** etc.):
 start / starting / started   help / helped / helped   long / longer / longest

we do *not* double the final consonant if there are *two* vowel letters before it (**-oil**, **-eed** etc.):
 boil / boiling / boiled   need / needing / needed   explain / explaining / explained
 cheap / cheaper / cheapest loud / louder / loudest   quiet / quieter / quietest

we do *not* double **y** or **w** at the end of words. (At the end of words **y** and **w** are not consonants.)
 stay / staying / stayed   grow / growing   new / newer / newest

---

American English

There are a few grammatical differences between British English and American English:

UNIT	BRITISH	AMERICAN

7A–B and 13A	The *present perfect* is used for an action in the past with a result now:
	• **I've lost** my key. **Have** you **seen** it?
	
	• Sally isn't here. She's **gone** out.
	
	The *present perfect* is used with **just, already** and **yet:**
	• I'm not hungry. **I've just had** lunch.
	
	• A: What time is he leaving?
	  B: He **has already left.**
	
	• **Have** you **finished** your work **yet?**
		The *present perfect* OR *past simple* can be used:
		• **I've lost** my key. **Have** you **seen** it?
		or I **lost** my key. **Did** you **see** it?
		• Sally isn't here. { She's **gone** out.
		                          She **went** out.
		The *present perfect* OR *past simple* can be used:
		• I'm not hungry. { **I've just had** lunch.
		                        I **just had** lunch.
		• A: What time is he leaving?
		  B: { He **has already left.**
		       { He **already left.**
		• **Have** you **finished** your work **yet?**
		or **Did** you **finish** your work **yet?**

8A	The *present perfect* is used with **ever** and **never** for a period that continues until now: • **Have** you **ever ridden** a horse? • I don't know who she is. **I've never seen** her before.	The *present perfect* OR *past simple* can be used: • **Have** you **ever ridden** a horse? *or* **Did** you **ever ride** a horse? • I don't know who she is. **I've never seen** her before. *or* I **never saw** her before.
17B	**have** a bath / **have** a shower	**take** a bath / **take** a shower
22D	**Will** or **shall** can be used with **I/we:** • I **will/shall** be late this evening. The questions **shall I...?** and **shall we...?** are used to ask for advice etc.: • Which way **shall we** go?	**Shall** is unusual: • I **will** be late this evening. **Should I...?** and **should we...?** are used to ask for advice etc.: • Which way **should we** go?
32B	You can use **needn't** (do) or **don't need to** (do): • We **needn't** hurry. *or* We **don't need to** hurry.	**Needn't** is unusual. The usual form is **don't need to:** • We **don't need to** hurry.
34A–B	After **demand, insist** etc. you can use **should:** • I demanded that he **should apologise.** • We insisted that something **should be** done about the problem.	The *subjunctive* is normally used. **Should** is unusual after **demand, insist** etc.: • I demanded that he **apologize.*** • We insisted that something **be** done about the problem.

* Many verbs ending in **-ise** in British English (apolog**ise**/organ**ise**/special**ise** etc.) are spelt with **-ize** (apolog**ize**/organ**ize**/special**ize** etc.) in American English.

UNIT	BRITISH	AMERICAN
73B	British speakers say 'to/in **hospital**' (without 'the'): • Three people were injured and taken to **hospital.**	American speakers say 'to/in **the** hospital': • Three people were injured and taken to **the** hospital.
78C	Nouns like **government/team/family** etc. can have a singular or plural verb: • The team **is/are** playing well.	These nouns normally take a singular verb in American English: • The team **is** playing well.
120B	**at the weekend / at weekends:** • Will you be here **at the weekend?**	**on the weekend / on weekends:** • Will you be here **on the weekend?**
123A	**in a street:** • Do you live **in this street?**	**on a street:** • Do you live **on this street?**
130C	**different from** or **different to:** • It was **different from** (*or* to) what I'd expected.	**different from** or **different than:** • It was **different from** (*or* than) what I'd expected.
131B	**write to** somebody: • Please **write to** me soon.	**write (to)** somebody (with or without 'to'): • Please **write** (to) me soon.

APPENDIX	BRITISH	AMERICAN
1.3	The verbs in this section (**burn, spoil** etc.) can be regular or irregular (**burned** *or* **burnt, spoiled** *or* **spoilt** etc.).	The verbs in this section are normally regular (**burned, spoiled** etc.).
1.4	The past participle of **get** is **got:** • Your English has **got** much better. (= has become much better) **Have got** is also an alternative to **have:** • **I've got** two brothers. (= I have two brothers.)	The past participle of **get** is **gotten:** • Your English has **gotten** much better. **Have got** = **have** (as in British English): • **I've got** two brothers.
6.6	travel → travelling / travelled cancel → cancelling / cancelled	travel → traveling / traveled cancel → canceling / canceled

ADDITIONAL EXERCISES

This section of exercises is divided into the following sections:

Present and past
Units 1–6, Appendix 2

1 *Put the verb into the correct form, present simple (**I do**), present continuous (**I am doing**), past simple (**I did**) or past continuous (**I was doing**).*

1 We can go out now. It ...**isn't raining**.... (not/rain) any more.

2 Ann ...**was waiting**... (wait) for me when I ...**arrived**.... (arrive).

3 I .... (get) hungry. Let's go and have something to eat.

4 What .... (you/do) in your spare time? Have you got any hobbies?

5 What speed .... (the car/do) at the time of the accident?

6 Mary usually .... (phone) me on Fridays but she .... (not/phone) last Friday.

7 A: When I last saw you, you .... (think) of moving to a new flat.
   B: That's right, but in the end I .... (decide) to stay where I was.

8 What's that noise? What .... (happen)?

9 It's usually dry here at this time of the year. It .... (not/rain) much.

10 Yesterday evening the phone .... (ring) three times while we .... (have) dinner.

11 Linda was busy when we .... (go) to see her yesterday. She .... (study) for an exam. We .... (not/want) to disturb her, so we .... (not/stay) very long.

12 When I first .... (tell) Tom the news, he .... (not/believe) me. He .... (think) that I .... (joke).

Present and past

2 *Choose the right alternative.*

1 Everything is going well. We ~~didn't have~~ / haven't had any problems so far. (haven't had *is right*)
2 Margaret <u>didn't go</u> / <u>hasn't gone</u> to work yesterday. She wasn't feeling well.
3 Look! That man over there <u>wears</u> / <u>is wearing</u> the same sweater as you.
4 Your son is much taller than when I last saw him. He <u>grew</u> / <u>has grown</u> a lot.
5 I still don't know what to do. I <u>didn't decide</u> / <u>haven't decided</u> yet.
6 I wonder why Jim <u>is</u> / <u>is being</u> so nice to me today. He isn't usually like that.
7 Jane had a book open in front of her but she <u>didn't read</u> / <u>wasn't reading</u> it.
8 I wasn't very busy. I <u>didn't have</u> / <u>wasn't having</u> much to do.
9 Mary wasn't happy in her new job at first but she <u>begins</u> / <u>is beginning</u> to enjoy it now.
10 After leaving school, Tim <u>found</u> / <u>has found</u> it very difficult to get a job.
11 When Sue heard the news, she <u>wasn't</u> / <u>hasn't been</u> very pleased.
12 This is a nice restaurant, isn't it? Is this the first time <u>you are</u> / <u>you've been</u> here?
13 I need a new job. <u>I'm doing</u> / <u>I've been doing</u> the same job for too long.
14 'Ann has gone out.' 'Oh, has she? What time <u>did she go</u> / <u>has she gone</u>?'
15 'You look tired.' 'Yes, <u>I've played</u> / <u>I've been playing</u> basketball.'
16 Where <u>are you coming</u> / <u>do you come</u> from? Are you American?
17 I'd like to see Tina again. It's a long time <u>since I saw her</u> / <u>that I didn't see her</u>.
18 Bob and Alice have been married <u>since 20 years</u> / <u>for 20 years</u>.

3 *Complete the questions using a suitable verb.*

1 A: I'm looking for Paul. ...Have you seen.... him?
  B: Yes, he was here a moment ago.
2 A: Why ...did you go.... to bed so early last night?
  B: Because I was feeling very tired.
3 A: Where ....?
  B: Just to the post box. I want to post these letters. I'll be back in a few minutes.
4 A: .... television every evening?
  B: No, only if there's a good programme on.
5 A: Your house is very beautiful. How long .... here?
  B: Nearly ten years.
6 A: How was your holiday? .... a nice time?
  B: Yes, thanks. It was great.
7 A: .... Julie recently?
  B: Yes, I met her a few days ago.
8 A: Can you describe the woman you saw? What ....?
  B: A red sweater and black jeans.
9 A: I'm sorry to keep you waiting. .... long?
  B: No, only about ten minutes.
10 A: How long .... you to get to work in the morning?
  B: Usually about 45 minutes. It depends on the traffic.
11 A: .... with that newspaper yet?
  B: No, I'm still reading it. I won't be long.
12 A: .... to the United States?
  B: No, never, but I went to Canada a few years ago.

4 *Use your own ideas to complete B's sentences.*

1 A: What's the new restaurant like? Is it good?
  B: I've no idea. ...*I've never been*.... there.

2 A: How well do you know Bill?
  B: Very well. We .... since we were children.

3 A: Did you enjoy your holiday?
  B: Yes, it was really good. It's the best holiday ....

4 A: Is Jack still here?
  B: No, I'm afraid he isn't. .... about ten minutes ago.

5 A: I like your suit. I haven't seen it before.
  B: It's new. It's the first time ....

6 A: How did you cut your knee?
  B: I slipped and fell when .... tennis.

7 A: Do you ever go swimming?
  B: Not these days. I haven't .... a long time.

8 A: How often do you go to the cinema?
  B: Very rarely. It's nearly a year .... to the cinema.

9 A: I've bought some new shoes. Do you like them?
  B: Yes, they're very nice. Where .... them?

Present and past

Units 1–17, 109, Appendix 2

5 *Put the verb in the correct form, past simple (**I did**), past continuous (**I was doing**), past perfect (**I had done**) or past perfect continuous (**I had been doing**).*

1

Yesterday afternoon Sharon ...*went*... (go) to the station to meet Paul. When she .... (get) there, Paul .... (already/wait) for her. His train .... (arrive) early.

2

When I got home, Bill .... (lie) on the sofa. The television was on but he .... (not/watch) it. He .... (fall) asleep and .... (snore) loudly. I .... (turn) the television off and just then he .... (wake) up.

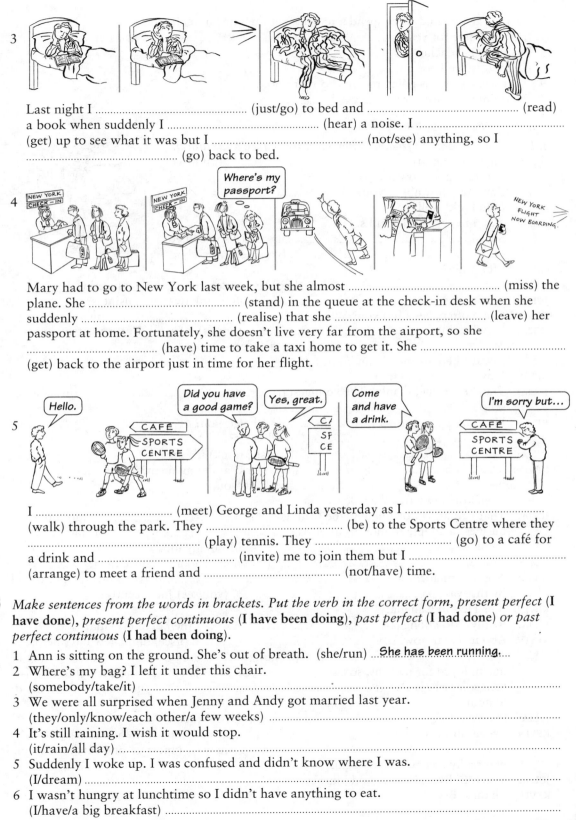

3

Last night I .... (just/go) to bed and .... (read) a book when suddenly I .... (hear) a noise. I .... (get) up to see what it was but I .... (not/see) anything, so I .... (go) back to bed.

4

Mary had to go to New York last week, but she almost .... (miss) the plane. She .... (stand) in the queue at the check-in desk when she suddenly .... (realise) that she .... (leave) her passport at home. Fortunately, she doesn't live very far from the airport, so she .... (have) time to take a taxi home to get it. She .... (get) back to the airport just in time for her flight.

5

I .... (meet) George and Linda yesterday as I .... (walk) through the park. They .... (be) to the Sports Centre where they .... (play) tennis. They .... (go) to a café for a drink and .... (invite) me to join them but I .... (arrange) to meet a friend and .... (not/have) time.

6 *Make sentences from the words in brackets. Put the verb in the correct form, present perfect (I have done), present perfect continuous (I have been doing), past perfect (I had done) or past perfect continuous (I had been doing).*

1 Ann is sitting on the ground. She's out of breath. (she/run) ..She.has.been.running...

2 Where's my bag? I left it under this chair.
(somebody/take/it) ....

3 We were all surprised when Jenny and Andy got married last year.
(they/only/know/each other/a few weeks) ....

4 It's still raining. I wish it would stop.
(it/rain/all day) ....

5 Suddenly I woke up. I was confused and didn't know where I was.
(I/dream) ....

6 I wasn't hungry at lunchtime so I didn't have anything to eat.
(I/have/a big breakfast) ....

7 Every year Bob and Alice spend a few days at the same hotel by the sea.
(they/go/there for years) ....

8 I've got a headache.
(I/have/it/since I got up) ....

9 Next week Gerry is going to run in a marathon.
(he/train/very hard for it) ....

7 *Put the verbs into the correct form.*

Julia and Kevin are old friends. They meet by chance at a station.

JULIA: Hello, Kevin. (1).. (I/not/see)
you for ages. How are you?

KEVIN: I'm fine. How about you? (2)..
(you/look) well.

JULIA: Yes, I'm very well thanks.
So, (3).. (you/go) somewhere
or (4).. (you/meet) somebody
off a train?

KEVIN: (5).. (I/go) to London for a business meeting.

JULIA: Oh. (6).. (you/often/go) away on business?

KEVIN: Quite often, yes. And you? Where (7).. (you/go)?

JULIA: Nowhere. (8).. (I/meet) a friend. Unfortunately, her train
(9).. (be) delayed – (10)..
(I/wait) here for nearly an hour.

KEVIN: How are your children?

JULIA: They're all fine, thanks. The youngest (11).. (just/start)
school.

KEVIN: How (12).. (she/get) on?
(13).. (she/like) it?

JULIA: Yes, (14).. (she/think) it's great.

KEVIN: (15).. (you/work) at the moment? When I last
(16).. (speak) to you, (17)..
(you/work) in a travel agency.

JULIA: That's right. Unfortunately, the firm (18).. (go) out of
business a couple of months after (19).. (I/start) work
there, so (20).. (I/lose) my job.

KEVIN: And (21).. (you/not/have) a job since then?

JULIA: Not a permanent job. (22).. (I/have) a few temporary jobs.
By the way, (23).. (you/see) Joe recently?

KEVIN: Joe? He's in Canada.

JULIA: Really? How long (24).. (he/be) in Canada?

KEVIN: About a year now. (25).. (I/see) him a few days before
(26).. (he/go). (27).. (he/be)
unemployed for months, so (28).. (he/decide) to try his
luck somewhere else. (29).. (he/really/look forward)
to going.

JULIA: So, what (30).. (he/do) there?

KEVIN: I've no idea. (31).. (I/not/hear) from him since
(32).. (he/leave). Anyway, I must go and catch my train. It
was really nice to see you again.

JULIA: You too. Bye. Have a good journey.

KEVIN: Thanks. Bye.

8 *Put the verb into the most suitable form.*

1 Who .... (invent) the bicycle?
2 'Do you still have a headache?'   'No, ... (it/go). I'm all right now.'
3 I was the last to leave the office. Everybody else .... (go) home.
4 What .... (you/do) last weekend? .... (you/go) away?
5 I like your car. How long .... (you/have) it?
6 We decided not to go out because .... (it/rain) quite hard.
7 Jill is an experienced teacher.   .... (she/teach) for 15 years.
8 .... (I/buy) a new jacket last week but .... (I/not/wear) it yet.
9 A few days ago .... (I/see) a man at a party whose face .... (be) very familiar. At first I couldn't think where .... (I/see) him before. Then suddenly .... (I/remember) who .... (it/be).
10 .... (you/hear) of Agatha Christie?   .... (she/be) a writer who .... (die) in 1976.   .... (she/write) more than 70 detective novels.   .... (you/read) any of them?
11 A: What .... (this word / mean)?
    B: I've no idea. .... (I/never/see) it before. Look it up in the dictionary.
12 A: .... (you/arrive) at the theatre in time for the play last night?
    B: No, we were late. By the time we got there, ... (it/already/begin).
13 I went to John's room and .... (knock) on the door but there .... (be) no answer. Either .... (he/go) out or .... (he/not/want) to see anyone.
14 Angela asked me how to use the photocopier.   .... (she/never/use) it before, so .... (she/not/know) what to do.
15 Mary .... (go) for a swim after work yesterday. .... (she/need) some exercise because .... (she/sit) in an office all day in front of a computer.

Past continuous and used to

Units 6 and 18

9 *Complete the sentences using the past continuous (**was doing**) or **used to**... . Use the verb in brackets.*

1 I haven't been to the cinema for ages now. We ...used to go... a lot. (go)
2 Ann didn't see me wave to her. She ...was looking... in the other direction. (look)
3 I .... a lot but I don't use my car very much these days. (drive)
4 I asked the driver to slow down. She .... too fast. (drive)
5 Rose and Jim met for the first time when they .... at university. (study)
6 When I was a child, I .... a lot of bad dreams. (have)
7 When the phone rang, I .... a shower. (have)
8 'Where were you yesterday afternoon?'   'I .... volleyball.' (play)
9 'Do you do any sports?'   'Not these days. I .... volleyball.' (play)
10 George looked very nice. He .... a very nice suit. (wear)

The future

10 *What do you say to your friend in these situations? Use the words given in brackets. Use the present continuous (**I am doing**), going to... or will (**I'll**).*

1 *You have made all your holiday arrangements. Your destination is Jamaica.*
   FRIEND: Have you decided where to go for your holiday yet?
   YOU: Yes, ...I'm going to Jamaica... (I/go)

2 *You have made an appointment with the dentist for Friday morning.*
   FRIEND: Shall we meet on Friday morning?
   YOU: I can't on Friday. .... (I/go)

3 *You and some friends are planning a holiday in Britain. You have decided to hire a car but you haven't arranged this yet.*
   FRIEND: How do you plan to travel round Britain? By train?
   YOU: No, ... (we/hire)

4 *Your friend has two young children. She wants to go out tomorrow evening. You offer to look after the children.*
   FRIEND: I want to go out tomorrow evening but I haven't got a baby-sitter.
   YOU: That's no problem. .... (I/look after)

5 *You have already arranged to have lunch with Sue tomorrow.*
   FRIEND: Are you free at lunchtime tomorrow?
   YOU: No, ... (have lunch)

6 *You are in a restaurant. You and your friend are looking at the menu. You ask your friend if he/she has decided what to have.*
   YOU: What ....? (you/have)
   FRIEND: I don't know. I can't make up my mind.

7 *You and a friend are reading. It's getting a bit dark and your friend is finding it difficult to read. You decide to turn on the light.*
   FRIEND: It's getting a bit dark, isn't it? It's difficult to read.
   YOU: .... (I/turn on)

8 *You and a friend are reading. It's getting a bit dark and you decide to turn on the light. You stand up and walk towards the light switch.*
   FRIEND: What are you doing?
   YOU: .... (I/turn on)

11 *Put the verb into the most suitable form. Use a present tense (simple or continuous),* **will (I'll)** *or* **shall.**

Conversation 1 (IN THE MORNING)

JENNY: (1)...**Are you doing**... (you/do) anything tomorrow evening, Helen?
HELEN: No, why?
JENNY: Well, do you fancy going to the cinema? *Strangers on a Plane* is on. I want to see it but I don't want to go alone.
HELEN: OK, (2).. (I/come) with you. What time
       (3).. (we/meet)?
JENNY: Well, the film (4).. (begin) at 8.45, so
       (5).. (I/meet) you at about 8.30 outside the cinema, OK?
HELEN: Fine. (6).. (I/see) Mary later this evening.
       (7).. (I/ask) her if she wants to come too?
JENNY: Yes, do that. (8).. (I/see) you tomorrow then. Bye.

Conversation 2 (LATER THE SAME DAY)

HELEN: Jenny and I (9)... (go) to the cinema tomorrow night to see
    Strangers on a Plane. Why don't you come with us?

MARY: I'd love to come. What time (10).. (the film/begin)?

HELEN: 8.45.

MARY: (11).. (you/meet) outside the cinema?

HELEN: Yes, at 8.30. Is that OK for you?

MARY: Yes, (12).. (I/be) there at 8.30.

12 *Put the verbs in the most suitable form. Sometimes there is more than one possibility.*

1 *A has decided to learn a language.*

A: I've decided to try and learn a foreign language.

B: Have you? Which language (1)...**are you going to learn**.... (you/learn)?

A: Spanish.

B: I see. And (2).. (you/do) a course?

A: Yes, (3)........................ (it/start) next week.

B: That's great. I'm sure (4).. (you/enjoy) it.

A: I hope so. But I think (5).. (it/be) quite difficult.

2 *A wants to know about B's holiday plans.*

A: I hear (1).. (you/go) on holiday soon.

B: That's right. (2).. (we/go) to Finland.

A: I hope (3).. (you/have) a nice time.

B: Thanks. (4)........................ (I/send) you a postcard and (5)...
    (I/get) in touch with you when (6).. (I/get) back.

3 *A invites B to a party.*

A: (1).. (I/have) a party next Saturday. Can you come?

B: On Saturday? I'm not sure. Some friends of mine (2).. (come) to
    stay with me next week but I think (3).. (they/go) by
    Saturday. But if (4)........................ (they/be) still here,
    (5)........................ (I/not/be) able to come to the party.

A: OK. Well, tell me as soon as (6).. (you/know).

B: Right. (7).. (I/phone) you during the week.

4 *A and B are two secret agents arranging a meeting. They are talking on the phone.*

A: Well, what time (1).. (we/meet)?

B: Come to the café by the station at four o'clock.
    (2).. (I/wait) for you
    when (3)........................ (you/arrive).
    (4)........................ (I/sit) by the window
    and (5)........................ (I/wear) a bright green sweater.

A: OK. (6)........................ (Agent 307/come) too?

B: No, she can't be there.

A: Oh. (7)........................ (I/bring) the documents?

B: Yes. (8)........................ (I/explain) everything when
    (9)........................ (I/see) you. And don't be late.

A: OK. (10)........................ (I/try) to be on time.

13 *Put the verb into the correct form. Choose from the following:*

present continuous (**I am doing**)   **will ('ll) / won't**
present simple (**I do**)   **will be doing**
going to (**I'm going to do**)   **shall**

1 I feel a bit hungry. I think .... (I/have) something to eat.
2 Why are you putting on your coat? .... (you/go) somewhere?
3 What time .... (I/phone) you this evening? About 7.30?
4 Look! That plane is flying towards the airport. .... (it/land).
5 We must do something soon, before .... (it/be) too late.
6 I'm sorry you've decided to leave the company. .... (I/miss)
   you when .... (you/go).
7 .... (I/give) you my address? If ....
   (I/give) you my address, ... (you/write) to me?
8 Are you still watching that programme? What time ....
   (it/end)?
9 .... (I/go) to London next weekend for a wedding. My sister
   .... (get) married.
10 I'm not ready yet. .... (I/tell) you when ....
   (I/be) ready. I promise .... (I/not/be) very long.
11 A: Where are you going?
    B: To the hairdresser's. .... (I/have) my hair cut.
12 She was very rude to me. I refuse to speak to her again until ....
   (she/apologise).
13 I wonder where .... (we/live) ten years from now?
14 What do you plan to do when .... (you/finish) your course at
   college?

Modal verbs (can/must/would) etc.   Units 26–40, Appendix 4

14 *Complete B's sentences using* **can / could / might / must / should / would** + *the verb in brackets.
In some sentences you need to use* **have: must have… / should have…** *etc. In some sentences you
need the negative (* **can't/couldn't** *etc.).*

1 A: I'm hungry.
   B: But you've just had lunch. You ...*can't be*.... hungry already. (be)
2 A: I haven't seen our neighbours for ages.
   B: No. They ...*must have gone*... away. (go)
3 A: What's the weather like? Is it raining?
   B: Not at the moment but it .... later. (rain)
4 A: Where has Julia gone?
   B: I'm not sure. She .... to the bank. (go)
5 A: I didn't see you at John's party last week.
   B: No, I had to work that evening, so I .... (go)
6 A: I saw you at John's party last week.
   B: No, you didn't. You .... me. I didn't go to John's
      party. (see)
7 A: When did you post the letter to Mary?
   B: This morning. So she .... it tomorrow. (get)

8 A: When was the last time you saw Bill?
   B: Years ago. I .... him if I saw him now. (recognise)
9 A: Did you hear the explosion?
   B: What explosion?
   A: There was a loud explosion a few minutes ago. You .... it. (hear)
10 A: We weren't sure which way to go. In the end we turned right.
   B: You went the wrong way. You .... left. (turn)

15 *Make sentences from the words in brackets.*

1 Don't phone Ann now. (she might / have / lunch)
   ...She might be having lunch...

2 I ate too much. Now I feel sick. (I shouldn't / eat / so much)
   ...I shouldn't have eaten so much...

3 I wonder why Tom didn't phone me. (he must / forget)
   ....

4 Why did you go home so early? (you needn't / go / home so early)
   ....

5 You've signed the contract. (it / can't / change / now)
   ....

6 'What's Linda doing?'   'I'm not sure.' (she may / watch / television)
   ....

7 Ann was standing outside the cinema. (she must / wait / for somebody)
   ....

8 He was in prison at the time that the crime was committed, so (he couldn't / do / it).
   ....

9 Why weren't you here earlier? (you ought / be / here earlier)
   ....

10 Why didn't you ask me to help you? (I would / help / you)
   ....

11 I'm surprised nobody told you that the road was very dangerous. (you should / warn)
   ....

12 George was in a strange mood yesterday. (he might not / feel / very well)
   ....

Conditionals   Units 25, 37–39

16 *Put the verb into the correct form.*

1 If you ...found... a wallet in the street, what would you do with it? (find)
2 I must hurry. My friend will be annoyed if I ...'m not... on time. (not/be)
3 I didn't realise that Gary was in hospital. If I ...had known... he was in hospital, I would have gone to visit him. (know)
4 If the phone ...., can you answer it? (ring)
5 I can't decide what to do. What would you do if you .... in my position? (be)
6 A: What shall we do tomorrow?
   B: Well, if it .... a nice day, we can go to the beach. (be)

7 A: Let's go to the beach.
   B: No, it's too cold. If it .... warmer, I wouldn't mind going to the beach. (be)

8 A: Did you go to the beach yesterday?
   B: No, it was too cold. If it .... warmer, we might have gone. (be)

9 If you .... enough money to go anywhere in the world, where would you go? (have)

10 I'm glad we had a map. I'm sure we would have got lost if we .... one. (not/have)

11 The accident was your fault. If you .... more carefully, it wouldn't have happened. (drive)

12 A: Why do you read newspapers?
   B: Well, if I .... newspapers, I wouldn't know what was happening in the world. (not/read)

17 *Complete the sentences.*

1 Liz is tired all the time. She shouldn't go to bed so late.
   If ...Liz didn't go to bed so late, she wouldn't be tired all the time.

2 It's rather late. I don't think Ann will come to see us now.
   I'd be surprised if Ann ....

3 I'm sorry I disturbed you. I didn't know you were busy.
   If I'd known you were busy, I ....

4 The dog attacked you, but only because you provoked it.
   If ....

5 I don't want them to be upset, so I've decided not to tell them what happened.
   They .... if ....

6 Unfortunately, I didn't have an umbrella and so I got very wet in the rain.
   I ....

7 Martin failed his driving test last week. He was very nervous and that's why he failed.
   If he ....

18 *Use your own ideas to complete these sentences.*

1 I'd go out this evening if ....

2 I'd have gone out last night if ....

3 If you hadn't reminded me, ...

4 We wouldn't have been late if ....

5 If I'd been able to get tickets, ...

6 Who would you phone if ....?

7 Cities would be nicer places if ....

8 If there was no television, ...

Wish

Units 38–40

19 *Put the verb into the correct form.*

1 I feel sick. I wish ...I hadn't eaten... so much cake. (I/not/eat)

2 I'm fed up with this rain. I wish ...it would stop... raining. (it/stop)

3 It's a difficult question. I wish .... the answer. (I/know)

4 I should have listened to you. I wish .... your advice. (I/take)

5 I wish .... here. She'd be able to help us. (Ann/be)
6 Aren't they ready yet? I wish .... (they/hurry up)
7 It would be nice to stay here. I wish .... to go now. (we/not/have)
8 When we were in London last year, we didn't have time to see all the things we wanted to see. I wish .... more time. (we/have)
9 It's freezing today. I wish .... so cold. I hate cold weather. (it/not/be)
10 What's her name again? I wish .... remember her name. (I/can)
11 What I said was stupid. I wish .... anything. (I/not/say)
12 (in a car) You're driving too fast. I wish .... a bit. (you/slow down)
13 It was a terrible film. I wish .... to see it. (we/not/go)
14 You're always tired. I wish .... to bed so late. (you/not/go)

Passive
Units 41–44

20 *Put the verb into the most suitable passive form.*

1 There's somebody behind us. I think we ...**are being followed**... (follow).
2 A mystery is something that ...**can't be explained**... (can't/explain).
3 We didn't play football yesterday. The match .... (cancel).
4 The television .... (repair). It's working again now.
5 The church tower .... (restore). The work is almost finished.
6 'How old is the tower?' 'It .... (believe) to be over 600 years old.'
7 If I didn't do my job properly, I .... (would/sack).
8 A: I left some papers on the desk last night and I can't find them now.
    B: They .... (might/throw) away.
9 I learnt to swim when I was very young. I .... (teach) by my mother.
10 After .... (arrest), I was taken to the police station.
11 '.. (you/ever/arrest)?' 'No, never.'
12 Two people .... (report) to .... (injure) in an explosion at a factory in Birmingham early this morning.

21 *Put the verb into the correct form, active or passive.*

1 This house is quite old. It ...**was built**... (build) over 100 years ago.
2 My grandfather was a builder. He ...**built**... (build) this house many years ago.
3 'Is your car still for sale?' 'No, I .... (sell) it.'
4 'Is the house at the end of the street still for sale?' 'No, it .... (sell).'
5 Sometimes mistakes .... (make). It's inevitable.
6 I wouldn't leave your car unlocked. It .... (might/steal).
7 My bag has disappeared. It .... (must/steal).
8 I can't find my hat. Somebody .... (must/take) it by mistake.
9 It's a serious problem. I don't know how it .... (can/solve).
10 We didn't leave early enough. We .... (should/leave) earlier.
11 Every time I travel by plane, my flight .... (delay).
12 A new bridge .... (build) across the river. Work started last year and the bridge .... (expect) to open next year.

22 *Read these newspaper reports and put the verbs into the most suitable form.*

---

1 **Castle fire**

Winton Castle (1)..<u>was damaged</u>.. (damage) in a fire last night. The fire, which (2).......................... (discover) at about 9 o'clock, spread very quickly. Nobody (3).......................... (injure) but two people had to (4).......................... (rescue) from an upstairs room. A number of paintings (5).......................... (believe/destroy). It (6).......................... (not/know) how the fire started.

---

3 **ROAD DELAYS**

Repair work started yesterday on the Paxham-Longworth road. The road (1).......................... (resurface) and there will be long delays. Drivers (2).......................... (ask) to use an alternative route if possible. The work (3).......................... (expect) to last two weeks. Next Sunday the road (4).......................... (close) and traffic (5).......................... (divert).

---

2 **SHOP ROBBERY**

In Paxham yesterday a shop assistant (1).......................... (force) to hand over £500 after (2).......................... (threaten) by a man with a knife. The man escaped in a car which (3).......................... (steal) earlier in the day. The car (4).......................... (later/find) in a car park where it (5).......................... (abandon) by the thief. A man (6).......................... (arrest) in connection with the robbery and (7).......................... (still/question) by the police.

---

4 **Accident**

A woman (1).......................... (take) to hospital after her car collided with a lorry near Norstock yesterday. She (2).......................... (allow) home later after treatment. The road (3).......................... (block) for an hour after the accident and traffic had to (4).......................... (divert). A police inspector said afterwards: 'The woman was lucky. She could (5).......................... (kill).'

-ing and the infinitive   **Units 52–65**

23 *Put the verb into the correct form.*

1 How old were you when you learnt ...<u>to drive?</u>.. (drive)
2 I don't mind ...<u>walking</u>... home but I'd rather ...<u>get</u>... a taxi. (walk, get)
3 I can't make a decision. I keep .... my mind. (change)
4 He had made his decision and refused .... his mind. (change)
5 Why did you change your decision? What made you .... your mind? (change)
6 It was a really good holiday. I really enjoyed .... by the sea again. (be)
7 Did I really tell you I was unhappy? I don't remember .... that. (say)
8 'Remember .... Tom tomorrow.'   'OK. I won't forget.' (phone)
9 The water here is not very good. I'd avoid .... it if I were you. (drink)
10 I pretended .... interested in the conversation but really it was very boring. (be)
11 I got up and looked out of the window .... what the weather was like. (see)
12 I have a friend who claims .... able to speak five languages. (be)

13 I like .... carefully about things before .... a
    decision. (think, make)
14 Steve used .... a footballer. He had to stop ....
    because of an injury. (be, play)
15 After .... by the police, the man admitted .... the
    car but denied .... at 100 miles an hour. (stop, steal, drive)
16 A: How do you make this machine ....? (work)
    B: I'm not sure. Try .... that button and see what happens. (press)

24 *Make sentences from the words in brackets.*

1   I can't find the tickets. (I/seem/lose/them) ...I seem to have lost them...
2   I haven't got far to go. (it/not/worth/take/a taxi) ...It's not worth taking a taxi...
3   I'm feeling a bit tired. (I/not/fancy/go/out) ....
4   Tim isn't very reliable. (he/tend/forget/things) ....
5   I've got a lot of luggage. (you/mind/help/me?) ....
6   There's nobody in the house. (everybody/seem/go out) ....
7   We don't like our flat. (we/think/move) ....
8   The vase was very valuable. (I/afraid/touch/it) ....
9   Bill never carries money with him. (he/afraid/robbed) ....
10 I wouldn't go to see the film. (it/not/worth/see) ....
11 I'm very tired after that long walk. (I/not/used/walk/so far)
    ....
12 Sue is on holiday. I received a postcard from her yesterday. (she/seem/enjoy/herself)
    ....
13 Dave had lots of holiday photographs. (he/insist/show/them to me)
    ....
14 I don't want to do the shopping. (I'd rather/somebody else/do/ it)
    ....

25 *Complete the second sentence so that the meaning is similar to the first.*

1   I was surprised I passed the exam. I didn't expect ...to pass the exam...
2   Did you manage to solve the problem? Did you succeed ...in solving the problem?...
3   I don't read newspapers any more. I've given up ....
4   I'd prefer not to go out tonight. I'd rather ....
5   He can't walk very well. He has difficulty ....
6   Shall I phone you this evening? Do you want ....?
7   Nobody saw me come in. I came in without ....
8   They said I was a cheat. I was accused ....
9   It will be good to see them again. I'm looking forward ....
10 What do you think I should do? What do you advise me ....?
11 It's a pity I couldn't go out with you. I'd like ....
12 I'm sorry that I didn't take your advice. I regret ....

Articles

26 *Put in* **a/an** *or* **the** *where necessary. Leave an empty space (–) if the sentence is already complete.*

1 I don't usually like staying at ...–... hotels, but last summer we spent a few days at
...*a*... very nice hotel by ...*the*... sea.
2 .... tennis is my favourite sport. I play once or twice .... week if I can, but I'm not
.... very good player.
3 I won't be home for .... dinner this evening. I'm meeting some friends after .... work
and we're going to .... cinema.
4 .... unemployment is very high at the moment and it's very difficult for .... people to
find .... work.
5 There was .... accident as I was going .... home last night. Two people were taken to
.... hospital. I think .... most accidents are caused by .... people driving too fast.
6 Carol is .... economist. She used to work in .... investment department of ....
Lloyds Bank. Now she works for .... American bank in .... United States.
7 A: What's .... name of .... hotel where you're staying?
B: .... Imperial. It's in .... Queen Street in .... city centre. It's near .... station.
8 I have two brothers. .... older one is training to be .... pilot with ....
British Airways. .... younger one is still at .... school. When he leaves .... school,
he hopes to go to .... university to study .... law.

Conjunctions

27 *Choose the right alternative.*

1 I'll try to be on time but don't worry ~~if/when~~ I'm late.   (if *is right*)
2 Don't throw that bag away. If/When you don't want it, I'll have it.
3 Please report to reception if/when you arrive at the hotel.
4 We've arranged to play tennis tomorrow but we won't play if/when it's raining.
5 Jennifer is in her final year at school. She still doesn't know what she's going to do
if/when she leaves.
6 What would you do if/when you lost your keys?
7 I hope I'll be able to come to the party but I'll let you know if/unless I can't.
8 I don't want to be disturbed, so don't phone me if/unless it's something important.
9 Please sign the contract if/unless you're happy with the conditions.
10 I like travelling by sea as long as / unless it's not rough.
11 You might not remember the name of the hotel, so write it down if / in case you forget it.
12 It's not cold now but take your coat with you if / in case it gets cold later.
13 Take your coat with you and then you can put it on if / in case it gets cold later.
14 The television is always on, even if / if nobody is watching it.
15 Even/Although we played very well, we lost the match.
16 We're not very close friends despite/although we've known each other a long time.
17 'When did you leave school?'   'As/When I was 16.'
18 Ann will be surprised when/as she hears the news.

Prepositions (time)

Units 12, 118–121

28 *Put in one of the following prepositions:* **at on in for since during by until**

1 Jack has gone away. He'll be back ...**in**... a week.
2 We're having a party .... Saturday. Can you come?
3 I've got an interview next week. It's .... 9.30 .... Tuesday morning.
4 Sue isn't usually here .... weekends. She goes away.
5 The train service is very good. The trains are nearly always .... time.
6 It was a confusing situation. Many things were happening .... the same time.
7 I couldn't decide whether or not to buy the sweater. .... the end I decided not to.
8 The road is busy all the time, even .... night.
9 I was woken up by a loud noise .... the night.
10 I saw Helen .... Friday but I haven't seen her .... then.
11 Brian has been doing the same job .... five years.
12 Ann's birthday is .... the end of March. I'm not sure exactly which day it is.
13 We've got some friends staying with us .... the moment. They're staying .... Friday.
14 If you're interested in applying for the job, your application must be received .... Friday.

Prepositions (place and other uses)

Units 122–127

29 *Put in the missing preposition.*

1 I'd love to be able to visit every country .... the world.
2 'Have you read any books .... Margaret White?' 'No, I've never heard of her.'
3 'Is there a bank near here?' 'Yes, there's one .... the end of this road.'
4 Tim is away at the moment. He's .... holiday.
5 You've got a dirty mark .... your cheek. Have a look .... the mirror.
6 We went .... a party .... Linda's house on Saturday.
7 Bombay is .... the west coast of India.
8 Look at the leaves .... that tree. They're a beautiful colour.
9 'Have you ever been .... Tokyo?' 'No, I've never been .... Japan.'
10 Mozart died .... Vienna in 1791 .... the age of 35.
11 'Are you .... this photograph?' 'Yes, that's me, ... the left.'
12 We went .... the theatre last night. We had seats .... the front row.
13 'Where's the light switch?' 'It's .... the wall .... the door.'
14 What time did you arrive .... the party?
15 I couldn't decide what to eat. There was nothing .... the menu that I liked.
16 We live .... a tower block. Our flat is .... the fifteenth floor.
17 'What did you think of the film?' 'Some parts were a bit stupid but .... the whole I enjoyed it.'
18 When you paid the hotel bill, did you pay .... cash or .... credit card?
19 'How did you get here? .... the bus?' 'No, ... car.'
20 A: I wonder what's .... television this evening. Have you got a newspaper?
   B: Yes, the TV programmes are .... the back page.

Noun/adjective + preposition

Units 128–130

30 *Put in the missing preposition.*

1 The plan has been changed but nobody seems to know the reason .... this.
2 Don't ask me to decide. I'm not very good .... making decisions.
3 Some people say that Sue is unfriendly but she's always very nice .... me.
4 What do you think is the best solution .... the problem?
5 There has been a big increase .... the price of land recently.
6 He lives a rather lonely life. He doesn't have much contact .... other people.
7 Paula is a keen photographer. She likes taking pictures .... people.
8 Gordon got married .... a woman he met when he was studying at college.
9 He's very brave. He's not afraid .... anything.
10 I'm surprised .... the amount of traffic today. I didn't think it would be so busy.
11 Thank you for lending me the guide book. It was full .... useful information.
12 Please come in and sit down. I'm sorry .... the mess.

Verb + preposition

Units 131–135

31 *Put in a preposition where necessary. If the sentence is already complete, leave an empty space (–).*

1 She works quite hard. You can't accuse her .... being lazy.
2 Who's going to look .... your children while you're at work?
3 The problem is becoming serious. We have to discuss .... it.
4 The problem is becoming serious. We have to do something .... it.
5 I prefer this chair .... the other one. It's more comfortable.
6 I must phone .... the office to tell them I won't be at work today.
7 The river divides the city .... two parts.
8 'What do you think .... the new manager?' 'She's all right, I suppose.'
9 Can somebody please explain .... me what I have to do?
10 'Do you like staying at hotels?' 'It depends .... the hotel.'
11 'Have you ever been to Borla?' 'No, I've never heard .... it. Where is it?'
12 You remind me .... somebody I knew a long time ago. You look just like her.
13 What's funny? What are you laughing .... ?
14 What have you done with all the money you had? What did you spend it .... ?

STUDY GUIDE

This guide is to help you decide which units you need to study. The sentences in the guide are grouped together (*Present and past*, *Articles and nouns* etc.) in the same way as the units in the *Contents* (page iii).

Each sentence can be completed using one or more of the alternatives (A, B, C etc.). There are between two and five alternatives each time. IN SOME SENTENCES MORE THAN ONE ALTERNATIVE IS POSSIBLE.

If you don't know or if you are not sure which alternatives are correct, then you probably need to study the unit(s) listed on the right. You will also find the correct sentence in this unit. (If two or three units are listed, you will find the correct sentence in the first one.)

There is a key to this study guide on page 343.

IF YOU ARE NOT SURE WHICH IS RIGHT	STUDY UNIT

Present and past

1.1 '............................. this week?' 'No, she's on holiday.'
A Is Susan working   B Does Susan work   C Does work Susan   **1, 3**

1.2 I don't understand this sentence. What ....?
A does mean this word   B does this word mean   C means this word   **2, 48**

1.3 John .... tennis once or twice a week.
A is playing usually   B is usually playing   C usually plays   D plays usually   **2, 3, 109**

1.4 How .... now? Better than before?
A you are feeling   B do you feel   C are you feeling   **4**

1.5 It was a boring weekend. .... anything.
A I didn't   B I don't do   C I didn't do   **5**

1.6 Tom .... his hand when he was cooking the dinner.
A burnt   B was burning   C has burnt   **6, 14**

Present perfect and past

2.1 Jim is away on holiday. He .... to Spain.
A is gone   B has gone   C has been   **7**

2.2 Everything is going well. We .... any problems so far.
A didn't have   B don't have   C haven't had   **8**

2.3 Linda has lost her passport again. It's the second time this ....
A has happened   B happens   C happened   **8, 13**

2.4 You're out of breath. ....?
A Are you running   B Have you run   C Have you been running   **9**

2.5 Where's the book I gave you? What .... with it?
A have you done   B have you been doing   C are you doing   **10**

2.6 We're good friends. We .... each other for a long time.
A know   B have known   C have been knowing   D knew   **11, 10**

2.7 Sally has been working here ....
A for six months   B since six months   C six months ago   **12**

301

2.8   It's two years .... Joe.

       A that I don't see B that I haven't seen C since I didn't see D since I saw

12

2.9   They .... out after lunch and they've just come back.

       A went B have gone C are gone

13, 14, 7

2.10   The Chinese .... printing.

       A invented B have invented C had invented

13, 15

2.11   Ian .... in Scotland for ten years. Now he lives in London.

       A lived B has lived C has been living

14, 11

2.12   The man sitting next to me on the plane was nervous because
he .... before.

       A hasn't flown B didn't fly C hadn't flown D wasn't flying

15

2.13   .... a car when they were living in London?

       A Had they B Did they have C Were they having D Have they had

17

2.14   I .... television a lot but I don't any more.

       A was watching B was used to watch C used to watch

18

Future

3.1   .... tomorrow, so we can go out somewhere.

       A I'm not working B I don't work C I won't work

19, 21

3.2   That bag looks heavy. .... you with it.

       A I'm helping B I help C I'll help

21

3.3   I think the weather .... be nice later.

       A will B shall C is going to

23, 22

3.4   'Ann is in hospital.' 'Yes, I know. .... her tomorrow.'

       A I visit B I'm going to visit C I'll visit

23, 20

3.5   We're late. The film .... by the time we get to the cinema.

       A will already start B will be already started C will already have started

24

3.6   Don't worry .... late tonight.

       A if I am B when I am C when I'll be D if I'll be

25

Modals

4.1   The fire spread through the building quickly but everybody ....

       A was able to escape B managed to escape C could escape

26

4.2   The phone is ringing. It .... be Tim.

       A might B can C could

27, 29

4.3   Why did you stay at a hotel when you went to New York? You
.... with Barbara.

       A can stay B could stay C could have stayed

27

4.4   I've lost one of my gloves. I .... it somewhere.

       A must drop B must have dropped C must be dropping
D must have been dropping

28

4.5   Take an umbrella with you when you go out. It .... rain later.   **30**
A may   B might   C can   D could

4.6   What was wrong with you? Why .... go to hospital?   **31**
A had you to   B did you have to   C must you

4.7   There's plenty of time. You .... hurry.   **31, 32**
A don't have to   B mustn't   C needn't

4.8   It was a great party last night. You .... come. Why didn't you?   **33**
A must have   B should have   C ought to have   D had to

4.9   Jane .... a car.   **34**
A suggested that I buy   B suggested that I should buy   C suggested me to buy

4.10   I think all drivers .... seat belts.   **35**
A should wear   B had better wear   C had better to wear

4.11   It's late. It's time .... home.   **35**
A we go   B we must go   C we should go   D we went

Conditionals and 'wish'

5.1   I'm not tired enough to go to bed yet. I wouldn't sleep if I **37**
to bed now.
A go   B went   C had gone   D would go

5.2   If I were you, I .... that coat. It's much too expensive.   **38**
A won't buy   B don't buy   C am not going to buy   D wouldn't buy

5.3   I decided to stay at home last night. I would have gone out if I **39**
so tired.
A wasn't   B weren't   C wouldn't have been   D hadn't been

5.4   I wish I .... a car. It would make life so much easier.   **40, 38**
A have   B had   C would have

Passive

6.1   We .... by a loud noise during the night.   **41**
A woke up   B are woken up   C were woken up   D were waking up

6.2   There's somebody walking behind us. I think **42**
A we are following   B we are being followed   C we are followed
D we are being following

6.3   'Where ....?' 'In London.'   **43**
A were you born   B are you born   C have you been born   D did you born

6.4   The train .... arrive at 11.30 but it was an hour late.   **44**
A supposed to   B is supposed to   C was supposed to

6.5   Where ....? Which hairdresser did you go to?   **45**
A did you cut your hair   B have you cut your hair
C did you have cut your hair   D did you have your hair cut

IF YOU ARE NOT SURE WHICH IS RIGHT	STUDY UNIT

Reported speech

7.1	Hello, Jim. I didn't expect to see you today. Sonia said you .... ill.	47, 46
	A are B were C was D should be	
7.2	Ann .... and left.	47
	A said goodbye to me B said me goodbye C told me goodbye	

Questions and auxiliary verbs

8.1	'How ....?' 'Nobody knows.'	48
	A happened the accident B did happen the accident	
	C did the accident happen	
8.2	'Do you know where ....?' 'No, he didn't say.'	49
	A Tom has gone B has Tom gone C has gone Tom	
8.3	The police officer stopped us and asked us where	49
	A were we going B are we going C we are going D we were going	
8.4	'Do you think it's going to rain?' '...................................'	50
	A I hope not B I don't hope C I don't hope so	
8.5	'You don't know where Karen is, ...?' 'Sorry, I've no idea.'	51
	A don't you B do you C is she	

-ing and the infinitive

9.1	You can't stop me .... what I want.	52
	A doing B do C to do D that I do	
9.2	I must go now. I promised .... late.	53, 40
	A not being B not to be C to not be D I wouldn't be	
9.3	Do you want .... with you or do you want to go alone?	54
	A me coming B me to come C that I come D that I will come	
9.4	I'm sure I locked the door. I clearly remember .... it.	55
	A locking B to lock C to have locked	
9.5	She tried to be serious but she couldn't help	56
	A laughing B to laugh C that she laughed	
9.6	I like .... the kitchen as often as possible.	57
	A cleaning B clean C to clean D that I clean	
9.7	I'm tired. I'd rather .... out this evening, if you don't mind.	58
	A not going B not to go C don't go D not go	
9.8	'Shall I stay here?' 'I'd rather .... with us.'	58
	A you come B you to come C you came D you would come	
9.9	Are you looking forward .... Ann again?	59, 61
	A seeing B to see C to seeing	
9.10	When Jane came to Britain, she had to get used .... on the left.	60
	A driving B to driving C to drive	
9.11	I'm thinking .... a house. Do you think that's a good idea?	61, 65
	A to buy B of to buy C of buying	

9.12   I'm sure you'll have no .... the exam.
       A difficulty to pass   B difficulties to pass   C difficulties passing
       D difficulty passing

62

9.13   A friend of mine phoned .... me to a party.
       A for invite   B to invite   C for inviting   D for to invite

63

9.14   Jim doesn't speak very clearly. ....
       A It is difficult to understand him.   B He is difficult to understand.
       C He is difficult to understand him.

64

9.15   The path was icy, so we walked very carefully. We were afraid ....
       A of falling   B from falling   C to fall

65

9.16   I didn't hear you .... in. You must have been very quiet.
       A come   B to come   C came

66

9.17   .... a hotel, we looked for somewhere to have dinner.
       A Finding   B After finding   C Having found   D We found

67

Articles and nouns

10.1   Call an ambulance. There's been ....
       A accident   B an accident   C some accident

68

10.2   'Where are you going?'   'I'm going to buy ....'
       A a bread   B some bread   C a loaf of bread

69

10.3   Sandra works at a big hospital. She's ....
       A nurse   B a nurse   C the nurse

70, 71

10.4   She works six days .... week.
       A in   B for   C a   D the

71

10.5   There are millions of stars in ....
       A space   B a space   C the space

72

10.6   Every day .... begins at 9 and finishes at 3.
       A school   B a school   C the school

73

10.7   .... a problem in most big cities.
       A Crime is   B The crime is   C The crimes are

74

10.8   When .... invented?
       A was telephone   B were telephones   C was the telephone
       D were the telephones

75

10.9   We visited ....
       A Canada and United States   B the Canada and the United States
       C Canada and the United States   D the Canada and United States

76

10.10 Julia is a student at ....
       A London University   B the London University   C the University of London

77

10.11 What time .... on television?
       A is the news   B are the news   C is news

78, 69

10.12 It took us quite a long time to get here. It was .... journey.
       A three hour   B a three-hours   C a three-hour

79

IF YOU ARE NOT SURE WHICH IS RIGHT	STUDY UNIT

10.13 Where is ....?
A the manager office   B the manager's office   C the office of the manager
D the office of the manager's

80

Pronouns and determiners

11.1 I'm going to a wedding on Saturday. .... is getting married.
A A friend of me   B A friend of mine   C One my friends

81

11.2 What time shall we .... this evening?
A meet   B meet us   C meet ourselves

82

11.3 They live on a busy road. .... a lot of noise from the traffic.
A It must be   B There must be   C There must have   D It must have

83

11.4 He's lazy. He never does .... work.
A some   B any   C no

84

11.5 'What would you like to eat?' 'I don't mind. .... – whatever you've got.'
A Something   B Anything   C Nothing

84, 85

11.6 We couldn't buy anything because .... of the shops were open.
A all   B no one   C none   D nothing

85

11.7 When we were on holiday, we spent .... money.
A a lot of   B much   C too much

86

11.8 .... don't visit this part of the town.
A The most tourists   B Most of tourists   C Most tourists

87

11.9 I asked two people the way to the station but .... of them knew.
A none   B either   C both   D neither

88

11.10 It was a great party. .... enjoyed it.
A Everybody   B All   C All of us   D Everybody of us

89

11.11 The bus service is very good. There's a bus .... ten minutes.
A each   B every   C all

89, 90

Relative clauses

12.1 I don't like stories .... have unhappy endings.
A that   B they   C which   D who

91

12.2 I didn't believe them at first but in fact everything .... was true.
A they said   B that they said   C what they said

92

12.3 What's the name of the man ....?
A you borrowed his car   B which car you borrowed
C whose car you borrowed   D his car you borrowed

93

12.4 Colin told me about his new job, ... very much.
A that he's enjoying   B which he's enjoying   C he's enjoying
D he's enjoying it

94

12.5 Sheila couldn't come to the party, ... was a pity.
A that   B it   C what   D which

95

IF YOU ARE NOT SURE WHICH IS RIGHT

12.6   Some of the people .... to the party can't come.   **96**
       A inviting   B invited   C who invited   D they were invited

Adjectives and adverbs

13.1   Jane doesn't enjoy her job. She's .... because she does the same   **97**
       thing every day.
       A boring   B bored

13.2   The woman was carrying a .... bag.   **98**
       A black small plastic   B small and black plastic   C small black plastic
       D plastic small black

13.3   Maria's English is excellent. She speaks **99**
       A perfectly English   B English perfectly   C perfect English   D English perfect

13.4   He .... to find a job but he had no luck.   **100**
       A tried hard   B tried hardly   C hardly tried

13.5   I haven't seen her for .... I've forgotten what she looks like.   **101**
       A so long   B a so long time   C a such long time   D such a long time

13.6   I haven't got .... on holiday at the moment.   **102**
       A money enough to go   B enough money to go   C money enough for going
       D enough money for going

13.7   Let's get a taxi. It's .... to walk.   **103**
       A a quite long way   B quite a long way   C rather a long way

13.8   The exam was quite easy – .... we expected.   **104**
       A more easy that   B more easy than   C easier than   D easier as

13.9   The more electricity you use, ...   **105**
       A your bill will be higher   B will be higher your bill
       C the higher your bill will be

13.10   He's a fast runner. I can't run as fast as **106**
       A he   B him   C he can

13.11   The film was really boring. It was .... I've ever seen.   **107**
       A most boring film   B the more boring film   C the film more boring
       D the most boring film

13.12   Tom likes walking. **108**
       A Every morning he walks to work.   B He walks to work every morning.
       C He walks every morning to work.

13.13   .... a long time for the bus.   **109**
       A Always we have to wait   B We always have to wait
       C We have always to wait   D We have to wait always

13.14   Ann .... She left last month.   **110**
       A still doesn't work here   B doesn't still work here   C no more works here
       D doesn't work here any more

13.15   .... she can't drive, she has bought a car.   **111, 112**
       A Even   B Even though   C Even if   D Even when

Conjunctions and prepositions

14.1 I couldn't sleep .... very tired.
A although I was   B despite I was   C despite of being   D in spite of being

112

14.2 You should insure your bicycle .... stolen.
A in case it will be   B if it will be   C in case it is   D if it is

113

14.3 The club is for members only. You .... you're a member.
A can't go in if   B can go in only if   C can't go in unless   D can go in unless

114

14.4 Angela has been married a long time. She got married .... she was 23 years old.
A when   B as

115

14.5 What a beautiful house! It's .... a palace.
A as   B like

116

14.6 They are very kind to me. They treat me .... their own son.
A like I am   B as if I am   C as if I was   D as if I were

117

14.7 I'll be in London next week. I hope to see Tom .... there.
A while I will be   B while I am   C during my visit   D during I am

118

14.8 Fred is away at the moment. I don't know exactly when he's coming back but I'm sure he'll be back .... Monday.
A by   B until

119

Prepositions

15.1 I'll be at home .... Friday morning. You can phone me then.
A at   B on   C in

120

15.2 I'm going away .... the end of January.
A at   B on   C in

121

15.3 When we were in Italy, we spent a few days .... Venice.
A at   B to   C in

122, 124

15.4 Our flat is .... the second floor of the building.
A at   B on   C in

123

15.5 I saw Jack .... a concert last Saturday.
A at   B on   C in

124

15.6 What time did they .... the hotel?
A arrive to   B arrive at   C arrive in   D get to   E get in

125

15.7 Tom's away at the moment. He's .... holiday in France.
A at   B on   C in   D for

126

15.8 We travelled .... 6.45 train, which arrived at 8.30.
A in the   B on the   C by the   D by

127

15.9 Have you read any books .... Agatha Christie?
A of   B from   C by

127

15.10 The accident was my fault, so I had to pay for the damage .... the other car.
A of   B for   C to   D on   E at

128

15.11 Why were you so unfriendly .... Tessa? Have you had an argument with her?   **129**
        A of   B for   C to   D with

15.12 I'm not very good .... repairing things.   **130**
        A at   B for   C in   D about

15.13 I don't understand this sentence. Can you ....?   **131**
        A explain to me this word   B explain me this word   C explain this word to me

15.14 If you're worried about the problem, you should do something .... it.   **132**
        A for   B about   C against   D with

15.15 'Who is Tom Madely?'   'I've no idea. I've never heard .... him.'   **133**
        A about   B from   C after   D of

15.16 'What time will you arrive?'   'I don't know. It depends .... the traffic.'   **134**
        A of   B for   C from   D on

15.17 I prefer tea .... coffee.   **135, 58**
        A to   B than   C against   D over

15.18 They gave me a form and told me to **136**
        A fill in   B fill it in   C fill in it

KEY TO EXERCISES

In some of the exercises, you have to use your own ideas to write sentences. Example answers are given in the key. If possible, check your answers with somebody who speaks English well.

UNIT 1

1.1

2 'm looking / am looking
3 's getting / is getting
4 're staying / are staying
5 'm coming / am coming
6 's starting / is starting
7 're making / are making ... 'm trying / am trying
8 's happening / is happening

1.2

2 are you looking
3 's she studying / is she studying
4 Is anybody listening
5 Is it getting

1.3

3 'm not enjoying / am not enjoying
4 's having / is having
5 'm not eating / am not eating
6 's learning / is learning
7 aren't speaking /'re not speaking / are not speaking

1.4

1 are you doing
2 'm training / am training
3 Are you enjoying
4 'm not working / am not working
5 'm trying / am trying
6 'm decorating / am decorating
7 Are you doing
8 are helping

1.5

2 's getting / is getting
3 is changing
4 is rising *or* is increasing
5 's getting / is getting

UNIT 2

2.1

2 drink
3 opens ... closes
4 causes
5 live
6 take place

2.2

2 do the banks close
3 does Martin come
4 do you do
5 takes ... does it take
6 play ... don't play
7 does this word mean

2.3

3 rises
4 make
5 don't eat
6 doesn't believe
7 translates
8 doesn't tell
9 flows

2.4

2 Does your sister play tennis?
3 Which newspaper do you read?
4 What does your brother do? *or* What is your brother's job?
5 How often do you go to the cinema?
6 Where does your mother live?

2.5

2 I promise
3 I insist
4 I apologise
5 I recommend

UNIT 3

3.1

3 *wrong* – is trying
4 *wrong* – are they talking
5 *right*
6 *wrong* – 's getting / is getting
7 *right*
8 *wrong* – 'm coming / am coming
9 *wrong* – are you getting

3.2

3 's waiting / is waiting
4 Are you listening
5 Do you listen
6 flows
7 's flowing / is flowing
8 grow ... aren't growing / 're not growing / are not growing
9 's improving / is improving
10 's staying / is staying ... always stays
11 'm starting / am starting
12 'm learning / am learning ... is teaching
13 finish ... 'm working / am working
14 live ... do your parents live
15 is looking ... 's staying / is staying

16 does your father do ... isn't working / 's not working / is not working
17 enjoy ... 'm not enjoying / am not enjoying
18 always leaves
19 's always leaving / is always leaving (always leaves *is also possible*)

3.3

2 It's always breaking down.
3 I'm always making the same mistake. / ...that mistake.
4 You're always leaving the lights on.

UNIT 4

4.1

2 *right*
3 *wrong* – Do you believe
4 *wrong* – It tastes
5 *wrong* – I think

4.2

2 What are you doing? I'm thinking.
3 Who does this umbrella belong to?
4 The dinner smells good.
5 Is anybody sitting here?
6 I'm having dinner.

4.3

2 doesn't belong / does not belong
3 'm using / am using
4 need
5 does he want
6 is he looking
7 believes
8 don't remember / do not remember
9 'm thinking / am thinking
10 think ... don't use / do not use
11 prefer
12 consists

4.4

2 is being
3 is
4 are you being
5 Is she

UNIT 5

5.1

2 had
3 She walked to work
4 It took her (about) half an hour
5 She started work
6 She didn't have (any) lunch. / ...eat (any) lunch.

7 She finished work
8 She was tired when she got home.
9 She cooked
10 She didn't go
11 She went to bed
12 She slept

5.2

2 taught
3 sold
4 drank
5 won
6 fell ... hurt
7 threw ... caught
8 spent ... bought ... cost

5.3

2 Did you go alone?
3 Was the food good?
4 How long did you stay there?
5 Did you stay at a hotel?
6 How did you travel?
7 Was the weather fine?
8 What did you do in the evenings?
9 Did you meet anybody interesting?

5.4

3 didn't disturb   8 laughed
4 went   9 flew
5 didn't sleep   10 didn't cost
6 didn't eat   11 didn't have
7 wasn't   12 were

UNIT 6

6.1

Example answers:
3 I was working.
4 I was in bed asleep.
5 I was having a meal in a restaurant.
6 I was watching TV at home.

6.2

Example answers:
2 was having a shower.
3 were waiting for the bus.
4 was reading the paper.
5 was watching it.

6.3

1 didn't see ... was looking
2 met ... were going ... was going ... had ... were waiting / waited
3 was cycling ... stepped ... was going ... managed ... didn't hit

6.4

2 were you doing
3 Did you go
4 was wearing (wore *is also possible*)
5 were you driving ... happened
6 took ... wasn't looking
7 didn't know

8 saw ... was trying
9 was walking ... heard ... was following ... started
10 wanted

UNIT 7

7.1

2 My father has started a new job.
3 I've given up smoking. / I have given...
4 Charles and Sarah have gone to Brazil.
5 Suzanne has had a baby.

7.2

2 She has broken her leg. / She's broken...
3 Her English has improved. / It has improved. / It's improved.
4 He has grown a beard. / He's grown...
5 The letter has arrived. / It has arrived. / It's arrived.
6 The bus fare has gone up. / It has gone up. / It's gone up.

7.3

2 've just seen / have just seen
3 's already left / has already left
4 haven't read it yet
5 's already seen / has already seen
6 've just arrived / have just arrived
7 haven't told him yet

7.4

2 he's just gone out / he has just gone out
3 I haven't finished yet.
4 I've already done / I have already done
5 Have you found a job yet?
6 she's just come back / she has just come back

7.5

2 been
3 gone
4 gone
5 been

UNIT 8

8.1

2 Have you ever been to California?
3 Have you ever run a marathon?
4 Have you ever spoken to a famous person?
5 Have you always lived in this town?
6 What's the most beautiful place you've ever visited?

8.2

2 haven't seen
3 haven't eaten
4 I haven't played (it)
5 I've had / I have had
6 I haven't read
7 I've never been / I haven't been
8 has been late / 's been late
9 I've never tried / I have never tried / I've never eaten
10 it's happened / it has happened / that's happened / that has happened
11 I've never seen her / I haven't seen her

8.3

2 haven't read one / a newspaper
3 it hasn't made a profit. / it has made a loss.
4 she hasn't worked (very) hard this term.
5 it hasn't snowed (much) this winter.
6 haven't won many/any games this season.

8.4

2 Have you played tennis before? No, this is the first time I've played tennis.
3 Have you ridden a horse before? / Have you been on a horse before? No, this is the first time I've ridden a horse. / ...I've been on a horse.
4 Have you been to London before? No, this is the first time I've been to London.

UNIT 9

9.1

2 have been playing tennis. / 've been playing tennis.
3 has been watching television. / 's been watching television.
4 has been running. / 's been running.

9.2

2 Have you been waiting long?
3 What have you been doing?
4 How long have you been living in Baker Street?
5 How long have you been selling computers?

9.3

2 have been waiting / 've been waiting
3 have been learning Spanish / 've been learning Spanish

4 She has been looking for a job /
   She's been looking… / Ann has
   been looking…
5 She has been working in London /
   She's been working… / Mary has
   been working…
6 have been writing to each other /
   've been writing…

9.4

2 have been looking / 've been
   looking
3 are you looking
4 have been going / 've been going
5 have been thinking / 've been
   thinking
6 is working / 's working
7 has been working / 's been working

UNIT 10

10.1

2 She has been travelling for three
   months.
   She has visited six countries so far.
3 He has won the national
   championship four times.
   He has been playing tennis since he
   was ten.
4 They have made ten films since
   they left college.
   They have been making films since
   they left college.

10.2

2 How long have you been waiting?
3 How many fish have you caught?
4 How many people have you
   invited?
5 How long have you been teaching?
6 How many books have you
   written?
   How long have you been writing
   books?
7 How long have you been saving?
   How much money have you saved?

10.3

2 has broken
3 Have you been working
4 Have you ever worked
5 has she gone
6 has appeared / 's appeared
7 haven't been waiting
8 has stopped / 's stopped
9 have lost / 've lost … Have you
   seen
10 have been reading / 've been
   reading … haven't finished
11 have read / 've read

UNIT 11

11.1

3 *wrong* – have been married
4 *right*
5 *wrong* – has been raining
6 *wrong* – have you been living
7 *wrong* – has been working
8 *right* (see Unit 19A)
9 *wrong* – haven't smoked
10 *wrong* – have you had it

11.2

2 How long have you been teaching
   English?
3 How long have you known Carol?
4 How long has your brother been in
   Australia?
5 How long have you had that
   jacket?
6 How long has Alan worked at the
   airport? *or* How long has Alan
   been working…
7 How long have you been having
   driving lessons?
8 Have you always lived in
   Glasgow?

11.3

3 has been / 's been
4 have been waiting / 've been
   waiting
5 have known / 've known
6 haven't played
7 has been watching / 's been
   watching
8 haven't watched
9 have had / 've had
10 hasn't been
11 have been feeling / 've been
   feeling *or* have felt / 've felt
12 has been living / 's been living
13 haven't been
14 have always wanted /
   've always wanted

UNIT 12

12.1

2 How long has she been learning
   Italian?
   When did she start learning
   Italian?
3 How long have you known him /
   …known Martin?
   When did you first meet
   (him/Martin)?
4 How long have they been married?
   When did they get married? (When
   did they marry? *is possible but less
   usual*)

12.2

3 been ill since Sunday
4 been ill for a few days
5 married two years ago
6 had it for ten years / had this
   camera for ten years
7 to France three weeks ago
8 been working in a hotel since June

12.3

2 for   5 Since   8 for
3 for   6 for   9 since
4 since   7 since

12.4

2 No, I haven't eaten in a restaurant
   for ages.
3 No, I haven't seen Sarah for about
   a month. / No, I haven't seen her
   for…
4 No, I haven't been to the cinema
   for a long time.
6 No, it's ages since I (last) ate in a
   restaurant.
7 No, it's about a month since I
   (last) saw Sarah.
8 No, it's a long time since I (last)
   went to the cinema.

UNIT 13

13.1

2 has gone to bed / 's gone to bed
3 has fallen / has dropped / has gone
   down
4 has turned on the light / has turned
   the light on / has turned it on
5 has grown / 's grown
6 has taken off

13.2

3 went
4 has gone / 's gone
5 have forgotten / 've forgotten
6 forgot
7 had
8 has been / 's been
9 haven't finished
10 has just gone / 's just gone
11 arrested
12 gave … lost   *or*
   have lost / 've lost
13 was … has disappeared /
   's disappeared
14 have improved / 've improved

13.3

3 *wrong* – did Shakespeare write
4 *right*
5 *wrong* – was
6 *right*
7 *wrong* – My grandparents got
   married…
8 *wrong* – were you born

9 *right*
10 *wrong* – <u>was</u> the scientist who
   <u>developed</u>…

13.4

2 has broken
   did that happen
   fell
3 Have you had
   cut … Did you go
   did

UNIT 14

14.1

3 *right*
4 *wrong* – I bought
5 *wrong* – were you
6 *wrong* – Jenny <u>left</u> school
7 *right*
8 *right*
9 *wrong* – wasn't
10 *wrong* – When <u>was this book</u>
   published

14.2

2 The weather has been cold
   recently.
3 It was cold last week.
4 I didn't read a newspaper
   yesterday.
5 I haven't read a newspaper today.
6 Ann has earned a lot of money this
   year.
7 She didn't earn so much last year.
8 Have you had a holiday recently?

14.3

2 got … was … went
3 Have you washed it? (Did you
   wash it? *is also possible*)
4 wasn't
5 worked
6 has lived / 's lived
7 Did you go … was … was
8 died … never met
9 have never met / 've never met
   him
10 I'm afraid he <u>has gone</u> out. /
   …he<u>'s gone</u> out.
   When exactly <u>did he go</u> out?
11 How long <u>have you lived</u> there?
   Where <u>did you live</u> before that?
   And how long <u>did you live</u> in
   Chicago?

14.4

Example answers:
2 I haven't bought anything today.
3 I didn't watch TV yesterday.
4 I went out with some friends
   yesterday evening.
5 I haven't been to the cinema
   recently.
6 I've been swimming a lot recently.

UNIT 15

15.1

2 It had changed a lot.
3 She had arranged to do something
   else. / She'd arranged…
4 The film had already begun.
5 I hadn't seen him for five years.
6 She had just had breakfast. /
   She'd just had…

15.2

2 I had never seen her before. /
   I'd never seen…
3 He had never played tennis before.
   / He'd never played…
4 We had never been there before. /
   We'd never been there before.   *or*
   …been to Denmark before.

15.3

1 called the police
2 there was … had gone / 'd gone
3 had just come back from holiday /
   'd just come…
   looked very well
4 had a phone call from Sally
   was
   had written to her / 'd written…
   had never replied to his letters /
   'd never replied…

15.4

2 went
3 had gone
4 broke
5 saw … had broken … stopped

UNIT 16

16.1

2 They had been playing football. /
   They'd been playing…
3 Somebody had been smoking in
   the room.
4 She had been dreaming. /
   She'd been dreaming.
5 He had been watching TV. /
   He'd been watching…

16.2

2 I <u>had been waiting</u> for 20 minutes
   when I <u>suddenly realised that I was</u>
   <u>in the wrong restaurant</u>.
3 At the time the factory <u>closed</u>
   <u>down</u>, Sarah <u>had been working</u>
   there for five years.
4 The orchestra <u>had been playing for</u>
   <u>about ten minutes</u> when <u>a man in</u>
   <u>the audience suddenly began</u>
   <u>shouting</u>.
5 *Example answer:*
   I had been walking along the road
   for about ten minutes when a car
   suddenly stopped just behind me.

16.3

3 was walking
4 had / 'd been running
5 were eating
6 had been eating (had eaten *is also
   possible*)
7 was looking
8 was waiting … had been waiting /
   'd been waiting
9 had had / 'd had
10 had / 'd been travelling

UNIT 17

17.1

3 I haven't got a ladder. /
   I don't have a ladder.
4 We didn't have enough time.
5 He didn't have a map.
6 She hasn't got any money. /
   She doesn't have any money.
7 They haven't got a key. /
   They don't have a key.
8 I didn't have a camera.

17.2

2 Have you got / Do you have
3 Did you have
4 Have you got / Do you have
5 did you have
6 Have you got / Do you have
7 Did you have

17.3

Example answers:
2 I've got a bicycle (now).
   I didn't have a bicycle (ten years
   ago).
3 I haven't got a guitar (now).
   I had a guitar (ten years ago).
4 I've got a dog (now).
   I had a dog (ten years ago).

17.4

2 has a swim
3 had a party
4 have a look
5 is having a rest / 's having a rest
6 had a chat
7 Did you have a nice time
8 had a baby
9 had a cigarette
10 was having a shower
11 Did you have a good flight

UNIT 18

18.1

2 used to have / used to ride
3 used to live
4 used to like / used to love / used to
   eat
5 used to be

6 used to take
7 used to be
8 did you use to go

18.2

3–6
He used to go to bed early.
He used to run three miles every morning.
He didn't use to go out in the evening.
He didn't use to spend much money. / ...spend a lot of money

18.3

2–10
She used to play the piano but she hasn't played (the piano) for years.
She used to be very lazy but she works very hard these days.
She didn't use to like cheese but she eats lots of cheese now.
She used to have a dog but it died two years ago.
She used to be a hotel receptionist but she works in a bookshop now.
She used to have lots of friends but she doesn't know many people these days.
She never used to read newspapers but she reads a newspaper every day now.
She didn't use to drink tea but she likes it now.
She used to go to a lot of parties but she hasn't been to a party for ages.

UNIT 19

19.1

2 How long are you staying?
3 When are you going?
4 Are you going alone?
5 Are you travelling by car?
6 Where are you staying?

19.2

2 am working late / 'm working late
   or ...working till 9 o'clock
3 I'm going to the theatre (with my mother)
4 I'm meeting Julia

19.3

Example answers:
2 I'm going to work tomorrow morning.
3 I'm not doing anything tomorrow evening.
4 I'm playing football next Sunday.
5 I'm going to a party this evening.

19.4

3 are having / 're having
4 opens ... finishes
5 am not going / 'm not going ...
   am staying / 'm staying
6 Are you doing
7 are going / 're going ... begins
8 does this train get
9 am going / 'm going ...
   Are you coming
10 is coming ... is travelling /
    's travelling ... arrives ...
    am meeting / 'm meeting
11 am not using / 'm not using
12 does it finish

UNIT 20

20.1

2 I'm going to phone her later.
3 I'm going to do it this afternoon.
4 Not yet. I'm going to read it after dinner.
5 (Not yet.) I'm just going to have it.

20.2

2 What are you going to wear?
3 Where are you going to put it?
4 Who are you going to invite?

20.3

2 I'm going to give it up.
3 I'm not going to take it.
4 I'm going to complain.

20.4

2 He is going to be late.
3 The boat is going to sink.
4 She is going to run out of petrol.

20.5

2 were going to play
3 was going to phone
4 was going to give up
5 were going to have

UNIT 21

21.1

2 I'll turn / I'll switch / I'll put
3 I'll go
4 I'll do
5 I'll show / I'll teach
6 I'll have
7 I'll send
8 I'll give / I'll bring
9 I'll stay / I'll wait

21.2

2 I'll go to bed.
3 I think I'll walk.
4 I'll play tennis (today).
5 I don't think I'll go swimming.

21.3

3 I'll meet
4 I'll lend
5 I'm having
6 I won't forget
7 does your train leave
8 won't tell
9 Are you doing
10 Will you come
11 I won't tell

21.4

2 Shall I buy it?
3 What shall I give/buy/get Ann (for her birthday)?
4 Where shall we go?
5 Shall we go by car or (shall we) walk? / ...or (shall we go) on foot?
6 What time shall I phone (you)?

UNIT 22

22.1

2 I'm going
3 will get
4 is coming
5 we are going
6 It won't hurt

22.2

2 will look
3 will like / 'll like
4 will get / 'll get
5 will be / 'll be
6 will meet / 'll meet
7 will come / 'll come
8 will be / 'll be

22.3

2 won't
3 will / 'll
4 won't
5 will / 'll
6 won't

22.4

Example answers:
2 I'll be in bed.
3 I'll be at work.
4 I expect I'll be at home.
5 I don't know where I'll be this time next year.

22.5

2 Do you think it will rain?
3 When do you think it will finish?
4 How much do you think it will cost?
5 Do you think they'll get married? / ...they will get married?
6 What time do you think you'll be back? / ...you will be back?
7 What do you think will happen?

UNIT 23

23.1

2 I'll lend
3 I'll get
4 I'm going to wash
5 are you going to paint
6 I'm going to buy
7 I'll show
8 I'll have
9 I'll do
10 it is going to fall
11 He's going to have ... he's going to do

23.2

1 I'll get
2 I'm going to sit ... I'll join
3 you'll find
4 I'm not going to apply
5 You'll wake (You're going to wake *is also possible*)
6 I'll take ... We'll leave ... Ann is going to take

UNIT 24

24.1

2 *b* is true
3 *a* and *c* are true
4 *b* and *d* are true
5 *c* and *d* are true
6 *c* is true

24.2

2 We'll have finished
3 we'll be playing
4 I'll be working
5 the meeting will have finished
6 he'll have spent
7 he'll have been
8 you'll still be doing
9 she'll have travelled
10 I'll be staying
11 Will you be seeing

UNIT 25

25.1

2 goes
3 will tell / 'll tell ... come
4 see ... won't recognise / will not recognise
5 is / 's
6 will wait / 'll wait ... are / 're
7 will be / 'll be ... gets
8 is
9 phones ... am / 'm

25.2

2 I'll give you my address when I find somewhere to live. *or* ...when I've found somewhere to live.

3 I'll come straight back home after I do the shopping. *or* ...after I've done the shopping.
4 Let's go home before it starts raining.
5 I won't speak to her until she apologises. *or* ...until she has apologised.

25.3

2 you leave / you go
3 you finish with it / when you finish reading it *or* you've finished with it / you've finished reading it / you've read it
4 you decide / you've decided
5 they finish the new road *or* they've finished the new road *or* they've built the new road

25.4

2	If	6	when
3	When	7	if
4	if	8	if
5	If		

UNIT 26

26.1

3 can
4 been able to
5 be able to
6 can
7 be able to

26.2

Example answers:
2 I used to be able to run fast.
3 I'd like to be able to play a musical instrument.
4 I've never been able to get up early.

26.3

2 could run
3 can wait
4 couldn't eat
5 can't hear
6 couldn't sleep

26.4

2 were able to find it.
3 I was able to finish it.
4 was able to get away.

26.5

4 couldn't / wasn't able to
5 was able to
6 could / was able to
7 was able to
8 could / was able to
9 were able to
10 couldn't / wasn't able to

UNIT 27

27.1

2 We could have fish.
3 You could give her a book.
4 You could phone her now.
5 We could go (and see him) on Friday.
6 We could hang it in the kitchen.

27.2

2	could	6	can
3	can / could	7	can / could
4	could	8	could
5	could		

27.3

2 could have gone
3 could apply
4 could have gone
5 could come

27.4

2 Ken couldn't have gone out (for a meal) on Friday evening (because he had to work).
3 Ken could have played tennis on Monday afternoon.
4 He couldn't have lent Jack £50 (because he was short of money). *or* He couldn't have lent him £50...
5 He could have come to Jane's party. *or* He could have gone to...
6 He couldn't have repaired her washing machine (because he doesn't know anything about machines).

UNIT 28

28.1

2	must	6	must
3	can't	7	must
4	must	8	can't
5	can't		

28.2

3 be
4 have been
5 be
6 go *or* have been
7 be going
8 have taken / have stolen
9 have been
10 be following

28.3

3 It must have been very expensive.
4 They must have gone away.
5 I must have left it in the restaurant last night.

6 The exam can't have been very difficult.
7 She must have been listening to our conversation. / She must have listened to…
8 She can't have understood what I said.
9 I must have forgotten to turn it off.
10 The driver can't have seen the red light.
11 The neighbours must have been having a party.

UNIT 29

29.1

2 She may/might be busy.
3 She may/might be working.
4 She may/might want to be alone.
5 She may/might have been ill yesterday.
6 She may/might have gone home early.
7 She may/might have had to go home early.
8 She may/might have been working yesterday.
9 She may/might not want to see me.
10 She may/might not be working today.
11 She may/might not have been feeling well yesterday.

29.2

2 be
3 have been
4 be waiting
5 have *or* have read

29.3

2 a She may/might be watching TV in her room.
  b She may/might have gone out.
3 a It may/might be in the car.
  b You may/might have left it in the restaurant last night.
4 a He may/might have been in the bath.
  b He may/might not have heard the bell.

29.4

3 might not have been invited.
4 couldn't have been invited.
5 couldn't have been an accident.
6 might not have been an accident.

UNIT 30

30.1

2 I may/might buy a Mercedes.
3 I may/might go to London.
4 I may/might hang it in the dining room.
5 He may/might come on Saturday.
6 She may/might go to university.

30.2

2 might wake
3 might bite
4 might need
5 might slip
6 might break

30.3

2 might be able to meet/see
3 might have to work
4 might have to go

30.4

2 I may/might not go out this evening.
3 Tom may/might not like the present I bought for him.
4 Sue may/might not be able to meet us this evening.

30.5

2 may/might as well go
3 may/might as well have another drink
4 We may/might as well watch it. *or* …watch the film.

UNIT 31

31.1

3 have to
4 must *or* have to
5 had to
6 must *or* have to
7 have to
8 had to
9 has to
10 have to
11 had to
12 has had to

31.2

2 do you have to get up / have you got to get up
3 does (she) have to go? / has (she) got to go?
4 did he have to pay?
5 did you have to wait?
6 do you have to phone her now? / have you got to phone her now?
7 does he have to leave? / has he got to leave?

31.3

2 don't have to pay
3 didn't have to wait
4 doesn't have to work
5 don't have to go
6 doesn't have to shave
7 don't have to do
8 didn't have to go

31.4

3 don't have to
4 mustn't
5 don't have to
6 mustn't
7 doesn't have to
8 mustn't
9 mustn't
10 don't have to

UNIT 32

32.1

2 needn't come
3 needn't walk
4 needn't ask
5 needn't tell
6 needn't explain

32.2

3 needn't
4 must
5 mustn't
6 needn't
7 needn't
8 must … mustn't
9 needn't … must

32.3

2 She needn't have bought any eggs.
3 You needn't have shouted (at me).
4 He needn't have sold his car.
5 We needn't have taken the camera.
6 I needn't have rushed / I needn't have hurried.

32.4

2 You needn't have walked home. You could have taken a taxi.
3 You needn't have stayed at a hotel. You could have stayed with us.
4 She needn't have phoned me in the middle of the night. She could have phoned me in the morning.
5 You needn't have left without saying anything. You could have said goodbye to me.

UNIT 33

33.1

2 You should look for another job.
3 He shouldn't go to bed so late.
4 You should take a photograph.

5 She shouldn't use her car so much.
6 He should put some pictures on the walls.

33.2
2 I think smoking should be banned in restaurants.
3 I don't think you should go out this evening.
4 I think the government should resign.

33.3
3 should come
4 should do
5 should have done
6 should win
7 should have won
8 should be
9 should have arrived

33.4
3 We should have reserved a table.
4 The shop should be open. / The shop should have opened by now. or It should…
5 She shouldn't be driving so fast. or She shouldn't be doing 50 miles an hour.
6 You should have come to see me.
7 The driver in front shouldn't have stopped without warning.
8 I should have been looking where I was going. or I should have looked where I was going.

UNIT 34

34.1
2 I should stay / I stay / I stayed a little longer.
3 they should visit / they visit / they visited the museum after lunch.
4 we should pay / we pay / we paid the rent by Friday.
5 I should go / I go / I went away for a few days.

34.2
1 b right c right d wrong
2 a right b wrong c right

34.3
2 should say
3 should worry
4 should leave
5 should ask
6 should listen

34.4
2 If Ann should arrive before I get home
3 If there should be some/any letters for me while I'm away

4 If you should need (any) help
5 Should there be some/any letters for me while I'm away
6 Should you need (any) help, let me know.

34.5
2 I should keep
3 I should phone
4 I should buy

UNIT 35

35.1
1 b had or 'd
  c close or shut
  d hadn't
2 a did
  b was done
  c thought

35.2
2 You'd better put a plaster on it.
3 We'd better reserve a table. / We'd better phone to reserve…
4 You'd better not go to work.
5 I'd better pay the phone bill. or …pay my phone bill.
6 I'd better not go out.
7 We'd better take a taxi. or …get a taxi

35.3
3 had better / 'd better or should
4 should
5 should
6 had better / 'd better
7 should
8 should

35.4
2 had a holiday.
3 was here.
4 It's time the train left.
5 It's time I had a party.
6 It's time some changes were made. / It's time there were some changes.

UNIT 36

36.1
2 Can/Could I leave a message? or Can/Could you give her a message?
3 Can/Could you tell me how to get to the station? or …the way to the station? or …where the station is?
4 Can/Could I try on these trousers? or Can/Could I try these (trousers) on?
5 Can I give you a lift?

36.2
2 Do you think I could use your phone?
3 Do you think you could check this letter (for me)?
4 Do you think I could leave work early?
5 Do you think you could turn the music down? or …turn it down?
6 Do you think I could come and see the flat?

36.3
1 Would you like something to eat? or Can I offer you something to eat?
2 Can/Could/Would you show me? or Do you think you could show me? or …do it for me?
3 Can/Could/May I have a look at your newspaper? or Do you think I could…?
4 Would you like to sit down? or Can I offer you a seat?
5 Can/Could/Would you slow down? or Do you think you could…?
6 Can/Could/May I/we have the bill, please? or Do you think I/we could have…? or Can/Could you bring me/us the bill, please?
7 Would you like to borrow it? or …to read it?

UNIT 37

37.1
3 would take / 'd take
4 refused
5 wouldn't get
6 closed down (or was/were closed down)
7 pressed
8 would be / 'd be
9 didn't come
10 borrowed
11 walked
12 would understand

37.2
2 What would you do if your car was stolen? or …were stolen?
3 What would you do if you lost your passport?
4 What would you do if there was a fire in the building? or …if there were a fire in the building?

37.3
2 If he took the examination, he'd fail. or …he would fail.
3 If we stayed at a hotel, it would cost too much money.

4 If she applied for the job, she wouldn't get it.

5 If we told them the truth, they wouldn't believe us.

6 If we invited Bill to the party, we'd have to invite his friends too.

37.4

Example answers:

2 somebody broke into my house.

3 I'd have a much nicer day than usual.

4 you were invited?

5 you'd look much nicer.

6 I didn't come out with you this evening?

UNIT 38

38.1

3 would help / 'd help
4 lived
5 would live / 'd live
6 would taste
7 was/were
8 wouldn't wait ... would go / 'd go
9 didn't go
10 weren't ... wouldn't be

38.2

2 If he spoke more clearly, people would understand him.

3 If the book wasn't/weren't so expensive, I'd buy it / I would buy it. *or* If the book was/were cheaper,...

4 If we could afford it, we'd / we would go out more often.

5 If it wasn't/weren't raining, we could have lunch in the garden.

6 If I didn't have to work tomorrow evening, I could / I would / I'd meet you. *or* ...I'd be able to meet you.

38.3

2 I had a key.
3 I wish Ann was/were here.
4 I wish it wasn't/weren't (so) cold.
5 I wish I didn't live in a big city.
6 I wish I could go to the party.
7 I wish I didn't have to work tomorrow.
8 I wish I knew something about cars.
9 I wish I was/were lying on a beautiful sunny beach.

38.4

Example answers:

1 I wish I was at home.
2 I wish I had a big garden.
3 I wish I could tell jokes.
4 I wish I was taller.

UNIT 39

39.1

2 he'd missed / he had missed ... he would have been / he'd have been

3 I would have forgotten / I'd have forgotten ... you hadn't reminded

4 I'd had / I had had ... I'd have sent / I would have sent

5 we'd have enjoyed / we would have enjoyed ... the weather had been

6 It would have been ... I'd walked / I had walked

7 I was / I were

8 I'd been tired / I had been tired

39.2

2 If the driver in front hadn't stopped so suddenly, the accident wouldn't have happened.

3 If I'd / I had known that George had to get up early, I'd / I would have woken him up.

4 If Jim hadn't lent me the money, I wouldn't have been able to buy the car. *or* ...I couldn't have bought the car.

5 If Margaret hadn't been wearing a seat belt, she'd / she would have been injured.

6 If you'd / you had had (some) breakfast, you wouldn't be hungry now.

7 If I'd / I had had some money on me, I'd / I would have got a taxi.

39.3

2 I wish I'd / I had applied for it. *or* ...for the job.

3 I wish I'd / I had learned to play a musical instrument.

4 I wish I hadn't painted it red. / ...painted the gate red.

5 I wish I'd / I had brought my camera.

6 I wish they'd / they had told me they were coming. *or* I wish I'd / I had known they were coming.

UNIT 40

40.1

2 would enjoy / 'd enjoy

3 would have enjoyed / 'd have enjoyed

4 would have phoned / 'd have phoned

5 would be / 'd be

6 would have stopped / 'd have stopped

40.2

2 He promised he would write to me.

3 They promised they would wait for us.

4 You promised you wouldn't tell Jill what I said.

40.3

2 I wish John would come. / I wish he would come.

3 I wish the baby would stop crying.

4 I wish somebody would give me a job.

5 I wish you would buy some new clothes. or ...get some new clothes.

6 I wish you wouldn't drive so fast.

7 I wish you wouldn't (always) leave the door open.

8 I wish people wouldn't drop litter in the street.

40.4

2 *right*
3 *wrong* – I wish I had more money.
4 *wrong* – I wish it wasn't/ weren't so cold today.
5 *right*
6 *right*
7 *wrong* – I wish everything wasn't/weren't so expensive.

40.5

2 would shake
3 would always forget
4 would share

UNIT 41

41.1

2 is made
3 was damaged
4 is included
5 were invited
6 are shown
7 are held
8 was written ... was translated
9 were overtaken

41.2

2 How is glass made?
3 When was Australia discovered?
4 What is silver used for?
5 When was television invented?

41.3

2 covers
3 is covered
4 are locked
5 was posted ... arrived
6 sank ... was rescued
7 died ... were brought
8 grew

9 was stolen
10 disappeared
11 did Sue resign
12 was Bill sacked
13 is owned
14 called ... was injured ... wasn't needed
15 were these photographs taken ... Did you take

41.4

2 All flights were cancelled because of fog.
3 This road isn't used very often.
4 I was accused of stealing money.
5 How are languages learnt?
6 We were advised not to go out alone.

UNIT 42

42.1

2 can't be broken.
3 can be eaten.
4 it can't be used.
5 it can't be seen.
6 it can be carried.

42.2

3 be made
4 be woken up
5 be spent
6 have been repaired
7 be carried
8 have been caused

42.3

2 The concert has been postponed.
3 The computer is being used at the moment.
4 I didn't realise that our conversation was being recorded.
5 ...we found that the game had been cancelled.
6 A new ring road is being built round the city.
7 A new hospital has been built near the airport.

42.4

3 It has been stolen! / It's been stolen!
4 Somebody has taken it. *or* ...taken my umbrella.
5 He has been promoted. / He's been promoted. *or* He was promoted.
6 It is being redecorated. / It's being redecorated.
7 It is working again. / It's working again ... It has been repaired. / It's been repaired.
8 Two people were arrested last night.

---

9 It had been blown down in the storm. *or* It was blown down...
10 Nobody has seen him since then.
11 Have you ever been mugged?

UNIT 43

43.1

2–6:
Beethoven was born in 1770.
Agatha Christie was born in 1891.
Galileo was born in 1564.
Mahatma Gandhi was born in 1869.
Martin Luther King was born in 1929.
Elvis Presley was born in 1935.
Leonardo da Vinci was born in 1452.
William Shakespeare was born in 1564.

7 I was born in...

43.2

2 I was asked some difficult questions at the interview.
3 Janet was given a present by her colleagues when she retired.
4 I wasn't told that George was ill.
5 How much will you be paid?
6 I think Tom should have been offered the job.
7 Have you been shown what to do?

43.3

2 being invited   5 being asked
3 being given   6 being paid
4 being attacked

43.4

2 got stung
3 get broken
4 get used
5 got stolen
6 got stopped
7 get paid
8 get damaged / get broken
9 get asked

UNIT 44

44.1

2 The weather is expected to be good tomorrow.
3 The thieves are believed to have got in through the kitchen window.
4 Many people are reported to be homeless after the floods.
5 The prisoner is thought to have escaped by climbing over a wall.

---

6 The man is alleged to have driven through the town at 90 miles an hour.
7 The building is reported to have been badly damaged by fire.
8 a The company is said to be losing a lot of money.
  b The company is believed to have lost a lot of money last year.
  c The company is expected to lose money this year.

44.2

2 He is supposed to be very rich.
3 He is supposed to write poetry.
4 He is supposed to have 12 children.
5 He is supposed to have robbed a bank a long time ago.

44.3

3 are / 're supposed to be
4 are / 're supposed to start
5 aren't / 're not supposed to block
6 was supposed to phone
7 weren't supposed to arrive *or* ...supposed to come

UNIT 45

45.1

1 b
2 a
3 a
4 b

45.2

2 To have it cleaned.
3 To have it repaired.
4 To have my hair cut.

45.3

2 I had it cut.
3 They had it painted.
4 She had them made.

45.4

2 have another key made
3 had your hair cut
4 Have you had your hair cut
5 Do you have a newspaper delivered
6 are having a swimming pool built
7 haven't had the film developed
8 have it cleaned
9 have your ears pierced

45.5

2 She had her bag stolen on a train.
3 He had his hat blown off in the wind.
4 She had her passport taken away from her by the police.

319

UNIT 46

46.1

2 He said that his father wasn't very well.
3 He said that Sharon and Paul were getting married next month.
4 He said that Margaret had had a baby.
5 He said that he didn't know what Fred was doing.
6 He said that he had / he'd seen Helen at a party in June and she had seemed fine. *or* He said that he saw Helen… and she seemed…
7 He said that he hadn't seen Diane recently.
8 He said that he wasn't enjoying his job very much.
9 He said that I could come and stay at his flat if I was ever in London.
10 He said that his car had been stolen a few weeks ago. *or* …that his car was stolen…
11 He said he wanted to go on holiday but he couldn't afford it.
12 He said he would / he'd tell Ann he had / he'd seen me. *or* …he saw me.

46.2

Example answers:

2 I thought you said she wasn't coming. / …she was going somewhere else.
3 I thought you said she didn't like him.
4 I thought you said you didn't know many people.
5 I thought you said you wouldn't be here next week. / …you would be away…
6 I thought you said you were staying at home. / …you weren't going out.
7 I thought you said you couldn't speak (any) French.
8 I thought you said you went to the cinema last week. / …you had been to the cinema last week.

UNIT 47

47.1

2 But you said you didn't like fish.
3 But you said you couldn't drive.
4 But you said Jane had a very well-paid job.
5 But you said you didn't have any brothers or sisters.
6 But you said you had never been to the United States.

7 But you said you were working tomorrow evening.
8 But you said Jane was a friend of yours.

47.2

2 Tell	7 tell … said
3 Say	8 tell … say
4 said	9 told
5 told	10 said
6 said	

47.3

2 her to slow down.
3 her not to worry.
4 asked Tom to give me a hand.
5 asked me to open my bag.
6 asked him to repeat what he (had) said.
7 told her not to wait for me if I was late.
8 asked her to marry him.
9 I told him to mind his own business.

UNIT 48

48.1

2 Where do you live now?
3 Are you married?
4 How long have you been married?
5 Have you got (any) children? *or* Do you have (any) children?
6 How old are they?
7 What does your husband do?
8 Does he enjoy his job?
9 Did he arrest anyone yesterday?
10 How often do you go on holiday?
11 Where are you going next year? *or* Where are you going to go…?

48.2

3 Who gave you the key? *or* Who gave it to you?
4 What happened?
5 What did she tell you? *or* What did Diane tell you?
6 Who does it belong to? *or* Who does this book…?
7 Who lives in that house? *or* Who lives there?
8 What did you fall over?
9 What fell on the floor?
10 What does it mean? *or* What does this word mean?
11 Who did you borrow it from? *or* …borrow the money from?
12 What are you worried about?

48.3

2 How is cheese made?
3 When was the computer invented?

4 Why isn't Sue working today?
5 What time are your friends coming?
6 Why was the concert cancelled?
7 Where was your mother born?
8 Why didn't you come to the party?
9 How did the accident happen?
10 Why doesn't this machine work?

48.4

2 Don't you like him?
3 Isn't it good?
4 Haven't you got any? / Don't you have any?

UNIT 49

49.1

2 Could you tell me where the post office is?
3 I wonder what the time is.
4 I want to know what this word means.
5 Do you know what time they left?
6 I don't know if/whether Sue is going out tonight.
7 Have you any idea where Carol lives?
8 I can't remember where I parked the car.
9 Can you tell me if/whether there is a bank near here?
10 Tell me what you want.
11 I don't know why Kay didn't come to the party.
12 Do you know if/whether you have to pay to park here?
13 I've no idea who that woman is.
14 Do you know if/whether Ann received my letter?
15 Can you tell me how far it is to the airport?

49.2

1 she has gone
2 when she will be back / when she'll be back
3 if/whether she went out alone

49.3

2 He asked me where I had been. *or* …where I'd been.
3 He asked me how long I had been back. *or* …how long I'd been back.
4 He asked me what I was doing now.
5 He asked me where I was living.
6 He asked me why I had come back / …why I'd come back / …why I came back.

7 He asked me if/whether I was glad to be back.

8 He asked me if/whether I had any plans to go away again.

9 He asked me if/whether I could lend him some money.

UNIT 50

50.1

2 doesn't
3 was
4 will
5 am ... isn't
6 should
7 won't
8 do
9 could
10 would ... could ... can't

50.2

3 Do you? I don't.
4 Didn't you? I did.
5 Haven't you? I have.
6 Did you? I didn't.

50.3

Example answers:

3 So did I.   *or*
   Did you? I didn't.
4 Neither will I.   *or*
   Won't you? Why not?
5 So do I.   *or*
   Do you? I live in a village.
6 So would I.   *or*
   Would you? I wouldn't.
7 Neither can I.   *or*
   Can't you? I can.

50.4

2 I hope so.
3 I expect so.
4 I don't think so.
5 I'm afraid not.
6 I'm afraid so.
7 I suppose so.
8 I hope not.
9 I think so.

UNIT 51

51.1

3	haven't you	11	shall we
4	were you	12	is it
5	does she	13	aren't I
6	isn't he	14	would you
7	hasn't she	15	will you
8	can't you	16	should I
9	will he	17	will you
10	aren't there	18	had he

51.2

2 It's (very) expensive, isn't it?
3 The film was great, wasn't it?
4 She has / She has got / She's got a lovely voice, hasn't she?   *or* She has a lovely voice, doesn't she?
5 It doesn't look very good, does it?
6 You've had your hair cut, haven't you?
7 This bridge isn't very safe, is it?

51.3

2 Jack, you couldn't get me some stamps, could you?
3 Kate, you don't know where Ann is, do you?   *or* ...you haven't seen Ann, have you?
4 Helen, you haven't got a bicycle pump, have you?   *or* ...you don't have a bicycle pump, do you?
5 Robin, you haven't seen my keys, have you?

UNIT 52

52.1

2	making	8	using
3	listening	9	seeing
4	applying	10	writing
5	washing	11	being
6	being	12	trying
7	working		

52.2

2 playing tennis
3 driving too fast
4 going for a swim
5 breaking into the shop
6 waiting a few minutes

52.3

2 travelling during the rush hour
3 going away (until) tomorrow
4 not having a licence
5 turning the radio down
6 not interrupting me all the time

52.4

Example answers:

2 going out
3 sitting on the floor
4 having a picnic
5 laughing
6 breaking down

UNIT 53

53.1

2 She agreed to help him.
3 He offered to carry her bag.
4 They arranged to meet at 8 o'clock.
5 She refused to tell him her name.

53.2

2 to get
3 to buy / to have / to drive
4 (how) to use / (how) to operate
5 to be
6 say *or* to say

53.3

2	to go	7	to call
3	going	8	having
4	waiting	9	missing
5	to go	10	to find
6	barking		

53.4

2 Tom appears to be worried about something.
3 You seem to know a lot of people.
4 My English seems to be getting better.
5 That car appears to have broken down.
6 David tends to forget things.
7 They claim to have solved the problem.

53.5

2 how to use
3 what to do
4 how to ride
5 what to say
6 whether to go

UNIT 54

54.1

2 do you want me to lend you some
3 would you like me to shut it
4 would you like me to show you
5 do you want me to repeat it
6 do you want me to wait

54.2

2 to stay (with them) for a few days.
3 She wouldn't let him use her phone.
4 She warned him to be careful.
5 He asked her to give him a hand.

54.3

2 I didn't expect it to rain.
3 Let him do what he wants.
4 Glasses make him look older.
5 I want you to know the truth.
6 Remind me to phone my sister.
7 Sarah persuaded me to apply for the job.
8 My lawyer advised me not to say anything to the police.
9 I was warned not to believe everything he says.
10 Having a car enables you to travel round more easily.

54.4

2 to go	6 to go
3 to do	7 eating
4 read	8 cry
5 to go	9 to study

UNIT 55

55.1

2 driving
3 to go
4 to go
5 raining
6 to buy
7 asking
8 asking
9 to answer
10 breaking
11 to pay
12 eating
13 to shut
14 meeting ... to see
15 crying *or* to cry
16 to get

55.2

2 He can remember going to Paris when he was eight.
3 He can't remember falling into a river.
4 He can remember crying on his first day at school.
5 He can't remember saying he wanted to be a doctor. *or* He can't remember wanting to be...
6 He can't remember being bitten by a dog.

55.3

1 b lending
  c to phone
  d to give
  e leaving/putting
2 a saying
  b to say *or* to tell you
3 a to become
  b working
  c reading

UNIT 56

56.1

2 Try turning it the other way.
3 Have you tried moving the aerial?
4 Why don't you try phoning him at work?
5 Have you tried taking an aspirin?

56.2

2 It needs cutting.
3 It needs redecorating.
4 They need tightening.
5 It needs emptying.

56.3

1 b knocking
  c to put
  d asking
  e to reach
  f to concentrate
2 a to go
  b looking
  c cleaning
  d to go
  e You don't need to iron ... It doesn't need ironing.
3 a overhearing
  b get *or* to get
  c smiling
  d make *or* to make

UNIT 57

57.1

3 likes taking / to take photographs.
4 doesn't like driving / to drive.
5 likes working / to work in the open air.
6 doesn't like taking / to take risks.
7 likes doing / to do nothing.
8 doesn't like being / to be kept waiting.

57.2

Example answers:
2 I don't mind playing cards.
3 I hate doing the ironing.
4 I enjoy going to museums.
5 I don't like lying on the beach all day.

57.3

Example answers:
2 I wouldn't like to be a dentist.
3 I'd like to be a hairdresser.
4 I'd hate to be an airline pilot.
5 I wouldn't mind being a tourist guide.

57.4

2 waiting
3 going / to go
4 writing
5 working/being
6 to come / to go
7 wearing / to wear
8 to sit
9 to get
10 to talk / to speak

57.5

2 I would like / I'd like to have seen the programme.
3 I would hate to have lost my watch.
4 I would love to have met Ann.
5 I wouldn't like to have been alone.

6 I would prefer to have travelled by train.

UNIT 58

58.1

2 I prefer tennis to football. *or* ...football to tennis.
3 I prefer phoning people to writing letters. *or* ...writing letters to phoning people.
4 I prefer going to the cinema to watching films on TV. *or* ...watching films on TV to going to the cinema.
6 I prefer to phone people rather than write letters. *or* ...to write letters rather than phone people.
7 I prefer to go to the cinema rather than watch films on TV. *or* ...to watch films on TV rather than go to the cinema.

58.2

3 I'd prefer to listen to some music.
4 I'd rather go for a swim.
5 I'd rather wait a few minutes.
6 I'd prefer to eat at home.
7 I'd rather think about it for a while.
8 I'd rather stand.
9 I'd prefer to go alone.
11 I'd rather go for a swim than play tennis.
12 I'd rather wait a few minutes than leave now.
13 I'd prefer to eat at home rather than go to a restaurant.
14 I'd rather think about it for a while than decide now.

58.3

2 I told her
3 would you rather I did it
4 would you rather I answered it

58.4

2 stayed	5 was
3 stay	6 didn't
4 didn't	

UNIT 59

59.1

2 lending you any money.
3 remembering names.
4 passing the exam.
5 being late?
6 eating at home, we went to a restaurant.
7 doing nothing.
8 telling any of their friends.
9 playing well.

59.2

2 by standing on a chair.
3 by turning a key.
4 by borrowing too much money.
5 by driving too fast.
6 by putting some posters up on the walls.

59.3

2 paying
3 going
4 saying
5 going
6 using
7 travelling / being
8 telling
9 doing / having

59.4

2 I'm looking forward to seeing her.
3 I'm not looking forward to going to the dentist.
4 She's looking forward to leaving school (next summer).
5 I'm looking forward to playing tennis (tomorrow).

UNIT 60

60.1

2 he wasn't used to having dinner so early, but after some time he got used to it. … He is used to having dinner at six o'clock. (or He is used to eating at six o'clock.)
3 She wasn't used to working nights … to get used to it … She is used to working nights.

60.2

2 No, I'm used to sleeping on the floor.
3 I'm used to working hard. / I'm used to hard work.
4 I'm not used to going to bed (so) late.

60.3

2 He wasn't used to the heat / …to the hot weather / …to living in a hot climate.
3 She had to get used to living
4 The children soon got used to her. / …to their new teacher.
5 (example answers) You would have to get used to the weather / to the food / to speaking a foreign language.

60.4

2 live		6 have	
3 drink		7 go	
4 eating		8 be	
5 having		9 being	

UNIT 61

61.1

2 doing
3 coming / going
4 doing / trying
5 buying
6 hearing
7 going
8 having
9 being
10 watching
11 inviting / asking

61.2

2 in solving
3 of living
4 of causing
5 (from) walking
6 for interrupting
7 of spending
8 from escaping
9 on helping
10 to playing

61.3

2 Tom insisted on driving Ann to the station.
3 Jim congratulated me on passing my exam.
4 Mrs Bond thanked Sue for coming to see her.
5 I warned Jack against staying at the hotel near the airport.
6 Mary apologised to me for not phoning (me) earlier.
7 Jane accused me of being selfish.

UNIT 62

62.1

2 It's no use asking Tom.
3 There's no point in going out
4 it's no good phoning her now
5 it's not worth complaining (about what happened)
6 I think it's a waste of time reading newspapers.

62.2

2 repairing.
3 visiting.
4 It's worth considering.
5 It's worth reading.
6 They aren't / They're not worth keeping.

62.3

2 There's no point in eating if you're not hungry.
3 There's no point in working if you don't need money.
4 There's no point in studying if you feel tired.

62.4

2 I have difficulty remembering people's names.
3 She had no difficulty getting a job.
4 Do you have difficulty understanding him?
5 You won't have any difficulty getting a ticket for the concert.

62.5

2 reading
3 writing
4 watching
5 climbing / going / walking

62.6

2 go skiing
3 went swimming
4 goes riding
5 go shopping

UNIT 63

63.1

2 I had to go to the bank to get some money.
3 I'm saving money to go to Canada.
4 I went into hospital to have an operation.
5 I'm wearing two pullovers to keep warm.
6 I phoned the police station to report that my car had been stolen.

63.2

2 to read
3 to walk   or   to go on foot
4 to drink
5 to put / to carry
6 to discuss / to consider / to talk about
7 to buy / to get
8 to talk / to speak
9 to wear / to put on
10 to celebrate
11 to help / to assist

63.3

2 for		6 to	
3 to		7 for	
4 to		8 for … to	
5 for			

63.4

2 We wore warm clothes so that we wouldn't get cold.
3 The man spoke very slowly so that I would understand what he said. or …so that I could understand…
4 I whispered so that nobody else could hear our conversation. or …would hear our conversation.
5 Please arrive early so that we can start the meeting on time.

6 She locked the door so that she wouldn't be disturbed.
7 I slowed down so that the car behind could overtake.

UNIT 64

64.1

2 This machine is quite easy to use.
3 The window was very difficult to open.
4 Some words are impossible to translate.
5 That chair isn't safe to stand on.
6 A car is expensive to maintain.

64.2

2 It's an easy mistake to make.
3 It's a nice place to live (in).
4 It was a good game to watch.

64.3

2 It's careless of you to make the same mistake again and again.
3 It was nice of Don and Jenny to invite me to stay with them.
4 It wasn't very considerate of John to make so much noise (when I was trying to sleep).

64.4

2 am/was glad to hear
3 were surprised to see
4 am/was sorry to hear

64.5

2 Paul was the last (person) to arrive.
3 Fiona was the only student / the only one to pass the exam.
4 I was the second customer/ person to complain (to the restaurant manager about the service).
5 Neil Armstrong was the first person/man to walk on the moon.

64.6

2 are bound to be
3 is sure to forget
4 is not / isn't likely to rain
5 is likely to be

UNIT 65

65.1

3 I'm afraid of losing it.
4 We were afraid to go swimming.
5 We were afraid of missing our train.
6 We were afraid to look.
7 She was afraid of spilling the drinks.
8 a I was afraid to eat it.
   b I was afraid of making myself ill.

65.2

2 in starting   5 to hear / in hearing
3 to read   6 in going
4 in getting

65.3

2 to disturb
3 for being late   or   I was late
4 for saying   or   I said
5 to hear

65.4

1 b to leave
   c from leaving
2 a to solve
   b in solving
3 a of going   4 a to buy
   b to go   b to buy
   c to going   c on buying
   d to go   d of buying

UNIT 66

66.1

2 arrive
3 take it / do it
4 it ring
5 him play / him playing
6 you lock it / you do it
7 her fall

66.2

2 We saw Dave and Helen playing tennis.
3 We saw Clare having a meal in a restaurant. / We saw Clare eating in a restaurant.
4 We heard Bill playing the guitar.
5 We could smell the dinner burning.
6 We saw Linda jogging.

66.3

3 happen   9 explode
4 tell   10 crawling
5 crying   11 slam
6 cycling   12 sleeping
7 say
8 run ... open ... climb

UNIT 67

67.1

2 Emma was sitting in an armchair reading a book.
3 Sue got home late feeling very tired.
4 Sarah went out saying she would be back in an hour.
5 Linda was in London for two years working as a tourist guide.
6 Mary walked round the town looking at the sights and taking photographs.

67.2

2 I fell asleep watching television.
3 The man slipped getting off a bus.
4 I got wet walking home in the rain.
5 Margaret had an accident driving to work yesterday.
6 Two firemen were overcome by smoke trying to put out the fire.

67.3

2 Having bought our tickets, we went into the theatre.
3 Having had dinner, they continued their journey.
4 Having done all her shopping, Lucy went for a cup of coffee.

67.4

2 Thinking they might be hungry, I offered them something to eat.
3 Being a foreigner, she needs a visa to stay in this country.
4 Not knowing his address, I wasn't able to contact him.
5 Having travelled a lot, Sarah knows a lot about other countries.
6 Not being able to understand English, the man didn't know what I wanted.
7 Having spent nearly all our money, we couldn't afford to stay in a hotel.

UNIT 68

68.1

3 a very nice restaurant
4 *right*
5 a toothbrush
6 a bank
7 an insurance company
8 *right*
9 *right*
10 a petrol station
11 a problem
12 an interview for a job
13 a necklace
14 a very good game

68.2

3 a key   8 a letter
4 a coat   9 blood
5 sugar   10 a question
6 a biscuit   11 a moment
7 electricity   12 a decision

68.3

2 days   8 air
3 meat   9 patience
4 a queue   10 languages
5 letters   11 countries
6 friends   12 space
7 people

UNIT 69

69.1

2 a a paper
  b any paper
3 a a light
  b Light
4 a a time
  b a wonderful time
5 advice
6 very good weather
7 bad luck
8 job
9 journey
10 total chaos
11 some
12 doesn't
13 Your hair is … it
14 the damage … was

69.2

2 information
3 chairs
4 furniture
5 hair
6 progress
7 job
8 work
9 permission
10 experience
11 experiences

69.3

2 I'd like some information about places to see (in this town).
3 Can you give me some advice about which examinations to take? / …some advice about examinations?
4 What time is the news (on TV)?
5 It's a beautiful view, isn't it? *or* It's beautiful scenery, isn't it?
6 What horrible weather!

UNIT 70

70.1

3 It's a vegetable.
4 It's a game.
5 They're musical instruments.
6 It's a (tall/high) building.
7 They're planets.
8 It's a flower.
9 They're rivers.
10 They're birds.
12 He was a writer / a dramatist / a playwright.
13 He was a scientist / a physicist.
14 They were American presidents / presidents of the United States.
15 She was an actress / a film actress / a film star.
16 They were singers/musicians.
17 They were painters/artists.

70.2

2 He's a waiter.
3 She's a travel agent.
4 He's a pilot.
5 She's a driving instructor.
6 He's a plumber.
7 She's a journalist.
8 He's an interpreter.

70.3

4 a
5 an
6 – (collect stamps)
7 a
8 Some
9 – (I've got sore feet.)
10 a
11 a … a
12 – (Those are nice shoes.)
13 some
14 a visa … some countries
15 a teacher. Her parents were teachers too.
16 – (going to concerts)
17 some
18 a liar … always telling lies

UNIT 71

71.1

1 …and a magazine. The newspaper is in my bag but I don't know where I put the magazine
2 I saw an accident this morning. A car crashed into a tree. The driver of the car wasn't hurt but the car was badly damaged.
3 …a blue one and a grey one. The blue one belongs to my neighbours; I don't know who the owner of the grey one is.
4 My friends live in an old house in a small village. There is a beautiful garden behind the house. I would like to have a garden like that.

71.2

1 a a
  b the
  c the
2 a a
  b a
  c the
3 a a
  b the
  c the
4 a an … The
  b the
  c the
5 a the
  b a
  c a

71.3

2 the dentist
3 the door
4 a mistake
5 the bus station
6 a problem
7 the post office
8 the floor
9 the book
10 a job in a bank

11 a small flat near the city centre
12 a small supermarket at the end of the street

71.4

Example answers:
3 Once or twice a year.
4 Thirty miles an hour.
5 About seven hours a night.
6 Two or three times a week.
7 About two hours a day.

UNIT 72

72.1

2 a nice holiday … the best holiday
3 the nearest shop … the end of this street
4 listen to the radio … I haven't got a radio
5 to travel in space … go to the moon
6 go to the cinema … a lot of films on television
7 a nice day … by the sea
8 for breakfast … eat breakfast
9 where Room 25 is … on the second floor
10 the most expensive hotel … a cheaper hotel

72.2

2 the … the
3 –
4 The
5 –
6 the
7 the information … the top of page 15.
8 a … The

72.3

2 in a small village in the country
3 The moon … the earth
4 the highest mountain in the world
5 the same thing
6 a very hot day … the hottest day of the year
7 have lunch … eat a good breakfast
8 live in a foreign country … the language
9 on the wrong platform. We were on Platform 3 instead of Platform 8.

72.4

2 the cinema
3 the sea
4 dinner
5 Question 8
6 the gate
7 Gate 21

UNIT 73

73.1

2 to school
3 at home
4 for school   *or*   for work
5 to work   *or*   to school
6 in hospital
7 at university
8 in bed
9 to prison

73.2

1 c school
  d school
  e get home from <u>school</u> ... <u>The school</u> isn't very far
  f school
  g the school
2 a university
  b university
  c the university
3 a the hospital
  b the hospital
  c hospital
  d hospital
4 a church
  b church
  c the church
5 a prison
  b the prison
  c prison

6 a bed
  b home
  c work
  d bed
  e work
  f work
7 a the sea
  b sea
  c the sea

UNIT 74

74.1

Example answers:
2 I like cats.
3 I don't like zoos.
4 I don't mind fast food restaurants.
5 I'm not interested in football.

74.2

3 spiders
4 meat
5 **the** questions
6 **the** people
7 History
8 lies
9 **the** hotels
10 **The** water
11 **the** grass
12 patience

74.3

3 Apples
4 the apples
5 Women ... men
6 tea
7 The vegetables
8 Life
9 skiing
10 the people
11 people ... aggression

12 All the books
13 the beds
14 war
15 The First World War
16 unemployment
17 the marriage
18 Most people ... marriage ... family life ... society

UNIT 75

75.1

1 b the cheetah
  c the kangaroo (and the rabbit)
2 a the swan
  b the penguin
  c the owl
3 a the wheel
  b the laser
  c the telescope
4 a the rupee
  b the escudo
  c the ...

75.2

2 a   6 the
3 the   7 a
4 a   8 (–)
5 the   9 The

75.3

2 the injured
3 the unemployed
4 the sick
5 the rich ... the poor

75.4

2 a German   the Germans
3 a Frenchman / a Frenchwoman the French
4 a Russian   the Russians
5 a Chinese   the Chinese
6 a Brazilian   the Brazilians
7 an Englishman / an Englishwoman the English
8 a/an... the...

UNIT 76

76.1

2 the   5 the
3 The ... the   6 –
4 –

76.2

3 *right*
4 **the** United States
5 **The** south ... **the** north
6 *right*
7 **the** Channel
8 **the** Middle East
9 *right*
10 *right*

11 **the** Swiss Alps
12 **The** United Kingdom
13 **The** Seychelles ... **the** Indian Ocean
14 **The** River Volga ... **the** Caspian Sea

76.3

2 In South America
3 The Nile
4 Sweden
5 The United States
6 The Rockies
7 The Mediterranean
8 Australia
9 The Pacific
10 The Indian Ocean
11 The Thames
12 The Danube
13 Thailand
14 The Panama Canal
15 The Amazon

UNIT 77

77.1

2 Turner's in Carter Road
3 **the** Park Hotel in Park Road
4 St Peter's in Baines Street
5 **the** Royal Oak in Union Street
6 **the** City Museum in Baines Street
7 Lloyds Bank in Forest Avenue
8 Victoria Park at the end of Baines Street
9 **the** New China House in Carter Road

77.2

2 **The** Eiffel Tower
3 **The** Vatican
4 Buckingham Palace
5 Broadway
6 **The** White House
7 **The** Acropolis
8 St Mark's Cathedral

77.3

2 Hyde Park
3 St James's Park
4 The Grand Hotel ... Baker Street
5 Gatwick Airport
6 Liverpool University
7 Harrison's
8 the Ship Inn
9 The Statue of Liberty ... New York harbour
10 the Science Museum
11 IBM ... British Telecom
12 The Classic
13 the Great Wall
14 the Independent ... the Herald
15 Cambridge University Press

UNIT 78

78.1
3 shorts
4 a means
5 means
6 some scissors *or*   a pair of scissors
7 a series
8 series
9 species

78.2
2 politics
3 economics
4 athletics
5 physics
6 gymnastics
7 electronics

78.3
2 don't
3 want
4 was
5 aren't
6 wasn't
7 does *or* do
8 isn't
9 they are
10 are
11 Do
12 is

78.4
2 wearing black jeans
3 *right* (is playing *is also correct*)
4 nice **people**
5 Ten pounds **is** not enough.
6 **some** new pyjamas *or* a new **pair of** pyjamas
7 *right* (hasn't *is also correct*)
8 Many people **have**
9 a police**man** / a police**woman** / a police **officer**
10 **Have** the police
11 **These** scissors **aren't**

UNIT 79

79.1
2 a computer magazine
3 holiday photographs
4 milk chocolate
5 a factory inspector
6 a central London hotel
7 examination results
8 the dining room carpet
9 a football club scandal
10 a two-part question
11 a seven-year-old girl

79.2
1 a a houseboat
  b a boathouse
2 a a race horse
  b a horse race
3 a a cardphone
  b a phonecard

79.3
2 room number
3 seat belt
4 credit card
5 weather forecast
6 newspaper editor
7 shop window

79.4
3 20-pound
4 15-minute
5 60 minutes
6 two-hour
7 five courses
8 two-year
9 500-year
10 five days
11 six-mile

UNIT 80

80.1
3 that man's jacket
4 the top of the page
5 Charles's daughter
6 the cause of the problem
7 yesterday's newspaper
8 my father's birthday
9 the name of this street
10 the children's toys
11 the new manager of the company *or*   the company's new manager
12 the result of the football match
13 our neighbours' garden
14 the ground floor of the building
15 Don and Mary's children
16 the economic policy of the government *or* the government's economic policy
17 Catherine's husband
18 the husband of the woman talking to Mary
19 Mike's parents' car
20 Helen's friend's wedding

80.2
2 a boy's name
3 children's clothes
4 a girls' school
5 a bird's nest
6 a women's magazine

80.3
2 Last week's storm caused a lot of damage.
3 The town's only cinema has closed down.
4 Britain's exports to the United States have fallen recently.
5 The region's main industry is tourism.

80.4
2 five minutes' walk *or* a five-minute walk
3 two weeks' holiday *or* a two-week holiday
4 an hour's sleep

UNIT 81

81.1
2 We met a relation of yours.
3 Henry borrowed a book of mine.
4 Ann invited some friends of hers to her flat.
5 We had dinner with a neighbour of ours.
6 I went on holiday with two friends of mine.
7 Is that man a friend of yours?
8 I met a friend of Jane's at the party.

81.2
2 my own television
3 her own money
4 her own business
5 his own private jet
6 his own ideas
7 its own parliament

81.3
2 your own fault
3 his own ideas
4 your own problems
5 her own decisions

81.4
2 makes her own clothes
3 writes his own songs
4 bake our own bread

81.5
2 my own
3 myself
4 himself
5 themselves
6 herself
7 their own
8 yourself
9 our own
10 her own

UNIT 82

82.1
2 hurt himself
3 blame herself
4 Put yourself
5 enjoyed themselves
6 burn yourself
7 express myself

82.2
2 me
3 myself
4 us
5 yourself
6 you
7 ourselves
8 themselves
9 them

82.3
2 feel
3 dried herself
4 concentrate
5 defend yourself
6 meeting
7 relax
8 wash

82.4

2 themselves
3 each other
4 each other
5 themselves
6 each other
7 ourselves
8 each other
9 <u>ourselves</u> to <u>each other</u>

82.5

2 He cut it himself.
3 I'll post it myself.
4 Linda told me herself. *or* Linda herself told me.
5 Why can't you phone him yourself? *or* ...do it yourself?

UNIT 83

83.1

3 Is there ... there is / there's
4 there was ... It was
5 It was
6 There was
7 is it
8 It was
9 It is / It's
10 there wasn't
11 Is it ... it's
12 there was ... There was
13 It was
14 There wasn't
15 There was ... it wasn't

83.2

2 There is a lot of salt in the soup.
3 There was nothing in the box.
4 There was a lot of violence in the film.
5 There were a lot of people in the shops.
6 *Example answers:*
   There is / There's a lot to do in this town. / ...a lot of life in this town. / ...a lot happening in this town.

83.3

2 There might be *or* There should be
3 there will be *or* there should be
4 There's going to be *or* There might be
5 There used to be
6 there should be
7 there wouldn't be

83.4

2 **there** was a lot of snow
3 *right*
4 **There** used to be a church here
5 *right*
6 **There** must have been a reason.

7 *right*
8 **There**'s sure to be a car park somewhere.
9 **there** will be an opportunity
10 *right*
11 **there** would be somebody to meet me at the station but **there** wasn't anybody.

UNIT 84

84.1

2 some
3 any
4 any ... some
5 some
6 any
7 any
8 some
9 any
10 any (some *is also possible*)

84.2

2 somebody/someone
3 anybody/anyone
4 anything
5 something
6 somebody/someone ... anybody/anyone
7 something ... anybody/anyone
8 Anybody/Anyone
9 anybody/anyone
10 anywhere
11 anywhere
12 somewhere
13 anywhere
14 anybody/anyone
15 something
16 Anybody/Anyone
17 She never tells <u>anybody anything</u> *or* ...<u>anyone anything</u>.

84.3

2 Any day
3 Anything
4 anywhere
5 Anything
6 Any time
7 Anybody/Anyone
8 Any newspaper / Any one

UNIT 85

85.1

2 Nobody/No one.
3 Nowhere.
4 None.
5 None.
6 Nobody/No one.
7 Nothing.
9 I wasn't talking to anybody/anyone.
10 I'm not going anywhere.

11 I haven't got any luggage.
12 They haven't got any children.
13 I didn't meet anybody/anyone.
14 I didn't buy anything.

85.2

3	no	7	No
4	any	8	any
5	None	9	any
6	none	10	none

85.3

2 nobody/no one
3 Nowhere
4 anything
5 Nothing ... anything
6 Nothing
7 anywhere
8 <u>Nobody/no one</u> said <u>anything</u>.

85.4

2 nobody
3 anybody
4 Anybody
5 Nothing
6 Anything
7 anything

UNIT 86

86.1

3 a lot of salt
4 *right*
5 *right*
6 a lot
7 many / a lot of
8 a lot
9 *right*

86.2

2 plenty of money
3 plenty of room
4 plenty to learn
5 are plenty of things to see
6 There are plenty of hotels.

86.3

2	little	5	many
3	many	6	few
4	much	7	little

86.4

3 **a** few dollars
4 **a** little time
5 *right*
6 *right*
7 only **a** few words

86.5

2	a little	6	A little
3	a few	7	little
4	few	8	a few
5	little		

UNIT 87

87.1

3 –	7 of
4 of	8 –
5 of	9 –
6 –	

87.2

3 of my spare time
4 of the houses
5 accidents
6 of her friends
7 of the population
8 birds
9 of the people I invited
10 of her opinions
11 European countries
12 (of) my dinner

87.3

3 Many people
4 Some of the photographs
5 Some people
6 most of the food
7 all (of) the money
8 all the time
9 most of the time
10 Most people
11 half (of) the questions

87.4

2 All of them	6 None of it
3 none of us	7 Some of them
4 some of it	8 all of it
5 none of them	

UNIT 88

88.1

2 Neither	5 Either
3 either (of them)	6 Neither
4 both	

88.2

2 either
3 both
4 Neither of
5 neither … both / both the / both of the
6 both / both of

88.3

2 either of them
3 both of them
4 neither of us
5 neither of them

88.4

3 Both Jim and Carol are on holiday.
4 George neither smokes nor drinks.
5 Neither Jim nor Carol has (got) a car.

6 The film was both long and boring.
7 That man's name is either Richard or Robert.
8 I've got neither the time nor the money to go on holiday.
9 We can leave either today or tomorrow.

88.5

2 either	6 either
3 any	7 neither
4 none	8 none
5 any	

UNIT 89

89.1

3 Everybody/Everyone
4 Everything
5 all
6 everybody/everyone
7 everything
8 All
9 everybody/everyone
10 All
11 everything
12 Everybody/Everyone
13 All
14 everything

89.2

2 The whole team played well.
3 He ate the whole box (of chocolates).
4 They searched the whole house.
5 Ann worked the whole day.
6 The whole family play/plays tennis.
7 It rained the whole week.
8 Ann worked all day.
9 It rained all week.

89.3

2 every four hours
3 every four years
4 every five minutes
5 every six months

89.4

2 every day
3 all day
4 The whole building
5 every time
6 all the time
7 all my luggage

UNIT 90

90.1

3 Each	6 every
4 Every	7 each
5 Each	8 every

90.2

3 Every	8 every
4 Each	9 every
5 every	10 each
6 every	11 Every
7 each	12 each

90.3

2 Sonia and I had ten pounds each. / …each had ten pounds.
3 Those postcards cost 40 pence each. / … are 40 pence each.
4 We paid £40 each. / We each paid £40.

90.4

2 everyone
3 every one
4 Everyone
5 every one

UNIT 91

91.1

2 A burglar is someone who breaks into a house to steal things.
3 A customer is someone who buys something from a shop.
4 A shoplifter is someone who steals from a shop.
5 A coward is someone who is not brave.
6 An atheist is someone who doesn't believe in God.
7 A pensioner is someone who no longer works and gets money from the state.
8 A tenant is someone who pays rent to live in a house or flat.

91.2

2 The man who/that answered the phone told me you were away.
3 The waitress who/that served us was very impolite and impatient.
4 The building that/which was destroyed in the fire has now been rebuilt.
5 The people who/that were arrested have now been released.
6 The bus that/which goes to the airport runs every half hour.

91.3

2 who/that runs away from home
3 that/which won the race
4 who/that stole my car
5 who/that invented the telephone
6 that/which were on the wall
7 that/which cannot be explained
8 that/which gives you the meaning of words
9 who/that are never on time
10 that/which can support life

329

UNIT 92

92.1

3	(who)	7	that
4	who	8	(that)
5	(who)	9	that
6	(that)		

92.2

2 (that/which) Ann is wearing
3 (that/which) we wanted to visit
4 (that/which) you're going to see
5 (who/that) I invited to the party
6 (that/which) you had to do
7 (that/which) we hired
8 (that/which) Tom recommended to us

92.3

2 (that/which) we were invited to
3 (who/that) I work with
4 (that/which) you told me about
5 (that/which) we went to last night
6 (that/which) I applied for
7 (who/that) you can rely on
8 (who/that) I saw you with

92.4

2	(that)	6	(that)
3	what	7	what
4	that	8	(that)
5	(that)		

UNIT 93

93.1

2 whose wife is an English teacher.
3 who owns a restaurant.
4 whose ambition is to climb Everest.
5 who have just got married.
6 whose parents used to work in a circus.

93.2

2 where we can have a really good meal
3 where I can buy some postcards
4 where we had the car repaired
5 where John is staying
6 where she (had) bought it

93.3

2	where	5	where
3	who	6	whose
4	whose	7	whom

93.4

Example answers:
2 we got stuck in a lift
3 I didn't write to you
4 you phoned
5 they haven't got a car
6 Mary got married

UNIT 94

94.1

3 which we enjoyed very much.
4 I went to see the doctor, who told me to rest for a few days.
5 John, who/whom I have known for a very long time, is one of my closest friends.
6 Sheila, whose job involves a lot of travelling, is away from home a lot.
7 The new stadium, which can hold 90,000 people, will be opened next month.
8 We often go to visit our friends in Bristol, which is only 30 miles away.
9 Glasgow, where my brother lives, is the largest city in Scotland.

94.2

3 The strike at the car factory, which lasted ten days, is now over.
4 I've found the book I was looking for.   *or*   ...the book that/which I was looking for.
5 The population of London, which was once the largest city in the world, is now falling.
6 Few of the people who/that applied for the job had the necessary qualifications.
7 Margaret showed me a photograph of her son, who is a policeman.

94.3

3 My office, which ... the building, is... (*commas*)
4 The office that/which... (*no commas*)
5 She told me her address, which... (*comma*)
6 There are some words that/which... (*no commas*)
7 The sun, which ... in the universe, provides... (*commas*)

UNIT 95

95.1

2 This is a photograph of our friends, with whom we went on holiday.   *or*   ...who we went on holiday with.
3 The wedding, to which only members of the family were invited, took place last Friday.   *or* The wedding, which only members of the family were invited to, took place...
4 Sheila, for whom we had been waiting, finally arrived.   *or* Sheila, who we had been waiting for, finally arrived.

5 We climbed to the top of the tower, from which we had a beautiful view.   *or*   ...which we had a beautiful view from.

95.2

2 We were given a lot of information, most of which was useless.
3 There were a lot of people at the party, only a few of whom I had met before.
4 I have sent her two letters, neither of which she has received.
5 Ten people applied for the job, none of whom were suitable.
6 Kate has got two cars, one of which she hardly ever uses.
7 Norman won £50,000, half of which he gave to his parents.
8 Julia has two sisters, both of whom are teachers.

95.3

2 Jill isn't on the phone, which makes it difficult to contact her.
3 Neil has passed his examinations, which is good news.
4 Our flight was delayed, which meant we had to wait four hours at the airport.
5 Ann offered to let me stay in her house, which was very nice of her.
6 The street I live in is very noisy at night, which makes it difficult to sleep.
7 Our car has broken down, which means we can't go away tomorrow.

UNIT 96

96.1

2 I didn't talk much to the man sitting next to me on the plane.
3 The taxi taking us to the airport broke down.
4 At the end of the street there is a path leading to the river.
5 A new factory employing 500 people has just opened in the town.
6 The company sent me a brochure containing all the information I needed.

96.2

2 The window broken in the storm last night has now been repaired.
3 Most of the suggestions made at the meeting were not very practical.
4 The paintings stolen from the museum haven't been found yet.
5 What was the name of the man arrested by the police?

96.3

3 living
4 offering
5 called
6 blown
7 sitting ... reading
8 working ... studying

96.4

3 There's somebody coming.
4 There were a lot of people travelling.
5 There was nobody else staying there.
6 There was nothing written on it.
7 There's a course beginning next Monday.

UNIT 97

97.1

2 a exhausting
  b exhausted
3 a depressing
  b depressed
  c depressed
4 a exciting
  b exciting
  c excited

97.2

2 interested
3 exciting
4 embarrassing
5 embarrassed
6 amazed
7 astonishing
8 amused
9 terrifying ... shocked
10 bored ... boring
11 boring ... interesting

97.3

2 bored   8 interested
3 confusing   9 exhausted
4 disgusting   10 excited
5 interested   11 amusing
6 annoyed   12 interesting
7 boring

UNIT 98

98.1

2 an unusual gold ring
3 a nice new pullover
4 a new green pullover
5 a beautiful old house
6 black leather gloves
7 an old American film
8 a long thin face
9 big black clouds
10 a lovely sunny day
11 a long wide avenue

12 a small black metal box
13 a big fat black cat
14 a lovely little old village
15 beautiful long black hair
16 an interesting old French painting
17 an enormous red and yellow umbrella

98.2

3 the last two days
4 the first two weeks of September
5 the next few days
6 the first three questions (of the examination)
7 the next two years
8 the last three days of our holiday

98.3

2 tastes awful   or   tasted awful
3 feel fine
4 smell nice
5 look wet
6 sounds quite interesting   or   sounded quite interesting

98.4

2 happy   5 terrible
3 happily   6 properly
4 violent

UNIT 99

99.1

2 badly   5 unexpectedly
3 easily   6 regularly
4 patiently

99.2

3 selfishly   8 badly
4 terribly   9 badly
5 sudden   10 safe
6 colourfully   11 angrily
7 colourful

99.3

2 careful
3 continuously
4 happily
5 fluent
6 specially
7 complete
8 perfectly
9 nervous
10 financially / completely

99.4

2 seriously ill
3 absolutely enormous
4 slightly damaged
5 unusually quiet
6 completely changed
7 unnecessarily long
8 badly planned

UNIT 100

100.1

2 good   6 well   9 well
3 well   7 well   10 good
4 good   8 good   11 well
5 well

100.2

2 well-known
3 well-kept
4 well-balanced
5 well-informed
6 well-dressed
7 well-paid
8 Well done! (*2 separate words*)

100.3

2 *right*
3 *right*
4 *wrong* – hard
5 *right*
6 *wrong* – slowly

100.4

2 hardly hear
3 hardly slept
4 hardly speak
5 hardly said
6 hardly changed
7 hardly recognised

100.5

2 hardly any
3 hardly anything
4 hardly anybody / hardly anyone
5 hardly ever
6 Hardly anybody / Hardly anyone
7 hardly anywhere
8 hardly ever
9 hardly any
10 hardly anything ... hardly anywhere

UNIT 101

101.1

4 so   10 such a
5 so   11 so
6 such a   12 so ... such
7 so   13 so
8 such   14 such a
9 such a   15 such a

101.2

3 I was so tired (that) I couldn't keep my eyes open.
4 We had such a good time on holiday (that) we didn't want to come home.
5 She speaks English so well (that) you would think it was her native language.   or   She speaks such good English (that)...

6 I've got such a lot of things to do (that) I don't know where to begin. *or* I've got so many things to do (that)…
7 The music was so loud (that) you could hear it from miles away.
8 I had such a big breakfast (that) I didn't eat anything else for the rest of the day.
9 It was such horrible weather (that) we spent the whole day indoors.

101.3
Example answers:
2 a It's so oppressive.
  b It's such an oppressive place.
3 a She's so friendly.
  b She's such a friendly person.
4 a It's so exhausting.
  b It's such an exhausting job.
5 a I haven't seen you for so long.
  b I haven't seen you for such a long time.

UNIT 102

102.1
2 enough money
3 enough milk
4 warm enough
5 enough room
6 well enough
7 enough time
8 enough qualifications
9 big enough
10 enough cups

102.2
2 too busy to talk
3 too late to go
4 warm enough to sit
5 too nice to be
6 enough energy to play
7 too far away to hear
8 enough English to read

102.3
2 This coffee is too hot to drink.
3 The piano was too heavy to move.
4 This coat isn't warm enough to wear in winter.
5 The situation is too complicated to explain.
6 This sofa isn't wide enough for three people to sit on.
7 The wall was too high to climb over.
8 Some things are too small to see without a microscope.

UNIT 103

103.1
2 quite a good voice.
3 quite a long way.
4 quite a busy day.
5 quite a nice time.
6 quite a strong wind.
7 quite a frightening experience.
8 quite a lot of mistakes.

103.2
2 <u>quite well</u> but it's <u>rather noisy</u>
3 <u>rather long</u> but <u>quite interesting</u>
4 <u>quite a hard worker</u> but he's <u>rather slow</u>
5 <u>rather disappointed</u> … <u>quite pleased</u>
6 <u>quite a well-paid</u> job but it's <u>rather hard</u> work
7 <u>quite near</u> us but it's <u>rather difficult</u>…

103.3
3 more than a little…
4 completely
5 more than a little…
6 more than a little…
7 completely

103.4
2 quite safe.
3 quite impossible.
4 quite right.
5 quite different.
6 quite unnecessary.
7 quite sure.
8 quite amazing.

UNIT 104

104.1
2 stronger
3 smaller
4 more expensive
5 warmer
6 more interesting
7 more difficult
8 better
9 worse
10 longer
11 more quietly
12 more often
13 further
14 happier / more cheerful

104.2
3 more serious than
4 thinner
5 bigger
6 more interested
7 more important than
8 simpler / more simple
9 more crowded than

10 more peaceful than
11 more easily
12 higher than

104.3
2 It takes longer by train than by car.
3 I ran further than Dave.
4 Joe did worse than Chris.
5 My friends arrived earlier than I expected.
6 The buses run more often than the trains. *or* …run more frequently than the trains. *or* The buses are more frequent than the trains.
7 We were busier than usual at work today. *or* We were busier at work today than usual.

UNIT 105

105.1
2 much bigger
3 much more complicated than
4 a bit happier
5 far more interesting than
6 a bit more slowly
7 a lot easier
8 slightly older

105.2
2 any earlier
3 no more expensive than
4 any further
5 no worse than

105.3
2 bigger and bigger
3 heavier and heavier
4 more and more nervous
5 worse and worse
6 more and more expensive
7 better and better
8 more and more talkative

105.4
2 the more I liked him *or* the more I got to like him
3 the more your profit (will be) *or* the higher your profit (will be) *or* the more profit you will make
4 the harder it is to concentrate
5 the more impatient she became

105.5
2 older
3 older *or* elder
4 older

UNIT 106

106.1

2 as high as yours.
3 You don't know as much about cars as me. *or* ...as I do.
4 It isn't as cold today as it was yesterday.
5 I don't feel as tired today as I felt yesterday. *or* ...as I did...
6 They haven't lived here as long as us. *or* ...as we have.
7 I wasn't as nervous before the interview as I usually am. *or* ...as usual.

106.2

3 The station wasn't as far as I thought.
4 The meal cost less than I expected. / ...was cheaper than I expected. / ...wasn't as expensive as I expected.
5 I don't go out as much as I used to. / ...as often as I used to.
6 She used to have longer hair.
7 You don't know them as well as me. *or* ...as I do.
8 There weren't as many people at this meeting as at the last one.

106.3

2 as well as
3 as long as
4 as soon as
5 as often as
6 as quietly as
7 just as comfortable as
8 just as well-qualified as
9 just as bad as

106.4

2 Your hair is the same colour as mine.
3 I arrived at the same time as you (did).
4 My birthday is (on) the same day as Tom's. *or* My birthday is the same as Tom's.

106.5

2 than him / than he does
3 as me / as I do
4 than us / than we were
5 than her / than she is
6 as them / as they have been

UNIT 107

107.1

2 It's <u>the cheapest restaurant in</u> the town.
3 It was <u>the happiest day of</u> my life.

4 She <u>is the most intelligent student in</u> the class.
5 It <u>is the most valuable painting in</u> the gallery.
6 It <u>is the busiest time of</u> the year.
8 He's one <u>of the richest men in</u> the world.
9 It <u>is one of the oldest castles in</u> Britain.
10 She <u>is one of the best players in</u> the team.
11 It <u>was one of the worst experiences of</u> my life.
12 He <u>is one of the most dangerous criminals in</u> the country.

107.2

3 larger
4 the longest
5 happier
6 the worst
7 the most popular
8 the highest ... higher
9 most enjoyable
10 more comfortable
11 the quickest
12 The oldest *or* The eldest

107.3

2 That's the funniest joke I've ever heard.
3 This is the best coffee I've ever tasted.
4 She is the most patient person I've ever met.
5 That's the furthest (*or* farthest) I've ever run.
6 It is/was the worst mistake I've ever made.
7 Who is the most famous person you've ever met?

UNIT 108

108.1

3 Jim doesn't like football very much.
4 *right*
5 I ate my dinner quickly...
6 Are you going to invite a lot of people to the party?
7 *right*
8 Did you go to bed late last night?
9 *right*
10 *right*
11 I met a friend of mine on my way home.
12 I fell off my bicycle yesterday.

108.2

2 We won the game easily.
3 I closed the door quietly.
4 Diane speaks German quite well.
5 Tim watches television all the time.

6 Please don't ask that question again.
7 Does Ken play football every weekend?
8 I borrowed some money from a friend of mine.

108.3

2 I go to the bank every Friday.
3 Why did you come home so late?
4 Ann drives her car to work every day.
5 I haven't been to the cinema recently.
6 Please write your name at the top of the page.
7 I remembered her name after a few minutes.
8 We walked around the town all morning.
9 I didn't see you at the party on Saturday night.
10 We found some interesting books in the library.
11 Sally took the children to the zoo yesterday.
12 They are building a new hotel opposite the park.

UNIT 109

109.1

3 I usually have...
4 *right*
5 Steve hardly ever gets angry.
6 I also went to the bank.
7 Jane always has to hurry...
8 We were all tired so we all fell asleep.
9 *right*

109.2

2 We were all on holiday.
3 We were all staying at the same hotel.
4 We all enjoyed ourselves.
5 Catherine is always very generous.
6 I don't usually have to work on Saturdays.
7 Do you always watch television in the evenings?
8 He is also learning Italian.
9 That hotel is probably very expensive.
10 It probably costs a lot to stay there.
11 I can probably help you.
12 I probably can't help you.

109.3

2 usually take
3 am usually
4 has probably gone

5 were both born
6 can also sing
7 often breaks
8 have never spoken
9 always have to wait
10 can only read
11 will probably be leaving
12 probably won't be
13 is hardly ever
14 are still living
15 would never have met
16 Yes, I <u>always am</u> at this time of day. (*but* I am always <u>tired</u>)

UNIT 110

110.1
3 He doesn't write poems any more.
4 He still wants to be a teacher.
5 He's not / He isn't interested in politics any more.
6 He's still single.
7 He doesn't go fishing any more.
8 He hasn't got a beard any more. / He doesn't have…
10–12
  He no longer writes poems.
  He is no longer interested in politics.
  He no longer goes fishing.
  He no longer has a beard. / He has no longer got a beard. / He's no longer got…

110.2
2 He hasn't gone yet.
3 They haven't finished their dinner yet.
4 They haven't woken up yet.
5 She hasn't found a job yet. *or* …found one yet.
6 I haven't decided (what to do) yet.
7 It hasn't taken off yet.

110.3
5 I don't want to go out yet.
6 she doesn't work there any more.
7 I still have a lot of friends there.
8 We've already met.
9 Do you still live in the same house
10 have you already eaten
11 He isn't here yet.
12 he still isn't here (he isn't here yet *is also possible*)
13 are you already a member
14 I can still remember it very clearly.
15 These trousers don't fit me any more.
16 Have you finished with the paper yet?
  No, I'm still reading it.

UNIT 111

111.1
2 even Angela
3 not even Sharon
4 even Angela
5 even Linda
6 not even Angela

111.2
2 She even has to work on Sundays.
3 They even painted the floor.
4 You could even hear the noise from the next street. *or* …hear it from…
5 They even have the windows open when it's freezing. *or* …have them open…
7 I can't even remember her name.
8 There isn't even a cinema.
9 He didn't even tell his wife (where he was going).

111.3
2 even older
3 even better
4 even more difficult
5 even worse
6 even less

111.4
2	if	6	Even
3	even if	7	Even though
4	even	8	even if
5	even though	9	Even though

UNIT 112

112.1
2 Although I had never seen her before
3 although it was quite cold
4 although we don't like them very much
5 Although I didn't speak the language
6 Although the heating was on
7 although I'd met her twice before
8 although we've known each other for a long time

112.2
2 a In spite of
  b Although
3 a because
  b although
4 a because of
  b in spite of
5 a although
  b because of
Example answers:
6 a he didn't study very hard.
  b he studied very hard.
7 a I was hungry.

b being hungry / my hunger / the fact that I was hungry

112.3
2 In spite of having very little money, they are happy.
3 Although my foot was injured, I managed to walk to the nearest village. *or* I managed to walk to the nearest village although my…
4 I enjoyed the film in spite of the silly story. / …in spite of the story being silly. / …in spite of the silliness of the story. / …in spite of the fact the story was silly. *or* In spite of…, I enjoyed the film.
5 Despite living in the same street, we hardly ever see each other. *or* Despite the fact that we live in… *or* We hardly ever see each other despite…
6 I got very wet in the rain even though I had an umbrella. *or* Even though I had an umbrella, I got…

112.4
2 It's a bit windy though.
3 We ate it though.
4 I don't like her husband though.

UNIT 113

113.1
2 she gets lost
3 She's going to take an umbrella in case it rains.
4 She's going to take her camera in case she wants to take some photographs.
5 She's going to take some water in case she gets thirsty.
6 She's going to take a towel in case she wants to have a swim.

113.2
1 in case you need to contact me.
2 I'll say goodbye now in case I don't see you again before you go.
3 Can you check the list in case we've forgotten something? *or* …forgotten anything?

113.3
2 He wrote down the name of the book in case he forgot it.
3 I phoned my parents in case they were worried about me.
4 I wrote to Jane again in case she hadn't received my first letter.
5 I gave them my address in case they came to London one day.

113.4

3	If	7	if
4	if	8	in case
5	in case	9	in case
6	if		

UNIT 114

114.1

2 unless you listen carefully.
3 I'll never speak to her again unless she apologises to me.
4 He won't be able to understand you unless you speak very slowly.
5 I'm going to look for another job unless the company offer (*or* offers) me more money.

114.2

2 I'm not going to the party unless you go too. *or* ...unless you come too.
3 The dog won't attack you unless you move suddenly.
4 He won't speak to you unless you ask him a question.
5 The doctor won't see you today unless it's an emergency.

114.3

2	unless	7	provided
3	providing	8	Unless
4	as long as	9	unless
5	unless	10	as long as
6	unless		

114.4

Example answers:
2 I have to work.
3 I don't have to work.
4 she has time.
5 it isn't raining.
6 I'm in a hurry.
7 you have something else to do.
8 you pay it back as soon as possible.
9 you take risks.

UNIT 115

115.1

3 *because*
4 *at the same time as*
5 *at the same time as*
6 *because*
7 *because*

115.2

2 As it was a nice day, we went for a walk by the sea.
3 As we didn't want to wake anybody up, we came in very quietly.

4 As the door was open, I walked in.
5 As none of us had a watch, we didn't know what time it was.

115.3

2 We all smiled as we posed for the photograph.
3 I burnt myself as I was taking a hot dish out of the oven.
4 The crowd cheered as the two teams ran onto the field.
5 A dog ran out in front of the car as we were driving along the road.

115.4

2	when	5	as
3	as	6	when
4	When		

115.5

Example answers:
1 you were getting into your car.
2 we started playing tennis.
3 I had to walk home.
4 somebody walked in front of the camera.

UNIT 116

116.1

3	like	8	As	13	like
4	like	9	as	14	like
5	as	10	like	15	as
6	like	11	as	16	as
7	like	12	like		

116.2

2 as a tourist guide
3 like blocks of ice
4 like a beginner
5 like a church
6 as a birthday present
7 as a problem
8 like winter
9 like a child

116.3

1	like	6	like	11	like
2	as	7	as	12	as
3	like	8	as	13	Like
4	like	9	as	14	as
5	as	10	like	15	as

UNIT 117

117.1

2 as if she had hurt her leg.
3 as if he meant what he was saying.
4 as if it has just been cut.
5 as if he hadn't eaten for a week.
6 as if she was enjoying it.
7 as if I'm going to be sick.
8 as if she didn't want to come.

117.2

2 You look as if you've seen a ghost.
3 You sound as if you're enjoying it. *or* ...as if you've been enjoying it.
4 I feel as if I've run a marathon.

117.3

2 It looks as if it's going to rain.
3 It sounds as if they are having an argument.
4 It looks as if there's been an accident.
5 It looks as if we'll have to walk.
6 It sounds as if you had a good time.

117.4

2 as if I was/were
3 as if she was/were
4 as if it was/were

UNIT 118

118.1

3	during	9	during
4	for	10	for
5	during	11	for
6	for	12	for
7	for	13	during
8	for	14	for

118.2

3	while	10	while
4	While	11	during
5	During	12	while
6	while	13	during
7	during	14	while
8	During	15	while
9	while		

118.3

Example answers:
3 I was doing the housework.
4 I make a quick phone call?
5 the lesson.
6 the interview.
7 the car is moving.
8 the meal.
9 the game.
10 we were playing football.

UNIT 119

119.1

2 by 10.30.
3 by Saturday whether you can come to the party.
4 Please make sure you're here by 2 o'clock. *or* Please be here...
5 If we leave now, we should arrive by lunchtime.

119.2

3	by	7	until	10	until
4	until	8	by	11	By
5	until … by	9	by	12	by
6	by				

119.3

Example answers:
3 until I come back.
4 by 5 o'clock.
5 by next Friday.
6 until midnight.

119.4

2 By the time I got to the station
3 By the time the police arrived
4 By the time the guards discovered what had happened
5 By the time I (had) finished my work

UNIT 120

120.1

2 on Sundays.
3 at night.
4 in the evening.
5 on 21 July 1969.
6 at the same time.
7 in the 1920s.
8 in about 20 minutes.
9 at the moment.
10 at Christmas.
11 in the Middle Ages.
12 in 11 seconds.

120.2

2 a	on	4 a	on	6 a	in		
b	at	b	–	b	on		
3 a	in	5 a	in	c	–		
b	on	b	at				

120.3

1 in
2 on
3 in
4 on
5 in
6 in
7 at
8 on
9 at
10 On Saturday night… at 11 o'clock
11 at
12 at 5 o'clock in the morning
13 on 7 January … in April
14 in
15 on Tuesday morning … in the afternoon
16 in
17 at
18 on
19 in

UNIT 121

121.1

2	on time	6	on time
3	in time	7	in time
4	on time	8	in time
5	in time	9	on time

121.2

2 I/we got home just in time.
3 I stopped him just in time.
4 I/we got to the cinema just in time for the beginning of the film.

121.3

2 at the end of the month
3 at the end of the course
4 at the end of the race
5 at the end of the interview

121.4

2 In the end she resigned.
3 In the end I gave up.
4 In the end we decided not to go. *or* …we didn't go.

121.5

2	In	5	in	8	at
3	at … at	6	at	9	in
4	in	7	in		

UNIT 122

122.1

2 At the traffic lights.
3 On his arm. *or* On the man's arm.
4 a On the door.
  b In the door.
5 In Paris.
6 On the wall.
7 a At the top of the stairs.
  b At the bottom (of the stairs).
8 a At the gate.
  b On the gate.
9 At the end of the queue.
10 On the beach.

122.2

2 on my guitar
3 at the next garage
4 in your coffee
5 on that tree
6 in the mountains
7 on the island
8 at the window

122.3

2	on the wall in the kitchen		
3	at		
4	on	8	in … in
5	At	9	on
6	on	10	in
7	at	11	on

UNIT 123

123.1

2 On the second floor.
3 On the corner. *or* At the corner.
4 In the corner.
5 In the back of the car.
6 in a mirror.
7 At the front.
8 In the back row.
9 a On the left.
  b On the right.
10 On a farm.

123.2

2 on the right
3 in the world
4 on my way to work
5 on the west coast
6 in the front row
7 at the back of the class
8 on the back of the envelope

123.3

1 in
2 on *or* at
3 in
4 on … on
5 at
6 in the paper … on the back page
7 in
8 in
9 in
10 on
11 on

UNIT 124

124.1

2 on a train
3 at a conference
4 in hospital
5 at the hairdresser / at the hairdresser's
6 on her bicycle
7 in New York
8 at the National Theatre

124.2

2 in bed
3 What's on at the cinema
4 in prison
5 at school
6 at the Sports Centre
7 in hospital
8 at the airport
9 on the plane
10 at sea

124.3

1 at
2 at
3 on
4 in
5 at
6 at/in a very nice hotel … in Amsterdam
7 in
8 at work … at home in bed
9 at
10 in
11 at
12 in London … at London University

UNIT 125

125.1

3 at
4 to
5 to
6 into
7 get home … going to bed
8 at
9 to France … in Brazil
10 to
11 in Chicago … moved to New York … lives in New York
12 to
13 into
14 to
15 at
16 to
17 Welcome to …

125.2

Example answers:

2 I've been to Sweden once.
3 I've never been to the United States.
4 I've been to Paris a few times.

125.3

2 in   4 at   6 –
3 –   5 to

125.4

2 I got on the bus.
3 I got out of the car.
4 I got off the train.
5 I got into the taxi. *or* I got in the taxi
6 I got off the plane.

UNIT 126

126.1

2 on the phone
3 on strike
4 on a tour
5 on holiday
6 on television

7 on purpose
8 on a diet
9 on business
10 on the whole

126.2

1 in cold weather
2 in pencil
3 in love
4 in block letters
5 in the shade
6 in my opinion
7 in cash

126.3

2 on
3 on
4 at
5 in
6 on
7 for
8 on
9 at
10 on
11 In my opinion … on television
12 on
13 on
14 at
15 on
16 at
17 on
18 in

UNIT 127

127.1

2 by mistake   5 by satellite
3 by hand   6 by chance
4 by cheque

127.2

2 on
3 by
4 on
5 by car … on my bike
6 in
7 on
8 by

127.3

Example answers:

3 *Ulysses* is a novel by James Joyce.
4 *Yesterday* is a song by Paul McCartney.
5 *Guernica* is a painting by Pablo Picasso.

127.4

1 by
2 with
3 by
4 by
5 with
6 by car … in your car

7 on
8 by
9 by the bed with a lamp and a clock on it
10 by

127.5

2 by ten pence.
3 by two votes.
4 Kate by five minutes. / her by five minutes.

UNIT 128

128.1

2 to the problem
3 with her brother
4 in prices
5 to your question
6 for a new road
7 in the number of people without jobs
8 for shoes like these any more
9 between your job and mine

128.2

2 invitation to
3 contact with
4 key to
5 cause of
6 reply to
7 connection between
8 pictures of
9 reason for
10 damage to

128.3

2 for   9 to *or* towards
3 of   10 with
4 to   11 in
5 in   12 for
6 for   13 to
7 of   14 of
8 in *or* to   15 for a rise in pay
                    16 to
                    17 with

UNIT 129

129.1

2 That was nice of her.
3 That was generous of him.
4 That wasn't very nice of them.
5 That's very kind of you.
6 That wasn't very polite of him.
7 That's a bit childish of them.

129.2

2 kind to
3 sorry for
4 annoyed with
5 annoyed about
6 impressed with / impressed by
7 bored with (*or* bored by)
8 astonished at / astonished by

129.3

2 of
3 to ... to
4 of
5 of
6 with
7 to
8 with
9 at/by
10 with
11 about
12 about
13 sorry <u>about</u> or sorry <u>for</u> ... angry
    <u>with</u>
14 furious <u>with</u> us <u>for</u> making
15 about
16 about
17 at/by
18 with/by
19 about
20 about
21 for

UNIT 130

130.1

2 of furniture
3 on sport
4 of time
5 at tennis
6 to a Russian (man)
7 of Robert
8 from yours / to yours

130.2

2 similar to
3 afraid of
4 interested in
5 responsible for
6 proud of
7 different from / different to

130.3

2	for	8	on	14	of
3	of	9	of	15	of
4	of	10	with	16	of
5	in	11	of	17	to
6	to	12	of	18	on
7	of ... of	13	in		

130.4

Example answers:
2 I'm hopeless at telling jokes.
3 I'm not very good at mathematics.
4 I'm quite good at remembering
    names.

UNIT 131

131.1

3 glanced at
4 invited to
5 listen to
6 <u>throw</u> stones <u>at</u>
7 <u>throw</u> it <u>to</u>
8 speaking to
9 wrote to
10 <u>point</u> them <u>at</u>

131.2

2	at	5	to	8	to
3	at	6	to	9	at
4	to	7	at	10	at

131.3

3 Can you explain this question to
    me?
4 Can you explain the system to me?
5 Can you explain to me how this
    machine works?
6 Can you explain to me what your
    problem is?

131.4

3	to	6	to	9	to
4	–	7	–	10	–
5	to	8	to		

UNIT 132

132.1

2	for	9	–	
3	for	10	for	
4	to	11	for	
5	for	12	about	
6	about	13	for	
7	–	14	for	
8	about			

132.2

2 waiting for
3 talk about
4 <u>asked</u> the waiter <u>for</u> the bill
5 applied for
6 <u>do</u> something <u>about</u> it
7 looks after *or* has looked after
8 <u>left</u> Boston <u>for</u> Paris

132.3

2	for	6	of	
3	about	7	about	
4	of	8	–	
5	for			

132.4

2 looking for
3 looked after
4 looking for
5 look for
6 looks after

UNIT 133

133.1

2 about
3 complained <u>to</u> us <u>about</u> the noise
4 of
5 of
6 about ... about ... about ... about
7 of
8 about
9 of *or* about

133.2

2 complaining about
3 think about
4 <u>warn</u> you <u>about</u>
5 heard of
6 dream of
7 <u>reminded</u> me <u>about</u>
8 <u>remind</u> you <u>of</u>

133.3

2	hear about	5	hear from	
3	heard from	6	hear about	
4	heard of	7	heard of	

133.4

2 think about
3 thinks about / thinks of
4 think of
5 think of
6 thinking of / thinking about
7 think of
8 thinking about / thinking of
9 thought about
10 <u>think</u> much <u>of</u>

UNIT 134

134.1

2 for the misunderstanding (which
    was my fault).
3 on winning the tournament.
4 from his enemies. / against his
    enemies.
5 of 11 players.
6 on bread and eggs.
8 for everything.
9 for the economic crisis?
10 violent crime on television.
11 is to blame for the economic
    crisis?
12 television is to blame for the
    increase in violent crime.

134.2

2 paid for
3 accused of
4 depends on
5 live on
6 <u>congratulated</u> him <u>on</u>
7 apologise to

134.3

2 from
3 on
4 of
5 for
6 for
7 –
8 on
9 on
10 on *or* –
11 from *or* against
12 of

UNIT 135

135.1

2 small towns to big cities.
3 with all the information I needed.
4 £60 on a pair of shoes.

135.2

2 happened to
3 drove into
4 divided into
5 believe in
6 <u>fill</u> it <u>with</u>
7 Concentrate on
8 succeeded in

135.3

2 to
3 on
4 in
5 to
6 in
7 with
8 into
9 in
10 on
11 into
12 to
13 into
14 on
15 <u>from</u> one language <u>into</u> another
16 happened <u>to</u> ... spend it <u>on</u>
17 into
18 with

135.4

Example answers:
2 on books.
3 into a wall.
4 to volleyball.
5 into many languages.

UNIT 136

136.1

2 turn up
3 moving in
4 closed down
5 dropped out
6 show off
7 dozed off
8 clears up

136.2

2 back at
3 out of
4 on with
5 up at
6 forward to
7 away with

136.3

2 cross it out
3 made it up
4 give them back
5 see her off
6 gave them away
7 show you round
8 turned it down

136.4

3 them up
4 the television off   *or*
  off the television
5 him down
6 a jacket on   *or*   on a jacket
7 your cigarette out   *or*
  out your cigarette
8 it out
9 a word up   *or*   up a word
10 it up

KEY TO ADDITIONAL EXERCISES

1

3 'm getting / am getting
4 do you do
5 was the car doing
6 phones ... didn't phone
7 were thinking ... decided
8 's happening / is happening
9 doesn't rain
10 rang ... were having
11 went ... was studying ... didn't want ... didn't stay
12 told ... didn't believe ... thought ... was joking

2

2 didn't go
3 is wearing
4 has grown
5 haven't decided
6 is being
7 wasn't reading
8 didn't have
9 is beginning
10 found
11 wasn't
12 you've been
13 I've been doing
14 did she go
15 I've been playing
16 do you come
17 since I saw her
18 for 20 years

3

3 are you going
4 Do you watch
5 have you lived / have you been living / have you been
6 Did you have
7 Have you seen
8 was she wearing
9 Have you been waiting / Have you been here
10 does it take
11 Have you finished
12 Have you (ever) been

4

2 have known each other / have been friends
3 I've ever had / I've ever been on / I've had for ages (etc.)
4 He went / He went home / He went out / He left
5 I've worn it
6 I was playing
7 been swimming for / had a swim for
8 since I've been / since I (last) went
9 did you buy / did you get

5

1 got ... was already waiting ... had arrived
2 was lying ... wasn't watching ... had fallen ... was snoring ... turned ... woke
3 had just gone ... was reading ... heard ... got ... didn't see ... went
4 missed ... was standing ... realised ... had left ... had ... got
5 met ... was walking ... had been ... had been playing ... were going ... invited ... had arranged ... didn't have

6

2 Somebody has taken it.
3 They had only known each other (for) a few weeks.
4 It has been raining all day. / It has rained all day.
5 I had been dreaming.
6 I'd had (= I had had) a big breakfast.
7 They've been going there for years.
8 I've had it since I got up.
9 He has been training very hard for it.

7

1 I haven't seen
2 You look / You're looking
3 are you going
4 are you meeting
5 I'm going
6 Do you often go
7 are you going
8 I'm meeting
9 has been
10 I've been waiting
11 has just started
12 is she getting
13 Does she like
14 she thinks
15 Are you working
16 spoke
17 you were working
18 went
19 I started / I had started
20 I lost
21 you haven't had
22 I've had
23 have you seen
24 has he been
25 I saw
26 he went
27 He had been
28 he decided / he'd decided
29 He was really looking forward
30 is he doing

31 I haven't heard
32 he left

8

1 invented
2 it's gone / it has gone
3 had gone
4 did you do ... Did you go
5 have you had
6 it was raining
7 She has been teaching
8 I bought ... I haven't worn
9 I saw ... was ... I'd seen / I had seen ... I remembered ... it was
10 Have you heard ... She was ... died ... She wrote ... Have you read
11 does this word mean ... I've never seen
12 Did you arrive ... it had already begun
13 knocked ... was ... he'd gone / he had gone ... he didn't want
14 She'd never used / She had never used ... she didn't know
15 went ... She needed ... she'd been sitting / she had been sitting

9

3 used to drive
4 was driving
5 were studying
6 used to have
7 was having
8 was playing
9 used to play
10 was wearing

10

2 I'm going to the dentist.
3 we're going to hire a car.
4 I'll look after the children.
5 I'm having lunch with Sue.
6 are you going to have?
7 I'll turn on the light.
8 I'm going to turn on the light.

11

2 I'll come
3 shall we meet
4 begins
5 I'll meet
6 I'm seeing
7 Shall I ask
8 I'll see
9 are going
10 does the film begin
11 Are you meeting
12 I'll be

12

1 (2) are you going to do
  (3) it starts
  (4) you'll enjoy
  (5) it will be / it's going to be
2 (1) you're going
  (2) We're going
  (3) you have / you'll have
  (4) I'll send
  (5) I'll get
  (6) I get
3 (1) I'm having / I'm going to have
  (2) are coming
  (3) they'll have gone
  (4) they're
  (5) I won't be able
  (6) you know
  (7) I'll phone
4 (1) shall we meet
  (2) I'll be waiting
  (3) you arrive
  (4) I'll be sitting
  (5) I'll be wearing
  (6) Is Agent 307 coming *or*
     Is Agent 307 going to come *or*
     Will Agent 307 be coming
  (7) Shall I bring
  (8) I'll explain
  (9) I see
  (10) I'll try

13

1 I'll have
2 Are you going
3 shall I phone
4 It's going to land
5 it is
6 I'll miss / I'm going to miss … you go / you've gone
7 Shall I give … I give … will you write
8 does it end
9 I'm going … is getting
10 I'll tell … I'm … I won't be
11 I'm going to have / I'm having
12 she apologises
13 we'll be living
14 you finish

14

3 could rain / might rain
4 might have gone / could have gone
5 couldn't go
6 couldn't have seen / can't have seen
7 should get
8 wouldn't recognise / might not recognise
9 must have heard
10 should have turned

15

3 He must have forgotten.
4 You needn't have gone home so early.
5 It can't be changed now.
6 She may be watching television.
7 She must have been waiting for somebody.
8 he couldn't have done it.
9 You ought to have been here earlier.
10 I would have helped you.
11 You should have been warned.
12 He might not have been feeling very well. / He might not have felt very well.

16

4 rings
5 were
6 is
7 was/were
8 had been
9 had
10 hadn't had
11 had driven / had been driving
12 didn't read

17

2 came (to see us now).
3 wouldn't have disturbed you.
4 If you hadn't provoked the dog, it wouldn't have attacked you.
5 They would be upset if I told them what happened. / …what had happened.
6 I wouldn't have got (so) wet if I'd had an umbrella.
7 If he hadn't been (so) nervous, he wouldn't have failed.

18

Example answers:
1 I wasn't feeling so tired.
2 I hadn't had so much to do.
3 I would have forgotten Jane's birthday.
4 you hadn't taken so long to get ready.
5 I would have gone to the concert.
6 you were in trouble?
7 there was no traffic.
8 people would go out more.

19

3 I knew
4 I'd taken / I had taken
5 Ann were / Ann was
6 they'd hurry up / they would hurry up
7 we didn't have
8 we'd had / we had had
9 it wasn't / it weren't
10 I could

11 I hadn't said
12 you'd slow down / you would slow down
13 we hadn't gone
14 you wouldn't go / you didn't go

20

3 was cancelled
4 has been repaired
5 is being restored
6 is believed
7 would be sacked
8 might have been thrown
9 was taught
10 being arrested
11 Have you ever been arrested
12 are reported … have been injured

21

3 have sold
4 has been sold
5 are made
6 might be stolen
7 must have been stolen
8 must have taken
9 can be solved
10 should have left
11 is delayed
12 is being built … is expected

22

Castle fire
2 was discovered
3 was injured
4 be rescued
5 are believed to have been destroyed
6 is not known

Shop robbery
1 was forced
2 being threatened
3 had been stolen
4 was later found
5 had been abandoned
6 has been arrested
7 is still being questioned

Road delays
1 is being resurfaced
2 are asked / are being asked / have been asked
3 is expected
4 will be closed
5 will be diverted

Accident
1 was taken
2 was allowed
3 was blocked
4 be diverted
5 have been killed

23

3 changing
4 to change
5 change
6 being
7 saying
8 to phone
9 drinking
10 to be
11 to see
12 to be
13 to think ... making
14 to be ... playing
15 being stopped ... stealing ... driving
16 work ... pressing

24

3 I don't fancy going out.
4 He tends to forget things.
5 Would you mind helping me?
6 Everybody seems to have gone out.
7 We're thinking of moving.
8 I was afraid to touch it.
9 He is afraid of being robbed.
10 It's not worth seeing.
11 I'm not used to walking so far.
12 She seems to be enjoying herself.
13 He insisted on showing them to me.
14 I'd rather somebody else did it.

25

3 reading newspapers.
4 not go out tonight / stay at home tonight.
5 walking *or* in walking.
6 me to phone you this evening?
7 anybody seeing me / being seen.
8 of being a cheat / of cheating.
9 to seeing them again.
10 to do?
11 to have gone out with you.
12 not taking your advice / not having taken your advice / that I didn't take your advice.

26

2 Tennis ... twice a week ... a very good player
3 for dinner ... after work ... to the cinema
4 Unemployment ... for people ... find work
5 an accident ... going home ... taken to hospital ... I think most accidents ... by people driving
6 an economist ... in the investment department ... of Lloyds Bank ... for an American bank ... in the United States

7 the name of the hotel ... The Imperial ... in Queen Street in the city centre ... near the station
8 The older one ... a pilot with British Airways ... The younger one ... at school ... he leaves school ... go to university ... study law

27

2 If
3 when
4 if
5 when
6 if
7 if
8 unless
9 if
10 as long as
11 in case
12 in case
13 if
14 even if
15 Although
16 although
17 When
18 when

28

2 on
3 at 9.30 on Tuesday
4 at
5 on
6 at
7 In
8 at
9 during / in
10 on Friday ... since then
11 for
12 at
13 at the moment ... until Friday
14 by

29

1 in
2 by
3 at
4 on
5 on your cheek ... in the mirror
6 to a party at Linda's house
7 on
8 on
9 to ... to
10 in Vienna ... at the age of 35
11 in this photograph ... on the left
12 to the theatre ... in the front row
13 on the wall by the door
14 at
15 on
16 in a tower block ... on the fifteenth floor
17 on
18 pay in cash *or* pay cash ... by credit card
19 On the bus ... by car
20 on ... on

30

1 for
2 at
3 to
4 to
5 in
6 with
7 of
8 to
9 of
10 at/by
11 of
12 about

31

1 of
2 after
3 – (*no preposition*)
4 about
5 to
6 – (*no preposition*)
7 into
8 of
9 to
10 on
11 of
12 of
13 at
14 on

KEY TO STUDY GUIDE (see page 301)

Note that sometimes more than one alternative is correct.

Present and past

1.1 A
1.2 B
1.3 C
1.4 B, C
1.5 C
1.6 A

Present perfect and past

2.1 B
2.2 C
2.3 A
2.4 C
2.5 A
2.6 B
2.7 A
2.8 D
2.9 A
2.10 A
2.11 A
2.12 C
2.13 B
2.14 C

Future

3.1 A
3.2 C
3.3 A, C
3.4 B
3.5 C
3.6 A

Modals

4.1 A, B
4.2 A, C
4.3 C
4.4 B
4.5 A, B, D
4.6 B
4.7 A, C
4.8 B, C
4.9 A, B
4.10 A
4.11 D

Conditionals and 'wish'

5.1 B
5.2 D
5.3 D
5.4 B

Passive

6.1 C
6.2 B
6.3 A
6.4 C
6.5 D

Reported speech

7.1 B
7.2 A

Questions and auxiliary verbs

8.1 C
8.2 A
8.3 D
8.4 A
8.5 B

-ing and the infinitive

9.1 A
9.2 B, D
9.3 B
9.4 A
9.5 A
9.6 C
9.7 D
9.8 C
9.9 C
9.10 B
9.11 C
9.12 D
9.13 B
9.14 A, B
9.15 A
9.16 A
9.17 B, C

Articles and nouns

10.1 B
10.2 B, C
10.3 B
10.4 C
10.5 A
10.6 A
10.7 A
10.8 C
10.9 C
10.10 A, C
10.11 A
10.12 C
10.13 B

Pronouns and determiners

11.1 B
11.2 A
11.3 B
11.4 B
11.5 B
11.6 C
11.7 A, C
11.8 C
11.9 D
11.10 A, C
11.11 B

Relative clauses

12.1 A, C
12.2 A, B
12.3 C
12.4 B
12.5 D
12.6 B

Adjectives and adverbs

13.1 B
13.2 C
13.3 B, C
13.4 A
13.5 A, D
13.6 B
13.7 B, C
13.8 C
13.9 C
13.10 B, C
13.11 D
13.12 A, B
13.13 B
13.14 D
13.15 B

Conjunctions and prepositions

14.1 A, D
14.2 C
14.3 B, C
14.4 A
14.5 B
14.6 C, D
14.7 B, C
14.8 A

Prepositions

15.1 B
15.2 A
15.3 C
15.4 B
15.5 A
15.6 B, D
15.7 B
15.8 B
15.9 C
15.10 C
15.11 C
15.12 A
15.13 C
15.14 B
15.15 D
15.16 D
15.17 A
15.18 B

INDEX